T0370319

Also by Tess Adams, *What the Restorative Approach Looks Like in My Classroom*

Creating

Joy

Daily

Tess Adams

BALBOA.
PRESS

A DIVISION OF HAY HOUSE

Balboa Press books may be ordered through booksellers or by contacting:

Balboa Press
A Division of Hay House
1663 Liberty Drive
Bloomington, IN 47403
www.balboapress.com
1 (877) 407-4847

Because of the dynamic nature of the Internet, any web addresses or links contained in this book may have changed since publication and may no longer be valid. The views expressed in this work are solely those of the author and do not necessarily reflect the views of the publisher, and the publisher hereby disclaims any responsibility for them.

The author of this book does not dispense medical advice or prescribe the use of any technique as a form of treatment for physical, emotional, or medical problems without the advice of a physician, either directly or indirectly. The intent of the author is only to offer information of a general nature to help you in your quest for emotional and spiritual well-being. In the event you use any of the information in this book for yourself, which is your constitutional right, the author and the publisher assume no responsibility for your actions.

Any people depicted in stock imagery provided by Thinkstock are models, and such images are being used for illustrative purposes only.
Certain stock imagery © Thinkstock.

ISBN: 978-1-4525-1407-9 (sc)
ISBN: 978-1-4525-1408-6 (e)

Library of Congress Control Number: 2014908139

Printed in the United States of America.

Balboa Press rev. date: 05/01/2014

Dedication

I lovingly dedicate this planner to three incredible women and two amazing men, Louise Hay, Esther Hicks, Christy Whitman, Mike Adams, and Fred Giffin.

Because of Louise Hay's love and work, I discovered the healing power of loving myself and using affirmations. Because of Esther Hicks, I have come to understand the abundant laws of the universe. Because of Christy Whitman, I am using all my talents and passions as a life coach to help people manifest their dreams. Because of Mike Adams, I have the perfect partner on my journey, I know unconditional love, and I know it is possible (if you want to) to marry someone just like your dad. Because of my dad, Fred Giffin, I am here! My dad has taught me how to love through everything, laugh with all my heart, and believe in the Omnipotent Power that is continually creating. He has also taught me that if you can't find it, make it! And that's exactly how this planner got started!

I send all of them much love!

Forward

When is the last time you felt truly joyful? If you hesitate in answering this simple question, then it has been too long. Tess Adams provides a delightful way to create joy in your life every day with her planner *Creating Joy Daily*. This is a tool that Tess developed for her own use in staying focused on joy and what she wanted to create in her life. When she realized how much it helped her, she wanted to share it with you. She believes that we can create whatever we want if we are grounded in a place of joy. Her life has changed in tremendously positive ways in a short time by using this basic principle.

When I approached Tess and asked her to be my coach as I transition into a new career, I had no idea that she would help me in every other aspect of my life as well. She helped me to understand that once you relax into a place of joy, anything you want can happen.

Look for joy in your own life every day and you will see positive changes that will bring you the life that you want. *Creating Joy Daily* won't be just a daily planner, it will become a way of life.

Janet Kangas

Preface

After my electronic device "crashed" and my data for my calendar was lost, I decided to purchase a printed planner that was not dependent on being charged or updated. But in my search for one, I discovered many of them did not have what I was looking for and many would not inspire me in my daily planning. So I decided to create a planner that would fill me with excitement and inspiration as I use it every day. I wanted it to have room to add color, and I wanted it to have room for me to set my intentions for the day. I wanted it to have room for keeping track of what I appreciate and what I have already manifested in my life, and what I would like the universe to handle for me. I also needed room to write down my affirmations. I love using this planner every day because I enjoy seeing all the wonderful experiences that are created because of it. It is my intention that when you use it, you will create a life full of joy, peace, and abundance daily.

Introduction

Here are some explanations for how to get the most out of this planner.

Five Things I Appreciate: I believe it is so important to be mindful of all that we have to appreciate, the small things as well as the big things in our lives. So I have given you room to record five of them that come to your mind on each daily page.

Three Things I Have Already Manifested: I also believe it is important to acknowledge the creations you have already manifested in your life. I have given you room to record three of them every day (although I am sure you will be creating far more than that!).

This is How I Want to Describe Myself Today: This is where you get to set your intentions for the kind of person you want to be that day.

Today's Affirmations: Record which affirmations you want to focus on each day.

Two Things I Will Do Just for Me: Self-care is vital if you want to be able to help others well. So please make plans for at least two things that you will do for yourself in taking good care of yourself every day. At first, you may find it a little challenging, but the more you make it a habit, the easier it will become.

Three Things I Want the Universe to Handle Today: Hand over what you need help with and be ready to amazed with what happens.

As you record what you will be doing each day, set an intention for how it will go and how you will feel while doing it. There is GREAT power in getting clear and setting intentions. The final explanation is that I have created lots of areas for you to put your own touch on this planner. Please color it in bright and fun colors and shapes that will delight you and give you joy as you begin to create your day!

Have fun!

Month: January

Sunday	Monday	Tuesday	Wednesday	Thursday	Friday	Saturday

Do at least one thing every day that brings you joy and record it on this page.

Affirmations:

"Life is supposed to be fun. All is really well."

—Abraham/Hicks

Today is:		3 Things I Have Manifested:
5 Things I Appreciate:		
		2 Things I Will Do Just for Me Today:
This Is How I Want to Describe Myself Today:		Today's Affirmations:
3 Things I Want the Universe to Handle:		

CREATE · YOUR · JOY

thank you · thank you

Time:	These Are My Intentions for Today:	I Intend to Feel:
6-7 AM		
7-8 AM		
8-9 AM		
9-10 AM		
10-11 AM		
11-12 AM		
12-1 PM		
1-2 PM		
2-3 PM		
3-4 PM		
4-5 PM		
5-6 PM		
6-7 PM		
7-8 PM		
8-9 PM		

© INTEND

FLOW

Today is:	3 Things I Have Manifested:
5 Things I Appreciate:	
	2 Things I Will Do Just for Me Today:
This Is How I Want to Describe Myself Today:	Today's Affirmations:
3 Things I Want the Universe to Handle:	

Time:	These Are My Intentions for Today:	I Intend to Feel:
6-7 AM		
7-8 AM		
8-9 AM		
9-10 AM		
10-11 AM		
11-12 AM		
12-1 PM		
1-2 PM		
2-3 PM		
3-4 PM		
4-5 PM		
5-6 PM		
6-7 PM		
7-8 PM		
8-9 PM		

CREATE . YOUR . JOY

thank you

INTEND

FLOW

Today is:	3 Things I Have Manifested:
5 Things I Appreciate:	
	2 Things I Will Do Just for Me Today:
This Is How I Want to Describe Myself Today:	Today's Affirmations:
3 Things I Want the Universe to Handle:	

Time:	These Are My Intentions for Today:	I Intend to Feel:
6-7 AM		
7-8 AM		
8-9 AM		
9-10 AM		
10-11 AM		
11-12 AM		
12-1 PM		
1-2 PM		
2-3 PM		
3-4 PM		
4-5 PM		
5-6 PM		
6-7 PM		
7-8 PM		
8-9 PM		

CREATE · YOUR · JOY

thank you

· INTEND

FLOW

Today is:	3 Things I Have Manifested:
5 Things I Appreciate:	
	2 Things I Will Do Just for Me Today:
This Is How I Want to Describe Myself Today:	Today's Affirmations:
3 Things I Want the Universe to Handle:	

Time:	These Are My Intentions for Today:	I Intend to Feel:
6-7 AM		
7-8 AM		
8-9 AM		
9-10 AM		
10-11 AM		
11-12 AM		
12-1 PM		
1-2 PM		
2-3 PM		
3-4 PM		
4-5 PM		
5-6 PM		
6-7 PM		
7-8 PM		
8-9 PM		

CREATE · YOUR · JOY

THANK YOU · INTEND

FLOW

Today is:	**3 Things I Have Manifested:**
5 Things I Appreciate:	
	2 Things I Will Do Just for Me Today:
This Is How I Want to Describe Myself Today:	**Today's Affirmations:**
3 Things I Want the Universe to Handle:	

Time:	These Are My Intentions for Today:	I Intend to Feel:
6-7 AM		
7-8 AM		
8-9 AM		
9-10 AM		
10-11 AM		
11-12 AM		
12-1 PM		
1-2 PM		
2-3 PM		
3-4 PM		
4-5 PM		
5-6 PM		
6-7 PM		
7-8 PM		
8-9 PM		

CREATE • YOUR • JOY

thank you

INTEND

· F L O W ·

Today is:	3 Things I Have Manifested:
5 Things I Appreciate:	
	2 Things I Will Do Just for Me Today:
This Is How I Want to Describe Myself Today:	Today's Affirmations:
3 Things I Want the Universe to Handle:	

Time:	These Are My Intentions for Today:	I Intend to Feel:
6-7 AM		
7-8 AM		
8-9 AM		
9-10 AM		
10-11 AM		
11-12 AM		
12-1 PM		
1-2 PM		
2-3 PM		
3-4 PM		
4-5 PM		
5-6 PM		
6-7 PM		
7-8 PM		
8-9 PM		

CREATE · YOUR · JOY

thank·you

© INTEND

FLOW

Today is:	3 Things I Have Manifested:
5 Things I Appreciate:	
	2 Things I Will Do Just for Me Today:
This Is How I Want to Describe Myself Today:	Today's Affirmations:
3 Things I Want the Universe to Handle:	

Time:	These Are My Intentions for Today:	I Intend to Feel:
6-7 AM		
7-8 AM		
8-9 AM		
9-10 AM		
10-11 AM		
11-12 AM		
12-1 PM		
1-2 PM		
2-3 PM		
3-4 PM		
4-5 PM		
5-6 PM		
6-7 PM		
7-8 PM		
8-9 PM		

CREATE • YOUR • JOY

thank you

INTEND

Today is:	3 Things I Have Manifested:
5 Things I Appreciate:	
	2 Things I Will Do Just for Me Today:
This Is How I Want to Describe Myself Today:	**Today's Affirmations:**
3 Things I Want the Universe to Handle:	

Time:	These Are My Intentions for Today:	I Intend to Feel:
6-7 AM		
7-8 AM		
8-9 AM		
9-10 AM		
10-11 AM		
11-12 AM		
12-1 PM		
1-2 PM		
2-3 PM		
3-4 PM		
4-5 PM		
5-6 PM		
6-7 PM		
7-8 PM		
8-9 PM		

CREATE . YOUR . JOY

thank you

INTEND

· F L O W ·

Today is:	**3 Things I Have Manifested:**
5 Things I Appreciate:	
	2 Things I Will Do Just for Me Today:
This Is How I Want to Describe Myself Today:	**Today's Affirmations:**
3 Things I Want the Universe to Handle:	

Time:	These Are My Intentions for Today:	I Intend to Feel:
6-7 AM		
7-8 AM		
8-9 AM		
9-10 AM		
10-11 AM		
11-12 AM		
12-1 PM		
1-2 PM		
2-3 PM		
3-4 PM		
4-5 PM		
5-6 PM		
6-7 PM		
7-8 PM		
8-9 PM		

CREATE · YOUR · JOY

thank you

· INTEND

FLOW

Today is:	3 Things I Have Manifested:
5 Things I Appreciate:	
	2 Things I Will Do Just for Me Today:
This Is How I Want to Describe Myself Today:	Today's Affirmations:
3 Things I Want the Universe to Handle:	

CREATE · YOUR · JOY

Time:	These Are My Intentions for Today:	I Intend to Feel:
6-7 AM		
7-8 AM		
8-9 AM		
9-10 AM		
10-11 AM		
11-12 AM		
12-1 PM		
1-2 PM		
2-3 PM		
3-4 PM		
4-5 PM		
5-6 PM		
6-7 PM		
7-8 PM		
8-9 PM		

thank you

INTEND

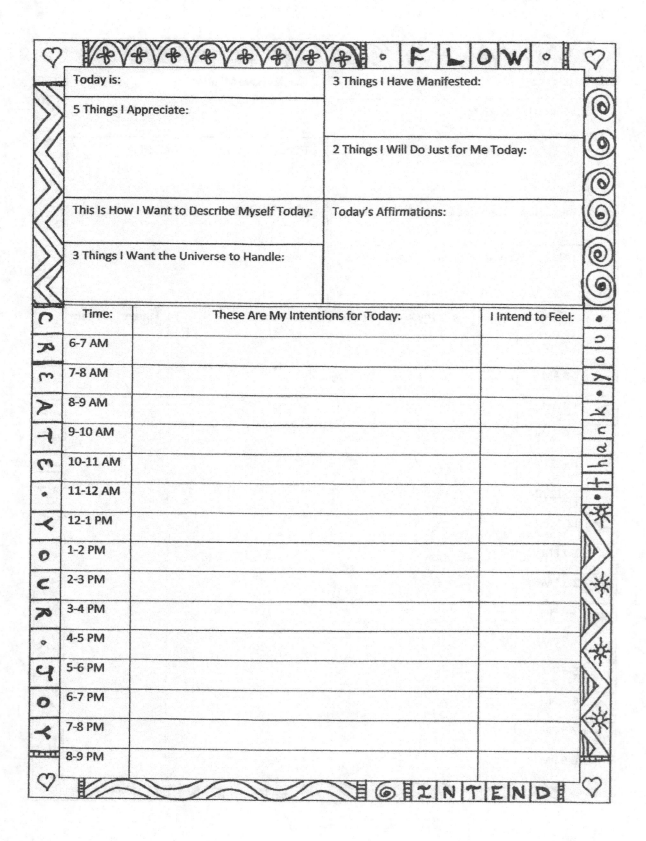

FLOW

Today is:	3 Things I Have Manifested:
5 Things I Appreciate:	
	2 Things I Will Do Just for Me Today:
This Is How I Want to Describe Myself Today:	Today's Affirmations:
3 Things I Want the Universe to Handle:	

Time:	These Are My Intentions for Today:	I Intend to Feel:
6-7 AM		
7-8 AM		
8-9 AM		
9-10 AM		
10-11 AM		
11-12 AM		
12-1 PM		
1-2 PM		
2-3 PM		
3-4 PM		
4-5 PM		
5-6 PM		
6-7 PM		
7-8 PM		
8-9 PM		

CREATE • YOUR • JOY

thank you

INTEND

· F L O W ·

Today is:	3 Things I Have Manifested:
5 Things I Appreciate:	
	2 Things I Will Do Just for Me Today:
This Is How I Want to Describe Myself Today:	**Today's Affirmations:**
3 Things I Want the Universe to Handle:	

Time:	These Are My Intentions for Today:	I Intend to Feel:
6-7 AM		
7-8 AM		
8-9 AM		
9-10 AM		
10-11 AM		
11-12 AM		
12-1 PM		
1-2 PM		
2-3 PM		
3-4 PM		
4-5 PM		
5-6 PM		
6-7 PM		
7-8 PM		
8-9 PM		

CREATE · YOUR · JOY

thank · you

© INTEND

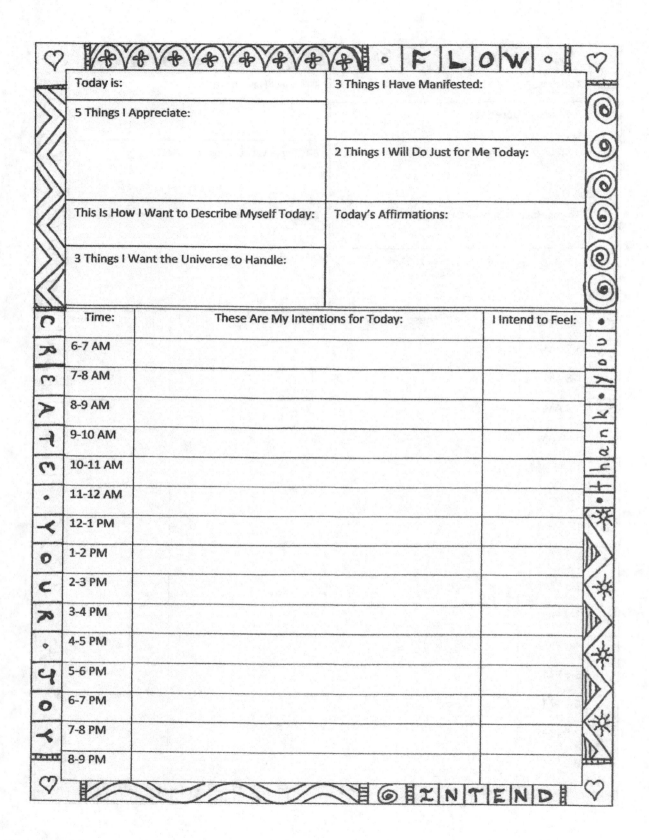

FLOW

Today is:	**3 Things I Have Manifested:**
5 Things I Appreciate:	
	2 Things I Will Do Just for Me Today:
This Is How I Want to Describe Myself Today:	**Today's Affirmations:**
3 Things I Want the Universe to Handle:	

Time:	These Are My Intentions for Today:	I Intend to Feel:
6-7 AM		
7-8 AM		
8-9 AM		
9-10 AM		
10-11 AM		
11-12 AM		
12-1 PM		
1-2 PM		
2-3 PM		
3-4 PM		
4-5 PM		
5-6 PM		
6-7 PM		
7-8 PM		
8-9 PM		

CREATE · YOUR · JOY

thank you

INTEND

FLOW

Today is:

5 Things I Appreciate:

3 Things I Have Manifested:

2 Things I Will Do Just for Me Today:

This Is How I Want to Describe Myself Today:

Today's Affirmations:

3 Things I Want the Universe to Handle:

Time:	These Are My Intentions for Today:	I Intend to Feel:
6-7 AM		
7-8 AM		
8-9 AM		
9-10 AM		
10-11 AM		
11-12 AM		
12-1 PM		
1-2 PM		
2-3 PM		
3-4 PM		
4-5 PM		
5-6 PM		
6-7 PM		
7-8 PM		
8-9 PM		

CREATE. YOUR. JOY

thank you

INTEND

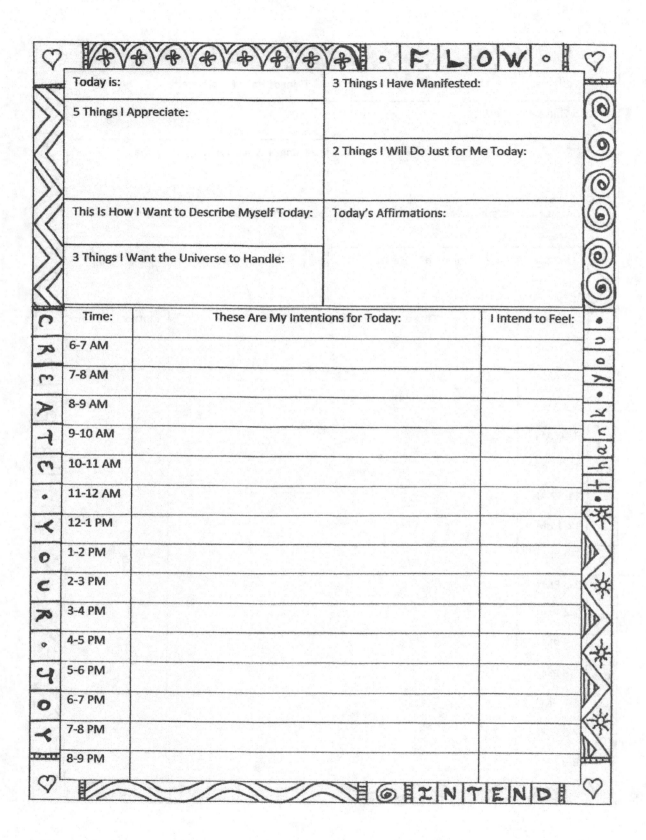

FLOW

Today is:	3 Things I Have Manifested:
5 Things I Appreciate:	
	2 Things I Will Do Just for Me Today:
This Is How I Want to Describe Myself Today:	**Today's Affirmations:**
3 Things I Want the Universe to Handle:	

Time:	These Are My Intentions for Today:	I Intend to Feel:
6-7 AM		
7-8 AM		
8-9 AM		
9-10 AM		
10-11 AM		
11-12 AM		
12-1 PM		
1-2 PM		
2-3 PM		
3-4 PM		
4-5 PM		
5-6 PM		
6-7 PM		
7-8 PM		
8-9 PM		

CREATE . YOUR . JOY

thank . you

INTEND

FLOW

Today is:	3 Things I Have Manifested:
5 Things I Appreciate:	
	2 Things I Will Do Just for Me Today:
This Is How I Want to Describe Myself Today:	Today's Affirmations:
3 Things I Want the Universe to Handle:	

Time:	These Are My Intentions for Today:	I Intend to Feel:
6-7 AM		
7-8 AM		
8-9 AM		
9-10 AM		
10-11 AM		
11-12 AM		
12-1 PM		
1-2 PM		
2-3 PM		
3-4 PM		
4-5 PM		
5-6 PM		
6-7 PM		
7-8 PM		
8-9 PM		

CREATE . YOUR . JOY

THANK . YOU

INTEND

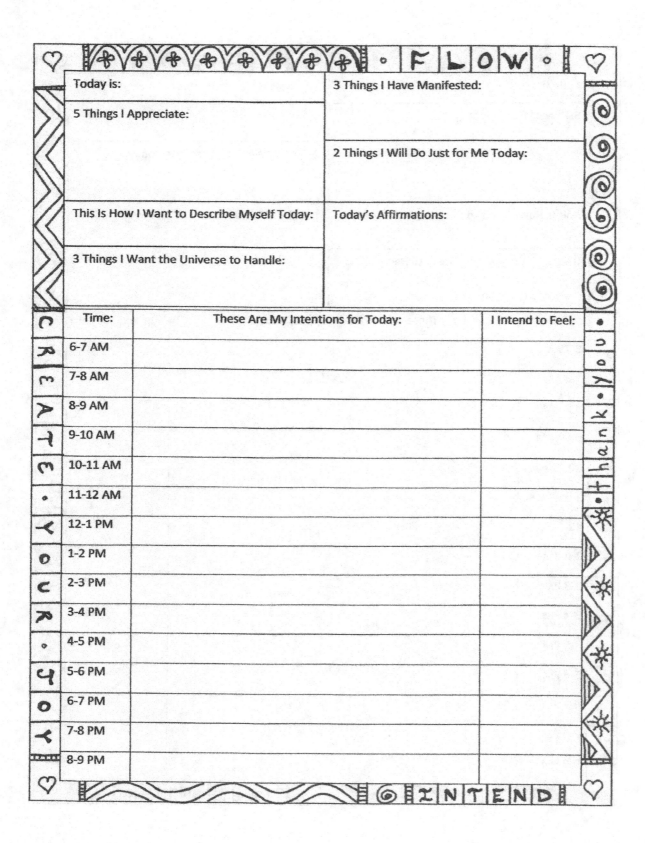

FLOW

Today is:	3 Things I Have Manifested:
5 Things I Appreciate:	
	2 Things I Will Do Just for Me Today:
This Is How I Want to Describe Myself Today:	Today's Affirmations:
3 Things I Want the Universe to Handle:	

CREATE • YOUR • JOY

thank you

Time:	These Are My Intentions for Today:	I Intend to Feel:
6-7 AM		
7-8 AM		
8-9 AM		
9-10 AM		
10-11 AM		
11-12 AM		
12-1 PM		
1-2 PM		
2-3 PM		
3-4 PM		
4-5 PM		
5-6 PM		
6-7 PM		
7-8 PM		
8-9 PM		

INTEND

FLOW

Today is:

5 Things I Appreciate:

3 Things I Have Manifested:

2 Things I Will Do Just for Me Today:

This Is How I Want to Describe Myself Today:

Today's Affirmations:

3 Things I Want the Universe to Handle:

Time:	These Are My Intentions for Today:	I Intend to Feel:
6-7 AM		
7-8 AM		
8-9 AM		
9-10 AM		
10-11 AM		
11-12 AM		
12-1 PM		
1-2 PM		
2-3 PM		
3-4 PM		
4-5 PM		
5-6 PM		
6-7 PM		
7-8 PM		
8-9 PM		

CREATE . YOUR . JOY

thank . you

INTEND

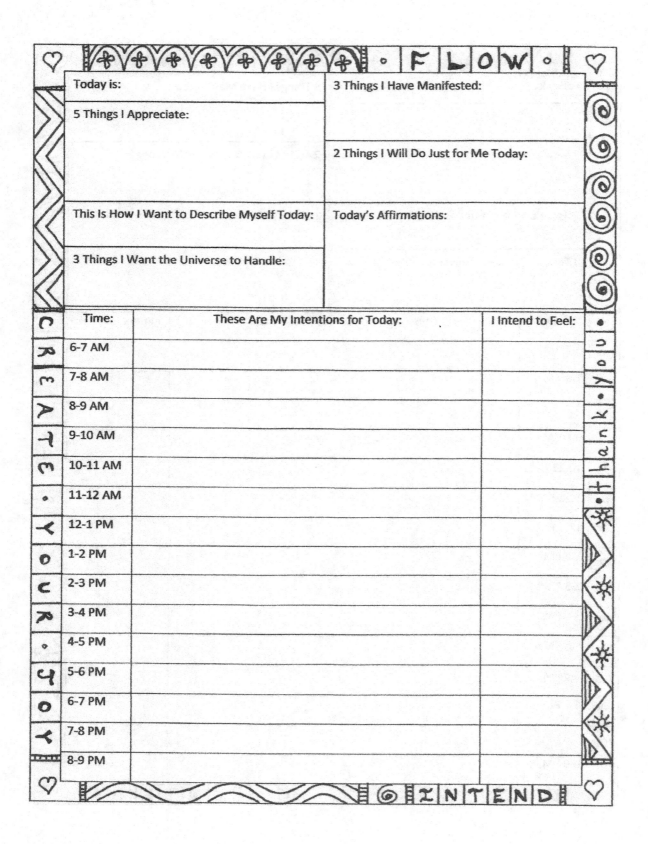

FLOW

Today is:	3 Things I Have Manifested:
5 Things I Appreciate:	
	2 Things I Will Do Just for Me Today:
This Is How I Want to Describe Myself Today:	**Today's Affirmations:**
3 Things I Want the Universe to Handle:	

	Time:	These Are My Intentions for Today:	I Intend to Feel:
C	6-7 AM		
R	7-8 AM		
E	8-9 AM		
A	9-10 AM		
T	10-11 AM		
E	11-12 AM		
.	12-1 PM		
Y	1-2 PM		
O	2-3 PM		
U	3-4 PM		
R	4-5 PM		
.	5-6 PM		
J	6-7 PM		
O	7-8 PM		
Y	8-9 PM		

INTEND

· F L O W ·

Today is:	3 Things I Have Manifested:
5 Things I Appreciate:	
	2 Things I Will Do Just for Me Today:
This Is How I Want to Describe Myself Today:	**Today's Affirmations:**
3 Things I Want the Universe to Handle:	

Time:	These Are My Intentions for Today:	I Intend to Feel:
6-7 AM		
7-8 AM		
8-9 AM		
9-10 AM		
10-11 AM		
11-12 AM		
12-1 PM		
1-2 PM		
2-3 PM		
3-4 PM		
4-5 PM		
5-6 PM		
6-7 PM		
7-8 PM		
8-9 PM		

CREATE · YOUR · JOY

· thank you ·

◎ INTEND

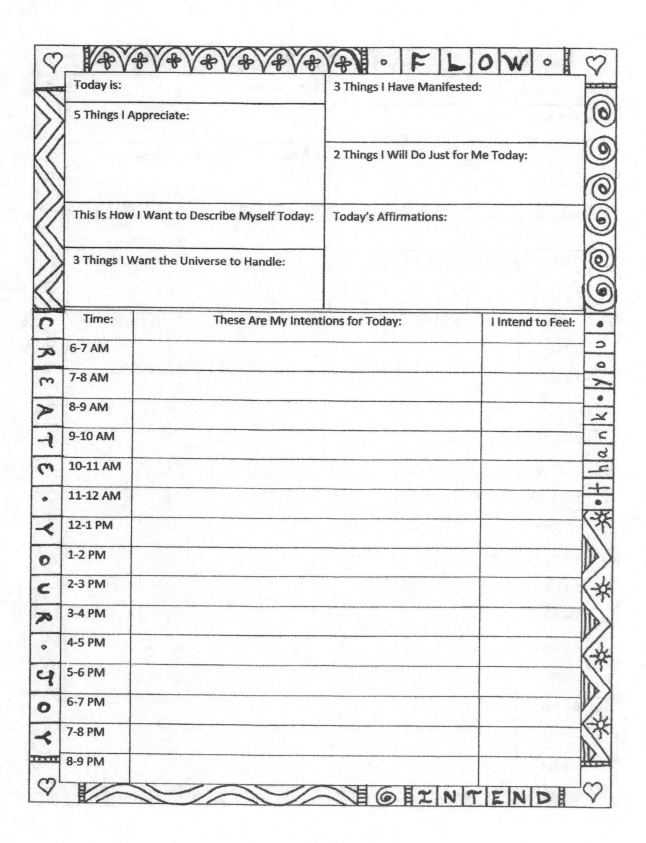

FLOW

Today is:	3 Things I Have Manifested:
5 Things I Appreciate:	
	2 Things I Will Do Just for Me Today:
This Is How I Want to Describe Myself Today:	**Today's Affirmations:**
3 Things I Want the Universe to Handle:	

Time:	These Are My Intentions for Today:	I Intend to Feel:
6-7 AM		
7-8 AM		
8-9 AM		
9-10 AM		
10-11 AM		
11-12 AM		
12-1 PM		
1-2 PM		
2-3 PM		
3-4 PM		
4-5 PM		
5-6 PM		
6-7 PM		
7-8 PM		
8-9 PM		

CREATE · YOUR · JOY

thank you

INTEND

FLOW

Today is:

5 Things I Appreciate:

This Is How I Want to Describe Myself Today:

3 Things I Want the Universe to Handle:

3 Things I Have Manifested:

2 Things I Will Do Just for Me Today:

Today's Affirmations:

Time:	These Are My Intentions for Today:	I Intend to Feel:
6-7 AM		
7-8 AM		
8-9 AM		
9-10 AM		
10-11 AM		
11-12 AM		
12-1 PM		
1-2 PM		
2-3 PM		
3-4 PM		
4-5 PM		
5-6 PM		
6-7 PM		
7-8 PM		
8-9 PM		

CREATE . YOUR . JOY

thank you

INTEND

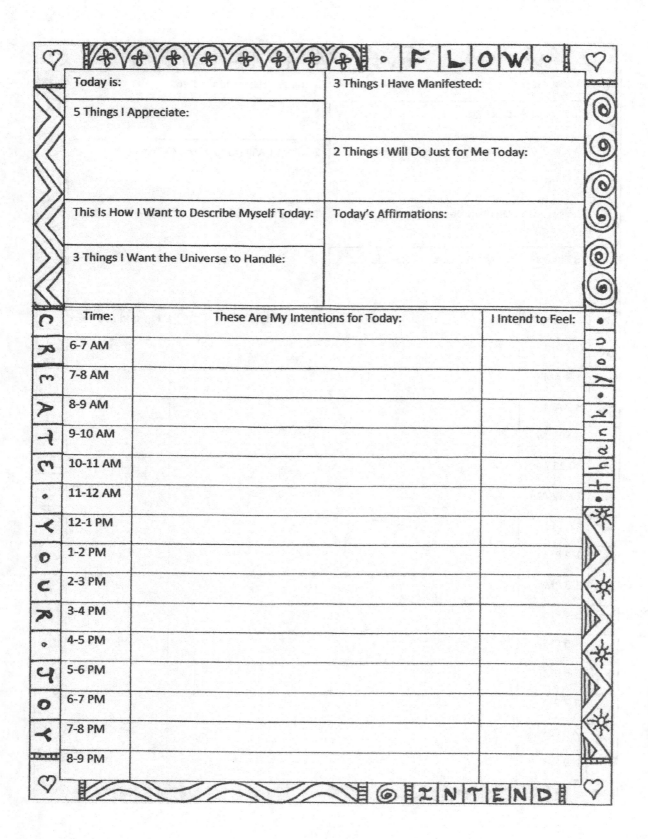

FLOW

Today is:

5 Things I Appreciate:

This Is How I Want to Describe Myself Today:

3 Things I Want the Universe to Handle:

3 Things I Have Manifested:

2 Things I Will Do Just for Me Today:

Today's Affirmations:

Time:	These Are My Intentions for Today:	I Intend to Feel:
6-7 AM		
7-8 AM		
8-9 AM		
9-10 AM		
10-11 AM		
11-12 AM		
12-1 PM		
1-2 PM		
2-3 PM		
3-4 PM		
4-5 PM		
5-6 PM		
6-7 PM		
7-8 PM		
8-9 PM		

CREATE . YOUR . JOY

thank . you

INTEND

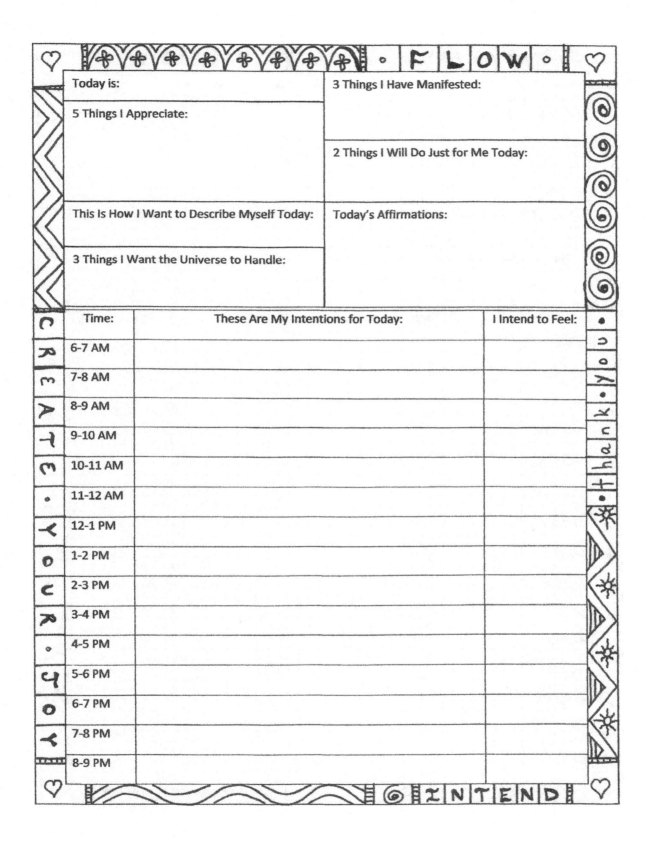

FLOW

Today is:	3 Things I Have Manifested:
5 Things I Appreciate:	
	2 Things I Will Do Just for Me Today:
This Is How I Want to Describe Myself Today:	Today's Affirmations:
3 Things I Want the Universe to Handle:	

CREATE · YOUR · JOY

thank you · thank

Time:	These Are My Intentions for Today:	I Intend to Feel:
6-7 AM		
7-8 AM		
8-9 AM		
9-10 AM		
10-11 AM		
11-12 AM		
12-1 PM		
1-2 PM		
2-3 PM		
3-4 PM		
4-5 PM		
5-6 PM		
6-7 PM		
7-8 PM		
8-9 PM		

INTEND

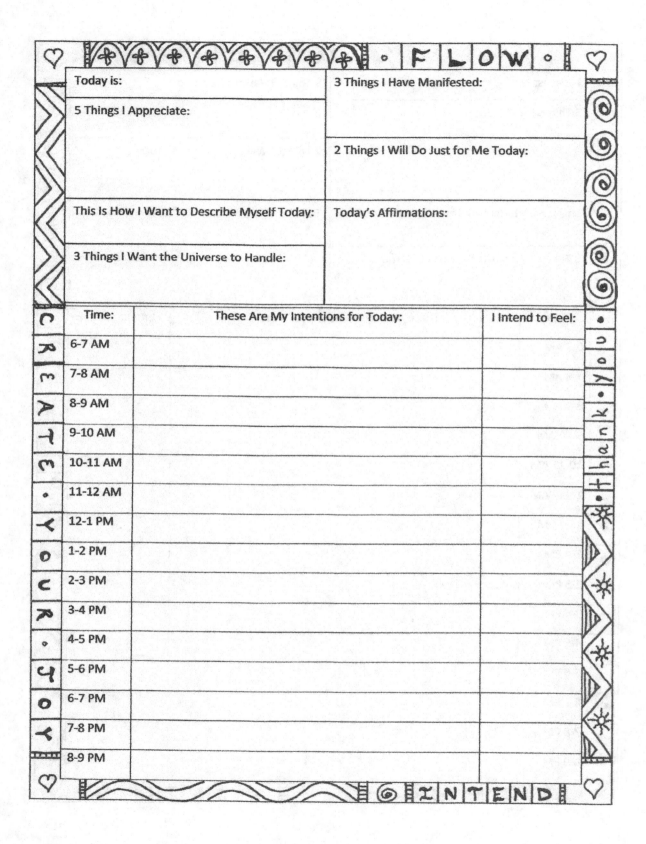

FLOW

Today is:	3 Things I Have Manifested:
5 Things I Appreciate:	
	2 Things I Will Do Just for Me Today:
This Is How I Want to Describe Myself Today:	Today's Affirmations:
3 Things I Want the Universe to Handle:	

CREATE • YOUR • JOY

Time:	These Are My Intentions for Today:	I Intend to Feel:
6-7 AM		
7-8 AM		
8-9 AM		
9-10 AM		
10-11 AM		
11-12 AM		
12-1 PM		
1-2 PM		
2-3 PM		
3-4 PM		
4-5 PM		
5-6 PM		
6-7 PM		
7-8 PM		
8-9 PM		

thank you

INTEND

FLOW

Today is:	**3 Things I Have Manifested:**
5 Things I Appreciate:	
	2 Things I Will Do Just for Me Today:
This Is How I Want to Describe Myself Today:	**Today's Affirmations:**
3 Things I Want the Universe to Handle:	

Time:	These Are My Intentions for Today:	I Intend to Feel:
6-7 AM		
7-8 AM		
8-9 AM		
9-10 AM		
10-11 AM		
11-12 AM		
12-1 PM		
1-2 PM		
2-3 PM		
3-4 PM		
4-5 PM		
5-6 PM		
6-7 PM		
7-8 PM		
8-9 PM		

CREATE . YOUR . JOY

thank . you

INTEND

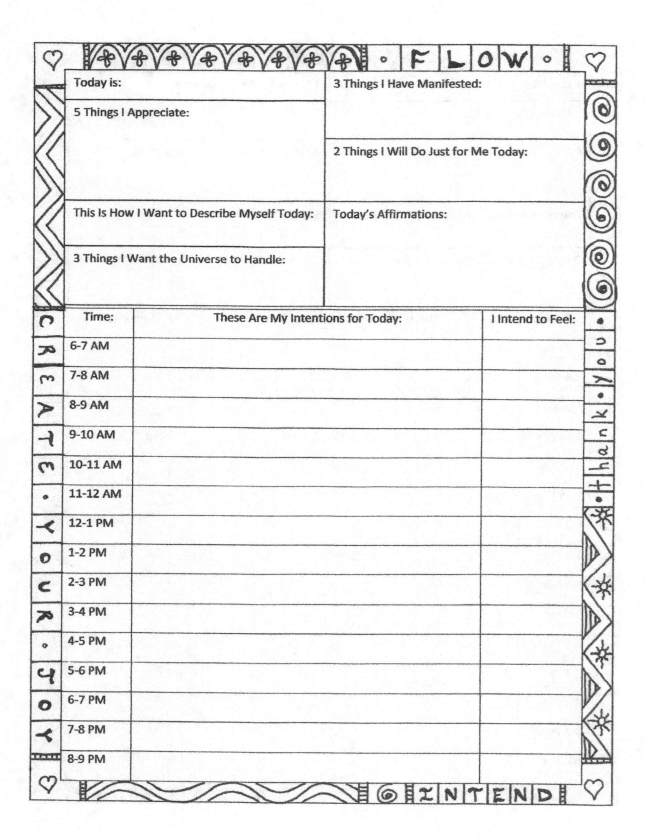

FLOW

Today is:	3 Things I Have Manifested:
5 Things I Appreciate:	
	2 Things I Will Do Just for Me Today:
This Is How I Want to Describe Myself Today:	Today's Affirmations:
3 Things I Want the Universe to Handle:	

Time:	These Are My Intentions for Today:	I Intend to Feel:
6-7 AM		
7-8 AM		
8-9 AM		
9-10 AM		
10-11 AM		
11-12 AM		
12-1 PM		
1-2 PM		
2-3 PM		
3-4 PM		
4-5 PM		
5-6 PM		
6-7 PM		
7-8 PM		
8-9 PM		

CREATE • YOUR • JOY

thank you

INTEND

FLOW

Today is:	3 Things I Have Manifested:
5 Things I Appreciate:	
	2 Things I Will Do Just for Me Today:
This Is How I Want to Describe Myself Today:	Today's Affirmations:
3 Things I Want the Universe to Handle:	

Time:	These Are My Intentions for Today:	I Intend to Feel:
6-7 AM		
7-8 AM		
8-9 AM		
9-10 AM		
10-11 AM		
11-12 AM		
12-1 PM		
1-2 PM		
2-3 PM		
3-4 PM		
4-5 PM		
5-6 PM		
6-7 PM		
7-8 PM		
8-9 PM		

CREATE YOUR JOY

thank you

INTEND

29

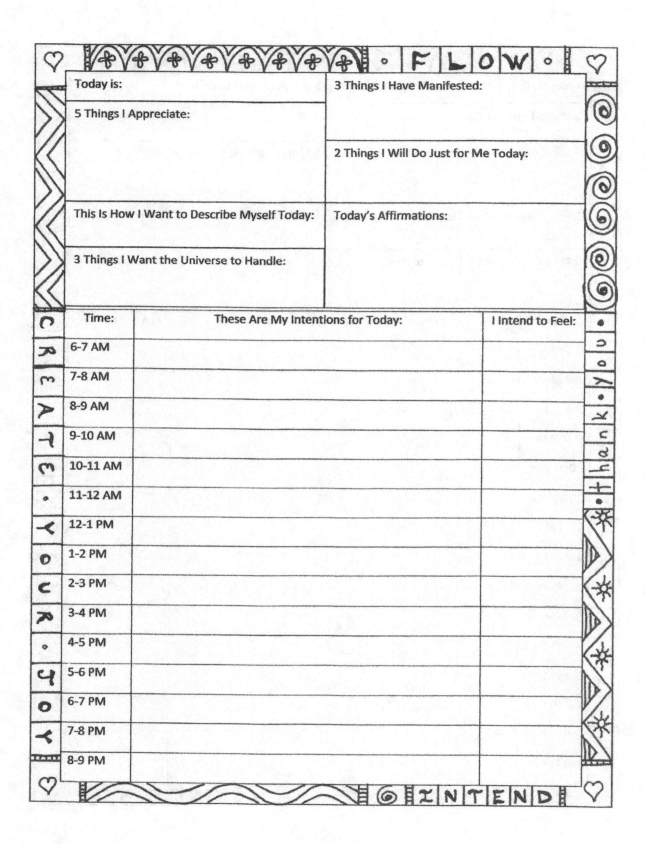

FLOW

Today is:

5 Things I Appreciate:

This Is How I Want to Describe Myself Today:

3 Things I Want the Universe to Handle:

3 Things I Have Manifested:

2 Things I Will Do Just for Me Today:

Today's Affirmations:

	Time:	These Are My Intentions for Today:	I Intend to Feel:
C	6-7 AM		
R	7-8 AM		
E	8-9 AM		
A	9-10 AM		
T	10-11 AM		
E	11-12 AM		
•	12-1 PM		
Y	1-2 PM		
O	2-3 PM		
U	3-4 PM		
R	4-5 PM		
•	5-6 PM		
J	6-7 PM		
O	7-8 PM		
Y	8-9 PM		

CREATE • YOUR • JOY

thank • you

INTEND

FLOW

Today is:

5 Things I Appreciate:

This Is How I Want to Describe Myself Today:

3 Things I Want the Universe to Handle:

3 Things I Have Manifested:

2 Things I Will Do Just for Me Today:

Today's Affirmations:

Time:	These Are My Intentions for Today:	I Intend to Feel:
6-7 AM		
7-8 AM		
8-9 AM		
9-10 AM		
10-11 AM		
11-12 AM		
12-1 PM		
1-2 PM		
2-3 PM		
3-4 PM		
4-5 PM		
5-6 PM		
6-7 PM		
7-8 PM		
8-9 PM		

CREATE · YOUR · JOY

thank you

INTEND

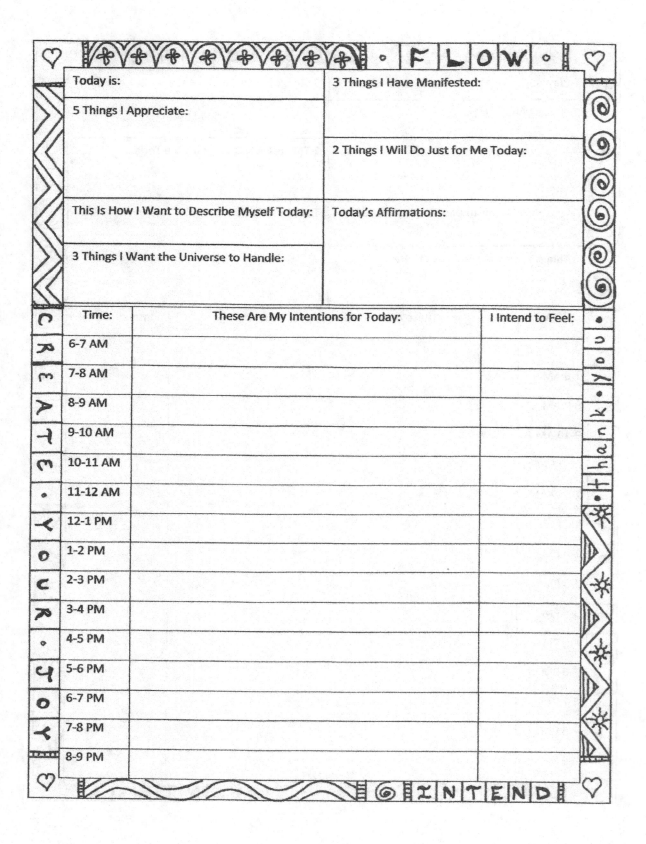

FLOW

Today is:	3 Things I Have Manifested:
5 Things I Appreciate:	
	2 Things I Will Do Just for Me Today:
This Is How I Want to Describe Myself Today:	Today's Affirmations:
3 Things I Want the Universe to Handle:	

CREATE . YOUR . JOY

thank you

Time:	These Are My Intentions for Today:	I Intend to Feel:
6-7 AM		
7-8 AM		
8-9 AM		
9-10 AM		
10-11 AM		
11-12 AM		
12-1 PM		
1-2 PM		
2-3 PM		
3-4 PM		
4-5 PM		
5-6 PM		
6-7 PM		
7-8 PM		
8-9 PM		

INTEND

Month: February

Sunday	Monday	Tuesday	Wednesday	Thursday	Friday	Saturday

Do at least one thing every day that brings you joy and record it on this page.

Affirmations:

" Everything exists for joy. There is not one other reason for life than joy.~ Abraham/Hicks

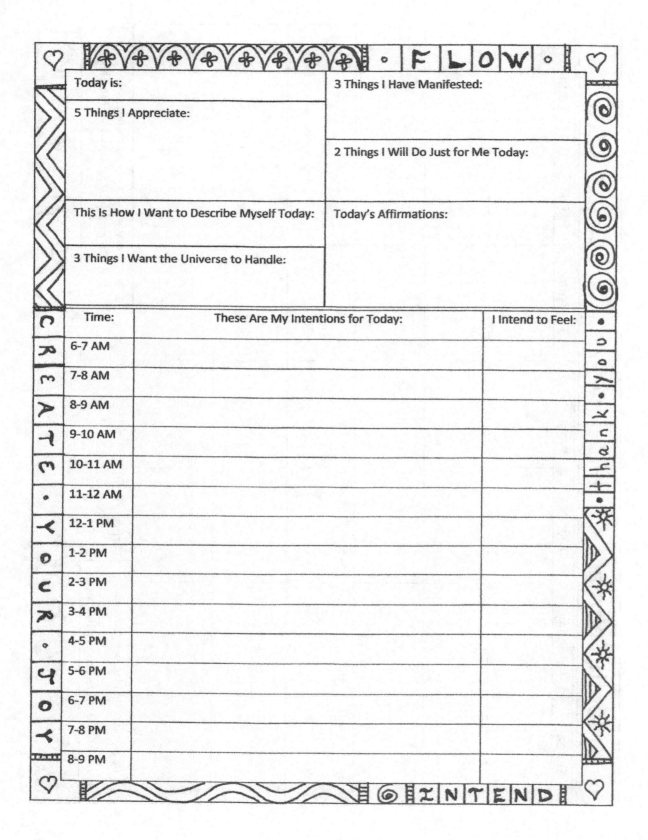

FLOW

| Today is: |
| 5 Things I Appreciate: |
| This Is How I Want to Describe Myself Today: |
| 3 Things I Want the Universe to Handle: |

| 3 Things I Have Manifested: |
| 2 Things I Will Do Just for Me Today: |
| Today's Affirmations: |

CREATE · YOUR · JOY

thank you · intend

Time:	These Are My Intentions for Today:	I Intend to Feel:
6-7 AM		
7-8 AM		
8-9 AM		
9-10 AM		
10-11 AM		
11-12 AM		
12-1 PM		
1-2 PM		
2-3 PM		
3-4 PM		
4-5 PM		
5-6 PM		
6-7 PM		
7-8 PM		
8-9 PM		

INTEND

FLOW

Today is:	3 Things I Have Manifested:

5 Things I Appreciate:

2 Things I Will Do Just for Me Today:

This Is How I Want to Describe Myself Today:	Today's Affirmations:

3 Things I Want the Universe to Handle:

Time:	These Are My Intentions for Today:	I Intend to Feel:
6-7 AM		
7-8 AM		
8-9 AM		
9-10 AM		
10-11 AM		
11-12 AM		
12-1 PM		
1-2 PM		
2-3 PM		
3-4 PM		
4-5 PM		
5-6 PM		
6-7 PM		
7-8 PM		
8-9 PM		

CREATE . YOUR . JOY

thank you

INTEND

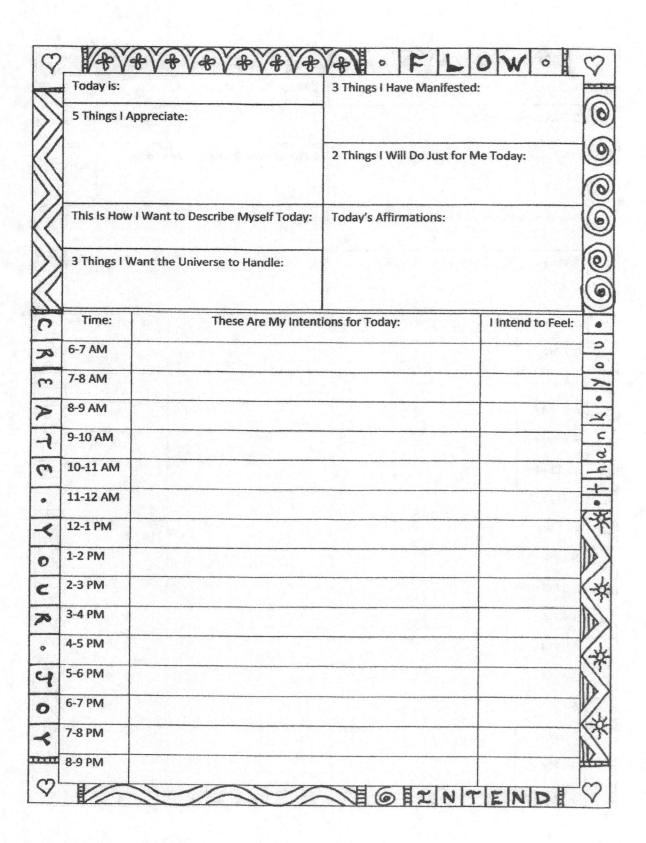

FLOW

Today is:	3 Things I Have Manifested:
5 Things I Appreciate:	
	2 Things I Will Do Just for Me Today:
This Is How I Want to Describe Myself Today:	Today's Affirmations:
3 Things I Want the Universe to Handle:	

Time:	These Are My Intentions for Today:	I Intend to Feel:
6-7 AM		
7-8 AM		
8-9 AM		
9-10 AM		
10-11 AM		
11-12 AM		
12-1 PM		
1-2 PM		
2-3 PM		
3-4 PM		
4-5 PM		
5-6 PM		
6-7 PM		
7-8 PM		
8-9 PM		

CREATE • YOUR • JOY

thank you

INTEND

36

FLOW

Today is:	3 Things I Have Manifested:
5 Things I Appreciate:	
	2 Things I Will Do Just for Me Today:
This Is How I Want to Describe Myself Today:	**Today's Affirmations:**
3 Things I Want the Universe to Handle:	

CREATE . YOUR . JOY

Time:	These Are My Intentions for Today:	I Intend to Feel:
6-7 AM		
7-8 AM		
8-9 AM		
9-10 AM		
10-11 AM		
11-12 AM		
12-1 PM		
1-2 PM		
2-3 PM		
3-4 PM		
4-5 PM		
5-6 PM		
6-7 PM		
7-8 PM		
8-9 PM		

thank you

INTEND

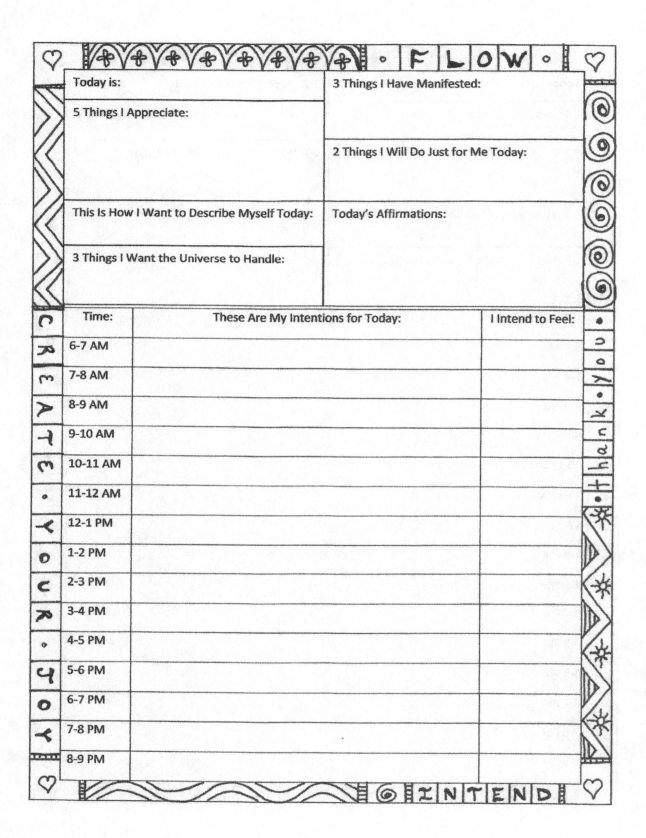

FLOW

Today is:	3 Things I Have Manifested:
5 Things I Appreciate:	
	2 Things I Will Do Just for Me Today:
This Is How I Want to Describe Myself Today:	Today's Affirmations:
3 Things I Want the Universe to Handle:	

CREATE · YOUR · JOY

thank you

INTEND

Time:	These Are My Intentions for Today:	I Intend to Feel:
6-7 AM		
7-8 AM		
8-9 AM		
9-10 AM		
10-11 AM		
11-12 AM		
12-1 PM		
1-2 PM		
2-3 PM		
3-4 PM		
4-5 PM		
5-6 PM		
6-7 PM		
7-8 PM		
8-9 PM		

· F L O W ·

Today is:	**3 Things I Have Manifested:**
5 Things I Appreciate:	
	2 Things I Will Do Just for Me Today:
This Is How I Want to Describe Myself Today:	**Today's Affirmations:**
3 Things I Want the Universe to Handle:	

Time:	These Are My Intentions for Today:	I Intend to Feel:
6-7 AM		
7-8 AM		
8-9 AM		
9-10 AM		
10-11 AM		
11-12 AM		
12-1 PM		
1-2 PM		
2-3 PM		
3-4 PM		
4-5 PM		
5-6 PM		
6-7 PM		
7-8 PM		
8-9 PM		

CREATE · YOUR · JOY

thank you

· INTEND

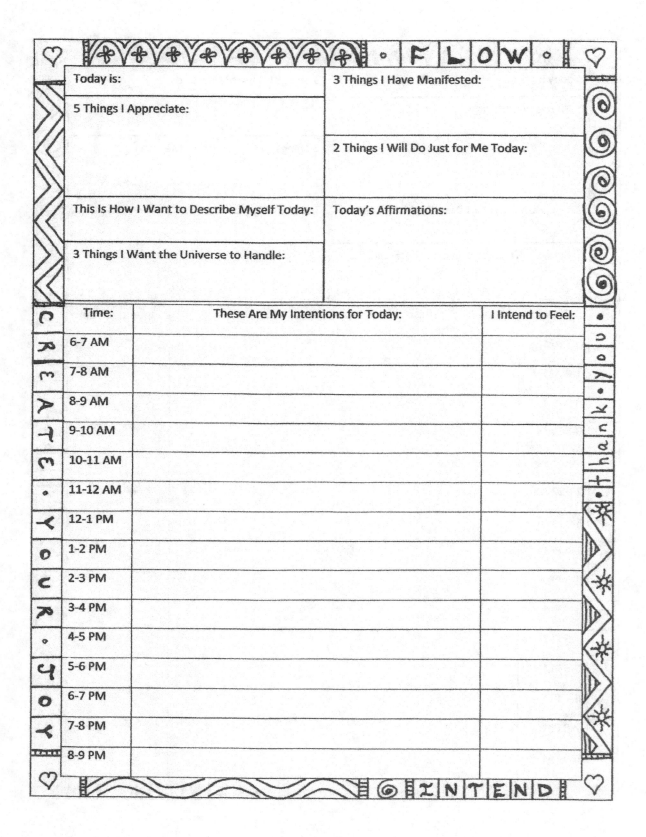

FLOW

Today is:	3 Things I Have Manifested:
5 Things I Appreciate:	
	2 Things I Will Do Just for Me Today:
This Is How I Want to Describe Myself Today:	**Today's Affirmations:**
3 Things I Want the Universe to Handle:	

CREATE • YOUR • JOY

Time:	These Are My Intentions for Today:	I Intend to Feel:
6-7 AM		
7-8 AM		
8-9 AM		
9-10 AM		
10-11 AM		
11-12 AM		
12-1 PM		
1-2 PM		
2-3 PM		
3-4 PM		
4-5 PM		
5-6 PM		
6-7 PM		
7-8 PM		
8-9 PM		

• thank you •

INTEND

FLOW

Today is:	3 Things I Have Manifested:
5 Things I Appreciate:	
	2 Things I Will Do Just for Me Today:
This Is How I Want to Describe Myself Today:	Today's Affirmations:
3 Things I Want the Universe to Handle:	

Time:	These Are My Intentions for Today:	I Intend to Feel:
6-7 AM		
7-8 AM		
8-9 AM		
9-10 AM		
10-11 AM		
11-12 AM		
12-1 PM		
1-2 PM		
2-3 PM		
3-4 PM		
4-5 PM		
5-6 PM		
6-7 PM		
7-8 PM		
8-9 PM		

CREATE . YOUR . JOY

thank you

INTEND

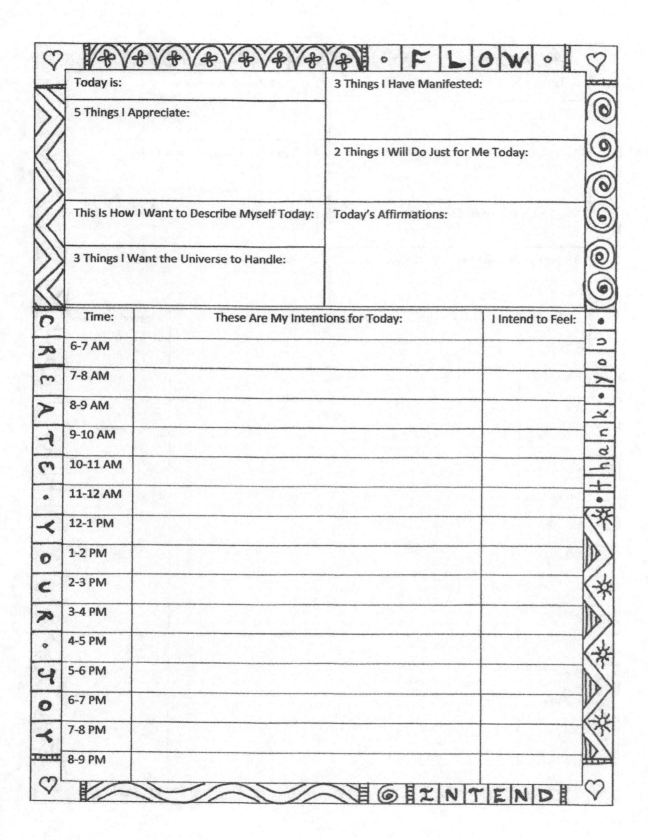

FLOW

Today is:

5 Things I Appreciate:

This Is How I Want to Describe Myself Today:

3 Things I Want the Universe to Handle:

3 Things I Have Manifested:

2 Things I Will Do Just for Me Today:

Today's Affirmations:

Time:	These Are My Intentions for Today:	I Intend to Feel:
6-7 AM		
7-8 AM		
8-9 AM		
9-10 AM		
10-11 AM		
11-12 AM		
12-1 PM		
1-2 PM		
2-3 PM		
3-4 PM		
4-5 PM		
5-6 PM		
6-7 PM		
7-8 PM		
8-9 PM		

CREATE · YOUR · JOY

thank · you

INTEND

FLOW

Today is:

5 Things I Appreciate:

This Is How I Want to Describe Myself Today:

3 Things I Want the Universe to Handle:

3 Things I Have Manifested:

2 Things I Will Do Just for Me Today:

Today's Affirmations:

Time:	These Are My Intentions for Today:	I Intend to Feel:
6-7 AM		
7-8 AM		
8-9 AM		
9-10 AM		
10-11 AM		
11-12 AM		
12-1 PM		
1-2 PM		
2-3 PM		
3-4 PM		
4-5 PM		
5-6 PM		
6-7 PM		
7-8 PM		
8-9 PM		

CREATE . YOUR . JOY

thank you

INTEND

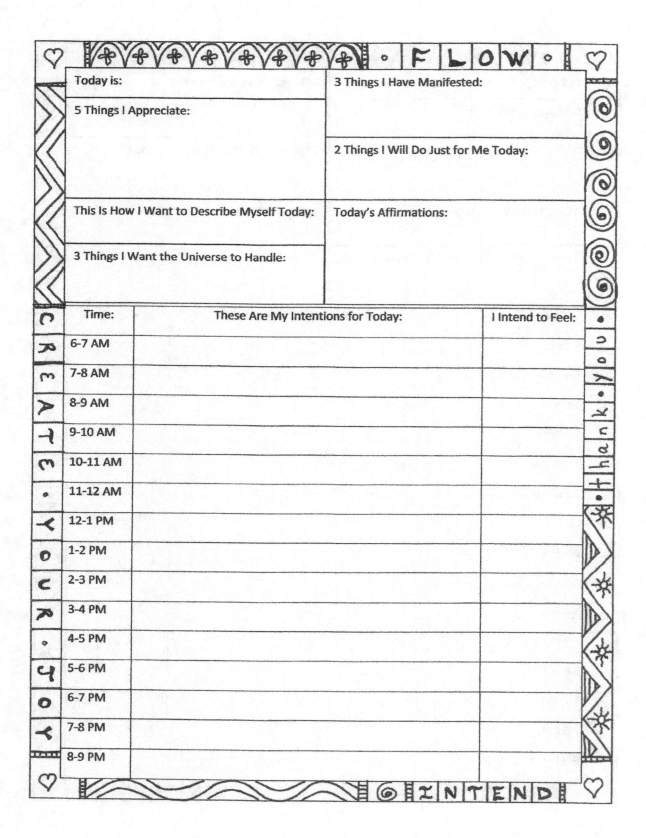

FLOW

Today is:	3 Things I Have Manifested:
5 Things I Appreciate:	
	2 Things I Will Do Just for Me Today:
This Is How I Want to Describe Myself Today:	Today's Affirmations:
3 Things I Want the Universe to Handle:	

	Time:	These Are My Intentions for Today:	I Intend to Feel:
C	6-7 AM		
R	7-8 AM		
E	8-9 AM		
A	9-10 AM		
T	10-11 AM		
E	11-12 AM		
•	12-1 PM		
Y	1-2 PM		
O	2-3 PM		
U	3-4 PM		
R	4-5 PM		
•	5-6 PM		
J	6-7 PM		
O	7-8 PM		
Y	8-9 PM		

CREATE • YOUR • JOY

thank you

INTEND

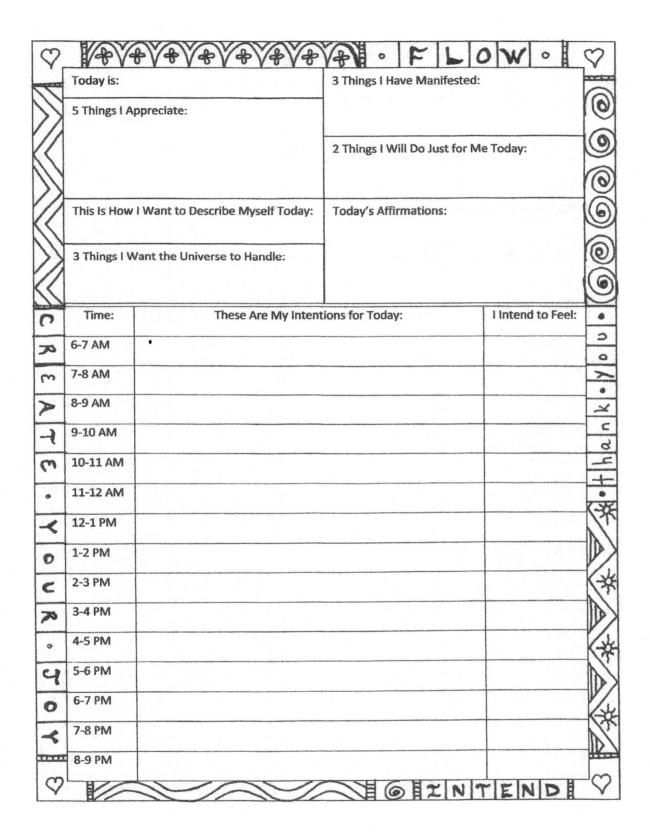

FLOW

Today is:	3 Things I Have Manifested:
5 Things I Appreciate:	
	2 Things I Will Do Just for Me Today:
This Is How I Want to Describe Myself Today:	Today's Affirmations:
3 Things I Want the Universe to Handle:	

CREATE • YOUR • JOY

thank • you

Time:	These Are My Intentions for Today:	I Intend to Feel:
6-7 AM		
7-8 AM		
8-9 AM		
9-10 AM		
10-11 AM		
11-12 AM		
12-1 PM		
1-2 PM		
2-3 PM		
3-4 PM		
4-5 PM		
5-6 PM		
6-7 PM		
7-8 PM		
8-9 PM		

INTEND

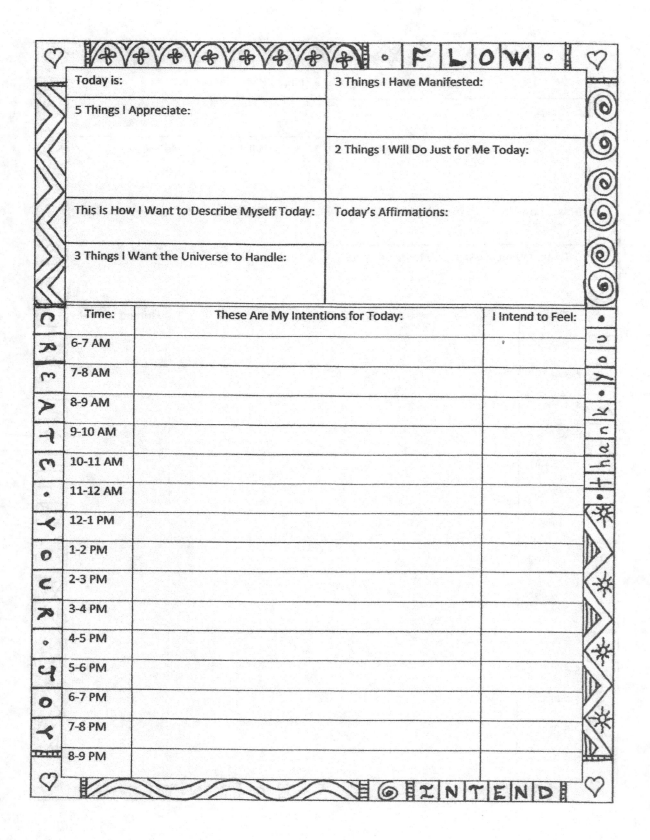

FLOW

Today is:	3 Things I Have Manifested:
5 Things I Appreciate:	
	2 Things I Will Do Just for Me Today:
This Is How I Want to Describe Myself Today:	Today's Affirmations:
3 Things I Want the Universe to Handle:	

CREATE • YOUR • JOY

thank you

Time:	These Are My Intentions for Today:	I Intend to Feel:
6-7 AM		
7-8 AM		
8-9 AM		
9-10 AM		
10-11 AM		
11-12 AM		
12-1 PM		
1-2 PM		
2-3 PM		
3-4 PM		
4-5 PM		
5-6 PM		
6-7 PM		
7-8 PM		
8-9 PM		

INTEND

FLOW

Today is:	3 Things I Have Manifested:
5 Things I Appreciate:	
	2 Things I Will Do Just for Me Today:
This Is How I Want to Describe Myself Today:	Today's Affirmations:
3 Things I Want the Universe to Handle:	

	Time:	These Are My Intentions for Today:	I Intend to Feel:
C	6-7 AM		
R	7-8 AM		
E	8-9 AM		
A	9-10 AM		
T	10-11 AM		
E	11-12 AM		
Y	12-1 PM		
O	1-2 PM		
U	2-3 PM		
R	3-4 PM		
	4-5 PM		
J	5-6 PM		
O	6-7 PM		
Y	7-8 PM		
	8-9 PM		

CREATE YOUR JOY · thank you · INTEND

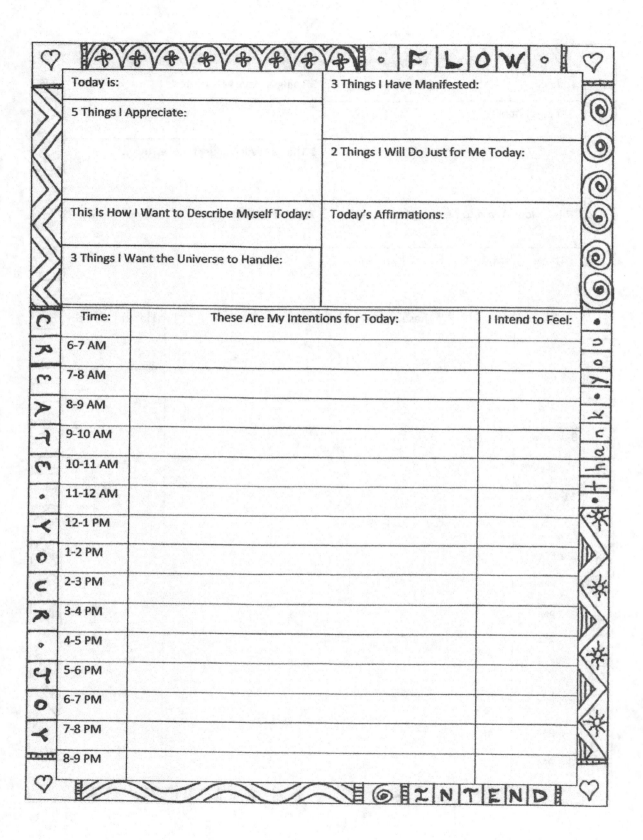

FLOW

Today is:	3 Things I Have Manifested:
5 Things I Appreciate:	
	2 Things I Will Do Just for Me Today:
This Is How I Want to Describe Myself Today:	Today's Affirmations:
3 Things I Want the Universe to Handle:	

Time:	These Are My Intentions for Today:	I Intend to Feel:
6-7 AM		
7-8 AM		
8-9 AM		
9-10 AM		
10-11 AM		
11-12 AM		
12-1 PM		
1-2 PM		
2-3 PM		
3-4 PM		
4-5 PM		
5-6 PM		
6-7 PM		
7-8 PM		
8-9 PM		

CREATE • YOUR • JOY

thank you

INTEND

48

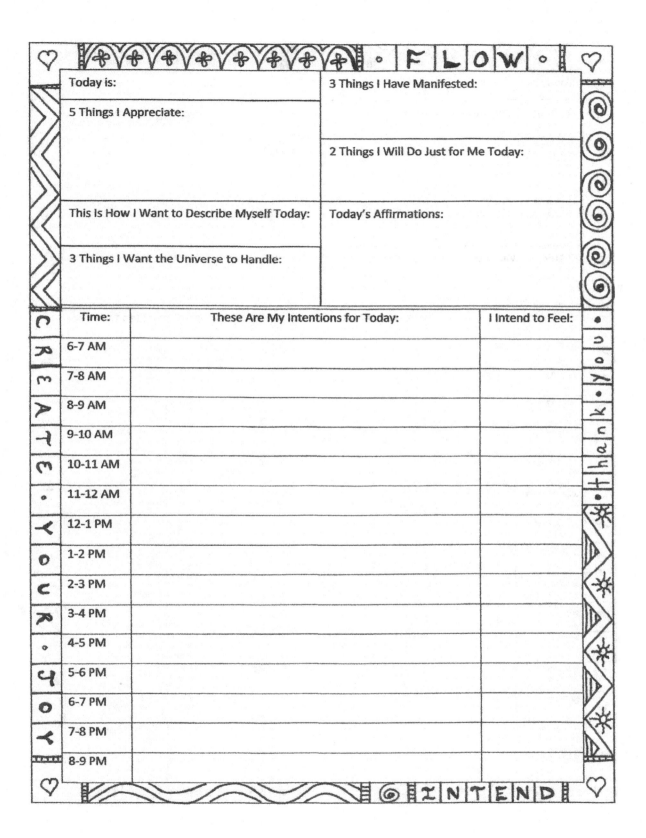

FLOW

Today is:	3 Things I Have Manifested:
5 Things I Appreciate:	
	2 Things I Will Do Just for Me Today:
This Is How I Want to Describe Myself Today:	Today's Affirmations:
3 Things I Want the Universe to Handle:	

	Time:	These Are My Intentions for Today:	I Intend to Feel:
C	6-7 AM		
R	7-8 AM		
E	8-9 AM		
A	9-10 AM		
T	10-11 AM		
E	11-12 AM		
Y	12-1 PM		
O	1-2 PM		
U	2-3 PM		
R	3-4 PM		
	4-5 PM		
J	5-6 PM		
O	6-7 PM		
Y	7-8 PM		
	8-9 PM		

thank you

INTEND

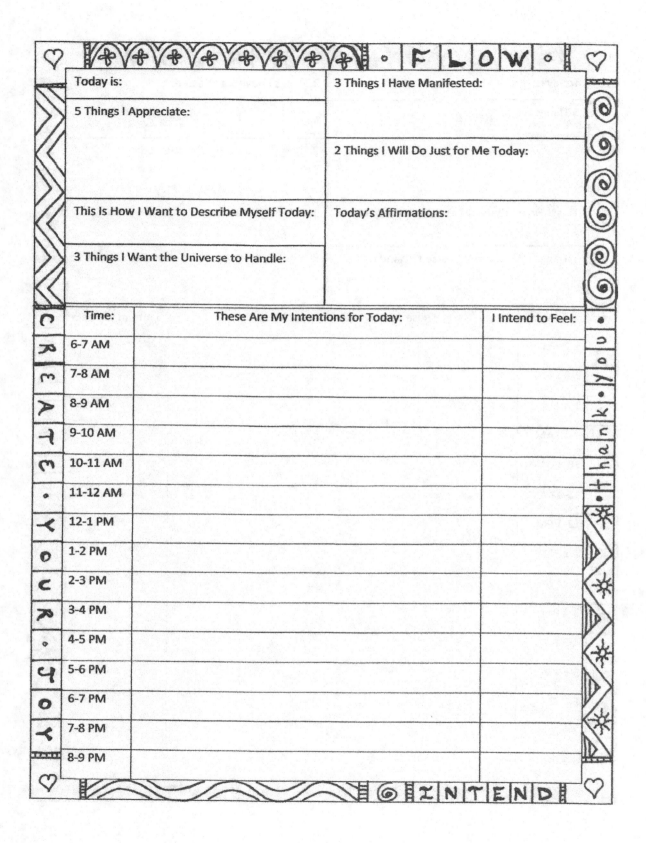

FLOW

Today is:	3 Things I Have Manifested:
5 Things I Appreciate:	
	2 Things I Will Do Just for Me Today:
This Is How I Want to Describe Myself Today:	Today's Affirmations:
3 Things I Want the Universe to Handle:	

CREATE · YOUR · JOY

thank you · thank you

Time:	These Are My Intentions for Today:	I Intend to Feel:
6-7 AM		
7-8 AM		
8-9 AM		
9-10 AM		
10-11 AM		
11-12 AM		
12-1 PM		
1-2 PM		
2-3 PM		
3-4 PM		
4-5 PM		
5-6 PM		
6-7 PM		
7-8 PM		
8-9 PM		

INTEND

· F L O W ·

Today is:	3 Things I Have Manifested:
5 Things I Appreciate:	
	2 Things I Will Do Just for Me Today:
This Is How I Want to Describe Myself Today:	**Today's Affirmations:**
3 Things I Want the Universe to Handle:	

	Time:	These Are My Intentions for Today:	I Intend to Feel:
C	6-7 AM		
R	7-8 AM		
E	8-9 AM		
A	9-10 AM		
T	10-11 AM		
E	11-12 AM		
Y	12-1 PM		
O	1-2 PM		
U	2-3 PM		
R	3-4 PM		
J	4-5 PM		
O	5-6 PM		
Y	6-7 PM		
	7-8 PM		
	8-9 PM		

CREATE · YOUR · JOY

thank you

· INTEND

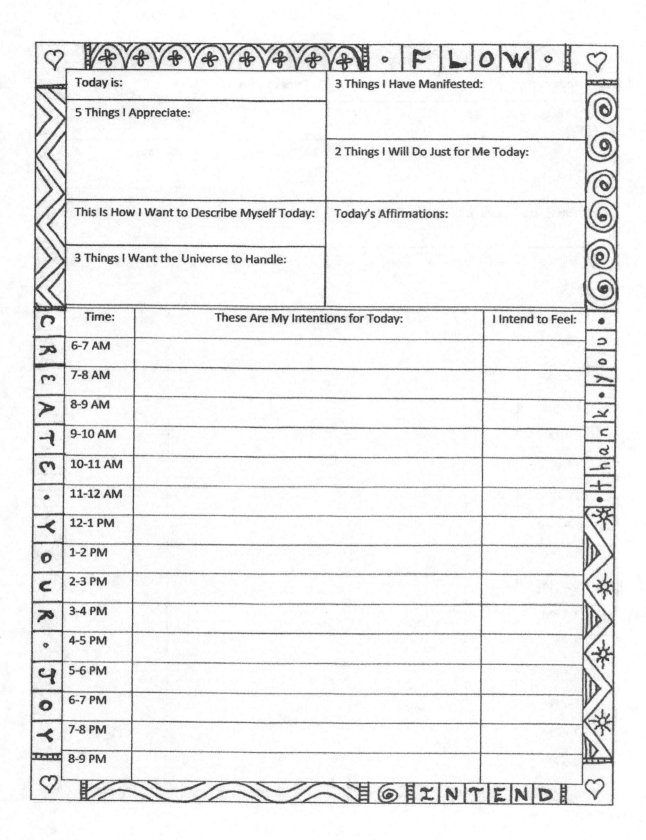

FLOW

Today is:	3 Things I Have Manifested:
5 Things I Appreciate:	
	2 Things I Will Do Just for Me Today:
This Is How I Want to Describe Myself Today:	Today's Affirmations:
3 Things I Want the Universe to Handle:	

CREATE • YOUR • JOY

Time:	These Are My Intentions for Today:	I Intend to Feel:
6-7 AM		
7-8 AM		
8-9 AM		
9-10 AM		
10-11 AM		
11-12 AM		
12-1 PM		
1-2 PM		
2-3 PM		
3-4 PM		
4-5 PM		
5-6 PM		
6-7 PM		
7-8 PM		
8-9 PM		

thank you

INTEND

FLOW

Today is:	3 Things I Have Manifested:
5 Things I Appreciate:	
	2 Things I Will Do Just for Me Today:
This Is How I Want to Describe Myself Today:	Today's Affirmations:
3 Things I Want the Universe to Handle:	

CREATE . YOUR . JOY

Time:	These Are My Intentions for Today:	I Intend to Feel:
6-7 AM		
7-8 AM		
8-9 AM		
9-10 AM		
10-11 AM		
11-12 AM		
12-1 PM		
1-2 PM		
2-3 PM		
3-4 PM		
4-5 PM		
5-6 PM		
6-7 PM		
7-8 PM		
8-9 PM		

thank you

INTEND

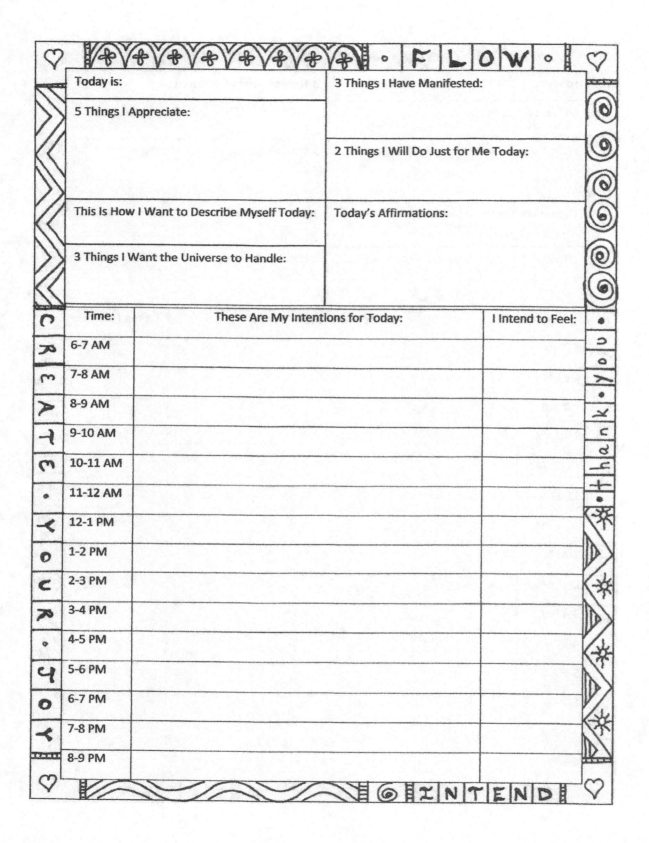

FLOW

Today is:	3 Things I Have Manifested:
5 Things I Appreciate:	
	2 Things I Will Do Just for Me Today:
This Is How I Want to Describe Myself Today:	Today's Affirmations:
3 Things I Want the Universe to Handle:	

Time:	These Are My Intentions for Today:	I Intend to Feel:
6-7 AM		
7-8 AM		
8-9 AM		
9-10 AM		
10-11 AM		
11-12 AM		
12-1 PM		
1-2 PM		
2-3 PM		
3-4 PM		
4-5 PM		
5-6 PM		
6-7 PM		
7-8 PM		
8-9 PM		

CREATE • YOUR • JOY

thank you

INTEND

· F L O W ·

Today is:

5 Things I Appreciate:

3 Things I Have Manifested:

2 Things I Will Do Just for Me Today:

This Is How I Want to Describe Myself Today:

Today's Affirmations:

3 Things I Want the Universe to Handle:

Time:	These Are My Intentions for Today:	I Intend to Feel:
6-7 AM		
7-8 AM		
8-9 AM		
9-10 AM		
10-11 AM		
11-12 AM		
12-1 PM		
1-2 PM		
2-3 PM		
3-4 PM		
4-5 PM		
5-6 PM		
6-7 PM		
7-8 PM		
8-9 PM		

CREATE. YOUR. JOY

do. you. thank t

© INTEND

FLOW

Today is:	3 Things I Have Manifested:
5 Things I Appreciate:	
	2 Things I Will Do Just for Me Today:
This Is How I Want to Describe Myself Today:	Today's Affirmations:
3 Things I Want the Universe to Handle:	

Time:	These Are My Intentions for Today:	I Intend to Feel:
6-7 AM		
7-8 AM		
8-9 AM		
9-10 AM		
10-11 AM		
11-12 AM		
12-1 PM		
1-2 PM		
2-3 PM		
3-4 PM		
4-5 PM		
5-6 PM		
6-7 PM		
7-8 PM		
8-9 PM		

CREATE · YOUR · JOY

thank you

INTEND

FLOW

Today is:	3 Things I Have Manifested:
5 Things I Appreciate:	
	2 Things I Will Do Just for Me Today:
This Is How I Want to Describe Myself Today:	**Today's Affirmations:**
3 Things I Want the Universe to Handle:	

	Time:	These Are My Intentions for Today:	I Intend to Feel:
C	6-7 AM		
R	7-8 AM		
E	8-9 AM		
A	9-10 AM		
T	10-11 AM		
E	11-12 AM		
Y	12-1 PM		
O	1-2 PM		
U	2-3 PM		
R	3-4 PM		
	4-5 PM		
J	5-6 PM		
O	6-7 PM		
Y	7-8 PM		
	8-9 PM		

INTEND

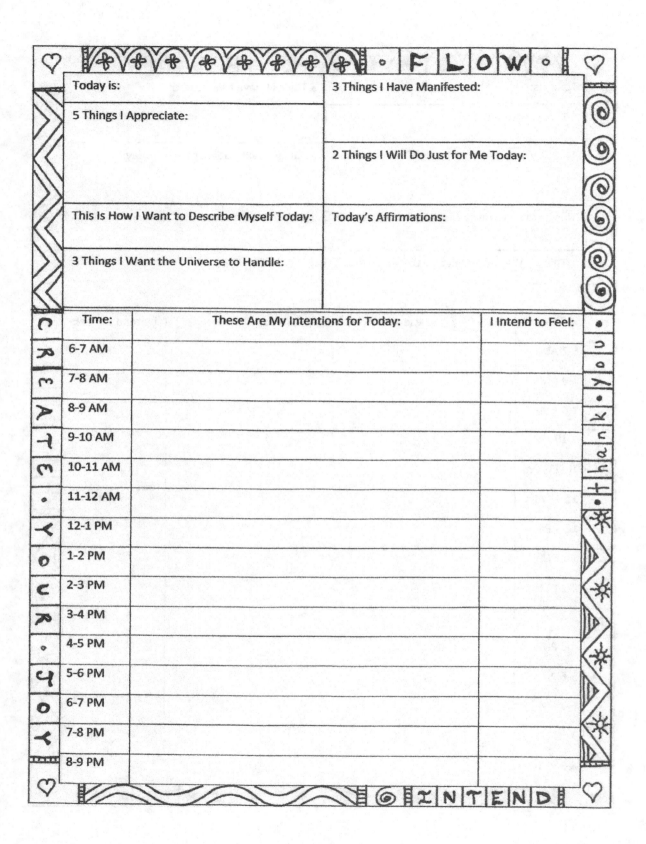

FLOW

Today is:	3 Things I Have Manifested:
5 Things I Appreciate:	2 Things I Will Do Just for Me Today:
This Is How I Want to Describe Myself Today:	Today's Affirmations:
3 Things I Want the Universe to Handle:	

CREATE • YOUR • JOY

thank you

Time:	These Are My Intentions for Today:	I Intend to Feel:
6-7 AM		
7-8 AM		
8-9 AM		
9-10 AM		
10-11 AM		
11-12 AM		
12-1 PM		
1-2 PM		
2-3 PM		
3-4 PM		
4-5 PM		
5-6 PM		
6-7 PM		
7-8 PM		
8-9 PM		

INTEND

FLOW

Today is:	3 Things I Have Manifested:
5 Things I Appreciate:	
	2 Things I Will Do Just for Me Today:
This Is How I Want to Describe Myself Today:	Today's Affirmations:
3 Things I Want the Universe to Handle:	

CREATE.YOUR.JOY

Time:	These Are My Intentions for Today:	I Intend to Feel:
6-7 AM		
7-8 AM		
8-9 AM		
9-10 AM		
10-11 AM		
11-12 AM		
12-1 PM		
1-2 PM		
2-3 PM		
3-4 PM		
4-5 PM		
5-6 PM		
6-7 PM		
7-8 PM		
8-9 PM		

thank you.

INTEND

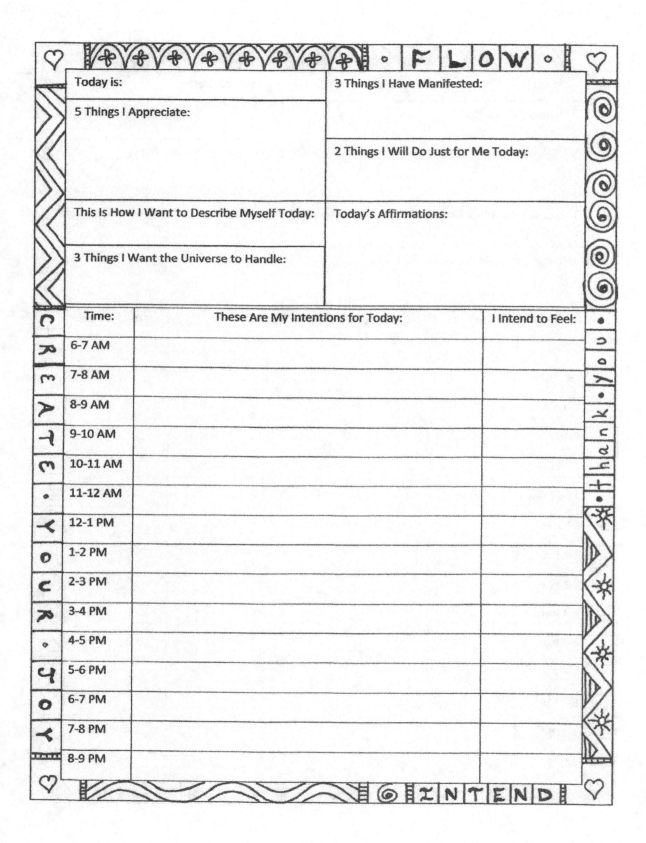

FLOW

Today is:

5 Things I Appreciate:

This Is How I Want to Describe Myself Today:

3 Things I Want the Universe to Handle:

3 Things I Have Manifested:

2 Things I Will Do Just for Me Today:

Today's Affirmations:

Time:	These Are My Intentions for Today:	I Intend to Feel:
6-7 AM		
7-8 AM		
8-9 AM		
9-10 AM		
10-11 AM		
11-12 AM		
12-1 PM		
1-2 PM		
2-3 PM		
3-4 PM		
4-5 PM		
5-6 PM		
6-7 PM		
7-8 PM		
8-9 PM		

INTEND

FLOW

Today is:

5 Things I Appreciate:

3 Things I Have Manifested:

2 Things I Will Do Just for Me Today:

This Is How I Want to Describe Myself Today:

Today's Affirmations:

3 Things I Want the Universe to Handle:

Time:	These Are My Intentions for Today:	I Intend to Feel:
6-7 AM		
7-8 AM		
8-9 AM		
9-10 AM		
10-11 AM		
11-12 AM		
12-1 PM		
1-2 PM		
2-3 PM		
3-4 PM		
4-5 PM		
5-6 PM		
6-7 PM		
7-8 PM		
8-9 PM		

CREATE . YOUR . JOY

thank you

INTEND

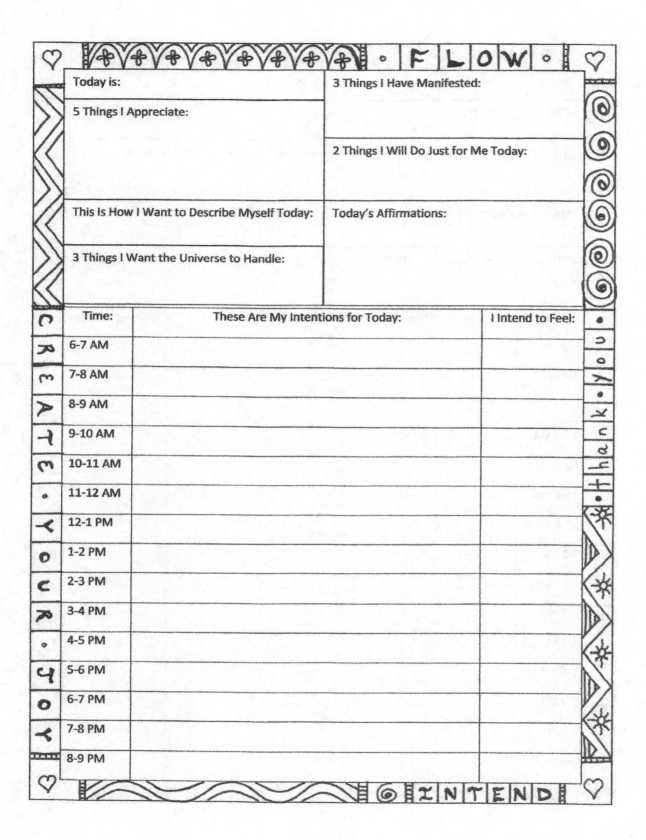

FLOW

Today is:

5 Things I Appreciate:

3 Things I Have Manifested:

2 Things I Will Do Just for Me Today:

This Is How I Want to Describe Myself Today:

Today's Affirmations:

3 Things I Want the Universe to Handle:

Time:	These Are My Intentions for Today:	I Intend to Feel:
6-7 AM		
7-8 AM		
8-9 AM		
9-10 AM		
10-11 AM		
11-12 AM		
12-1 PM		
1-2 PM		
2-3 PM		
3-4 PM		
4-5 PM		
5-6 PM		
6-7 PM		
7-8 PM		
8-9 PM		

CREATE • YOUR • JOY

thank you

INTEND

62

Month: March

Sunday	Monday	Tuesday	Wednesday	Thursday	Friday	Saturday

Do at least one thing every day that brings you joy and record it on this page.

Affirmations:

" There is no shortage. "

— Abraham/Hicks

FLOW

Today is:	3 Things I Have Manifested:
5 Things I Appreciate:	
	2 Things I Will Do Just for Me Today:
This Is How I Want to Describe Myself Today:	Today's Affirmations:
3 Things I Want the Universe to Handle:	

Time:	These Are My Intentions for Today:	I Intend to Feel:
6-7 AM		
7-8 AM		
8-9 AM		
9-10 AM		
10-11 AM		
11-12 AM		
12-1 PM		
1-2 PM		
2-3 PM		
3-4 PM		
4-5 PM		
5-6 PM		
6-7 PM		
7-8 PM		
8-9 PM		

CREATE · YOUR · JOY

thank you

INTEND

FLOW

Today is:	**3 Things I Have Manifested:**
5 Things I Appreciate:	
	2 Things I Will Do Just for Me Today:
This Is How I Want to Describe Myself Today:	**Today's Affirmations:**
3 Things I Want the Universe to Handle:	

Time:	These Are My Intentions for Today:	I Intend to Feel:
6-7 AM		
7-8 AM		
8-9 AM		
9-10 AM		
10-11 AM		
11-12 AM		
12-1 PM		
1-2 PM		
2-3 PM		
3-4 PM		
4-5 PM		
5-6 PM		
6-7 PM		
7-8 PM		
8-9 PM		

CREATE . YOUR . JOY

thank you .

INTEND

65

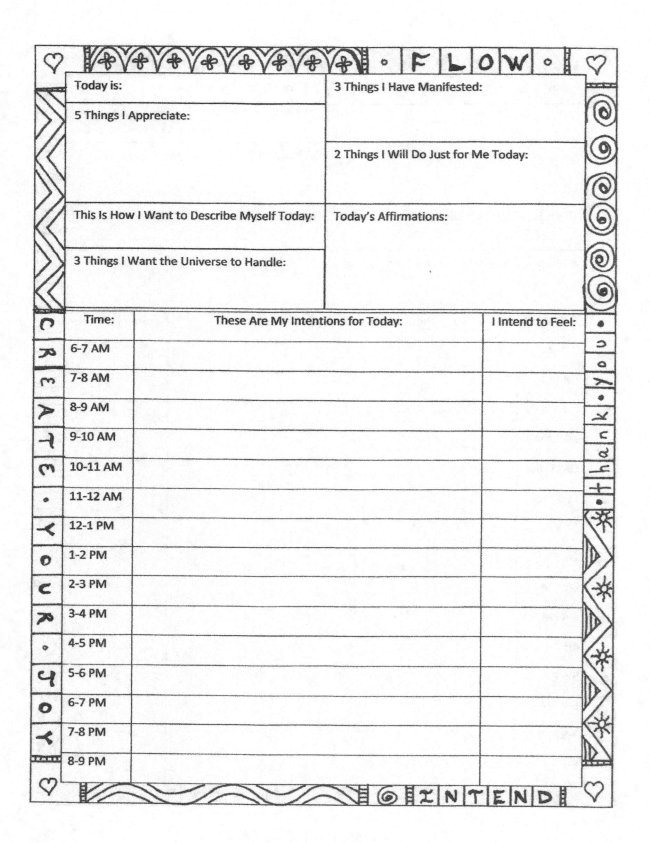

FLOW

Today is:	3 Things I Have Manifested:
5 Things I Appreciate:	
	2 Things I Will Do Just for Me Today:
This Is How I Want to Describe Myself Today:	Today's Affirmations:
3 Things I Want the Universe to Handle:	

CREATE . YOUR . JOY

Time:	These Are My Intentions for Today:	I Intend to Feel:
6-7 AM		
7-8 AM		
8-9 AM		
9-10 AM		
10-11 AM		
11-12 AM		
12-1 PM		
1-2 PM		
2-3 PM		
3-4 PM		
4-5 PM		
5-6 PM		
6-7 PM		
7-8 PM		
8-9 PM		

thank you

INTEND

FLOW

Today is:	3 Things I Have Manifested:
5 Things I Appreciate:	
	2 Things I Will Do Just for Me Today:
This Is How I Want to Describe Myself Today:	Today's Affirmations:
3 Things I Want the Universe to Handle:	

	Time:	These Are My Intentions for Today:	I Intend to Feel:
C	6-7 AM		
R	7-8 AM		
E	8-9 AM		
A	9-10 AM		
T	10-11 AM		
E	11-12 AM		
Y	12-1 PM		
O	1-2 PM		
U	2-3 PM		
R	3-4 PM		
	4-5 PM		
J	5-6 PM		
O	6-7 PM		
Y	7-8 PM		
	8-9 PM		

CREATE . YOUR . JOY

thank you

INTEND

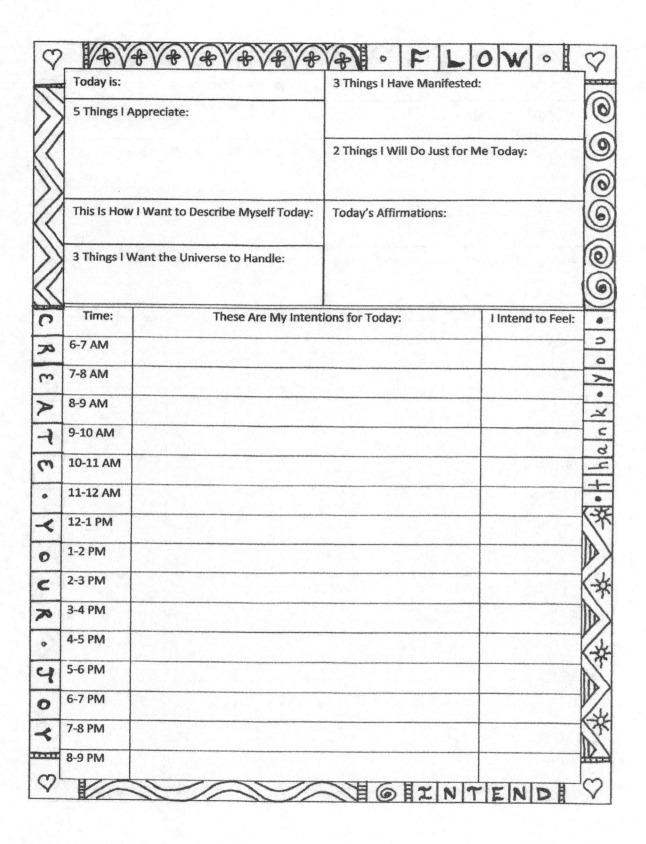

FLOW

Today is:

5 Things I Appreciate:

This Is How I Want to Describe Myself Today:

3 Things I Want the Universe to Handle:

3 Things I Have Manifested:

2 Things I Will Do Just for Me Today:

Today's Affirmations:

Time:	These Are My Intentions for Today:	I Intend to Feel:
6-7 AM		
7-8 AM		
8-9 AM		
9-10 AM		
10-11 AM		
11-12 AM		
12-1 PM		
1-2 PM		
2-3 PM		
3-4 PM		
4-5 PM		
5-6 PM		
6-7 PM		
7-8 PM		
8-9 PM		

CREATE . YOUR . JOY

thank you

INTEND

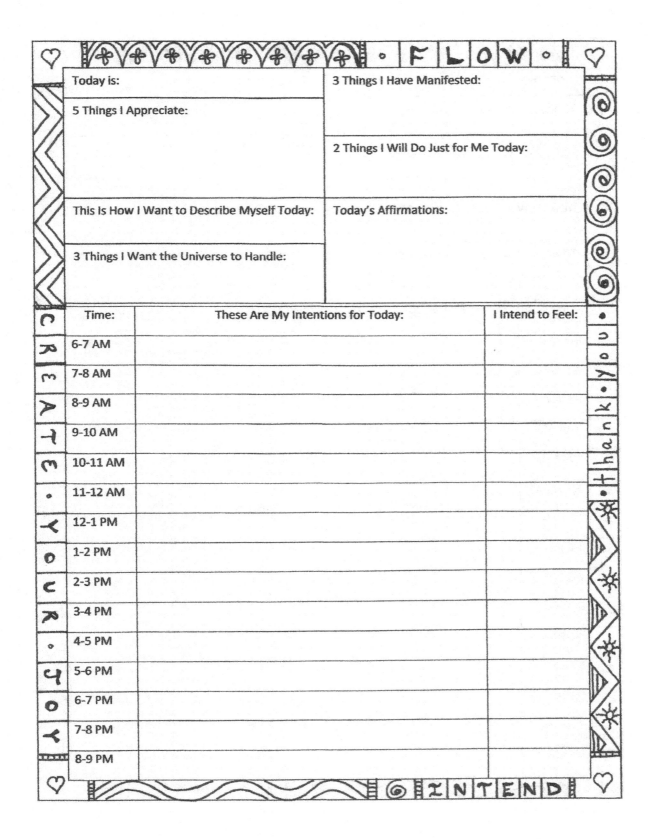

FLOW

Today is:	3 Things I Have Manifested:
5 Things I Appreciate:	
	2 Things I Will Do Just for Me Today:
This Is How I Want to Describe Myself Today:	**Today's Affirmations:**
3 Things I Want the Universe to Handle:	

Time:	These Are My Intentions for Today:	I Intend to Feel:
6-7 AM		
7-8 AM		
8-9 AM		
9-10 AM		
10-11 AM		
11-12 AM		
12-1 PM		
1-2 PM		
2-3 PM		
3-4 PM		
4-5 PM		
5-6 PM		
6-7 PM		
7-8 PM		
8-9 PM		

CREATE · YOUR · JOY

thank you

INTEND

FLOW

Today is:	3 Things I Have Manifested:
5 Things I Appreciate:	
	2 Things I Will Do Just for Me Today:
This Is How I Want to Describe Myself Today:	Today's Affirmations:
3 Things I Want the Universe to Handle:	

CREATE · YOUR · JOY

thank you

Time:	These Are My Intentions for Today:	I Intend to Feel:
6-7 AM		
7-8 AM		
8-9 AM		
9-10 AM		
10-11 AM		
11-12 AM		
12-1 PM		
1-2 PM		
2-3 PM		
3-4 PM		
4-5 PM		
5-6 PM		
6-7 PM		
7-8 PM		
8-9 PM		

INTEND

70

FLOW

Today is:	**3 Things I Have Manifested:**
5 Things I Appreciate:	
	2 Things I Will Do Just for Me Today:
This Is How I Want to Describe Myself Today:	**Today's Affirmations:**
3 Things I Want the Universe to Handle:	

Time:	These Are My Intentions for Today:	I Intend to Feel:
6-7 AM		
7-8 AM		
8-9 AM		
9-10 AM		
10-11 AM		
11-12 AM		
12-1 PM		
1-2 PM		
2-3 PM		
3-4 PM		
4-5 PM		
5-6 PM		
6-7 PM		
7-8 PM		
8-9 PM		

CREATE . YOUR . JOY

thank you

INTEND

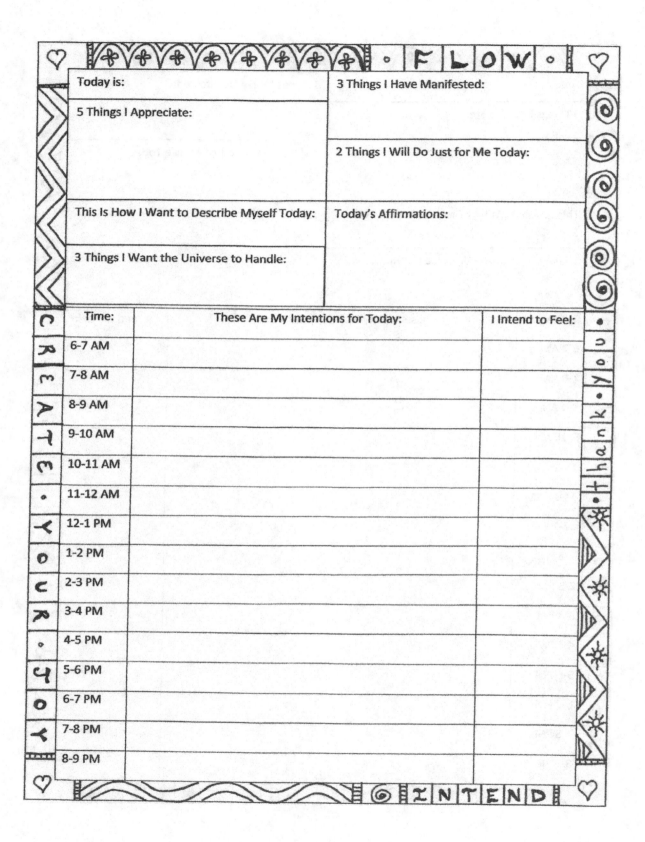

FLOW

Today is:	3 Things I Have Manifested:
5 Things I Appreciate:	
	2 Things I Will Do Just for Me Today:
This Is How I Want to Describe Myself Today:	**Today's Affirmations:**
3 Things I Want the Universe to Handle:	

CREATE . YOUR . CRE . JOY

thank . you

Time:	These Are My Intentions for Today:	I Intend to Feel:
6-7 AM		
7-8 AM		
8-9 AM		
9-10 AM		
10-11 AM		
11-12 AM		
12-1 PM		
1-2 PM		
2-3 PM		
3-4 PM		
4-5 PM		
5-6 PM		
6-7 PM		
7-8 PM		
8-9 PM		

INTEND

· F L O W ·

Today is:	3 Things I Have Manifested:
5 Things I Appreciate:	
	2 Things I Will Do Just for Me Today:
This Is How I Want to Describe Myself Today:	**Today's Affirmations:**
3 Things I Want the Universe to Handle:	

Time:	These Are My Intentions for Today:	I Intend to Feel:
6-7 AM		
7-8 AM		
8-9 AM		
9-10 AM		
10-11 AM		
11-12 AM		
12-1 PM		
1-2 PM		
2-3 PM		
3-4 PM		
4-5 PM		
5-6 PM		
6-7 PM		
7-8 PM		
8-9 PM		

CREATE · YOUR · JOY

thank · you

INTEND

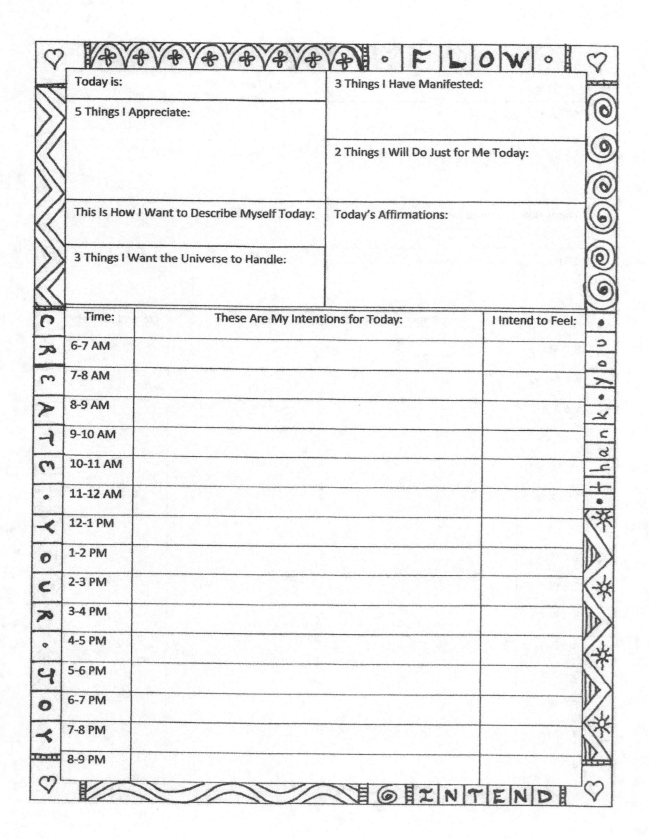

FLOW

Today is:

5 Things I Appreciate:

This Is How I Want to Describe Myself Today:

3 Things I Want the Universe to Handle:

3 Things I Have Manifested:

2 Things I Will Do Just for Me Today:

Today's Affirmations:

CREATE · YOUR · JOY

thank you

Time:	These Are My Intentions for Today:	I Intend to Feel:
6-7 AM		
7-8 AM		
8-9 AM		
9-10 AM		
10-11 AM		
11-12 AM		
12-1 PM		
1-2 PM		
2-3 PM		
3-4 PM		
4-5 PM		
5-6 PM		
6-7 PM		
7-8 PM		
8-9 PM		

INTEND

. F L O W .

Today is:	3 Things I Have Manifested:
5 Things I Appreciate:	
	2 Things I Will Do Just for Me Today:
This Is How I Want to Describe Myself Today:	**Today's Affirmations:**
3 Things I Want the Universe to Handle:	

Time:	These Are My Intentions for Today:	I Intend to Feel:
6-7 AM		
7-8 AM		
8-9 AM		
9-10 AM		
10-11 AM		
11-12 AM		
12-1 PM		
1-2 PM		
2-3 PM		
3-4 PM		
4-5 PM		
5-6 PM		
6-7 PM		
7-8 PM		
8-9 PM		

CREATE. YOUR. JOY

thank you

INTEND

FLOW

Today is:	**3 Things I Have Manifested:**
5 Things I Appreciate:	
	2 Things I Will Do Just for Me Today:
This Is How I Want to Describe Myself Today:	**Today's Affirmations:**
3 Things I Want the Universe to Handle:	

CREATE • YOUR • JOY

thank you • thank you

Time:	These Are My Intentions for Today:	I Intend to Feel:
6-7 AM		
7-8 AM		
8-9 AM		
9-10 AM		
10-11 AM		
11-12 AM		
12-1 PM		
1-2 PM		
2-3 PM		
3-4 PM		
4-5 PM		
5-6 PM		
6-7 PM		
7-8 PM		
8-9 PM		

INTEND

FLOW

Today is:	**3 Things I Have Manifested:**
5 Things I Appreciate:	
	2 Things I Will Do Just for Me Today:
This Is How I Want to Describe Myself Today:	**Today's Affirmations:**
3 Things I Want the Universe to Handle:	

CREATE · YOUR · JOY

THANK YOU

Time:	These Are My Intentions for Today:	I Intend to Feel:
6-7 AM		
7-8 AM		
8-9 AM		
9-10 AM		
10-11 AM		
11-12 AM		
12-1 PM		
1-2 PM		
2-3 PM		
3-4 PM		
4-5 PM		
5-6 PM		
6-7 PM		
7-8 PM		
8-9 PM		

INTEND

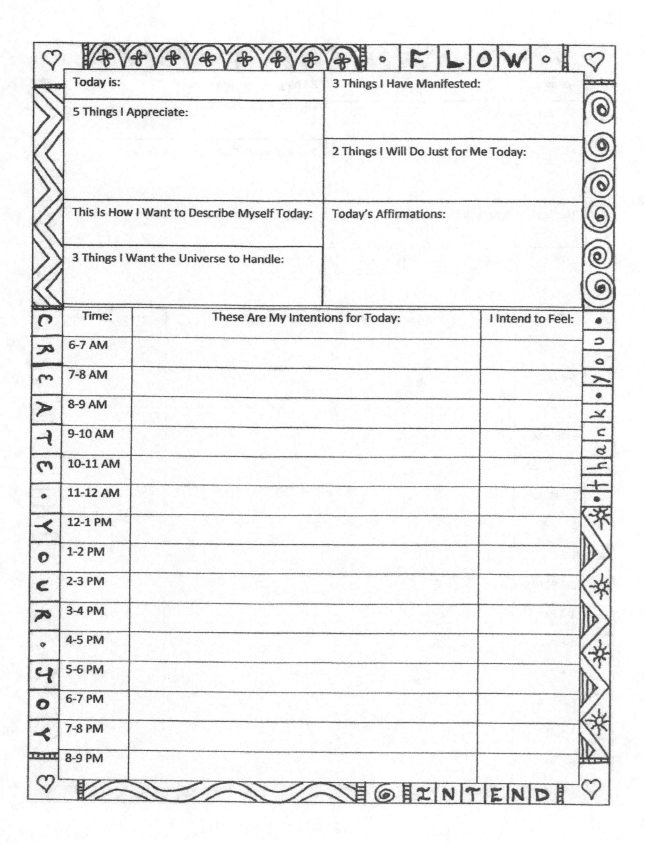

FLOW

Today is:	3 Things I Have Manifested:
5 Things I Appreciate:	
	2 Things I Will Do Just for Me Today:
This Is How I Want to Describe Myself Today:	Today's Affirmations:
3 Things I Want the Universe to Handle:	

Time:	These Are My Intentions for Today:	I Intend to Feel:
6-7 AM		
7-8 AM		
8-9 AM		
9-10 AM		
10-11 AM		
11-12 AM		
12-1 PM		
1-2 PM		
2-3 PM		
3-4 PM		
4-5 PM		
5-6 PM		
6-7 PM		
7-8 PM		
8-9 PM		

CREATE • YOUR • JOY

thank you

INTEND

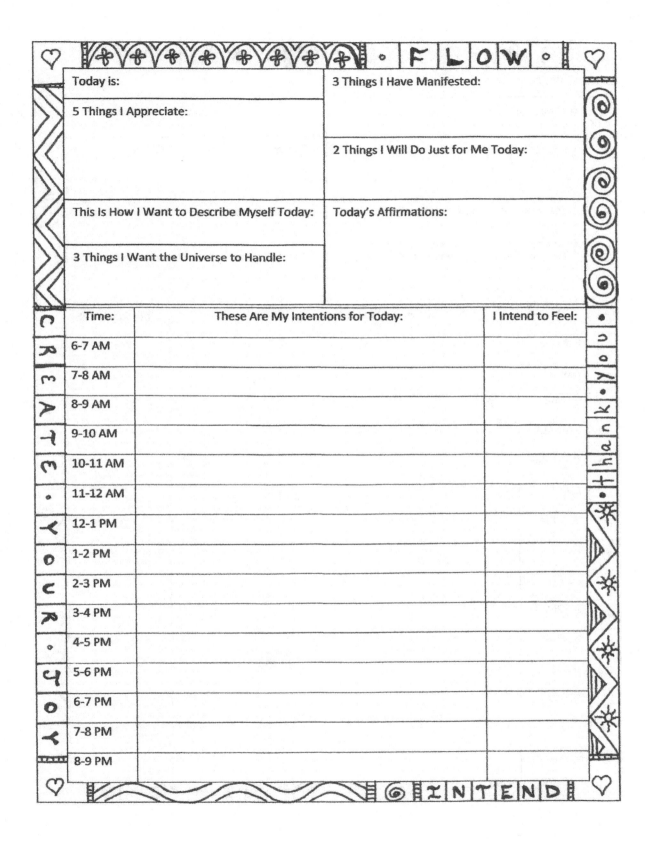

FLOW

Today is:	3 Things I Have Manifested:
5 Things I Appreciate:	
	2 Things I Will Do Just for Me Today:
This Is How I Want to Describe Myself Today:	Today's Affirmations:
3 Things I Want the Universe to Handle:	

CREATE • YOUR • JOY

thank you • INTEND

Time:	These Are My Intentions for Today:	I Intend to Feel:
6-7 AM		
7-8 AM		
8-9 AM		
9-10 AM		
10-11 AM		
11-12 AM		
12-1 PM		
1-2 PM		
2-3 PM		
3-4 PM		
4-5 PM		
5-6 PM		
6-7 PM		
7-8 PM		
8-9 PM		

· F L O W ·

Today is:	3 Things I Have Manifested:
5 Things I Appreciate:	
	2 Things I Will Do Just for Me Today:
This Is How I Want to Describe Myself Today:	**Today's Affirmations:**
3 Things I Want the Universe to Handle:	

Time:	These Are My Intentions for Today:	I Intend to Feel:
6-7 AM		
7-8 AM		
8-9 AM		
9-10 AM		
10-11 AM		
11-12 AM		
12-1 PM		
1-2 PM		
2-3 PM		
3-4 PM		
4-5 PM		
5-6 PM		
6-7 PM		
7-8 PM		
8-9 PM		

CREATE · YOUR · JOY

thank you

INTEND

· F L O W ·

Today is:	3 Things I Have Manifested:
5 Things I Appreciate:	
	2 Things I Will Do Just for Me Today:
This Is How I Want to Describe Myself Today:	Today's Affirmations:
3 Things I Want the Universe to Handle:	

Time:	These Are My Intentions for Today:	I Intend to Feel:
6-7 AM		
7-8 AM		
8-9 AM		
9-10 AM		
10-11 AM		
11-12 AM		
12-1 PM		
1-2 PM		
2-3 PM		
3-4 PM		
4-5 PM		
5-6 PM		
6-7 PM		
7-8 PM		
8-9 PM		

CREATE · YOUR · JOY

thank you

· INTEND

Today is:	3 Things I Have Manifested:
5 Things I Appreciate:	
	2 Things I Will Do Just for Me Today:
This Is How I Want to Describe Myself Today:	Today's Affirmations:
3 Things I Want the Universe to Handle:	

CREATE • YOUR • JOY

thank you

Time:	These Are My Intentions for Today:	I Intend to Feel:
6-7 AM		
7-8 AM		
8-9 AM		
9-10 AM		
10-11 AM		
11-12 AM		
12-1 PM		
1-2 PM		
2-3 PM		
3-4 PM		
4-5 PM		
5-6 PM		
6-7 PM		
7-8 PM		
8-9 PM		

INTEND

FLOW

Today is:

5 Things I Appreciate:

This Is How I Want to Describe Myself Today:

3 Things I Want the Universe to Handle:

3 Things I Have Manifested:

2 Things I Will Do Just for Me Today:

Today's Affirmations:

Time:	These Are My Intentions for Today:	I Intend to Feel:
6-7 AM		
7-8 AM		
8-9 AM		
9-10 AM		
10-11 AM		
11-12 AM		
12-1 PM		
1-2 PM		
2-3 PM		
3-4 PM		
4-5 PM		
5-6 PM		
6-7 PM		
7-8 PM		
8-9 PM		

CREATE . YOUR . JOY

thank you

INTEND

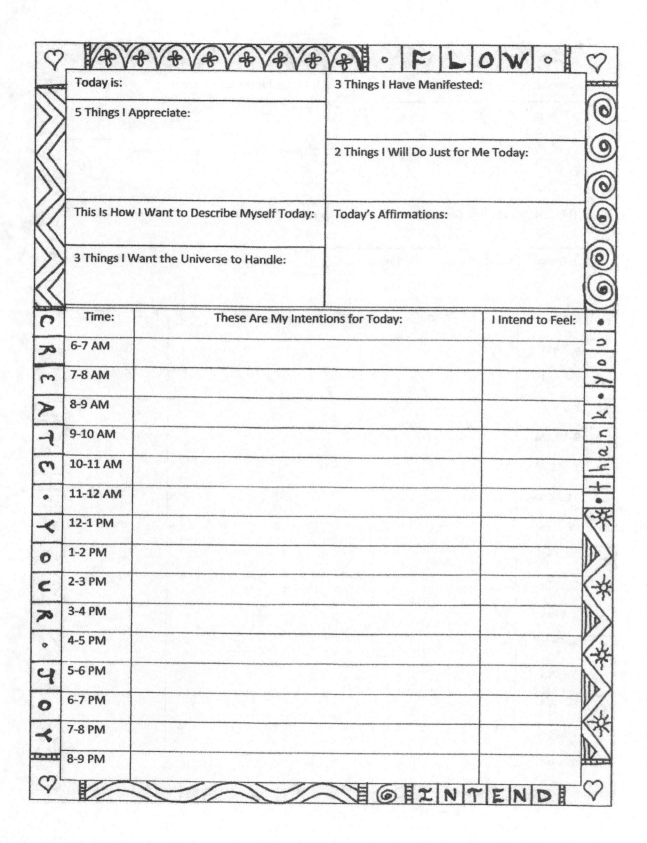

FLOW

Today is:

5 Things I Appreciate:

This Is How I Want to Describe Myself Today:

3 Things I Want the Universe to Handle:

3 Things I Have Manifested:

2 Things I Will Do Just for Me Today:

Today's Affirmations:

Time:	These Are My Intentions for Today:	I Intend to Feel:
6-7 AM		
7-8 AM		
8-9 AM		
9-10 AM		
10-11 AM		
11-12 AM		
12-1 PM		
1-2 PM		
2-3 PM		
3-4 PM		
4-5 PM		
5-6 PM		
6-7 PM		
7-8 PM		
8-9 PM		

CREATE • YOUR • JOY

thank you

INTEND

· F L O W ·

Today is:	**3 Things I Have Manifested:**
5 Things I Appreciate:	
	2 Things I Will Do Just for Me Today:
This Is How I Want to Describe Myself Today:	**Today's Affirmations:**
3 Things I Want the Universe to Handle:	

Time:	These Are My Intentions for Today:	I Intend to Feel:
6-7 AM		
7-8 AM		
8-9 AM		
9-10 AM		
10-11 AM		
11-12 AM		
12-1 PM		
1-2 PM		
2-3 PM		
3-4 PM		
4-5 PM		
5-6 PM		
6-7 PM		
7-8 PM		
8-9 PM		

CREATE. YOUCROR. JOY

thank you.

· INTEND

Today is:		**3 Things I Have Manifested:**
5 Things I Appreciate:		
		2 Things I Will Do Just for Me Today:
This Is How I Want to Describe Myself Today:		**Today's Affirmations:**
3 Things I Want the Universe to Handle:		

CREATE • YOUR • JOY

Time:	These Are My Intentions for Today:	I Intend to Feel:
6-7 AM		
7-8 AM		
8-9 AM		
9-10 AM		
10-11 AM		
11-12 AM		
12-1 PM		
1-2 PM		
2-3 PM		
3-4 PM		
4-5 PM		
5-6 PM		
6-7 PM		
7-8 PM		
8-9 PM		

thank you

INTEND

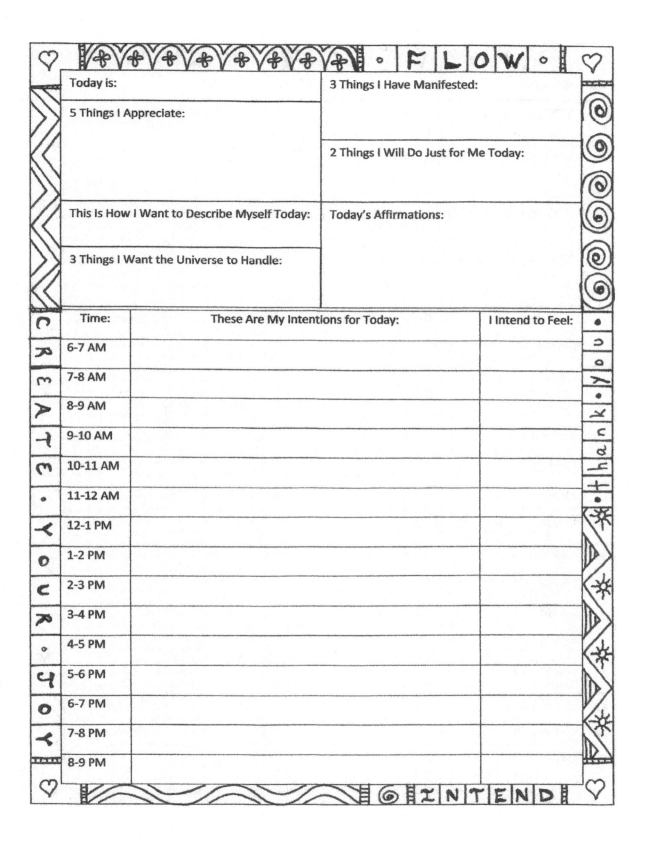

FLOW

Today is:

5 Things I Appreciate:

This Is How I Want to Describe Myself Today:

3 Things I Want the Universe to Handle:

3 Things I Have Manifested:

2 Things I Will Do Just for Me Today:

Today's Affirmations:

Time:	These Are My Intentions for Today:	I Intend to Feel:
6-7 AM		
7-8 AM		
8-9 AM		
9-10 AM		
10-11 AM		
11-12 AM		
12-1 PM		
1-2 PM		
2-3 PM		
3-4 PM		
4-5 PM		
5-6 PM		
6-7 PM		
7-8 PM		
8-9 PM		

CREATE . YOUR . JOY

thank you

INTEND

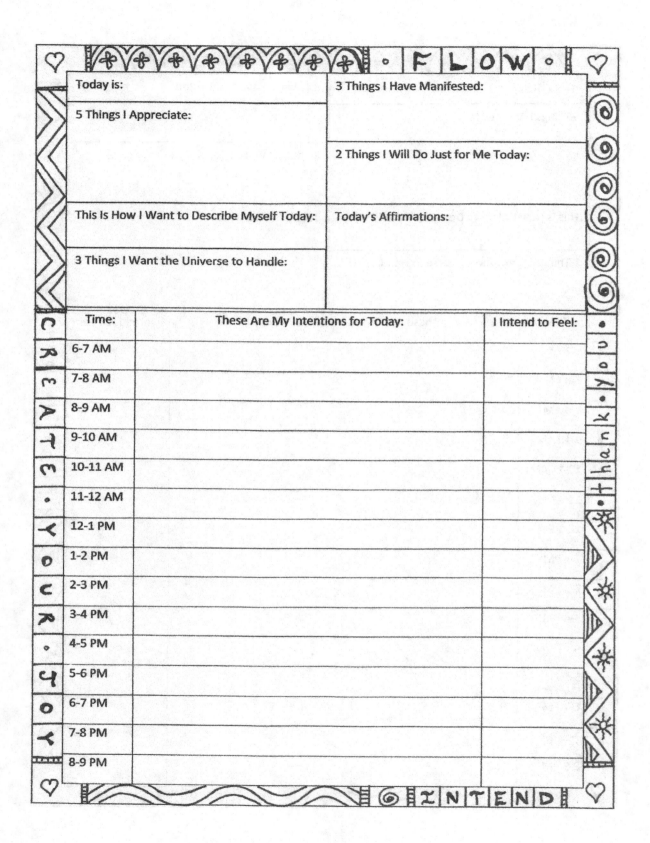

FLOW

Today is:

5 Things I Appreciate:

This Is How I Want to Describe Myself Today:

3 Things I Want the Universe to Handle:

3 Things I Have Manifested:

2 Things I Will Do Just for Me Today:

Today's Affirmations:

Time:	These Are My Intentions for Today:	I Intend to Feel:
6-7 AM		
7-8 AM		
8-9 AM		
9-10 AM		
10-11 AM		
11-12 AM		
12-1 PM		
1-2 PM		
2-3 PM		
3-4 PM		
4-5 PM		
5-6 PM		
6-7 PM		
7-8 PM		
8-9 PM		

CREATE · YOUR · JOY

thank you

INTEND

· F L O W ·

Today is:	3 Things I Have Manifested:
5 Things I Appreciate:	
	2 Things I Will Do Just for Me Today:
This Is How I Want to Describe Myself Today:	**Today's Affirmations:**
3 Things I Want the Universe to Handle:	

Time:	These Are My Intentions for Today:	I Intend to Feel:
6-7 AM		
7-8 AM		
8-9 AM		
9-10 AM		
10-11 AM		
11-12 AM		
12-1 PM		
1-2 PM		
2-3 PM		
3-4 PM		
4-5 PM		
5-6 PM		
6-7 PM		
7-8 PM		
8-9 PM		

CREATE · YOUR · JOY

thank you

· INTEND

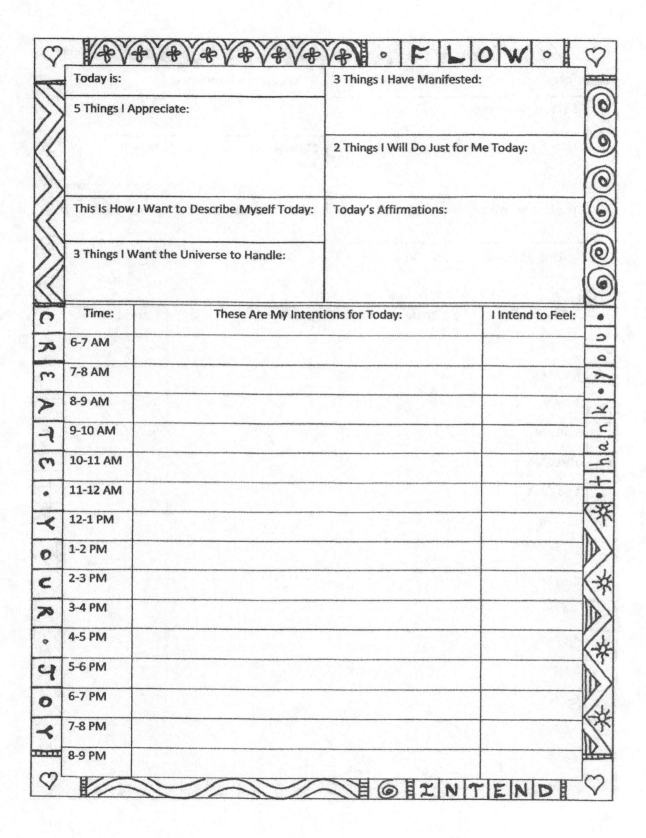

FLOW

Today is:

5 Things I Appreciate:

3 Things I Have Manifested:

2 Things I Will Do Just for Me Today:

This Is How I Want to Describe Myself Today:

Today's Affirmations:

3 Things I Want the Universe to Handle:

CREATE • YOUR • JOY

thank you

Time:	These Are My Intentions for Today:	I Intend to Feel:
6-7 AM		
7-8 AM		
8-9 AM		
9-10 AM		
10-11 AM		
11-12 AM		
12-1 PM		
1-2 PM		
2-3 PM		
3-4 PM		
4-5 PM		
5-6 PM		
6-7 PM		
7-8 PM		
8-9 PM		

INTEND

· F L O W ·

Today is:	3 Things I Have Manifested:
5 Things I Appreciate:	
	2 Things I Will Do Just for Me Today:
This Is How I Want to Describe Myself Today:	**Today's Affirmations:**
3 Things I Want the Universe to Handle:	

Time:	These Are My Intentions for Today:	I Intend to Feel:
6-7 AM		
7-8 AM		
8-9 AM		
9-10 AM		
10-11 AM		
11-12 AM		
12-1 PM		
1-2 PM		
2-3 PM		
3-4 PM		
4-5 PM		
5-6 PM		
6-7 PM		
7-8 PM		
8-9 PM		

CREATE · YOUR · JOY

THANK YOU

INTEND

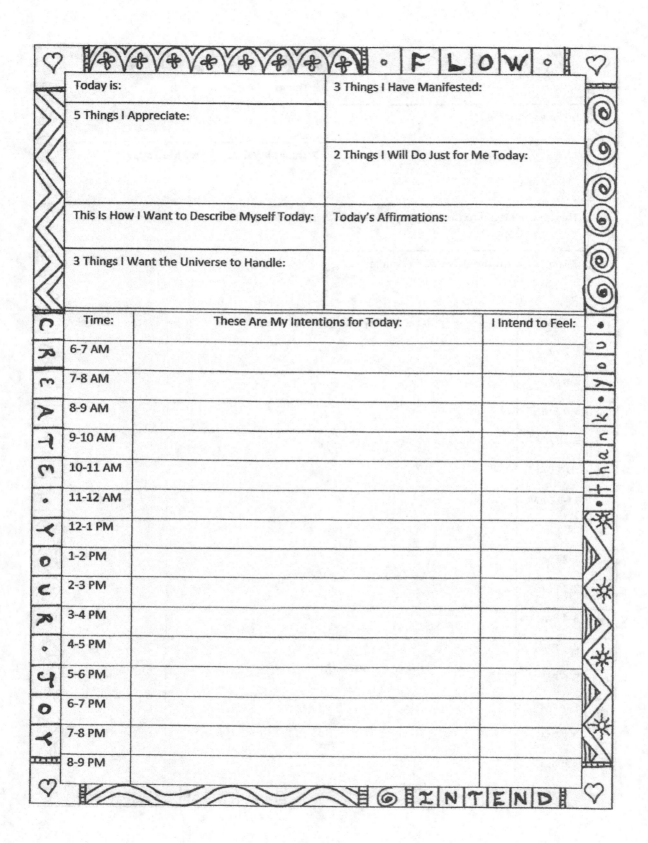

FLOW

Today is:	3 Things I Have Manifested:
5 Things I Appreciate:	
	2 Things I Will Do Just for Me Today:
This Is How I Want to Describe Myself Today:	Today's Affirmations:
3 Things I Want the Universe to Handle:	

Time:	These Are My Intentions for Today:	I Intend to Feel:
6-7 AM		
7-8 AM		
8-9 AM		
9-10 AM		
10-11 AM		
11-12 AM		
12-1 PM		
1-2 PM		
2-3 PM		
3-4 PM		
4-5 PM		
5-6 PM		
6-7 PM		
7-8 PM		
8-9 PM		

CREATE • YOUR • JOY

thank you

INTEND

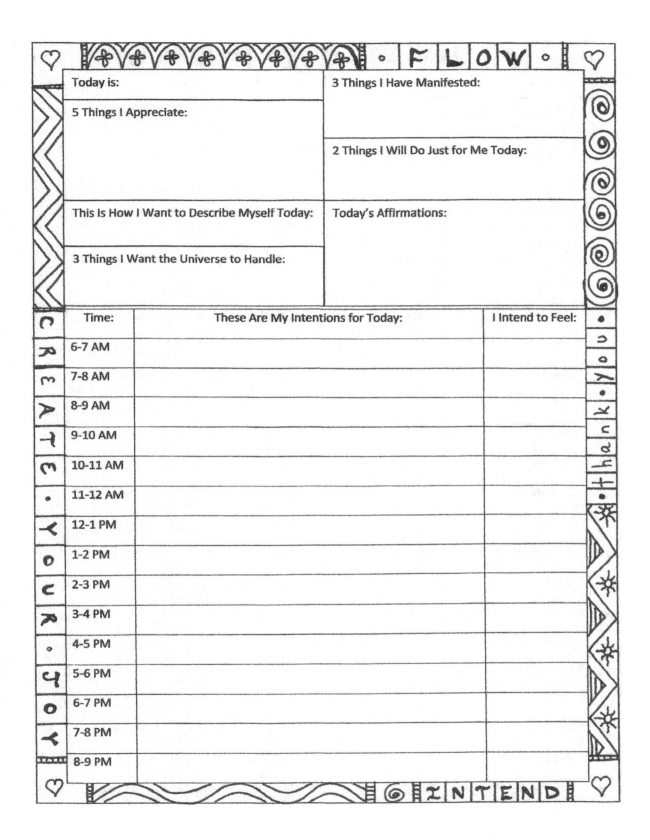

FLOW

Today is:	3 Things I Have Manifested:
5 Things I Appreciate:	
	2 Things I Will Do Just for Me Today:
This Is How I Want to Describe Myself Today:	Today's Affirmations:
3 Things I Want the Universe to Handle:	

Time:	These Are My Intentions for Today:	I Intend to Feel:
6-7 AM		
7-8 AM		
8-9 AM		
9-10 AM		
10-11 AM		
11-12 AM		
12-1 PM		
1-2 PM		
2-3 PM		
3-4 PM		
4-5 PM		
5-6 PM		
6-7 PM		
7-8 PM		
8-9 PM		

CREATE • YOUR • JOY

thank you

INTEND

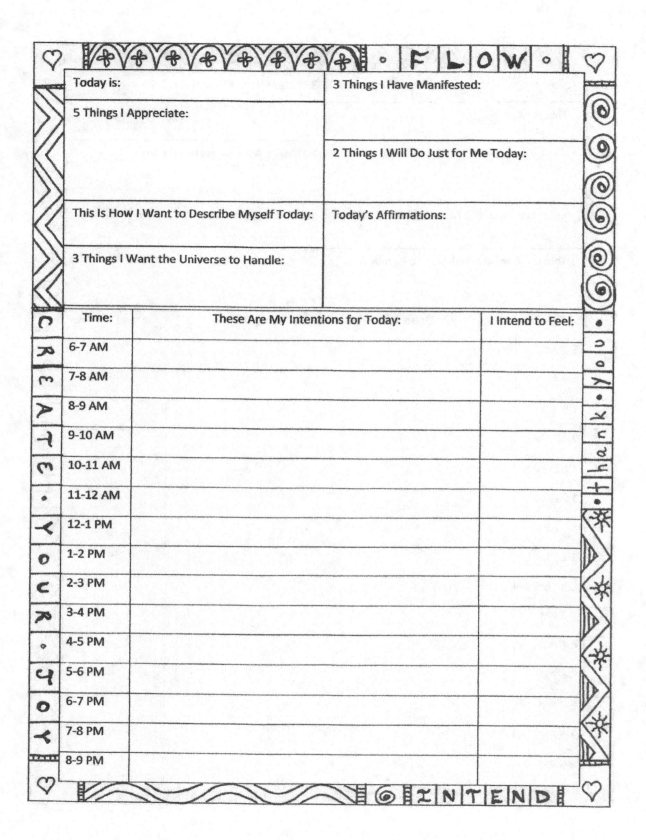

FLOW

| Today is: | 3 Things I Have Manifested: |

5 Things I Appreciate:

2 Things I Will Do Just for Me Today:

This Is How I Want to Describe Myself Today:

Today's Affirmations:

3 Things I Want the Universe to Handle:

CREATE • YOUR • JOY

thank you

Time:	These Are My Intentions for Today:	I Intend to Feel:
6-7 AM		
7-8 AM		
8-9 AM		
9-10 AM		
10-11 AM		
11-12 AM		
12-1 PM		
1-2 PM		
2-3 PM		
3-4 PM		
4-5 PM		
5-6 PM		
6-7 PM		
7-8 PM		
8-9 PM		

INTEND

Month: April

Sunday	Monday	Tuesday	Wednesday	Thursday	Friday	Saturday

Do at least one thing every day that brings you joy and record it on this page.

Affirmations:

" The basis of your life is absolute freedom, the goal is joy."—Abraham/Hicks

FLOW

Today is:	3 Things I Have Manifested:
5 Things I Appreciate:	
	2 Things I Will Do Just for Me Today:
This Is How I Want to Describe Myself Today:	Today's Affirmations:
3 Things I Want the Universe to Handle:	

CREATE • YOUR • JOY

Time:	These Are My Intentions for Today:	I Intend to Feel:
6-7 AM		
7-8 AM		
8-9 AM		
9-10 AM		
10-11 AM		
11-12 AM		
12-1 PM		
1-2 PM		
2-3 PM		
3-4 PM		
4-5 PM		
5-6 PM		
6-7 PM		
7-8 PM		
8-9 PM		

thank you • **INTEND**

· F L O W ·

Today is:	3 Things I Have Manifested:
5 Things I Appreciate:	
	2 Things I Will Do Just for Me Today:
This Is How I Want to Describe Myself Today:	**Today's Affirmations:**
3 Things I Want the Universe to Handle:	

	Time:	These Are My Intentions for Today:	I Intend to Feel:
C	6-7 AM		
R	7-8 AM		
E	8-9 AM		
A	9-10 AM		
T	10-11 AM		
E	11-12 AM		
·	12-1 PM		
Y	1-2 PM		
O	2-3 PM		
U	3-4 PM		
R	4-5 PM		
·	5-6 PM		
J	6-7 PM		
O	7-8 PM		
Y	8-9 PM		

· INTEND

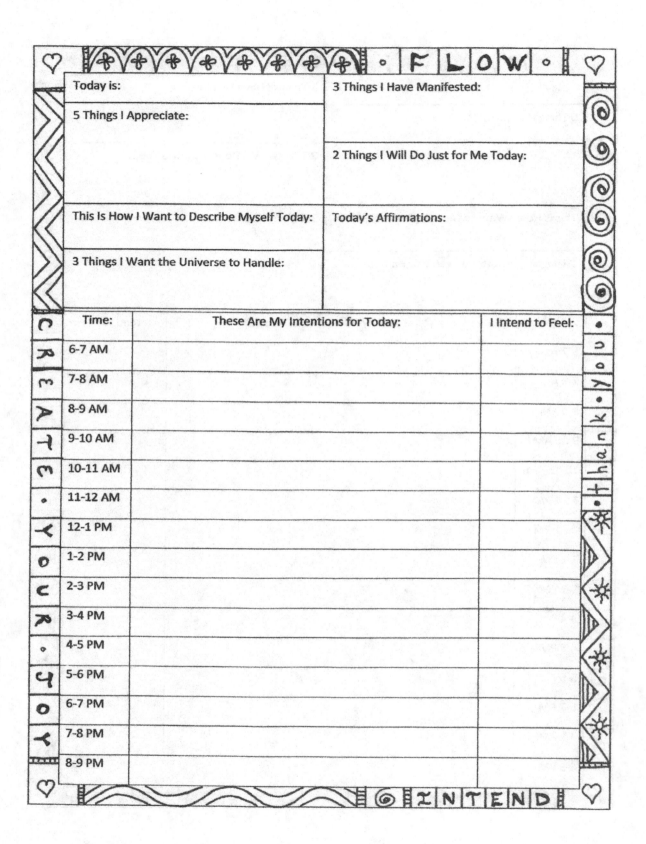

FLOW

Today is:	3 Things I Have Manifested:
5 Things I Appreciate:	
	2 Things I Will Do Just for Me Today:
This Is How I Want to Describe Myself Today:	Today's Affirmations:
3 Things I Want the Universe to Handle:	

Time:	These Are My Intentions for Today:	I Intend to Feel:
6-7 AM		
7-8 AM		
8-9 AM		
9-10 AM		
10-11 AM		
11-12 AM		
12-1 PM		
1-2 PM		
2-3 PM		
3-4 PM		
4-5 PM		
5-6 PM		
6-7 PM		
7-8 PM		
8-9 PM		

CREATE YOUR JOY

thank you

INTEND

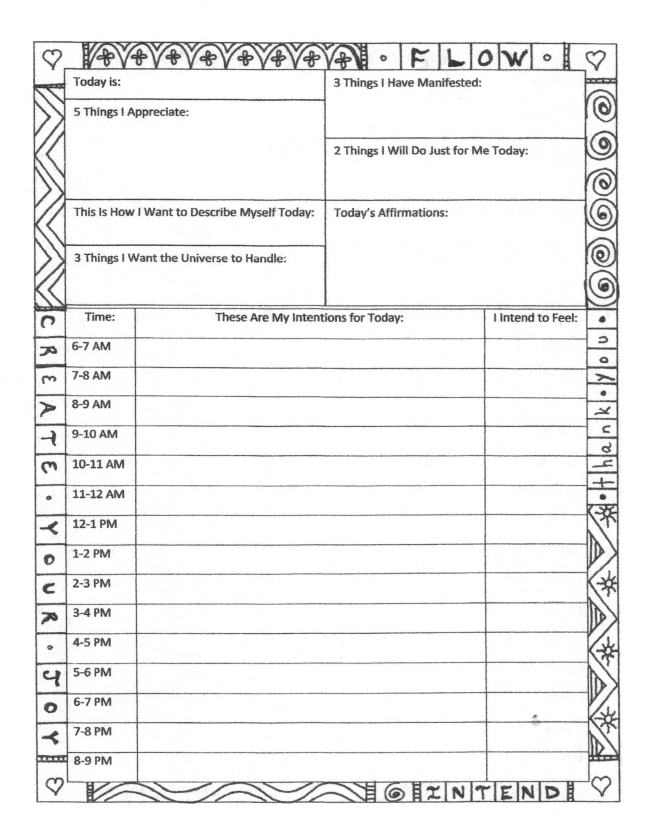

FLOW

Today is:	3 Things I Have Manifested:
5 Things I Appreciate:	
	2 Things I Will Do Just for Me Today:
This Is How I Want to Describe Myself Today:	**Today's Affirmations:**
3 Things I Want the Universe to Handle:	

Time:	These Are My Intentions for Today:	I Intend to Feel:
6-7 AM		
7-8 AM		
8-9 AM		
9-10 AM		
10-11 AM		
11-12 AM		
12-1 PM		
1-2 PM		
2-3 PM		
3-4 PM		
4-5 PM		
5-6 PM		
6-7 PM		
7-8 PM		
8-9 PM		

INTEND

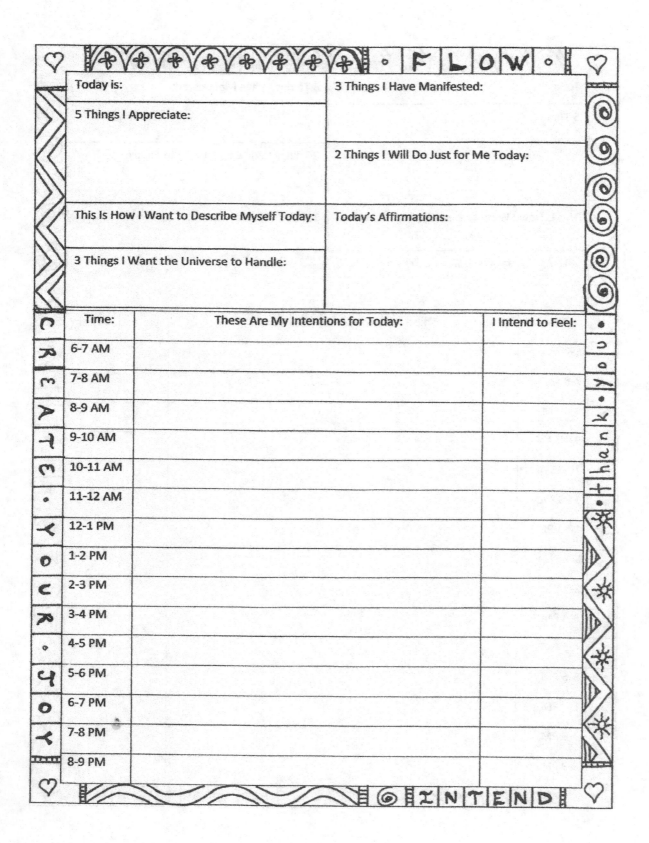

FLOW

Today is:	3 Things I Have Manifested:
5 Things I Appreciate:	
	2 Things I Will Do Just for Me Today:
This Is How I Want to Describe Myself Today:	Today's Affirmations:
3 Things I Want the Universe to Handle:	

Time:	These Are My Intentions for Today:	I Intend to Feel:
6-7 AM		
7-8 AM		
8-9 AM		
9-10 AM		
10-11 AM		
11-12 AM		
12-1 PM		
1-2 PM		
2-3 PM		
3-4 PM		
4-5 PM		
5-6 PM		
6-7 PM		
7-8 PM		
8-9 PM		

CREATE . YOUR . JOY

thank you

INTEND

FLOW

Today is:	3 Things I Have Manifested:
5 Things I Appreciate:	
	2 Things I Will Do Just for Me Today:
This Is How I Want to Describe Myself Today:	**Today's Affirmations:**
3 Things I Want the Universe to Handle:	

Time:	These Are My Intentions for Today:	I Intend to Feel:
6-7 AM		
7-8 AM		
8-9 AM		
9-10 AM		
10-11 AM		
11-12 AM		
12-1 PM		
1-2 PM		
2-3 PM		
3-4 PM		
4-5 PM		
5-6 PM		
6-7 PM		
7-8 PM		
8-9 PM		

CREATE . YOUR . JOY

thank you

INTEND

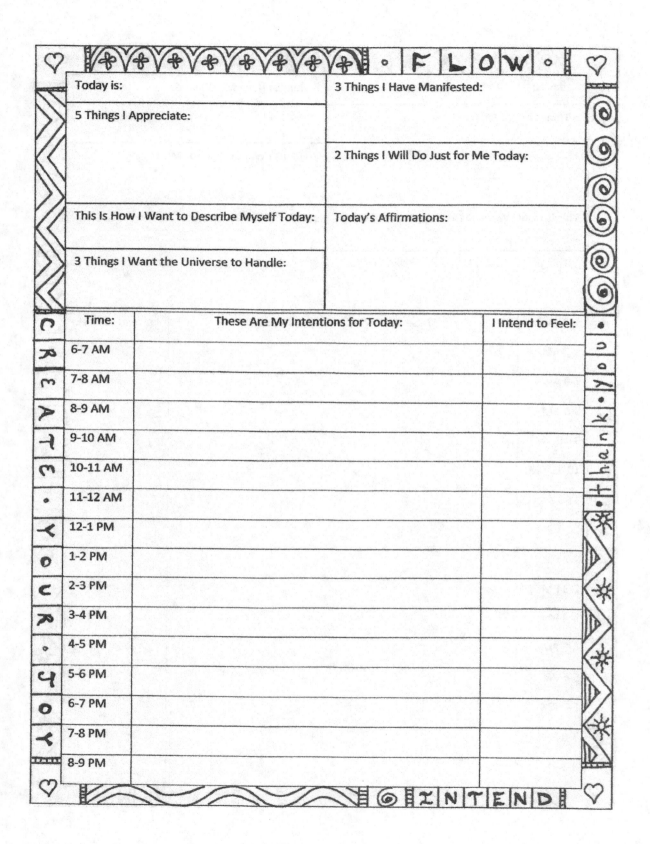

FLOW

Today is:	3 Things I Have Manifested:
5 Things I Appreciate:	
	2 Things I Will Do Just for Me Today:
This Is How I Want to Describe Myself Today:	Today's Affirmations:
3 Things I Want the Universe to Handle:	

CREATE • YOUR • JOY

thank you •

Time:	These Are My Intentions for Today:	I Intend to Feel:
6-7 AM		
7-8 AM		
8-9 AM		
9-10 AM		
10-11 AM		
11-12 AM		
12-1 PM		
1-2 PM		
2-3 PM		
3-4 PM		
4-5 PM		
5-6 PM		
6-7 PM		
7-8 PM		
8-9 PM		

INTEND

102

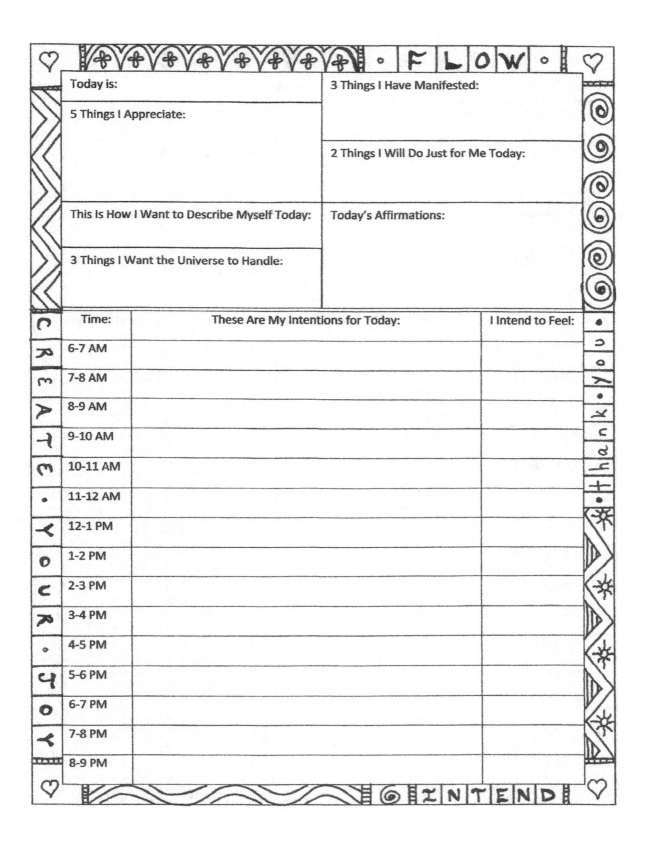

FLOW

Today is:	3 Things I Have Manifested:
5 Things I Appreciate:	
	2 Things I Will Do Just for Me Today:
This Is How I Want to Describe Myself Today:	Today's Affirmations:
3 Things I Want the Universe to Handle:	

Time:	These Are My Intentions for Today:	I Intend to Feel:
6-7 AM		
7-8 AM		
8-9 AM		
9-10 AM		
10-11 AM		
11-12 AM		
12-1 PM		
1-2 PM		
2-3 PM		
3-4 PM		
4-5 PM		
5-6 PM		
6-7 PM		
7-8 PM		
8-9 PM		

CREATE . YOUR . JOY

Thank You

I INTEND

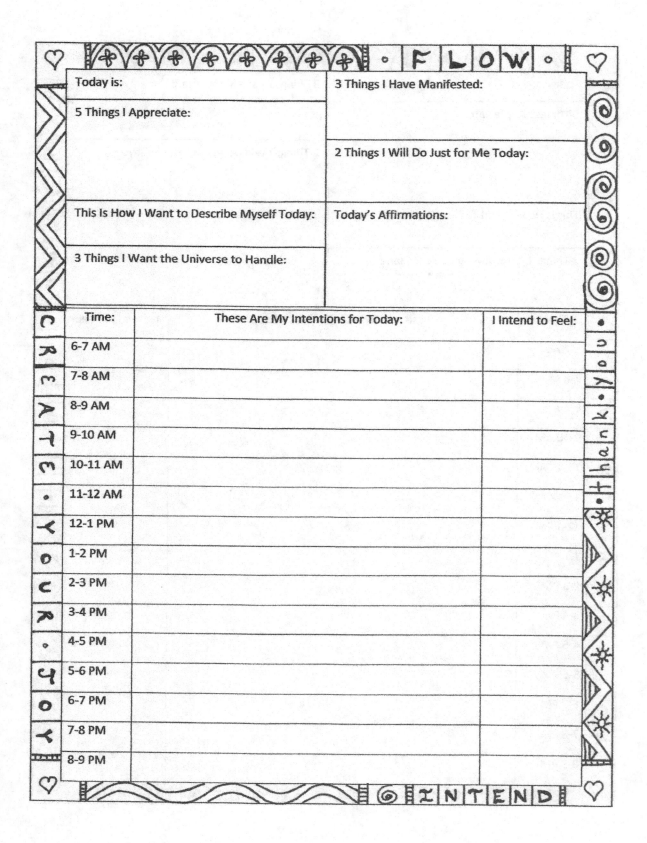

FLOW

Today is:	3 Things I Have Manifested:
5 Things I Appreciate:	
	2 Things I Will Do Just for Me Today:
This Is How I Want to Describe Myself Today:	Today's Affirmations:
3 Things I Want the Universe to Handle:	

CREATE · YOUR · JOY

Time:	These Are My Intentions for Today:	I Intend to Feel:
6-7 AM		
7-8 AM		
8-9 AM		
9-10 AM		
10-11 AM		
11-12 AM		
12-1 PM		
1-2 PM		
2-3 PM		
3-4 PM		
4-5 PM		
5-6 PM		
6-7 PM		
7-8 PM		
8-9 PM		

thank you

INTEND

FLOW

Today is:	3 Things I Have Manifested:
5 Things I Appreciate:	
	2 Things I Will Do Just for Me Today:
This Is How I Want to Describe Myself Today:	**Today's Affirmations:**
3 Things I Want the Universe to Handle:	

Time:	These Are My Intentions for Today:	I Intend to Feel:
6-7 AM		
7-8 AM		
8-9 AM		
9-10 AM		
10-11 AM		
11-12 AM		
12-1 PM		
1-2 PM		
2-3 PM		
3-4 PM		
4-5 PM		
5-6 PM		
6-7 PM		
7-8 PM		
8-9 PM		

CREATE • YOUR • JOY

thank you

INTEND

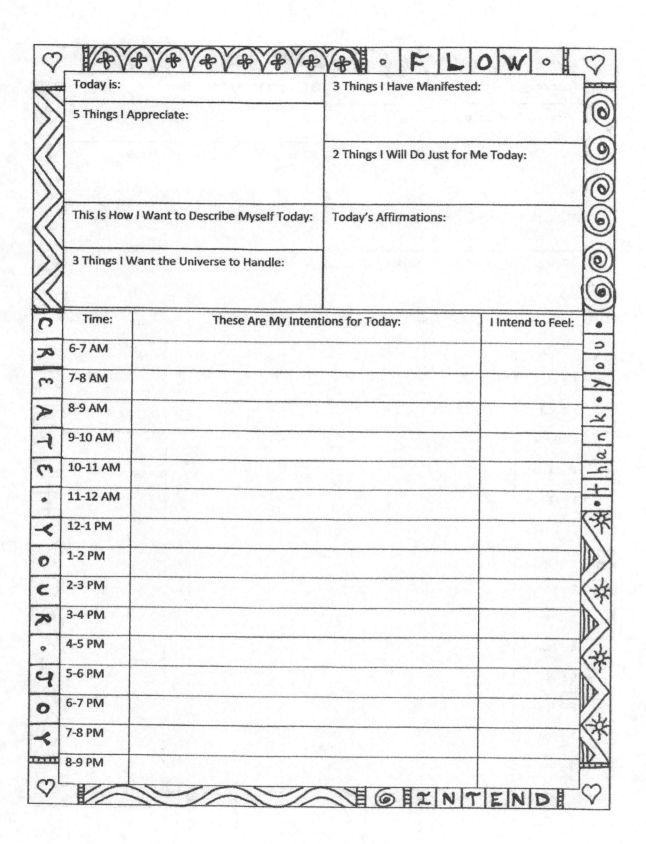

FLOW

Today is:	3 Things I Have Manifested:
5 Things I Appreciate:	
	2 Things I Will Do Just for Me Today:
This Is How I Want to Describe Myself Today:	Today's Affirmations:
3 Things I Want the Universe to Handle:	

CREATE · YOUR · JOY

thank you

Time:	These Are My Intentions for Today:	I Intend to Feel:
6-7 AM		
7-8 AM		
8-9 AM		
9-10 AM		
10-11 AM		
11-12 AM		
12-1 PM		
1-2 PM		
2-3 PM		
3-4 PM		
4-5 PM		
5-6 PM		
6-7 PM		
7-8 PM		
8-9 PM		

INTEND

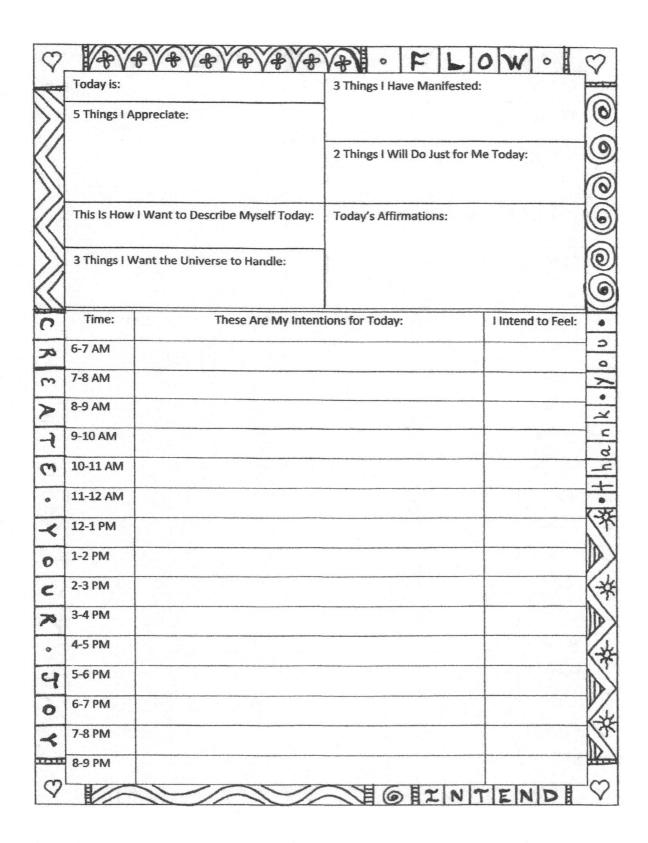

FLOW

Today is:	**3 Things I Have Manifested:**
5 Things I Appreciate:	
	2 Things I Will Do Just for Me Today:
This Is How I Want to Describe Myself Today:	**Today's Affirmations:**
3 Things I Want the Universe to Handle:	

CREATE . YOUR . JOY

Time:	These Are My Intentions for Today:	I Intend to Feel:
6-7 AM		
7-8 AM		
8-9 AM		
9-10 AM		
10-11 AM		
11-12 AM		
12-1 PM		
1-2 PM		
2-3 PM		
3-4 PM		
4-5 PM		
5-6 PM		
6-7 PM		
7-8 PM		
8-9 PM		

thank you

INTEND

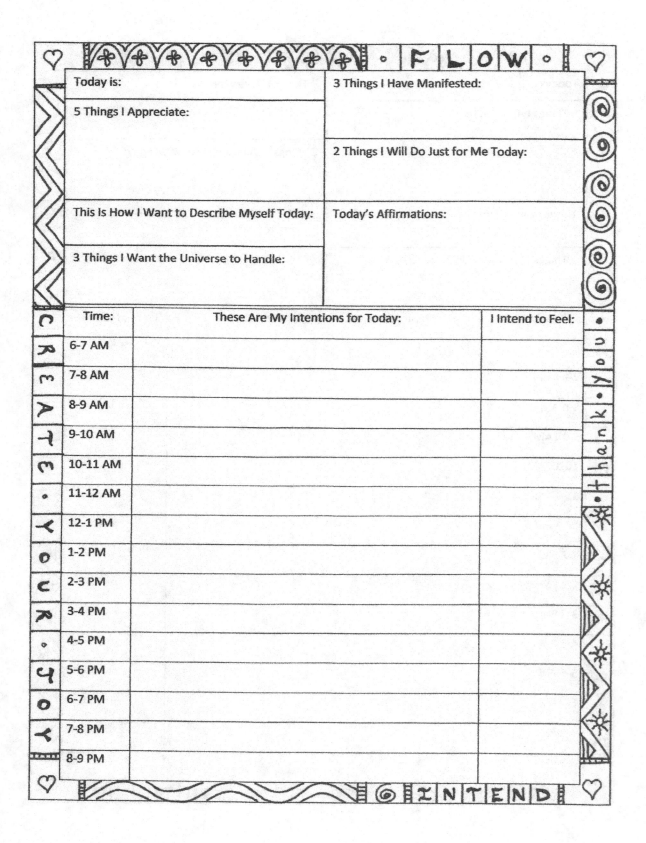

FLOW

Today is:
5 Things I Appreciate:

This Is How I Want to Describe Myself Today:

3 Things I Want the Universe to Handle:

3 Things I Have Manifested:

2 Things I Will Do Just for Me Today:

Today's Affirmations:

Time:	These Are My Intentions for Today:	I Intend to Feel:
6-7 AM		
7-8 AM		
8-9 AM		
9-10 AM		
10-11 AM		
11-12 AM		
12-1 PM		
1-2 PM		
2-3 PM		
3-4 PM		
4-5 PM		
5-6 PM		
6-7 PM		
7-8 PM		
8-9 PM		

CREATE • YOUR • JOY

thank • you

INTEND

108

· F L O W ·

Today is:	3 Things I Have Manifested:
5 Things I Appreciate:	
	2 Things I Will Do Just for Me Today:
This Is How I Want to Describe Myself Today:	**Today's Affirmations:**
3 Things I Want the Universe to Handle:	

Time:	These Are My Intentions for Today:	I Intend to Feel:
6-7 AM		
7-8 AM		
8-9 AM		
9-10 AM		
10-11 AM		
11-12 AM		
12-1 PM		
1-2 PM		
2-3 PM		
3-4 PM		
4-5 PM		
5-6 PM		
6-7 PM		
7-8 PM		
8-9 PM		

CREATE · YOUR · JOY

thank · you

INTEND

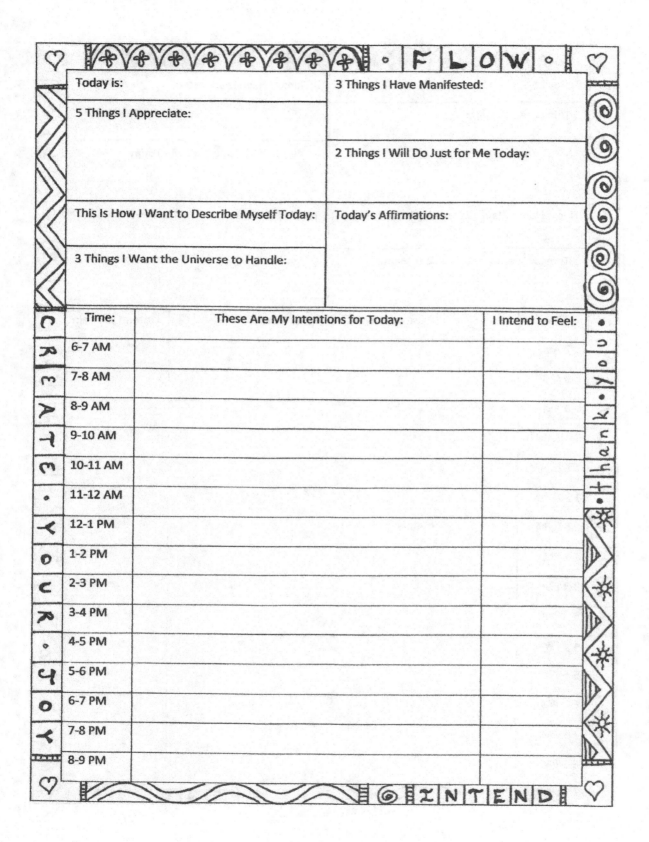

FLOW

Today is:	3 Things I Have Manifested:
5 Things I Appreciate:	
	2 Things I Will Do Just for Me Today:
This Is How I Want to Describe Myself Today:	Today's Affirmations:
3 Things I Want the Universe to Handle:	

Time:	These Are My Intentions for Today:	I Intend to Feel:
6-7 AM		
7-8 AM		
8-9 AM		
9-10 AM		
10-11 AM		
11-12 AM		
12-1 PM		
1-2 PM		
2-3 PM		
3-4 PM		
4-5 PM		
5-6 PM		
6-7 PM		
7-8 PM		
8-9 PM		

CREATE YOUR JOY

thank you

INTEND

FLOW

Today is:	3 Things I Have Manifested:
5 Things I Appreciate:	
	2 Things I Will Do Just for Me Today:
This Is How I Want to Describe Myself Today:	Today's Affirmations:
3 Things I Want the Universe to Handle:	

Time:	These Are My Intentions for Today:	I Intend to Feel:
6-7 AM		
7-8 AM		
8-9 AM		
9-10 AM		
10-11 AM		
11-12 AM		
12-1 PM		
1-2 PM		
2-3 PM		
3-4 PM		
4-5 PM		
5-6 PM		
6-7 PM		
7-8 PM		
8-9 PM		

CREATE . YOUR . JOY

thank . you

INTEND

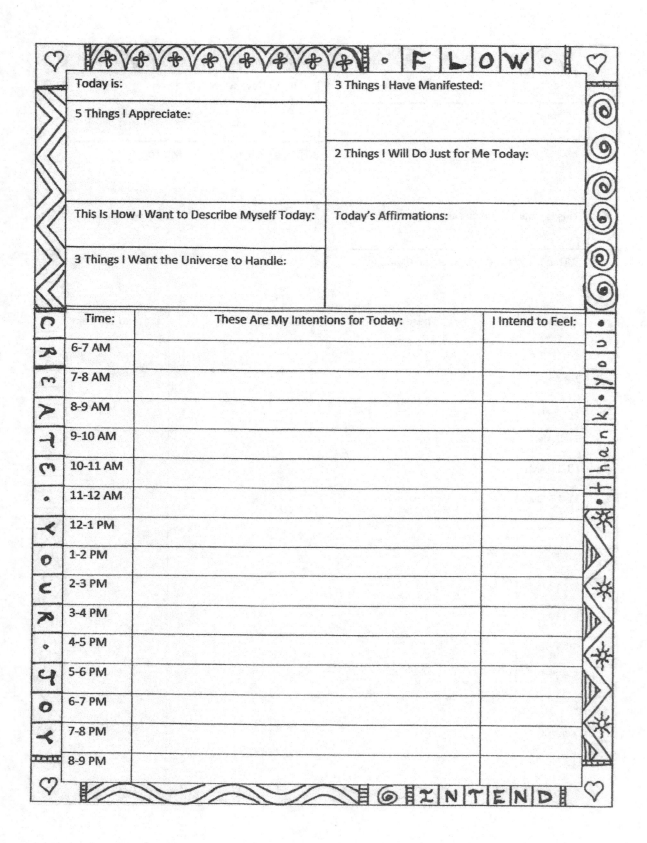

FLOW

Today is:	3 Things I Have Manifested:
5 Things I Appreciate:	
	2 Things I Will Do Just for Me Today:
This Is How I Want to Describe Myself Today:	Today's Affirmations:
3 Things I Want the Universe to Handle:	

CREATE • YOUR • JOY

thank you • thank you

Time:	These Are My Intentions for Today:	I Intend to Feel:
6-7 AM		
7-8 AM		
8-9 AM		
9-10 AM		
10-11 AM		
11-12 AM		
12-1 PM		
1-2 PM		
2-3 PM		
3-4 PM		
4-5 PM		
5-6 PM		
6-7 PM		
7-8 PM		
8-9 PM		

INTEND

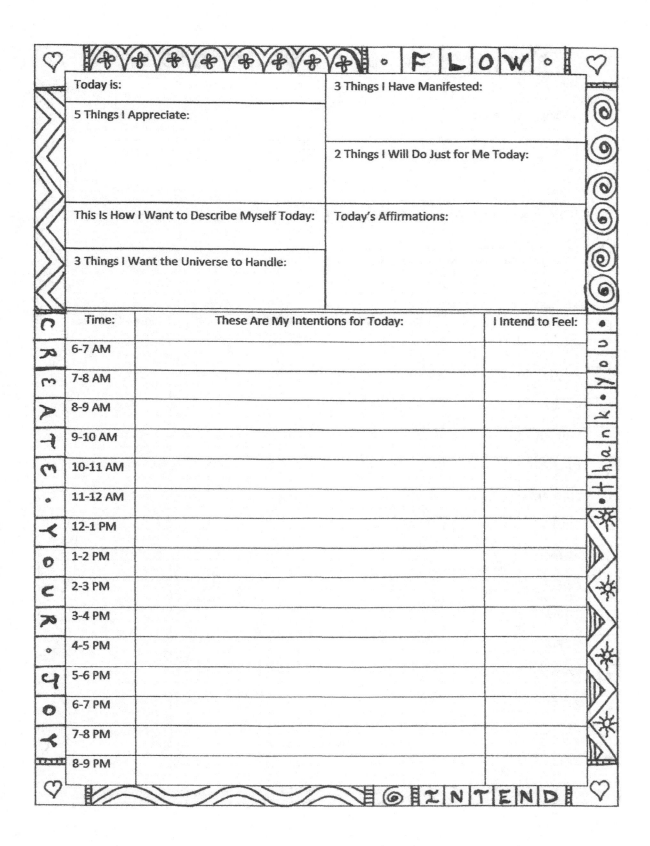

FLOW

Today is:	**3 Things I Have Manifested:**
5 Things I Appreciate:	
	2 Things I Will Do Just for Me Today:
This Is How I Want to Describe Myself Today:	**Today's Affirmations:**
3 Things I Want the Universe to Handle:	

CREATE • YOUR • JOY

• thank you •

Time:	These Are My Intentions for Today:	I Intend to Feel:
6-7 AM		
7-8 AM		
8-9 AM		
9-10 AM		
10-11 AM		
11-12 AM		
12-1 PM		
1-2 PM		
2-3 PM		
3-4 PM		
4-5 PM		
5-6 PM		
6-7 PM		
7-8 PM		
8-9 PM		

INTEND

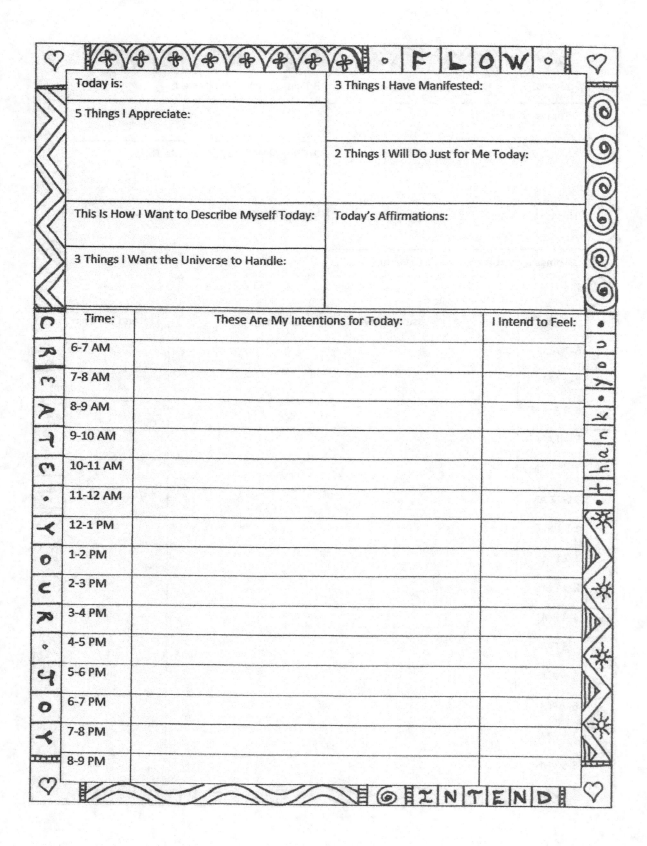

FLOW

Today is:

5 Things I Appreciate:

This Is How I Want to Describe Myself Today:

3 Things I Want the Universe to Handle:

3 Things I Have Manifested:

2 Things I Will Do Just for Me Today:

Today's Affirmations:

CREATE • YOUR • JOY	Time:	These Are My Intentions for Today:	I Intend to Feel:
	6-7 AM		
	7-8 AM		
	8-9 AM		
	9-10 AM		
	10-11 AM		
	11-12 AM		
	12-1 PM		
	1-2 PM		
	2-3 PM		
	3-4 PM		
	4-5 PM		
	5-6 PM		
	6-7 PM		
	7-8 PM		
	8-9 PM		

thank you

INTEND

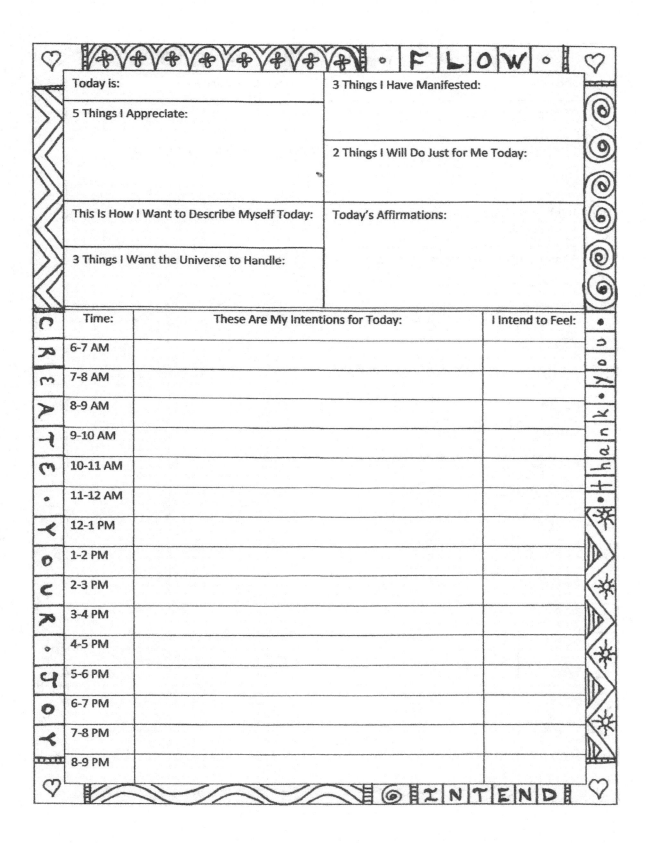

FLOW

Today is:

5 Things I Appreciate:

This Is How I Want to Describe Myself Today:

3 Things I Want the Universe to Handle:

3 Things I Have Manifested:

2 Things I Will Do Just for Me Today:

Today's Affirmations:

	Time:	These Are My Intentions for Today:	I Intend to Feel:
C	6-7 AM		
R	7-8 AM		
E	8-9 AM		
A	9-10 AM		
T	10-11 AM		
E	11-12 AM		
•	12-1 PM		
Y	1-2 PM		
O	2-3 PM		
U	3-4 PM		
R	4-5 PM		
•	5-6 PM		
J	6-7 PM		
O	7-8 PM		
Y	8-9 PM		

INTEND

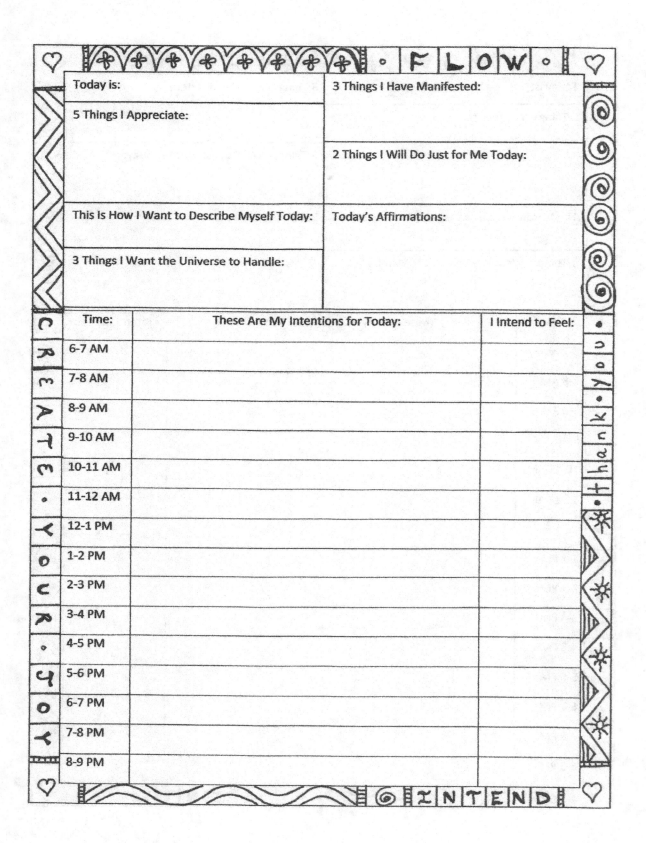

FLOW

Today is:

5 Things I Appreciate:

This Is How I Want to Describe Myself Today:

3 Things I Want the Universe to Handle:

3 Things I Have Manifested:

2 Things I Will Do Just for Me Today:

Today's Affirmations:

Time:	These Are My Intentions for Today:	I Intend to Feel:
6-7 AM		
7-8 AM		
8-9 AM		
9-10 AM		
10-11 AM		
11-12 AM		
12-1 PM		
1-2 PM		
2-3 PM		
3-4 PM		
4-5 PM		
5-6 PM		
6-7 PM		
7-8 PM		
8-9 PM		

CREATE . YOUR . JOY

thank you

INTEND

FLOW

Today is:	3 Things I Have Manifested:
5 Things I Appreciate:	
	2 Things I Will Do Just for Me Today:
This Is How I Want to Describe Myself Today:	Today's Affirmations:
3 Things I Want the Universe to Handle:	

Time:	These Are My Intentions for Today:	I Intend to Feel:
6-7 AM		
7-8 AM		
8-9 AM		
9-10 AM		
10-11 AM		
11-12 AM		
12-1 PM		
1-2 PM		
2-3 PM		
3-4 PM		
4-5 PM		
5-6 PM		
6-7 PM		
7-8 PM		
8-9 PM		

INTEND

CREATE . YOUR . JOY

thank you

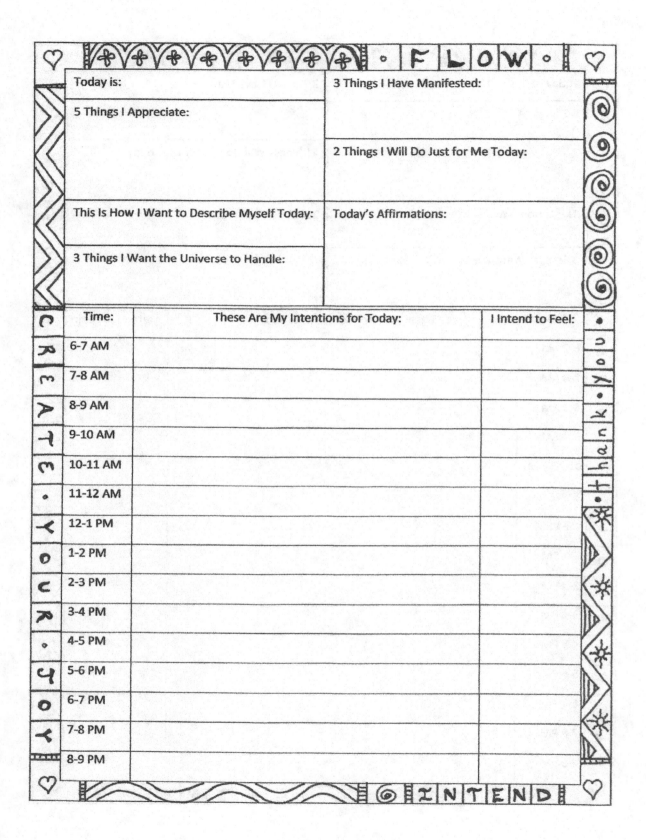

FLOW

Today is:

5 Things I Appreciate:

This Is How I Want to Describe Myself Today:

3 Things I Want the Universe to Handle:

3 Things I Have Manifested:

2 Things I Will Do Just for Me Today:

Today's Affirmations:

Time:	These Are My Intentions for Today:	I Intend to Feel:
6-7 AM		
7-8 AM		
8-9 AM		
9-10 AM		
10-11 AM		
11-12 AM		
12-1 PM		
1-2 PM		
2-3 PM		
3-4 PM		
4-5 PM		
5-6 PM		
6-7 PM		
7-8 PM		
8-9 PM		

CREATE • YOUR • JOY

thank • you

INTEND

118

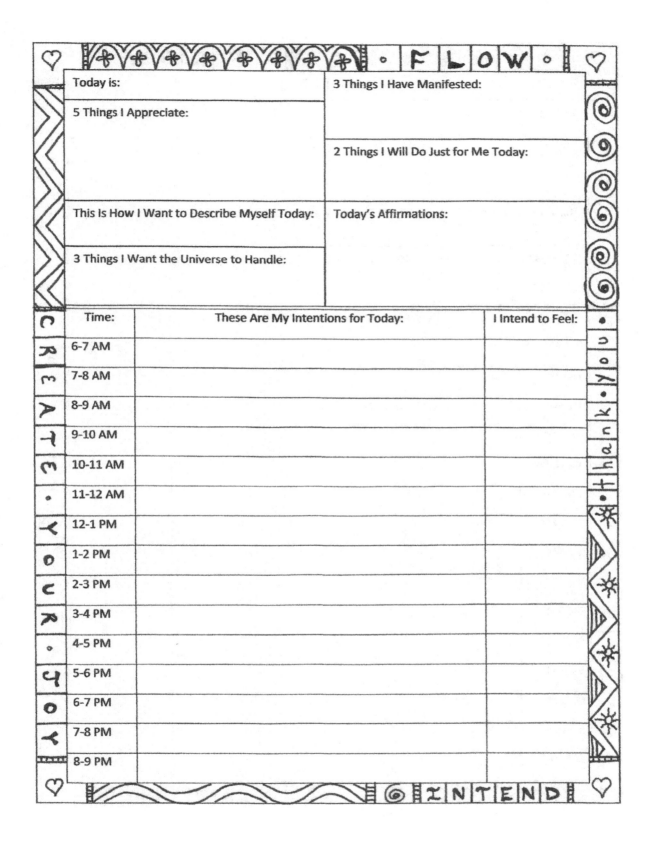

FLOW

Today is:	3 Things I Have Manifested:
5 Things I Appreciate:	
	2 Things I Will Do Just for Me Today:
This Is How I Want to Describe Myself Today:	Today's Affirmations:
3 Things I Want the Universe to Handle:	

	Time:	These Are My Intentions for Today:	I Intend to Feel:	
C	6-7 AM			
R	7-8 AM			
E	8-9 AM			
A	9-10 AM			
T	10-11 AM			
E	11-12 AM			
Y	12-1 PM			
O	1-2 PM			
U	2-3 PM			
R	3-4 PM			
J	4-5 PM			
O	5-6 PM			
Y	6-7 PM			
	7-8 PM			
	8-9 PM			

INTEND

119

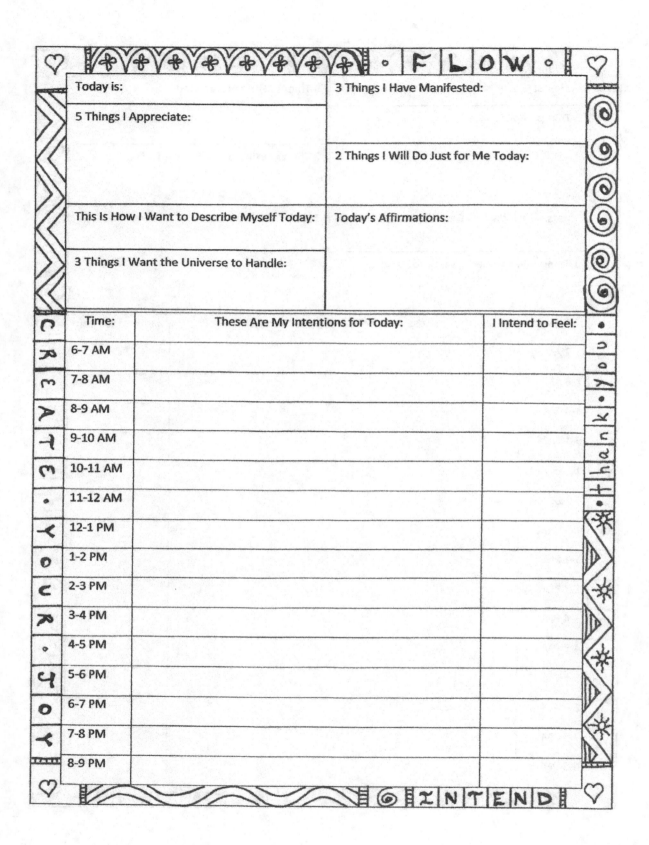

FLOW

Today is:	3 Things I Have Manifested:
5 Things I Appreciate:	
	2 Things I Will Do Just for Me Today:
This Is How I Want to Describe Myself Today:	Today's Affirmations:
3 Things I Want the Universe to Handle:	

Time:	These Are My Intentions for Today:	I Intend to Feel:
6-7 AM		
7-8 AM		
8-9 AM		
9-10 AM		
10-11 AM		
11-12 AM		
12-1 PM		
1-2 PM		
2-3 PM		
3-4 PM		
4-5 PM		
5-6 PM		
6-7 PM		
7-8 PM		
8-9 PM		

CREATE . YOUR . JOY

thank you .

INTEND

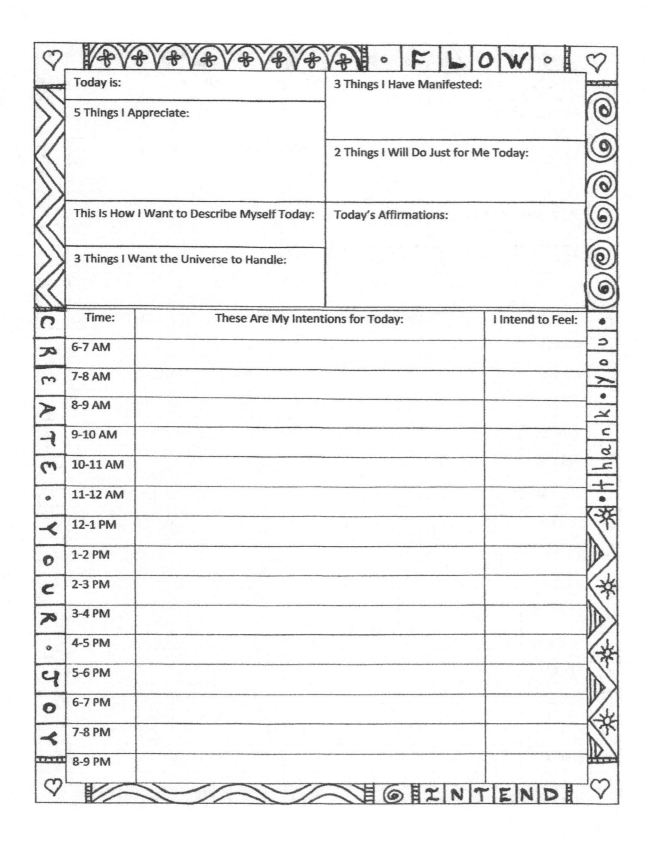

FLOW

Today is:	3 Things I Have Manifested:
5 Things I Appreciate:	
	2 Things I Will Do Just for Me Today:
This Is How I Want to Describe Myself Today:	Today's Affirmations:
3 Things I Want the Universe to Handle:	

Time:	These Are My Intentions for Today:	I Intend to Feel:
6-7 AM		
7-8 AM		
8-9 AM		
9-10 AM		
10-11 AM		
11-12 AM		
12-1 PM		
1-2 PM		
2-3 PM		
3-4 PM		
4-5 PM		
5-6 PM		
6-7 PM		
7-8 PM		
8-9 PM		

CREATE . YOUR . JOY

thank you

INTEND

121

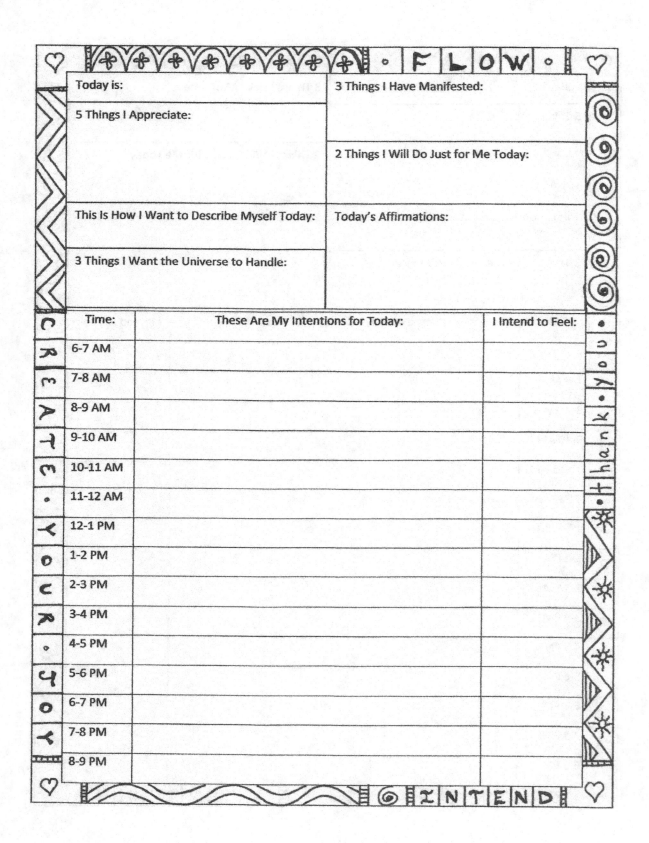

FLOW

Today is:

5 Things I Appreciate:

This Is How I Want to Describe Myself Today:

3 Things I Want the Universe to Handle:

3 Things I Have Manifested:

2 Things I Will Do Just for Me Today:

Today's Affirmations:

Time:	These Are My Intentions for Today:	I Intend to Feel:
6-7 AM		
7-8 AM		
8-9 AM		
9-10 AM		
10-11 AM		
11-12 AM		
12-1 PM		
1-2 PM		
2-3 PM		
3-4 PM		
4-5 PM		
5-6 PM		
6-7 PM		
7-8 PM		
8-9 PM		

CREATE YOUR JOY

thank you

INTEND

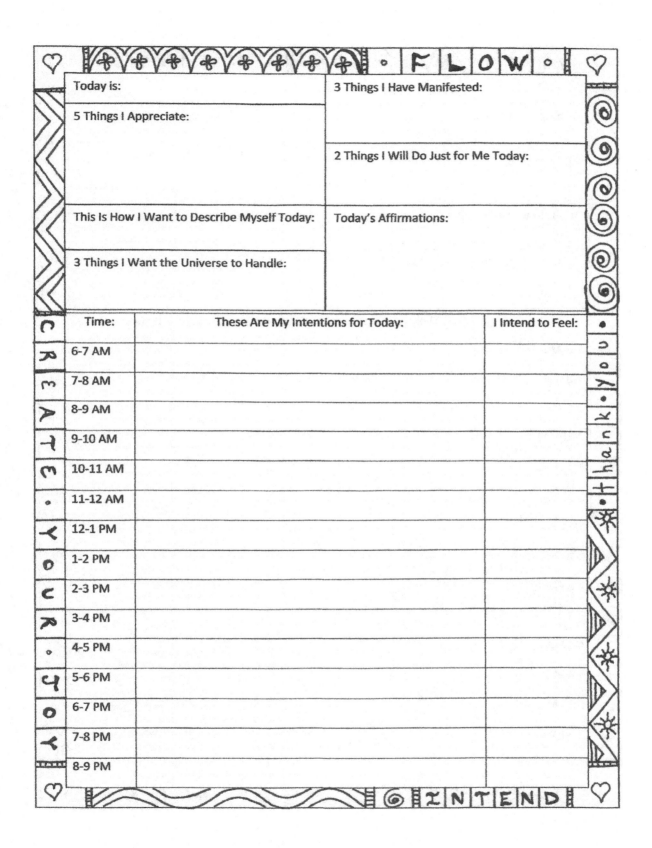

FLOW

Today is:	3 Things I Have Manifested:
5 Things I Appreciate:	
	2 Things I Will Do Just for Me Today:
This Is How I Want to Describe Myself Today:	Today's Affirmations:
3 Things I Want the Universe to Handle:	

Time:	These Are My Intentions for Today:	I Intend to Feel:
6-7 AM		
7-8 AM		
8-9 AM		
9-10 AM		
10-11 AM		
11-12 AM		
12-1 PM		
1-2 PM		
2-3 PM		
3-4 PM		
4-5 PM		
5-6 PM		
6-7 PM		
7-8 PM		
8-9 PM		

CREATE · YOUR · JOY

Thank you.

INTEND

123

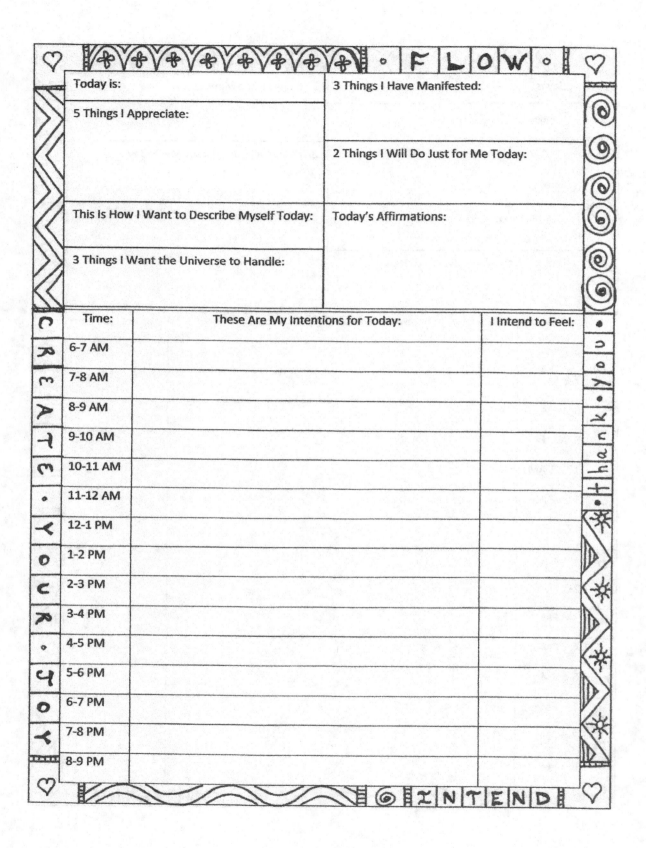

FLOW

Today is:	3 Things I Have Manifested:
5 Things I Appreciate:	
	2 Things I Will Do Just for Me Today:
This Is How I Want to Describe Myself Today:	Today's Affirmations:
3 Things I Want the Universe to Handle:	

CREATE • YOUR • JOY

thank you.

Time:	These Are My Intentions for Today:	I Intend to Feel:
6-7 AM		
7-8 AM		
8-9 AM		
9-10 AM		
10-11 AM		
11-12 AM		
12-1 PM		
1-2 PM		
2-3 PM		
3-4 PM		
4-5 PM		
5-6 PM		
6-7 PM		
7-8 PM		
8-9 PM		

INTEND

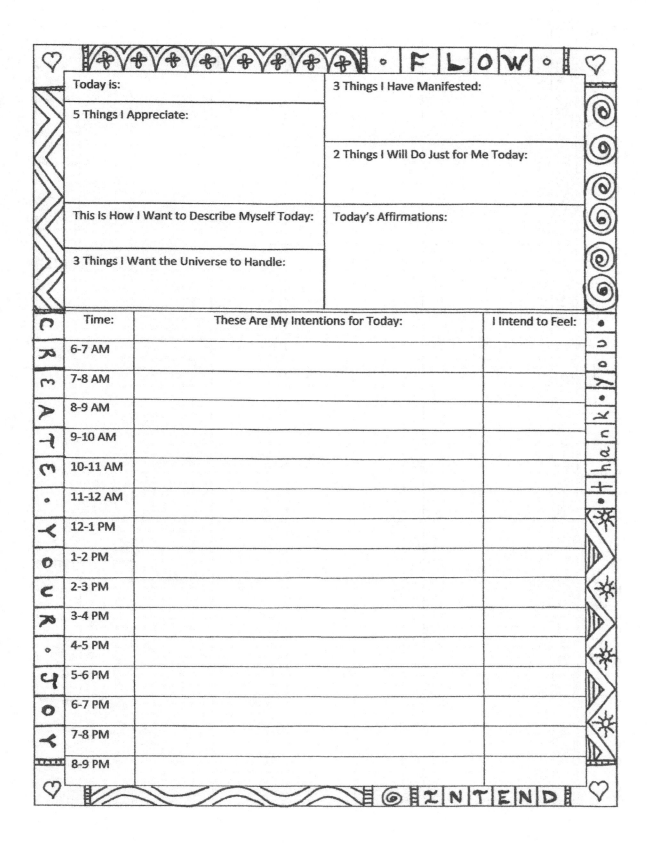

FLOW

Today is:	3 Things I Have Manifested:
5 Things I Appreciate:	
	2 Things I Will Do Just for Me Today:
This Is How I Want to Describe Myself Today:	Today's Affirmations:
3 Things I Want the Universe to Handle:	

Time:	These Are My Intentions for Today:	I Intend to Feel:
6-7 AM		
7-8 AM		
8-9 AM		
9-10 AM		
10-11 AM		
11-12 AM		
12-1 PM		
1-2 PM		
2-3 PM		
3-4 PM		
4-5 PM		
5-6 PM		
6-7 PM		
7-8 PM		
8-9 PM		

CREATE . YOUR . JOY

INTEND

thank . you

Month: May

Sunday	Monday	Tuesday	Wednesday	Thursday	Friday	Saturday

Do at least one thing every day that brings you joy and record it on this page.

Affirmations:

" You are all adored and worthy. "

--Abraham/Hicks

126

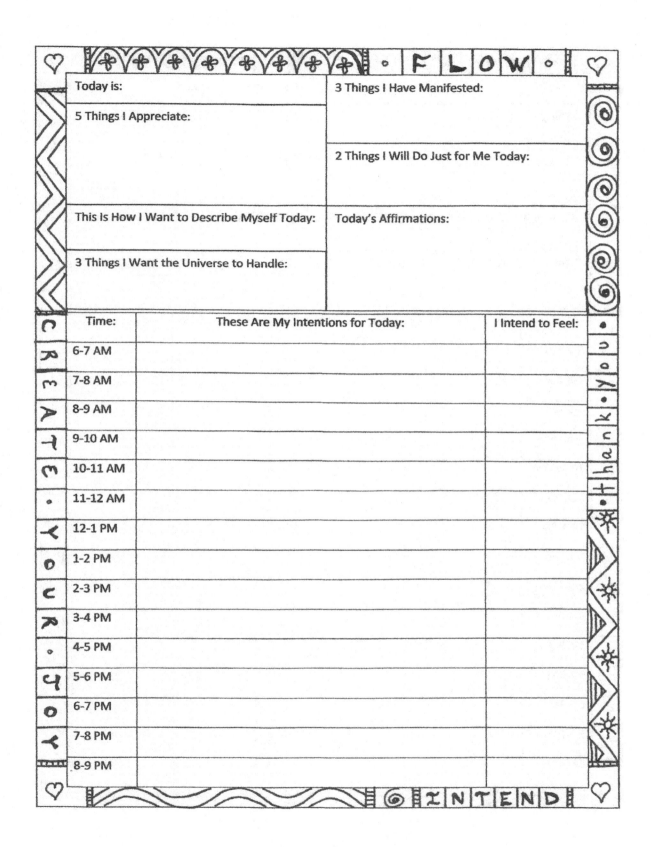

FLOW

Today is:		3 Things I Have Manifested:

5 Things I Appreciate:

	2 Things I Will Do Just for Me Today:

This Is How I Want to Describe Myself Today:	Today's Affirmations:

3 Things I Want the Universe to Handle:

Time:	These Are My Intentions for Today:	I Intend to Feel:
6-7 AM		
7-8 AM		
8-9 AM		
9-10 AM		
10-11 AM		
11-12 AM		
12-1 PM		
1-2 PM		
2-3 PM		
3-4 PM		
4-5 PM		
5-6 PM		
6-7 PM		
7-8 PM		
8-9 PM		

CREATE . YOUCR . JOY

Thank You . INTEND

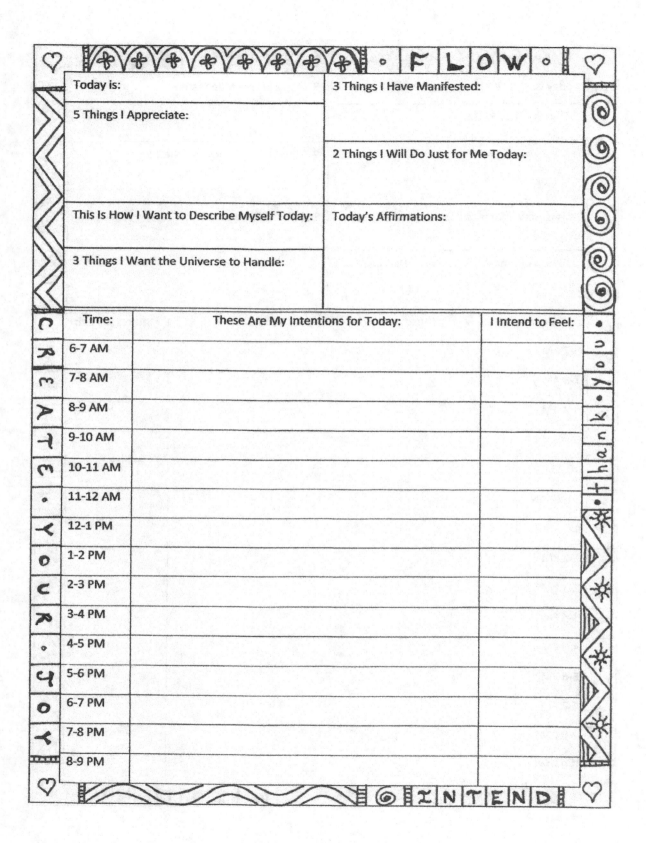

FLOW

Today is:

5 Things I Appreciate:

This Is How I Want to Describe Myself Today:

3 Things I Want the Universe to Handle:

3 Things I Have Manifested:

2 Things I Will Do Just for Me Today:

Today's Affirmations:

CREATE • YOUR • JOY

thank you •

Time:	These Are My Intentions for Today:	I Intend to Feel:
6-7 AM		
7-8 AM		
8-9 AM		
9-10 AM		
10-11 AM		
11-12 AM		
12-1 PM		
1-2 PM		
2-3 PM		
3-4 PM		
4-5 PM		
5-6 PM		
6-7 PM		
7-8 PM		
8-9 PM		

INTEND

FLOW

Today is:	**3 Things I Have Manifested:**
5 Things I Appreciate:	
	2 Things I Will Do Just for Me Today:
This Is How I Want to Describe Myself Today:	**Today's Affirmations:**
3 Things I Want the Universe to Handle:	

Time:	These Are My Intentions for Today:	I Intend to Feel:
6-7 AM		
7-8 AM		
8-9 AM		
9-10 AM		
10-11 AM		
11-12 AM		
12-1 PM		
1-2 PM		
2-3 PM		
3-4 PM		
4-5 PM		
5-6 PM		
6-7 PM		
7-8 PM		
8-9 PM		

CREATE . YOUR . JOY

thank you

INTEND

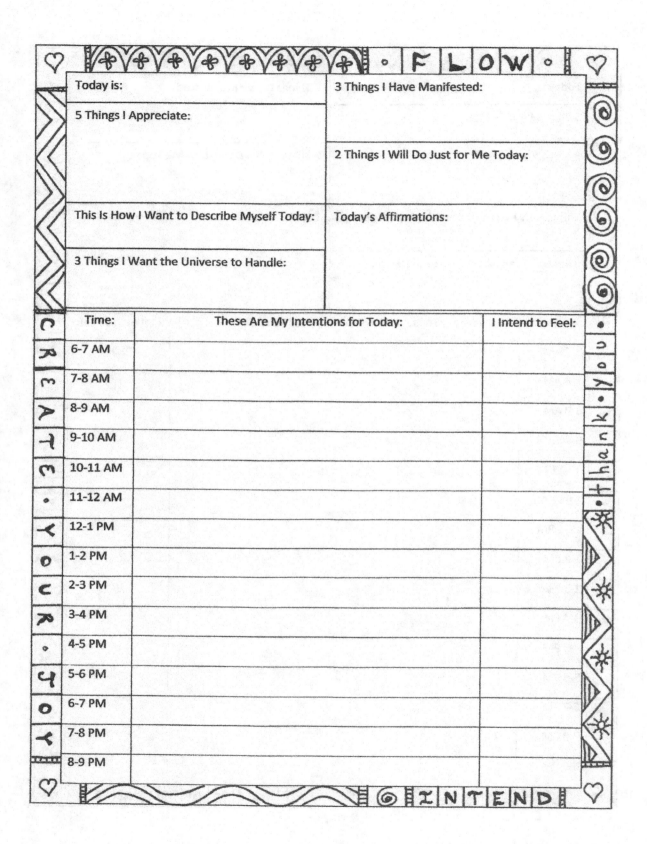

FLOW

Today is:	3 Things I Have Manifested:
5 Things I Appreciate:	
	2 Things I Will Do Just for Me Today:
This Is How I Want to Describe Myself Today:	Today's Affirmations:
3 Things I Want the Universe to Handle:	

Time:	These Are My Intentions for Today:	I Intend to Feel:
6-7 AM		
7-8 AM		
8-9 AM		
9-10 AM		
10-11 AM		
11-12 AM		
12-1 PM		
1-2 PM		
2-3 PM		
3-4 PM		
4-5 PM		
5-6 PM		
6-7 PM		
7-8 PM		
8-9 PM		

CREATE • YOUR • JOY

thank you

INTEND

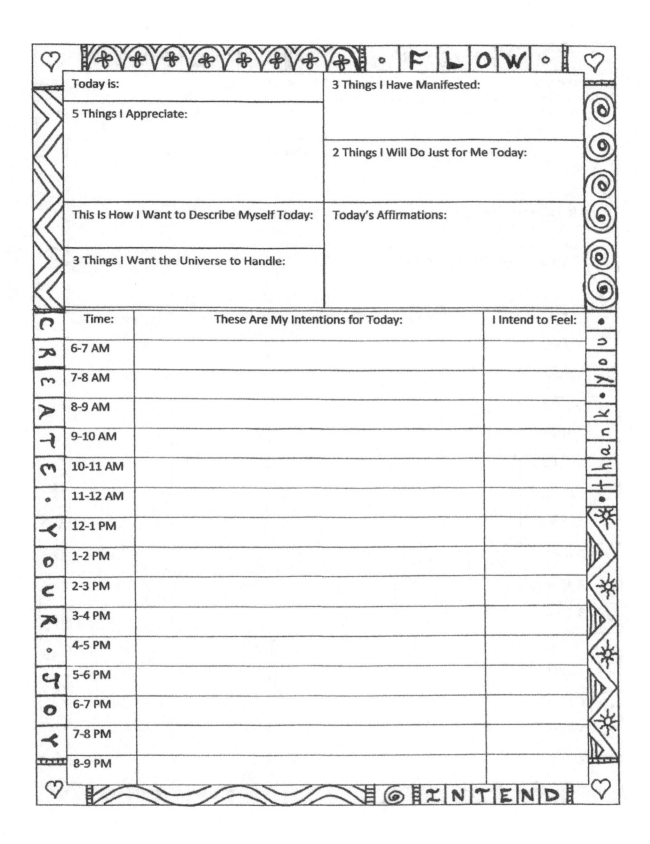

FLOW

Today is:	3 Things I Have Manifested:
5 Things I Appreciate:	
	2 Things I Will Do Just for Me Today:
This Is How I Want to Describe Myself Today:	Today's Affirmations:
3 Things I Want the Universe to Handle:	

Time:	These Are My Intentions for Today:	I Intend to Feel:
6-7 AM		
7-8 AM		
8-9 AM		
9-10 AM		
10-11 AM		
11-12 AM		
12-1 PM		
1-2 PM		
2-3 PM		
3-4 PM		
4-5 PM		
5-6 PM		
6-7 PM		
7-8 PM		
8-9 PM		

CREATE . YOUR . JOY

thank you

INTEND

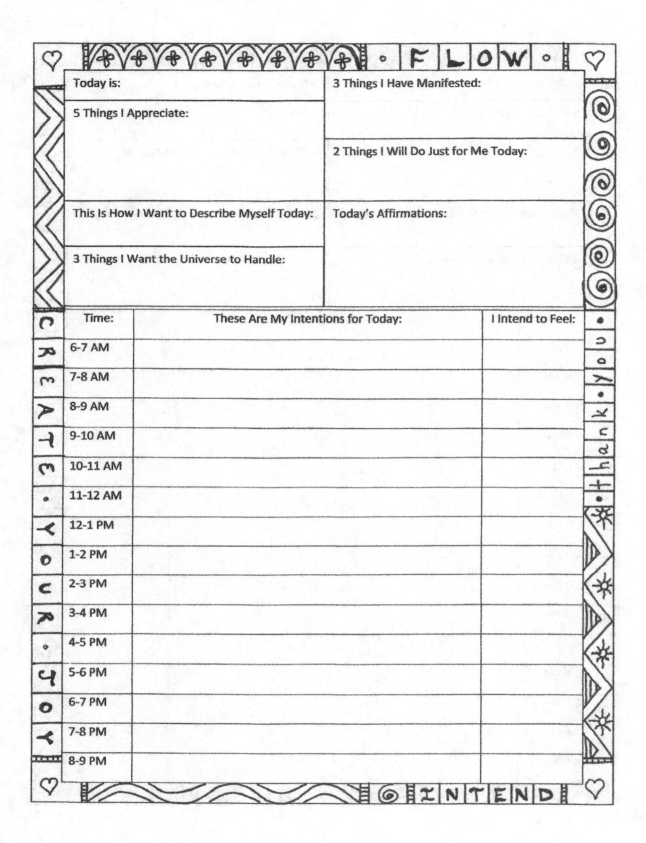

FLOW

Today is:	3 Things I Have Manifested:
5 Things I Appreciate:	
	2 Things I Will Do Just for Me Today:
This Is How I Want to Describe Myself Today:	Today's Affirmations:
3 Things I Want the Universe to Handle:	

Time:	These Are My Intentions for Today:	I Intend to Feel:
6-7 AM		
7-8 AM		
8-9 AM		
9-10 AM		
10-11 AM		
11-12 AM		
12-1 PM		
1-2 PM		
2-3 PM		
3-4 PM		
4-5 PM		
5-6 PM		
6-7 PM		
7-8 PM		
8-9 PM		

CREATE . YOUR . JOY

thank you

INTEND

FLOW

Today is:

5 Things I Appreciate:

3 Things I Have Manifested:

2 Things I Will Do Just for Me Today:

This Is How I Want to Describe Myself Today:

Today's Affirmations:

3 Things I Want the Universe to Handle:

Time:	These Are My Intentions for Today:	I Intend to Feel:
6-7 AM		
7-8 AM		
8-9 AM		
9-10 AM		
10-11 AM		
11-12 AM		
12-1 PM		
1-2 PM		
2-3 PM		
3-4 PM		
4-5 PM		
5-6 PM		
6-7 PM		
7-8 PM		
8-9 PM		

CREATE • YOUR • JOY

thank you

INTEND

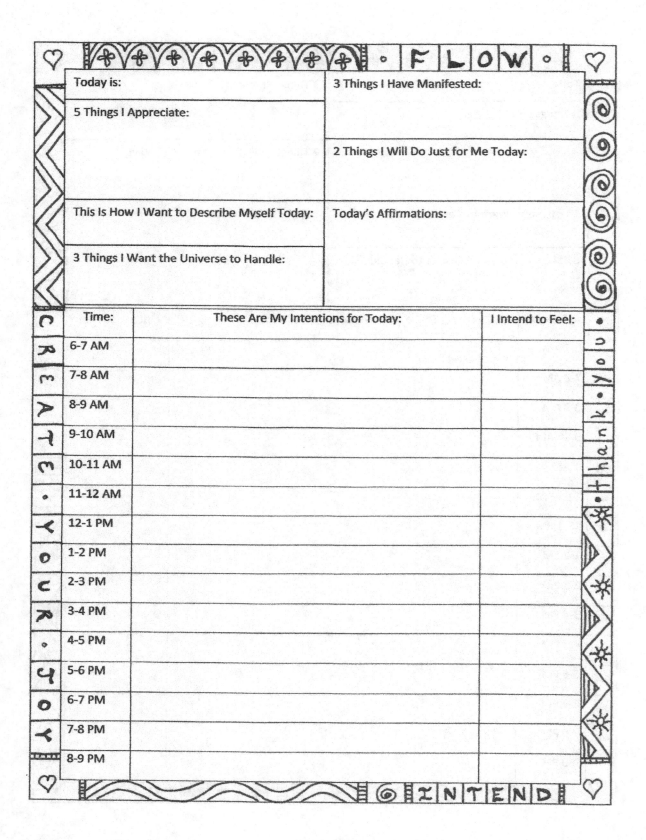

FLOW

Today is:	3 Things I Have Manifested:
5 Things I Appreciate:	
	2 Things I Will Do Just for Me Today:
This Is How I Want to Describe Myself Today:	Today's Affirmations:
3 Things I Want the Universe to Handle:	

Time:	These Are My Intentions for Today:	I Intend to Feel:
6-7 AM		
7-8 AM		
8-9 AM		
9-10 AM		
10-11 AM		
11-12 AM		
12-1 PM		
1-2 PM		
2-3 PM		
3-4 PM		
4-5 PM		
5-6 PM		
6-7 PM		
7-8 PM		
8-9 PM		

CREATE YOUR JOY

thank you

INTEND

134

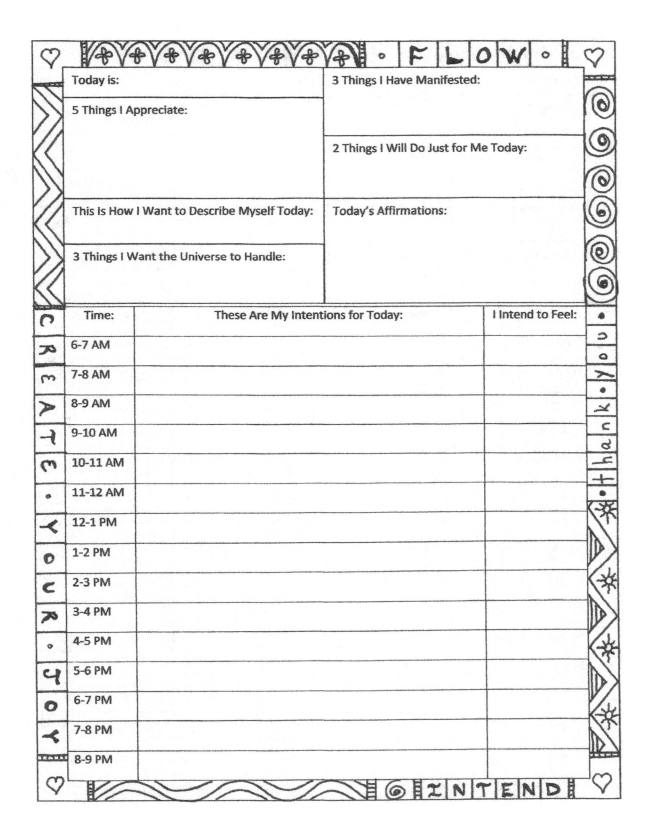

FLOW

Today is:	3 Things I Have Manifested:
5 Things I Appreciate:	
	2 Things I Will Do Just for Me Today:
This Is How I Want to Describe Myself Today:	Today's Affirmations:
3 Things I Want the Universe to Handle:	

Time:	These Are My Intentions for Today:	I Intend to Feel:
6-7 AM		
7-8 AM		
8-9 AM		
9-10 AM		
10-11 AM		
11-12 AM		
12-1 PM		
1-2 PM		
2-3 PM		
3-4 PM		
4-5 PM		
5-6 PM		
6-7 PM		
7-8 PM		
8-9 PM		

CREATE . YOUR . JOY

thank you

INTEND

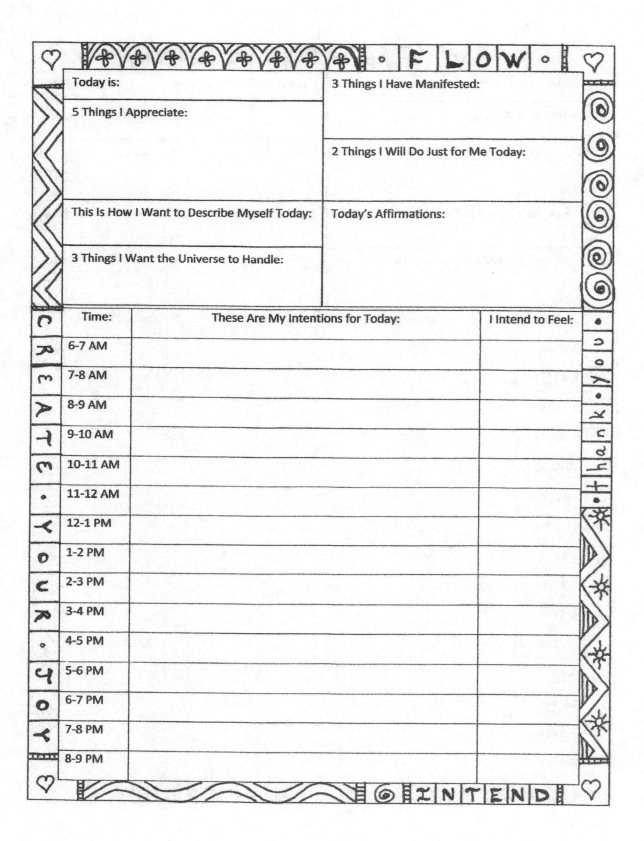

FLOW

Today is:		3 Things I Have Manifested:
5 Things I Appreciate:		
		2 Things I Will Do Just for Me Today:
This Is How I Want to Describe Myself Today:		Today's Affirmations:
3 Things I Want the Universe to Handle:		

CREATE · YOUR · JOY

Time:	These Are My Intentions for Today:	I Intend to Feel:
6-7 AM		
7-8 AM		
8-9 AM		
9-10 AM		
10-11 AM		
11-12 AM		
12-1 PM		
1-2 PM		
2-3 PM		
3-4 PM		
4-5 PM		
5-6 PM		
6-7 PM		
7-8 PM		
8-9 PM		

· thank you ·

INTEND

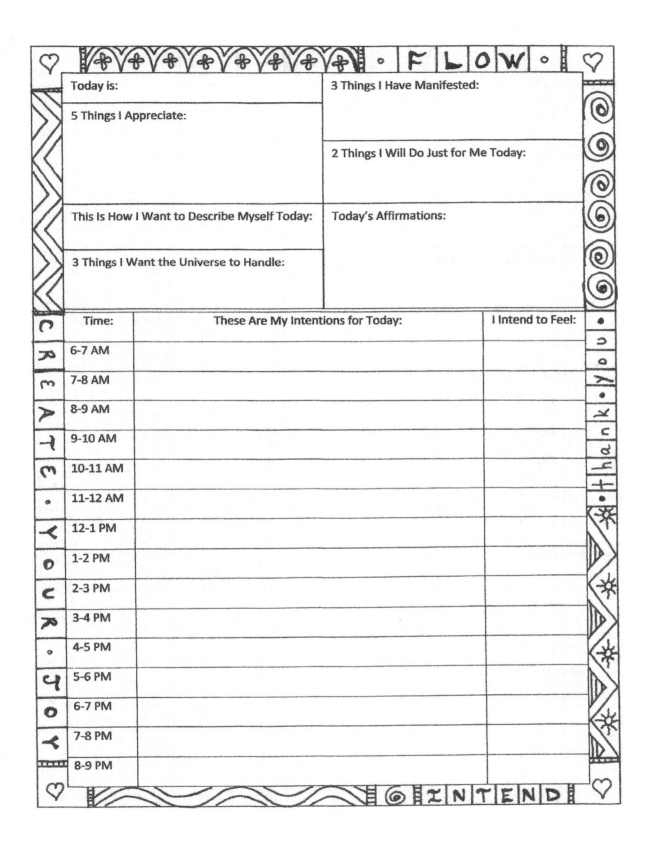

FLOW

Today is:	3 Things I Have Manifested:
5 Things I Appreciate:	
	2 Things I Will Do Just for Me Today:
This Is How I Want to Describe Myself Today:	Today's Affirmations:
3 Things I Want the Universe to Handle:	

CREATE . YOUR . JOY

Time:	These Are My Intentions for Today:	I Intend to Feel:
6-7 AM		
7-8 AM		
8-9 AM		
9-10 AM		
10-11 AM		
11-12 AM		
12-1 PM		
1-2 PM		
2-3 PM		
3-4 PM		
4-5 PM		
5-6 PM		
6-7 PM		
7-8 PM		
8-9 PM		

INTEND

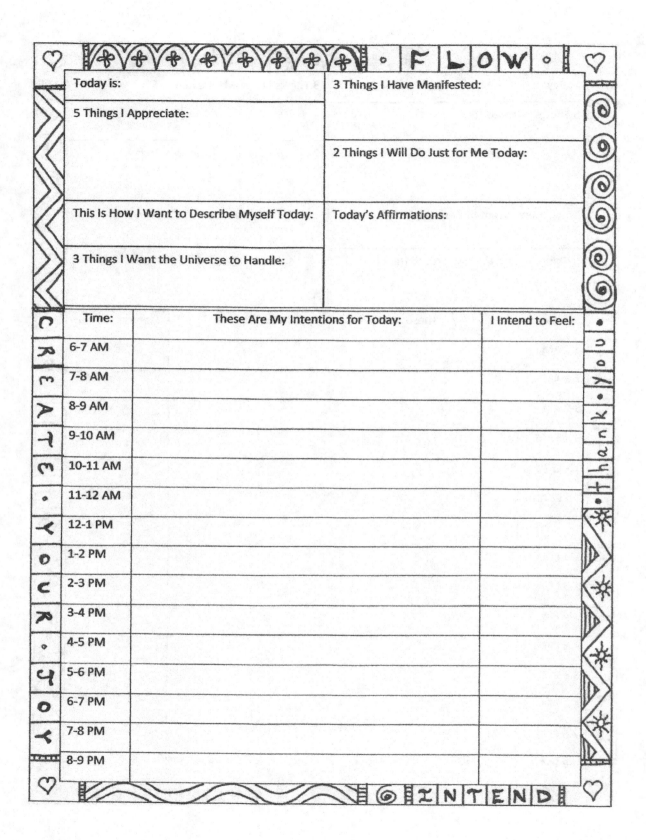

FLOW

Today is:	3 Things I Have Manifested:
5 Things I Appreciate:	
	2 Things I Will Do Just for Me Today:
This Is How I Want to Describe Myself Today:	**Today's Affirmations:**
3 Things I Want the Universe to Handle:	

Time:	These Are My Intentions for Today:	I Intend to Feel:
6-7 AM		
7-8 AM		
8-9 AM		
9-10 AM		
10-11 AM		
11-12 AM		
12-1 PM		
1-2 PM		
2-3 PM		
3-4 PM		
4-5 PM		
5-6 PM		
6-7 PM		
7-8 PM		
8-9 PM		

CREATE. YOUR. JOY

thank.you

INTEND

FLOW

Today is:

5 Things I Appreciate:

3 Things I Have Manifested:

2 Things I Will Do Just for Me Today:

This Is How I Want to Describe Myself Today:

Today's Affirmations:

3 Things I Want the Universe to Handle:

Time:	These Are My Intentions for Today:	I Intend to Feel:
6-7 AM		
7-8 AM		
8-9 AM		
9-10 AM		
10-11 AM		
11-12 AM		
12-1 PM		
1-2 PM		
2-3 PM		
3-4 PM		
4-5 PM		
5-6 PM		
6-7 PM		
7-8 PM		
8-9 PM		

CREATE . YOUR . JOY

. thank you .

INTEND

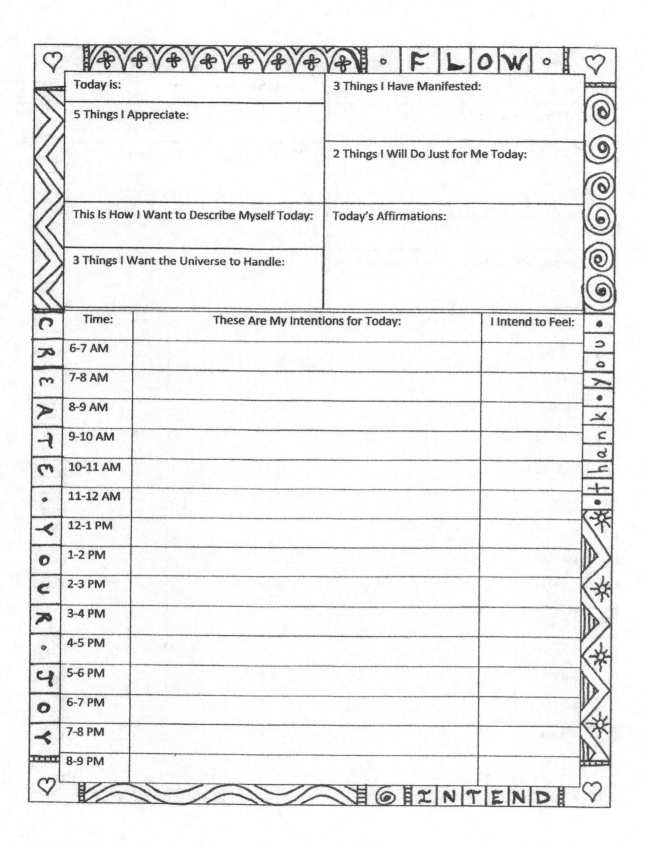

FLOW

Today is:	3 Things I Have Manifested:
5 Things I Appreciate:	
	2 Things I Will Do Just for Me Today:
This Is How I Want to Describe Myself Today:	**Today's Affirmations:**
3 Things I Want the Universe to Handle:	

Time:	These Are My Intentions for Today:	I Intend to Feel:
6-7 AM		
7-8 AM		
8-9 AM		
9-10 AM		
10-11 AM		
11-12 AM		
12-1 PM		
1-2 PM		
2-3 PM		
3-4 PM		
4-5 PM		
5-6 PM		
6-7 PM		
7-8 PM		
8-9 PM		

CREATE • YOUR • JOY

thank you

INTEND

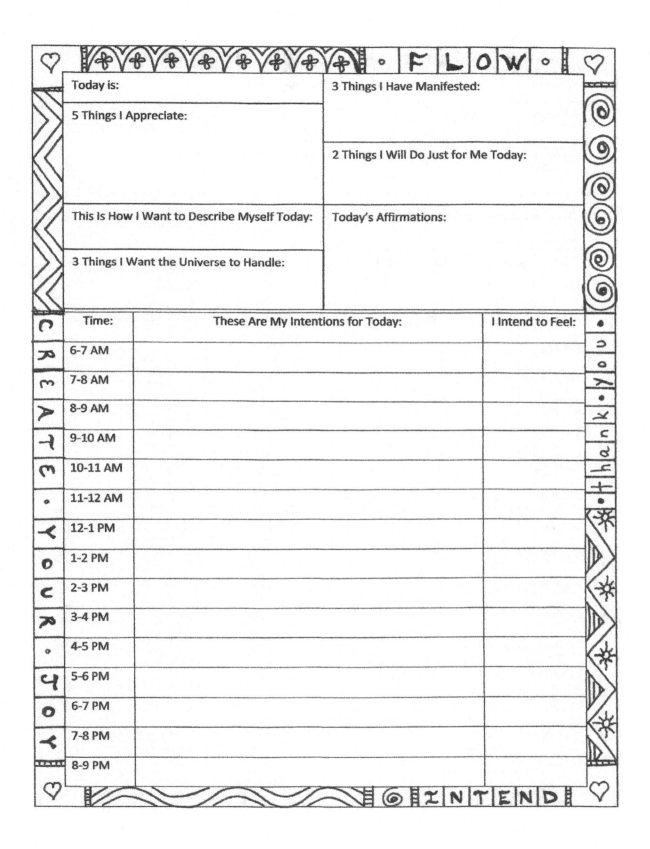

FLOW

Today is:	3 Things I Have Manifested:
5 Things I Appreciate:	
	2 Things I Will Do Just for Me Today:
This Is How I Want to Describe Myself Today:	**Today's Affirmations:**
3 Things I Want the Universe to Handle:	

CREATE • YOUR • JOY

thank you •

Time:	These Are My Intentions for Today:	I Intend to Feel:
6-7 AM		
7-8 AM		
8-9 AM		
9-10 AM		
10-11 AM		
11-12 AM		
12-1 PM		
1-2 PM		
2-3 PM		
3-4 PM		
4-5 PM		
5-6 PM		
6-7 PM		
7-8 PM		
8-9 PM		

INTEND

141

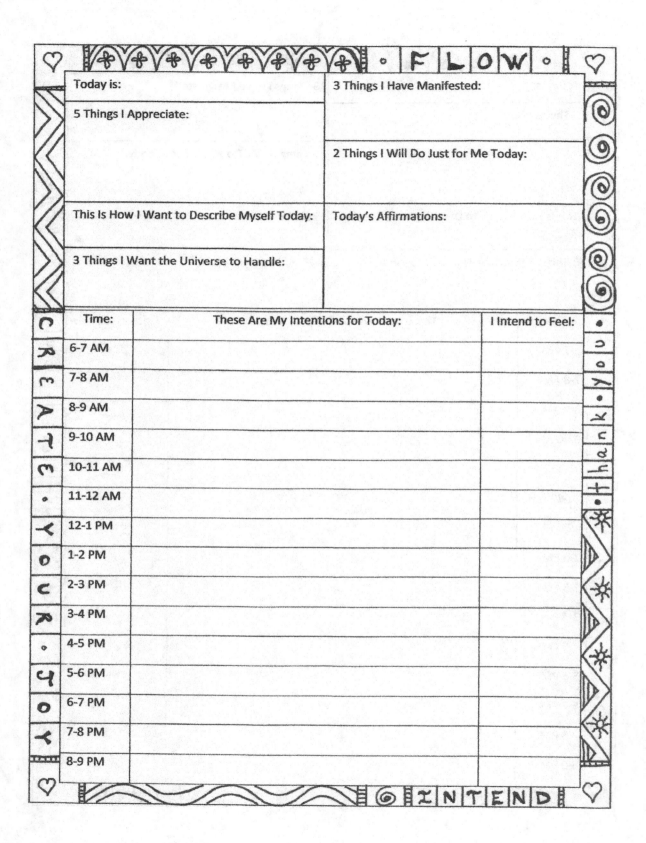

FLOW

Today is:

5 Things I Appreciate:

This Is How I Want to Describe Myself Today:

3 Things I Want the Universe to Handle:

3 Things I Have Manifested:

2 Things I Will Do Just for Me Today:

Today's Affirmations:

Time:	These Are My Intentions for Today:	I Intend to Feel:
6-7 AM		
7-8 AM		
8-9 AM		
9-10 AM		
10-11 AM		
11-12 AM		
12-1 PM		
1-2 PM		
2-3 PM		
3-4 PM		
4-5 PM		
5-6 PM		
6-7 PM		
7-8 PM		
8-9 PM		

CREATE . YOUR . JOY

thank you

INTEND

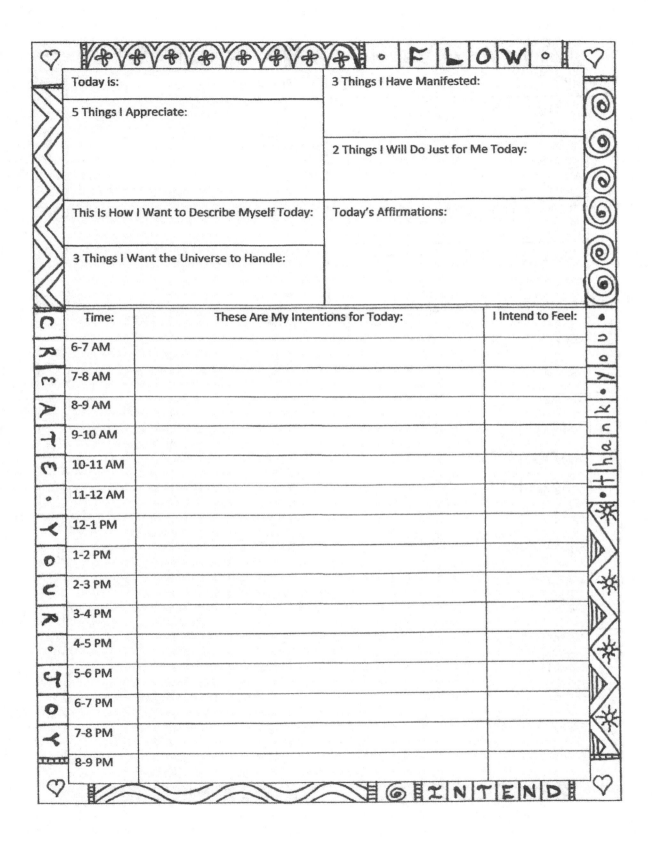

FLOW

Today is:	3 Things I Have Manifested:
5 Things I Appreciate:	
	2 Things I Will Do Just for Me Today:
This Is How I Want to Describe Myself Today:	Today's Affirmations:
3 Things I Want the Universe to Handle:	

CREATE • YOUR • JOY

thank you

Time:	These Are My Intentions for Today:	I Intend to Feel:
6-7 AM		
7-8 AM		
8-9 AM		
9-10 AM		
10-11 AM		
11-12 AM		
12-1 PM		
1-2 PM		
2-3 PM		
3-4 PM		
4-5 PM		
5-6 PM		
6-7 PM		
7-8 PM		
8-9 PM		

INTEND

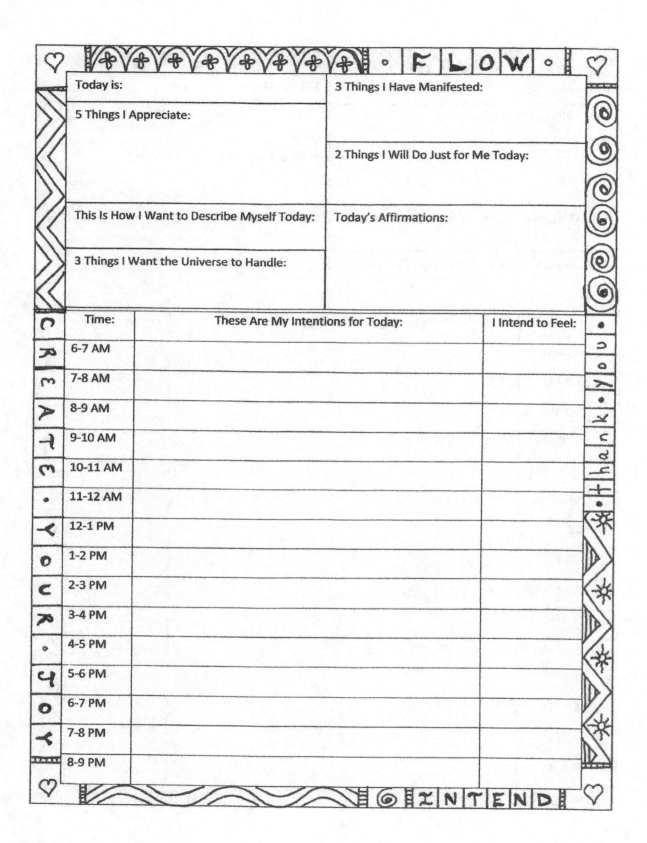

FLOW

Today is:	3 Things I Have Manifested:
5 Things I Appreciate:	
	2 Things I Will Do Just for Me Today:
This Is How I Want to Describe Myself Today:	**Today's Affirmations:**
3 Things I Want the Universe to Handle:	

CREATE . YOUR . JOY

thank you . thank you

Time:	These Are My Intentions for Today:	I Intend to Feel:
6-7 AM		
7-8 AM		
8-9 AM		
9-10 AM		
10-11 AM		
11-12 AM		
12-1 PM		
1-2 PM		
2-3 PM		
3-4 PM		
4-5 PM		
5-6 PM		
6-7 PM		
7-8 PM		
8-9 PM		

INTEND

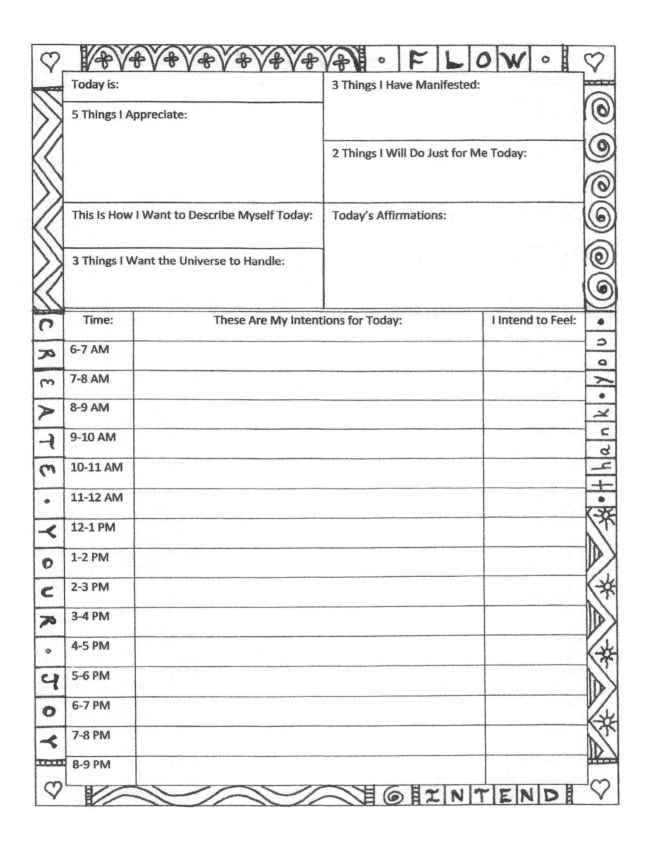

FLOW

Today is:	**3 Things I Have Manifested:**
5 Things I Appreciate:	
	2 Things I Will Do Just for Me Today:
This Is How I Want to Describe Myself Today:	**Today's Affirmations:**
3 Things I Want the Universe to Handle:	

Time:	These Are My Intentions for Today:	I Intend to Feel:
6-7 AM		
7-8 AM		
8-9 AM		
9-10 AM		
10-11 AM		
11-12 AM		
12-1 PM		
1-2 PM		
2-3 PM		
3-4 PM		
4-5 PM		
5-6 PM		
6-7 PM		
7-8 PM		
8-9 PM		

CREATE • YOUR • JOY

thank • you

INTEND

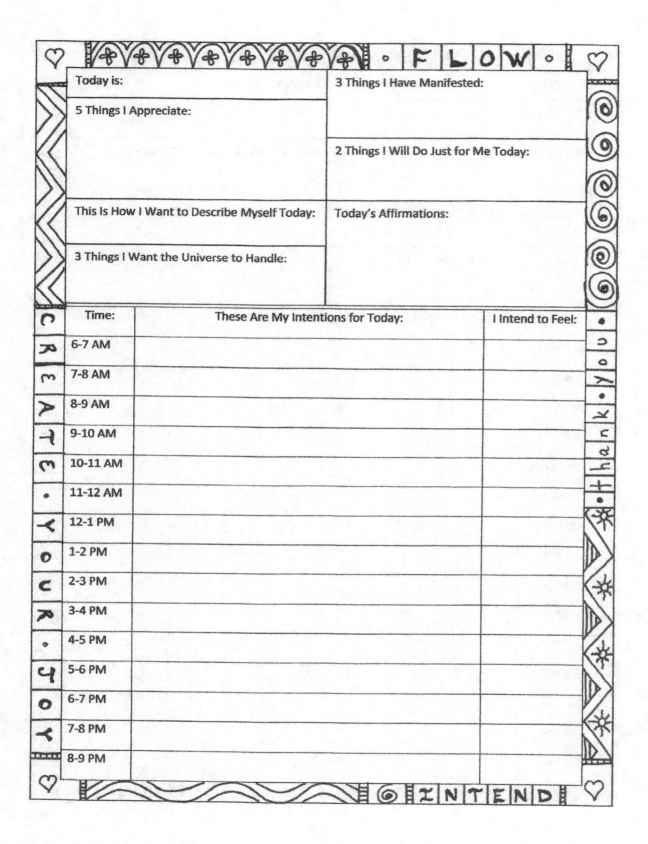

FLOW

Today is:		3 Things I Have Manifested:
5 Things I Appreciate:		
		2 Things I Will Do Just for Me Today:
This Is How I Want to Describe Myself Today:		Today's Affirmations:
3 Things I Want the Universe to Handle:		

CREATE • YOUR • JOY

Time:	These Are My Intentions for Today:	I Intend to Feel:
6-7 AM		
7-8 AM		
8-9 AM		
9-10 AM		
10-11 AM		
11-12 AM		
12-1 PM		
1-2 PM		
2-3 PM		
3-4 PM		
4-5 PM		
5-6 PM		
6-7 PM		
7-8 PM		
8-9 PM		

thank you

INTEND

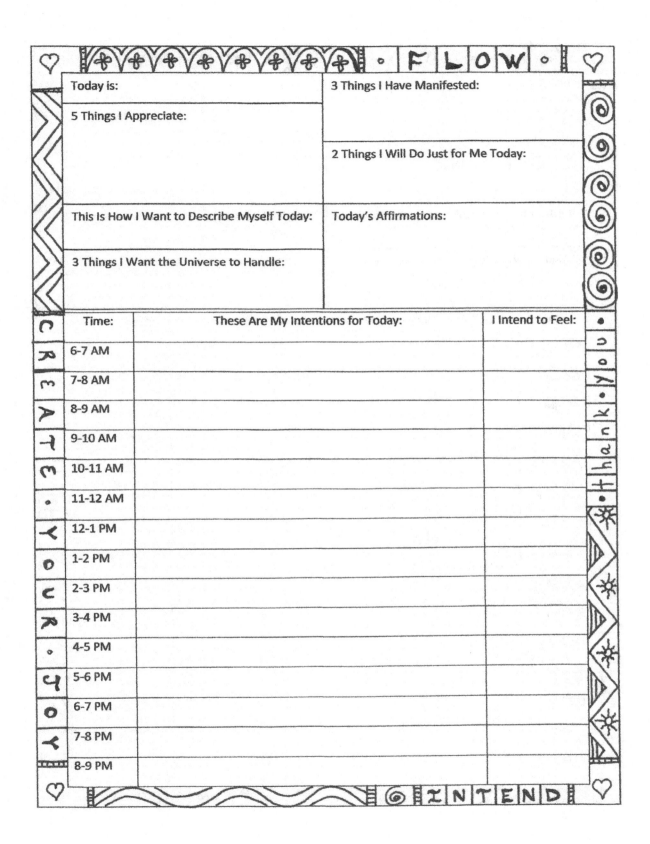

FLOW

Today is:	3 Things I Have Manifested:
5 Things I Appreciate:	
	2 Things I Will Do Just for Me Today:
This Is How I Want to Describe Myself Today:	Today's Affirmations:
3 Things I Want the Universe to Handle:	

Time:	These Are My Intentions for Today:	I Intend to Feel:
6-7 AM		
7-8 AM		
8-9 AM		
9-10 AM		
10-11 AM		
11-12 AM		
12-1 PM		
1-2 PM		
2-3 PM		
3-4 PM		
4-5 PM		
5-6 PM		
6-7 PM		
7-8 PM		
8-9 PM		

CREATE • YOUR • JOY

thank you

INTEND

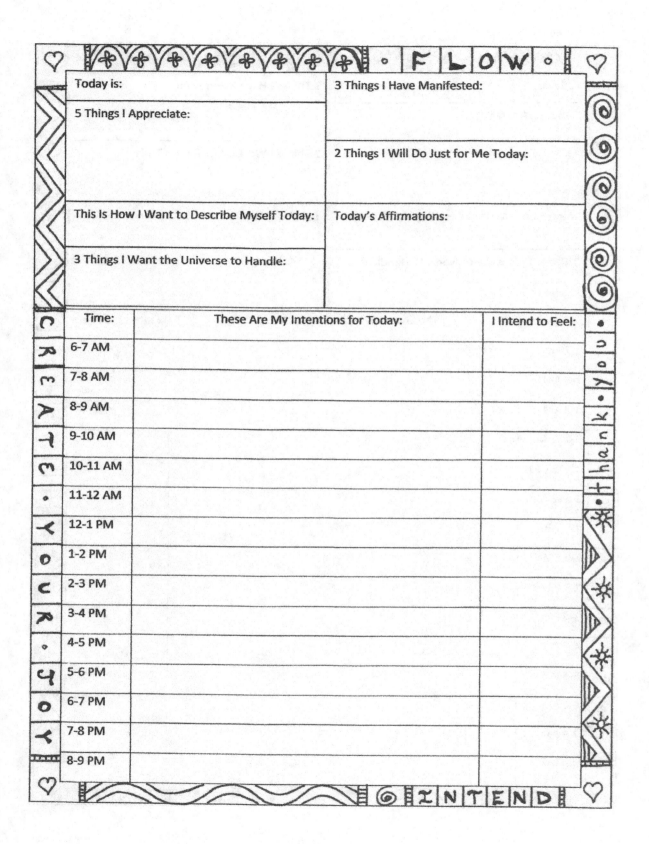

FLOW

Today is:	3 Things I Have Manifested:
5 Things I Appreciate:	
	2 Things I Will Do Just for Me Today:
This Is How I Want to Describe Myself Today:	**Today's Affirmations:**
3 Things I Want the Universe to Handle:	

CREATE • YOUR • JOY

thank you •

Time:	These Are My Intentions for Today:	I Intend to Feel:
6-7 AM		
7-8 AM		
8-9 AM		
9-10 AM		
10-11 AM		
11-12 AM		
12-1 PM		
1-2 PM		
2-3 PM		
3-4 PM		
4-5 PM		
5-6 PM		
6-7 PM		
7-8 PM		
8-9 PM		

INTEND

FLOW

Today is:	**3 Things I Have Manifested:**
5 Things I Appreciate:	
	2 Things I Will Do Just for Me Today:
This Is How I Want to Describe Myself Today:	**Today's Affirmations:**
3 Things I Want the Universe to Handle:	

CREATE . YOUR . JOY

Time:	These Are My Intentions for Today:	I Intend to Feel:
6-7 AM		
7-8 AM		
8-9 AM		
9-10 AM		
10-11 AM		
11-12 AM		
12-1 PM		
1-2 PM		
2-3 PM		
3-4 PM		
4-5 PM		
5-6 PM		
6-7 PM		
7-8 PM		
8-9 PM		

thank . you

INTEND

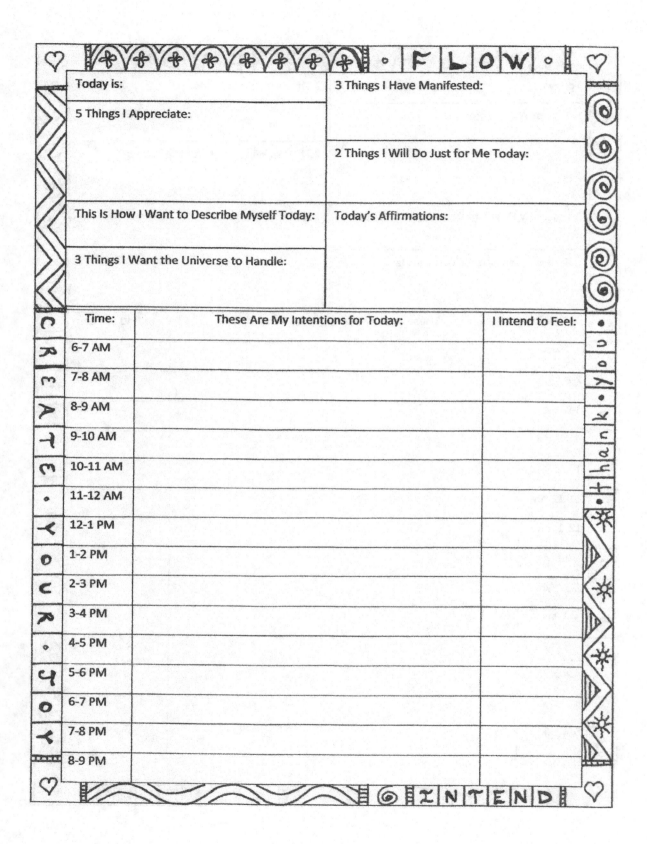

FLOW

Today is:

5 Things I Appreciate:

This Is How I Want to Describe Myself Today:

3 Things I Want the Universe to Handle:

3 Things I Have Manifested:

2 Things I Will Do Just for Me Today:

Today's Affirmations:

Time:	These Are My Intentions for Today:	I Intend to Feel:
6-7 AM		
7-8 AM		
8-9 AM		
9-10 AM		
10-11 AM		
11-12 AM		
12-1 PM		
1-2 PM		
2-3 PM		
3-4 PM		
4-5 PM		
5-6 PM		
6-7 PM		
7-8 PM		
8-9 PM		

CREATE . YOUR . JOY

thank you

INTEND

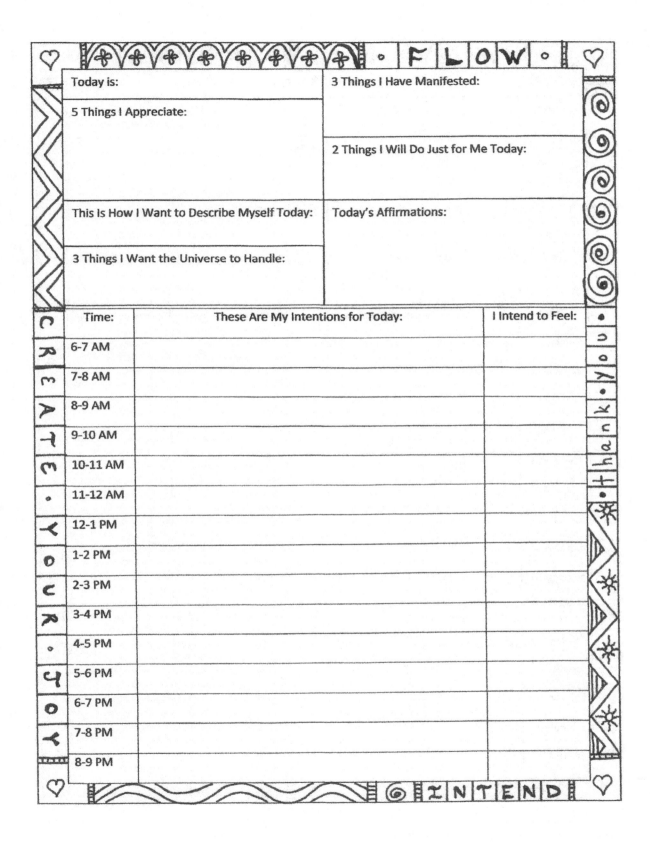

FLOW

Today is:	3 Things I Have Manifested:
5 Things I Appreciate:	
	2 Things I Will Do Just for Me Today:
This Is How I Want to Describe Myself Today:	**Today's Affirmations:**
3 Things I Want the Universe to Handle:	

CREATE · YOUR · JOY

Time:	These Are My Intentions for Today:	I Intend to Feel:
6-7 AM		
7-8 AM		
8-9 AM		
9-10 AM		
10-11 AM		
11-12 AM		
12-1 PM		
1-2 PM		
2-3 PM		
3-4 PM		
4-5 PM		
5-6 PM		
6-7 PM		
7-8 PM		
8-9 PM		

INTEND

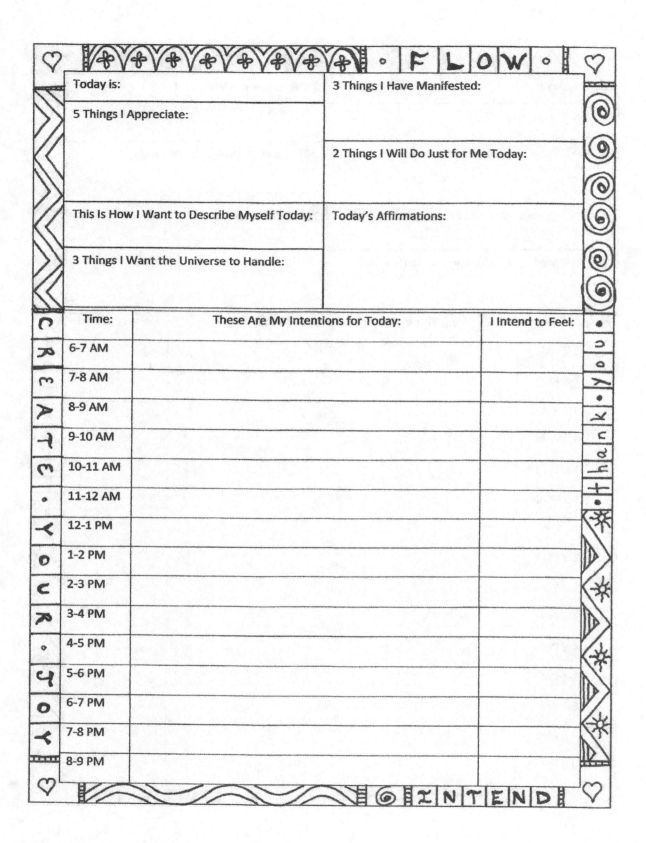

FLOW

Today is:	3 Things I Have Manifested:
5 Things I Appreciate:	
	2 Things I Will Do Just for Me Today:
This Is How I Want to Describe Myself Today:	Today's Affirmations:
3 Things I Want the Universe to Handle:	

Time:	These Are My Intentions for Today:	I Intend to Feel:
6-7 AM		
7-8 AM		
8-9 AM		
9-10 AM		
10-11 AM		
11-12 AM		
12-1 PM		
1-2 PM		
2-3 PM		
3-4 PM		
4-5 PM		
5-6 PM		
6-7 PM		
7-8 PM		
8-9 PM		

CREATE • YOUR • JOY

thank you

INTEND

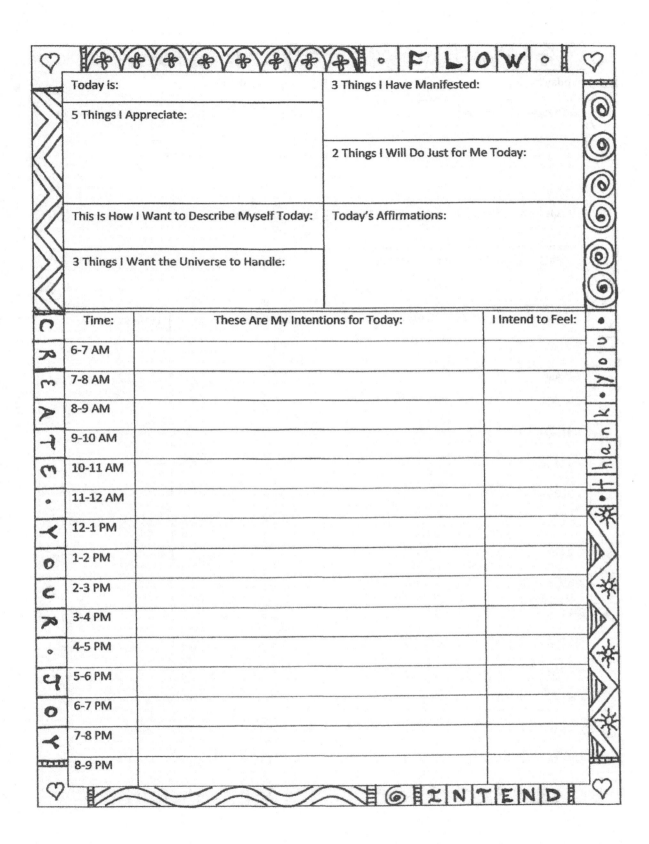

FLOW

Today is:	3 Things I Have Manifested:
5 Things I Appreciate:	
	2 Things I Will Do Just for Me Today:
This Is How I Want to Describe Myself Today:	Today's Affirmations:
3 Things I Want the Universe to Handle:	

CREATE · YOUR · JOY

Time:	These Are My Intentions for Today:	I Intend to Feel:
6-7 AM		
7-8 AM		
8-9 AM		
9-10 AM		
10-11 AM		
11-12 AM		
12-1 PM		
1-2 PM		
2-3 PM		
3-4 PM		
4-5 PM		
5-6 PM		
6-7 PM		
7-8 PM		
8-9 PM		

INTEND

153

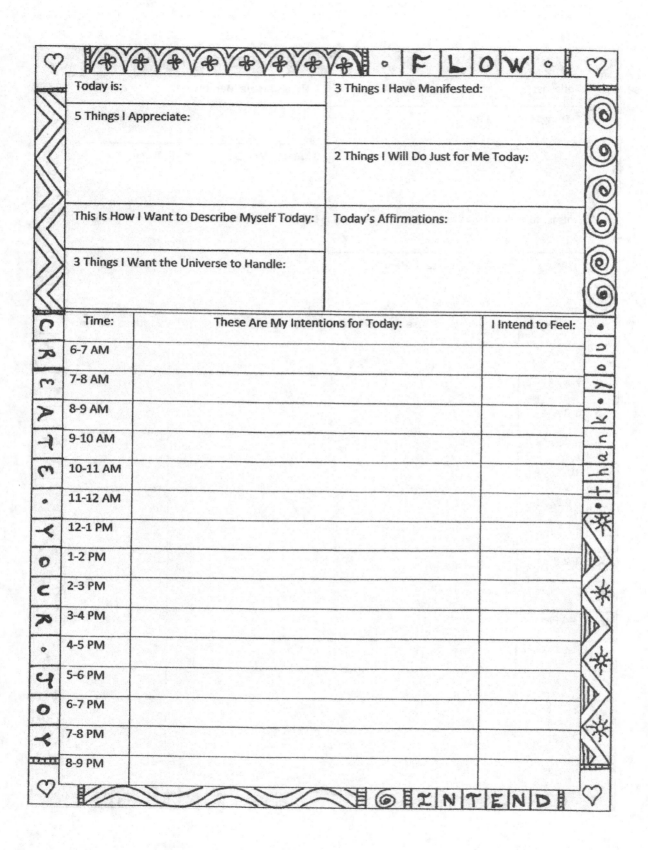

FLOW

Today is:	3 Things I Have Manifested:
5 Things I Appreciate:	
	2 Things I Will Do Just for Me Today:
This Is How I Want to Describe Myself Today:	Today's Affirmations:
3 Things I Want the Universe to Handle:	

	Time:	These Are My Intentions for Today:	I Intend to Feel:
C	6-7 AM		
R	7-8 AM		
E	8-9 AM		
A	9-10 AM		
T	10-11 AM		
E	11-12 AM		
·	12-1 PM		
Y	1-2 PM		
O	2-3 PM		
U	3-4 PM		
R	4-5 PM		
·	5-6 PM		
J	6-7 PM		
O	7-8 PM		
Y	8-9 PM		

INTEND

FLOW

Today is:

5 Things I Appreciate:

3 Things I Have Manifested:

2 Things I Will Do Just for Me Today:

This Is How I Want to Describe Myself Today:

Today's Affirmations:

3 Things I Want the Universe to Handle:

Time:	These Are My Intentions for Today:	I Intend to Feel:
6-7 AM		
7-8 AM		
8-9 AM		
9-10 AM		
10-11 AM		
11-12 AM		
12-1 PM		
1-2 PM		
2-3 PM		
3-4 PM		
4-5 PM		
5-6 PM		
6-7 PM		
7-8 PM		
8-9 PM		

CREATE. YOUR. JOY

thank you

INTEND

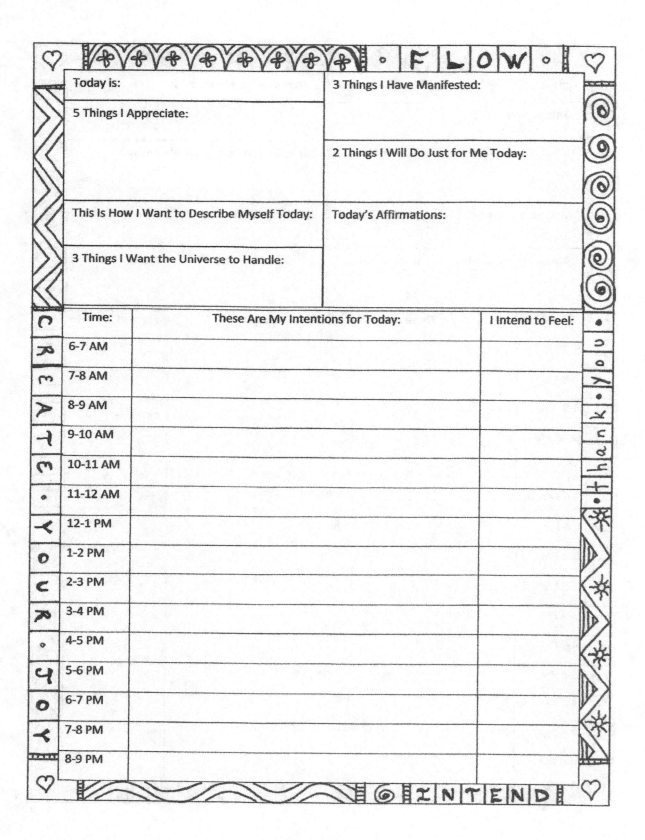

FLOW

Today is:

5 Things I Appreciate:

This Is How I Want to Describe Myself Today:

3 Things I Want the Universe to Handle:

3 Things I Have Manifested:

2 Things I Will Do Just for Me Today:

Today's Affirmations:

CREATE · YOUR · JOY	Time:	These Are My Intentions for Today:	I Intend to Feel:	thank you
	6-7 AM			
	7-8 AM			
	8-9 AM			
	9-10 AM			
	10-11 AM			
	11-12 AM			
	12-1 PM			
	1-2 PM			
	2-3 PM			
	3-4 PM			
	4-5 PM			
	5-6 PM			
	6-7 PM			
	7-8 PM			
	8-9 PM			

INTEND

· F L O W ·

Today is:

5 Things I Appreciate:

3 Things I Have Manifested:

2 Things I Will Do Just for Me Today:

This Is How I Want to Describe Myself Today:

Today's Affirmations:

3 Things I Want the Universe to Handle:

Time:	These Are My Intentions for Today:	I Intend to Feel:
6-7 AM		
7-8 AM		
8-9 AM		
9-10 AM		
10-11 AM		
11-12 AM		
12-1 PM		
1-2 PM		
2-3 PM		
3-4 PM		
4-5 PM		
5-6 PM		
6-7 PM		
7-8 PM		
8-9 PM		

CREATE · YOUR · JOY

thank you ·

INTEND

Month: June

Sunday	Monday	Tuesday	Wednesday	Thursday	Friday	Saturday

Do at least one thing every day that brings you joy and record it on this page.

Affirmations:

"Remember that your natural state is joy."

– Wayne Dyer

158

FLOW

Today is:		3 Things I Have Manifested:
5 Things I Appreciate:		
		2 Things I Will Do Just for Me Today:
This Is How I Want to Describe Myself Today:		Today's Affirmations:
3 Things I Want the Universe to Handle:		

Time:	These Are My Intentions for Today:	I Intend to Feel:
6-7 AM		
7-8 AM		
8-9 AM		
9-10 AM		
10-11 AM		
11-12 AM		
12-1 PM		
1-2 PM		
2-3 PM		
3-4 PM		
4-5 PM		
5-6 PM		
6-7 PM		
7-8 PM		
8-9 PM		

CREATE. YOUR. JOY

thank you.

INTEND

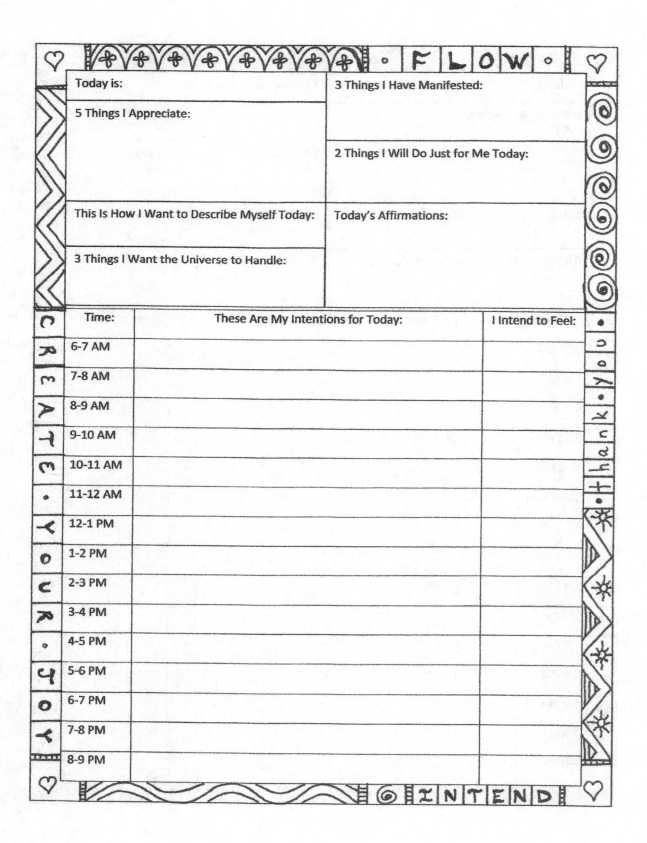

FLOW

Today is:

5 Things I Appreciate:

This Is How I Want to Describe Myself Today:

3 Things I Want the Universe to Handle:

3 Things I Have Manifested:

2 Things I Will Do Just for Me Today:

Today's Affirmations:

	Time:	These Are My Intentions for Today:	I Intend to Feel:
C	6-7 AM		
R	7-8 AM		
E	8-9 AM		
A	9-10 AM		
T	10-11 AM		
E	11-12 AM		
•	12-1 PM		
Y	1-2 PM		
O	2-3 PM		
U	3-4 PM		
R	4-5 PM		
•	5-6 PM		
J	6-7 PM		
O	7-8 PM		
Y	8-9 PM		

CREATE • YOUR • JOY

thank you

INTEND

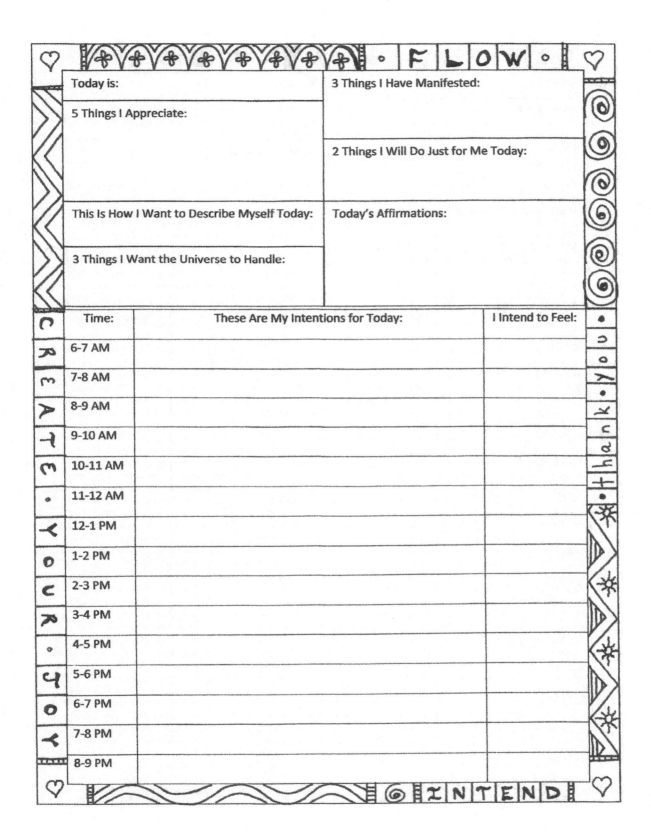

FLOW

Today is:	3 Things I Have Manifested:
5 Things I Appreciate:	
	2 Things I Will Do Just for Me Today:
This Is How I Want to Describe Myself Today:	Today's Affirmations:
3 Things I Want the Universe to Handle:	

Time:	These Are My Intentions for Today:	I Intend to Feel:
6-7 AM		
7-8 AM		
8-9 AM		
9-10 AM		
10-11 AM		
11-12 AM		
12-1 PM		
1-2 PM		
2-3 PM		
3-4 PM		
4-5 PM		
5-6 PM		
6-7 PM		
7-8 PM		
8-9 PM		

CREATE · YOUR · JOY

thank you

INTEND

161

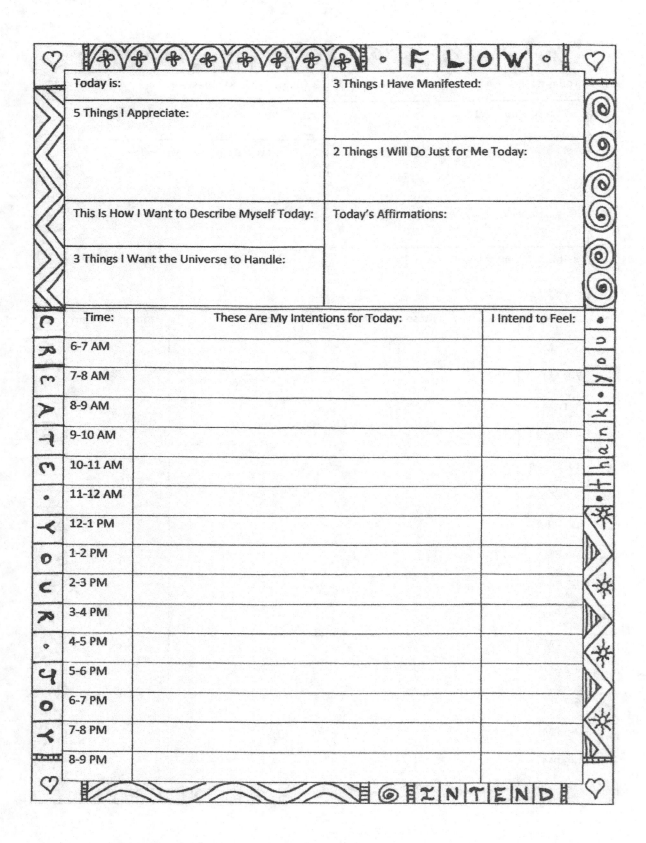

FLOW

| Today is: | 3 Things I Have Manifested: |

5 Things I Appreciate:

2 Things I Will Do Just for Me Today:

This Is How I Want to Describe Myself Today: Today's Affirmations:

3 Things I Want the Universe to Handle:

Time:	These Are My Intentions for Today:	I Intend to Feel:
6-7 AM		
7-8 AM		
8-9 AM		
9-10 AM		
10-11 AM		
11-12 AM		
12-1 PM		
1-2 PM		
2-3 PM		
3-4 PM		
4-5 PM		
5-6 PM		
6-7 PM		
7-8 PM		
8-9 PM		

CREATE . YOUR . JOY

thank . you

INTEND

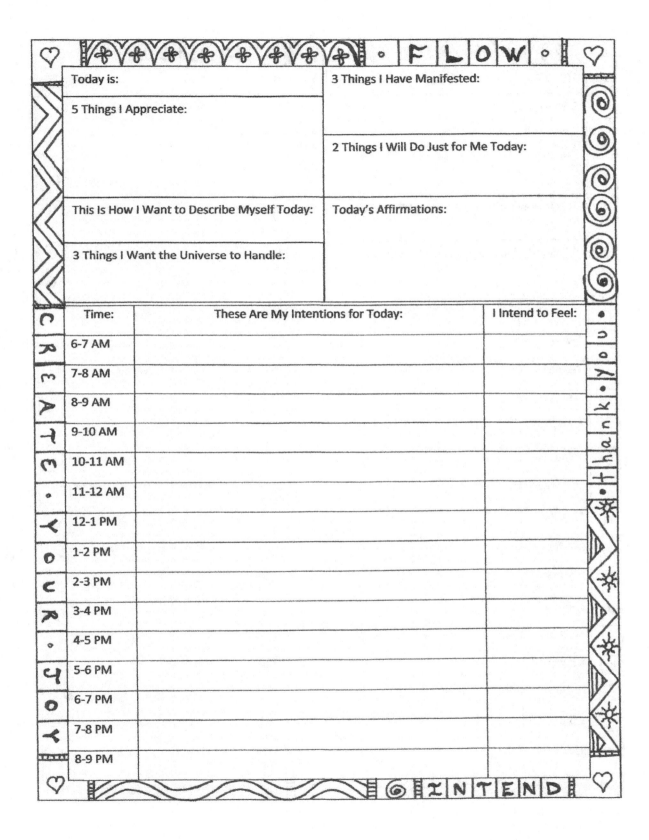

FLOW

Today is:	3 Things I Have Manifested:
5 Things I Appreciate:	
	2 Things I Will Do Just for Me Today:
This Is How I Want to Describe Myself Today:	Today's Affirmations:
3 Things I Want the Universe to Handle:	

Time:	These Are My Intentions for Today:	I Intend to Feel:
6-7 AM		
7-8 AM		
8-9 AM		
9-10 AM		
10-11 AM		
11-12 AM		
12-1 PM		
1-2 PM		
2-3 PM		
3-4 PM		
4-5 PM		
5-6 PM		
6-7 PM		
7-8 PM		
8-9 PM		

CREATE . YOUR . JOY

INTEND

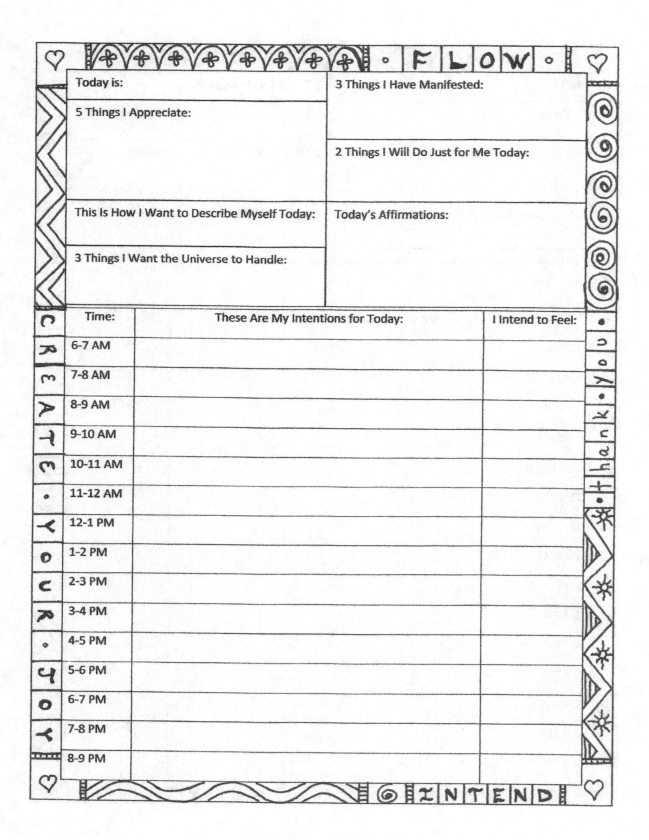

FLOW

Today is:	3 Things I Have Manifested:
5 Things I Appreciate:	
	2 Things I Will Do Just for Me Today:
This Is How I Want to Describe Myself Today:	Today's Affirmations:
3 Things I Want the Universe to Handle:	

Time:	These Are My Intentions for Today:	I Intend to Feel:
6-7 AM		
7-8 AM		
8-9 AM		
9-10 AM		
10-11 AM		
11-12 AM		
12-1 PM		
1-2 PM		
2-3 PM		
3-4 PM		
4-5 PM		
5-6 PM		
6-7 PM		
7-8 PM		
8-9 PM		

CREATE · YOUR · JOY

thank you

INTEND

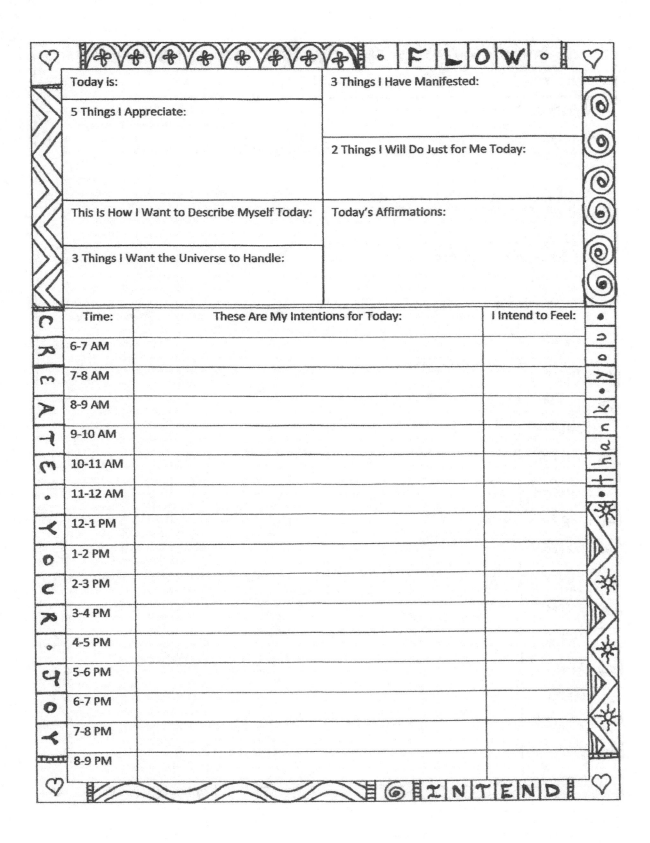

FLOW

Today is:	3 Things I Have Manifested:
5 Things I Appreciate:	
	2 Things I Will Do Just for Me Today:
This Is How I Want to Describe Myself Today:	Today's Affirmations:
3 Things I Want the Universe to Handle:	

Time:	These Are My Intentions for Today:	I Intend to Feel:
6-7 AM		
7-8 AM		
8-9 AM		
9-10 AM		
10-11 AM		
11-12 AM		
12-1 PM		
1-2 PM		
2-3 PM		
3-4 PM		
4-5 PM		
5-6 PM		
6-7 PM		
7-8 PM		
8-9 PM		

CREATE • YOUR • JOY

thank you

INTEND

165

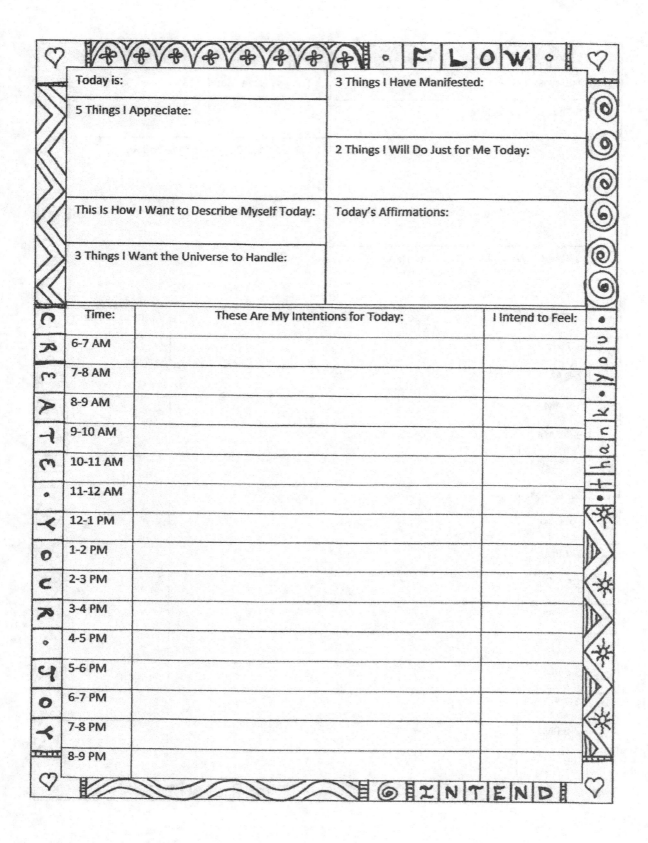

FLOW

Today is:

5 Things I Appreciate:

This Is How I Want to Describe Myself Today:

3 Things I Want the Universe to Handle:

3 Things I Have Manifested:

2 Things I Will Do Just for Me Today:

Today's Affirmations:

Time:	These Are My Intentions for Today:	I Intend to Feel:
6-7 AM		
7-8 AM		
8-9 AM		
9-10 AM		
10-11 AM		
11-12 AM		
12-1 PM		
1-2 PM		
2-3 PM		
3-4 PM		
4-5 PM		
5-6 PM		
6-7 PM		
7-8 PM		
8-9 PM		

CREATE . YOUR . JOY

thank you

INTEND

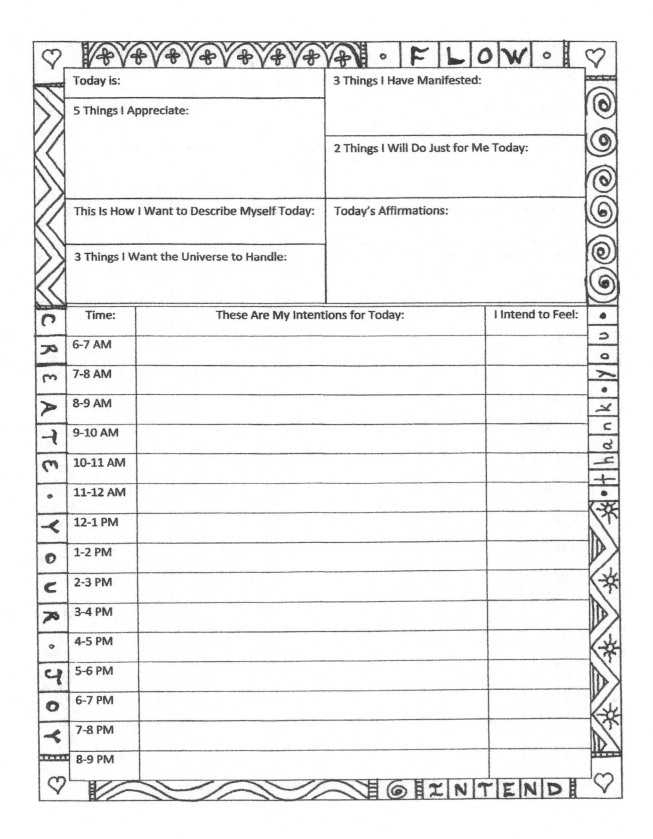

FLOW

| Today is: | 3 Things I Have Manifested: |

5 Things I Appreciate:

2 Things I Will Do Just for Me Today:

This Is How I Want to Describe Myself Today:

Today's Affirmations:

3 Things I Want the Universe to Handle:

CREATE · YOUR · JOY

Time:	These Are My Intentions for Today:	I Intend to Feel:
6-7 AM		
7-8 AM		
8-9 AM		
9-10 AM		
10-11 AM		
11-12 AM		
12-1 PM		
1-2 PM		
2-3 PM		
3-4 PM		
4-5 PM		
5-6 PM		
6-7 PM		
7-8 PM		
8-9 PM		

thank you

INTEND

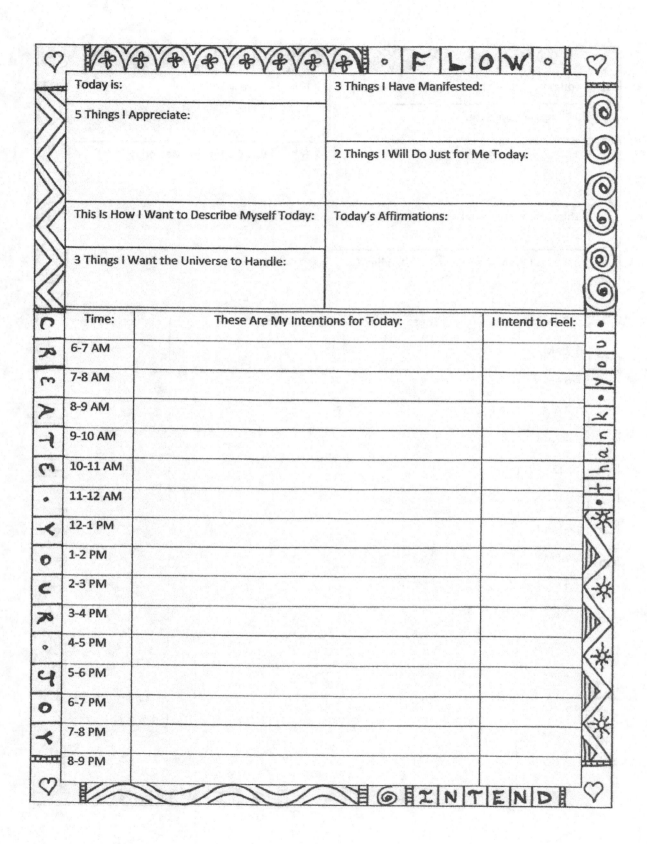

FLOW

Today is:	3 Things I Have Manifested:
5 Things I Appreciate:	
	2 Things I Will Do Just for Me Today:
This Is How I Want to Describe Myself Today:	Today's Affirmations:
3 Things I Want the Universe to Handle:	

Time:	These Are My Intentions for Today:	I Intend to Feel:
6-7 AM		
7-8 AM		
8-9 AM		
9-10 AM		
10-11 AM		
11-12 AM		
12-1 PM		
1-2 PM		
2-3 PM		
3-4 PM		
4-5 PM		
5-6 PM		
6-7 PM		
7-8 PM		
8-9 PM		

CREATE . YOUR . JOY

thank you

INTEND

168

FLOW

Today is:	3 Things I Have Manifested:
5 Things I Appreciate:	
	2 Things I Will Do Just for Me Today:
This Is How I Want to Describe Myself Today:	Today's Affirmations:
3 Things I Want the Universe to Handle:	

Time:	These Are My Intentions for Today:	I Intend to Feel:
6-7 AM		
7-8 AM		
8-9 AM		
9-10 AM		
10-11 AM		
11-12 AM		
12-1 PM		
1-2 PM		
2-3 PM		
3-4 PM		
4-5 PM		
5-6 PM		
6-7 PM		
7-8 PM		
8-9 PM		

CREATE. YOUR. JOY

thank. you

INTEND

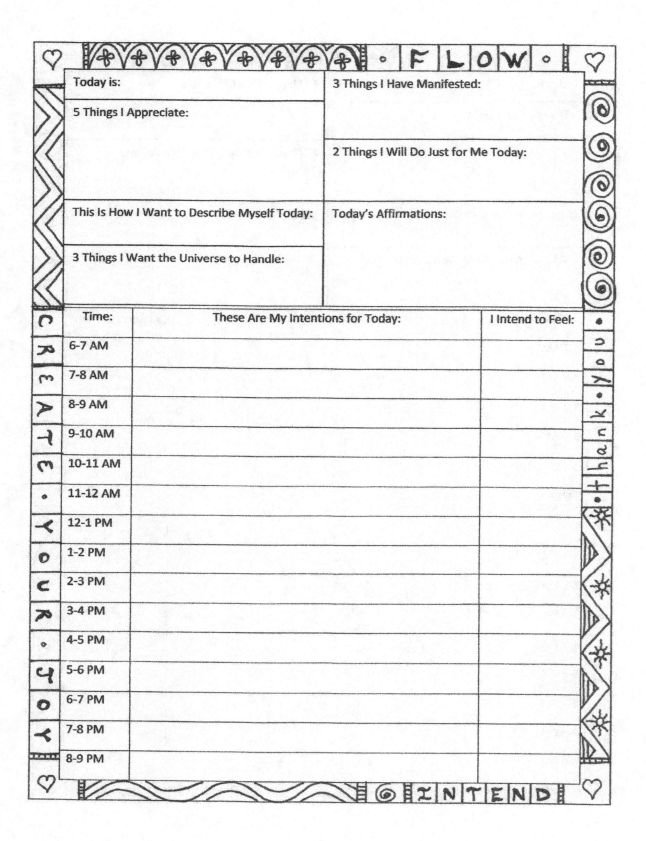

FLOW

Today is:	3 Things I Have Manifested:
5 Things I Appreciate:	
	2 Things I Will Do Just for Me Today:
This Is How I Want to Describe Myself Today:	**Today's Affirmations:**
3 Things I Want the Universe to Handle:	

CREATE • YOUR • JOY

thank you

Time:	These Are My Intentions for Today:	I Intend to Feel:
6-7 AM		
7-8 AM		
8-9 AM		
9-10 AM		
10-11 AM		
11-12 AM		
12-1 PM		
1-2 PM		
2-3 PM		
3-4 PM		
4-5 PM		
5-6 PM		
6-7 PM		
7-8 PM		
8-9 PM		

INTEND

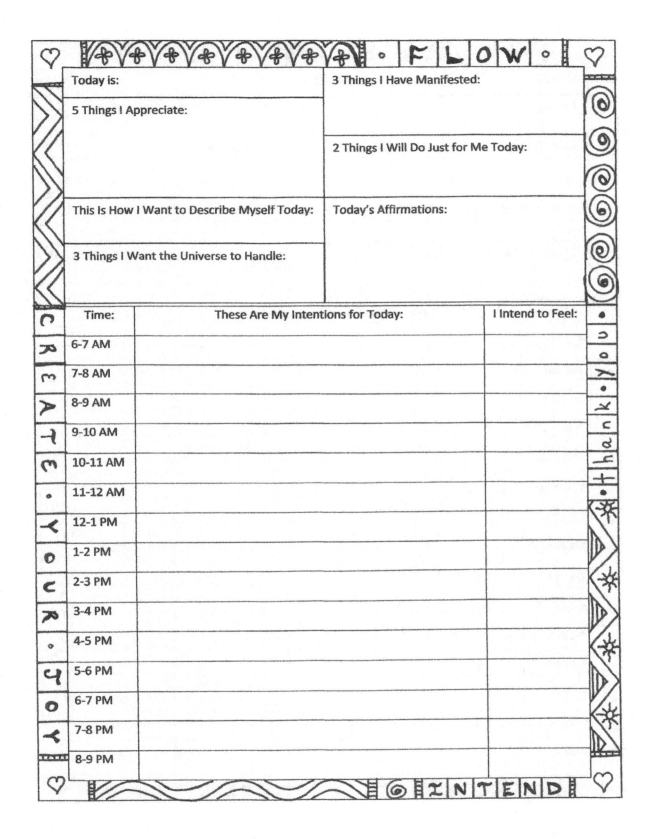

FLOW

Today is:	3 Things I Have Manifested:
5 Things I Appreciate:	
	2 Things I Will Do Just for Me Today:
This Is How I Want to Describe Myself Today:	Today's Affirmations:
3 Things I Want the Universe to Handle:	

Time:	These Are My Intentions for Today:	I Intend to Feel:
6-7 AM		
7-8 AM		
8-9 AM		
9-10 AM		
10-11 AM		
11-12 AM		
12-1 PM		
1-2 PM		
2-3 PM		
3-4 PM		
4-5 PM		
5-6 PM		
6-7 PM		
7-8 PM		
8-9 PM		

CREATE . YOUR . JOY

thank you

INTEND

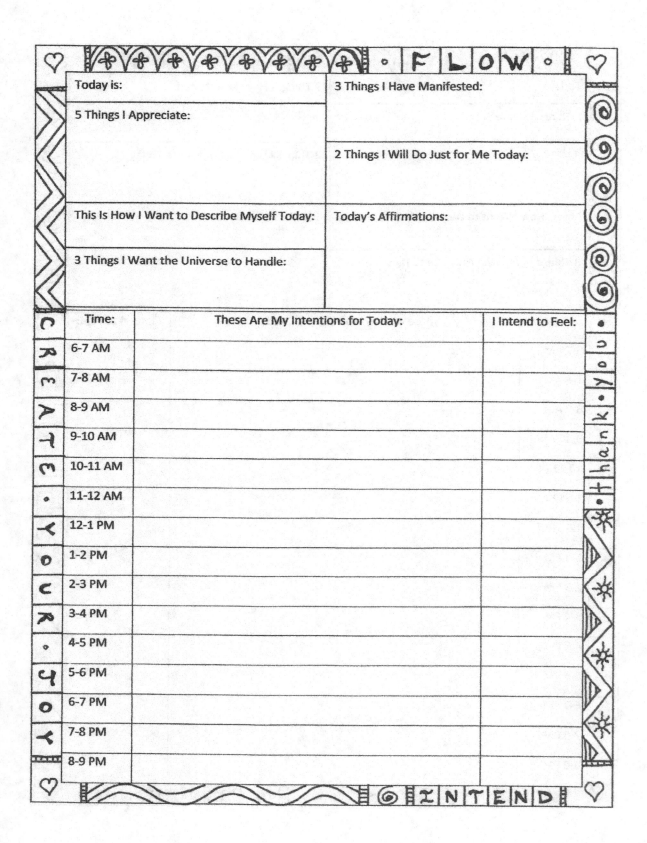

FLOW

Today is:	3 Things I Have Manifested:
5 Things I Appreciate:	
	2 Things I Will Do Just for Me Today:
This Is How I Want to Describe Myself Today:	Today's Affirmations:
3 Things I Want the Universe to Handle:	

Time:	These Are My Intentions for Today:	I Intend to Feel:
6-7 AM		
7-8 AM		
8-9 AM		
9-10 AM		
10-11 AM		
11-12 AM		
12-1 PM		
1-2 PM		
2-3 PM		
3-4 PM		
4-5 PM		
5-6 PM		
6-7 PM		
7-8 PM		
8-9 PM		

INTEND

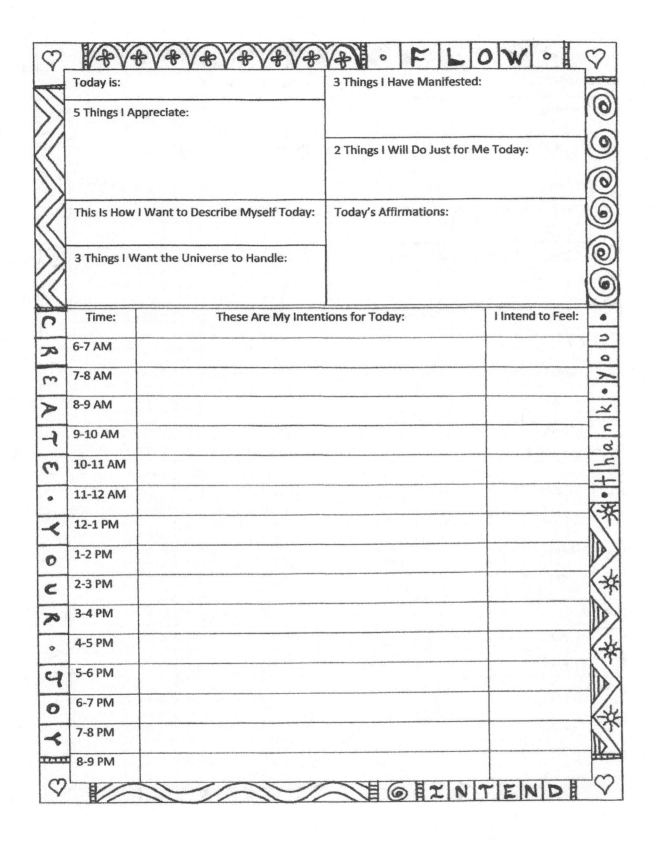

FLOW

Today is:	3 Things I Have Manifested:
5 Things I Appreciate:	
	2 Things I Will Do Just for Me Today:
This Is How I Want to Describe Myself Today:	Today's Affirmations:
3 Things I Want the Universe to Handle:	

Time:	These Are My Intentions for Today:	I Intend to Feel:
6-7 AM		
7-8 AM		
8-9 AM		
9-10 AM		
10-11 AM		
11-12 AM		
12-1 PM		
1-2 PM		
2-3 PM		
3-4 PM		
4-5 PM		
5-6 PM		
6-7 PM		
7-8 PM		
8-9 PM		

CREATE . YOUR . JOY

Thank you.

INTEND

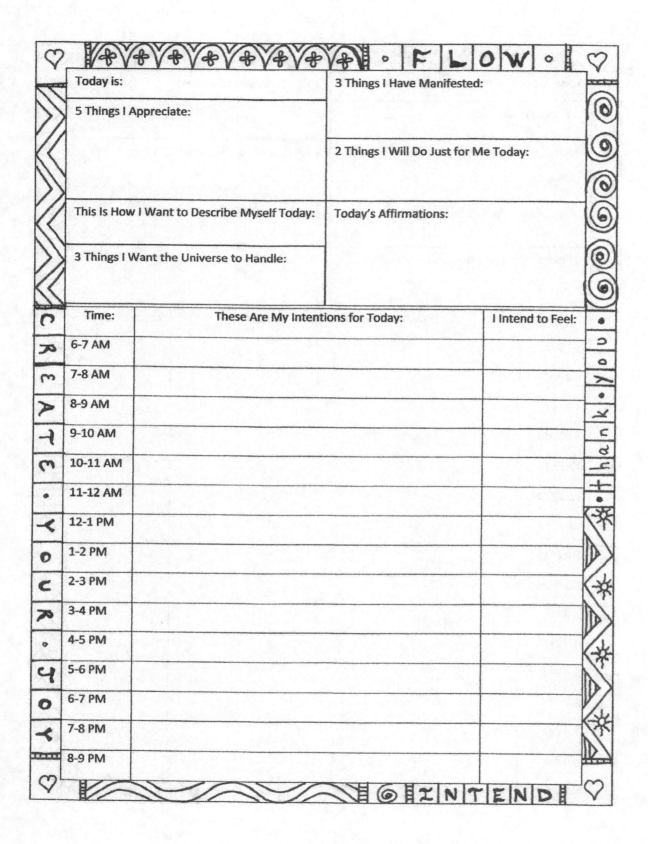

FLOW

Today is:

5 Things I Appreciate:

This Is How I Want to Describe Myself Today:

3 Things I Want the Universe to Handle:

3 Things I Have Manifested:

2 Things I Will Do Just for Me Today:

Today's Affirmations:

Time:	These Are My Intentions for Today:	I Intend to Feel:
6-7 AM		
7-8 AM		
8-9 AM		
9-10 AM		
10-11 AM		
11-12 AM		
12-1 PM		
1-2 PM		
2-3 PM		
3-4 PM		
4-5 PM		
5-6 PM		
6-7 PM		
7-8 PM		
8-9 PM		

CREATE · YOUR · JOY

thank you

INTEND

174

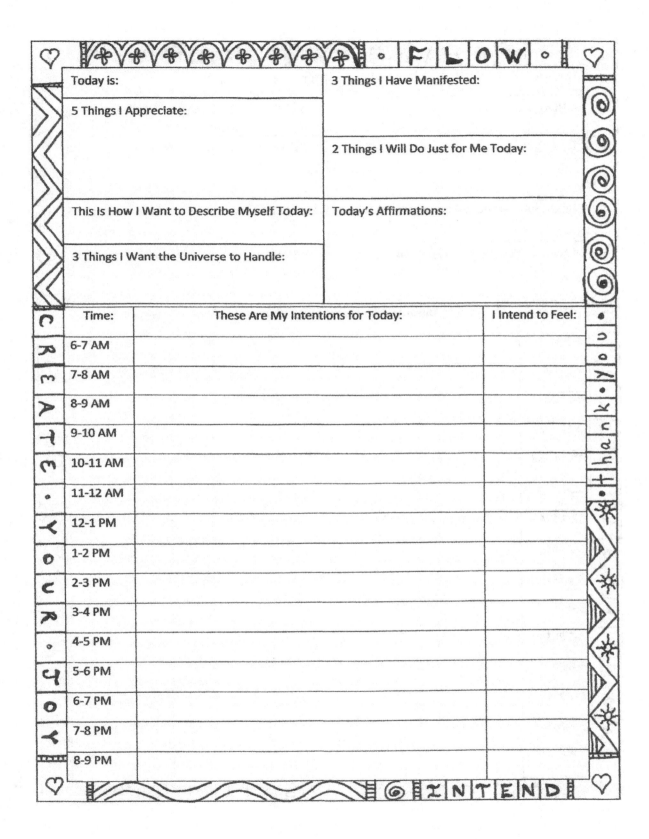

FLOW

| Today is: | 3 Things I Have Manifested: |

5 Things I Appreciate:

2 Things I Will Do Just for Me Today:

This Is How I Want to Describe Myself Today:

Today's Affirmations:

3 Things I Want the Universe to Handle:

Time:	These Are My Intentions for Today:	I Intend to Feel:
6-7 AM		
7-8 AM		
8-9 AM		
9-10 AM		
10-11 AM		
11-12 AM		
12-1 PM		
1-2 PM		
2-3 PM		
3-4 PM		
4-5 PM		
5-6 PM		
6-7 PM		
7-8 PM		
8-9 PM		

CREATE YOUR JOY

THANK YOU

INTEND

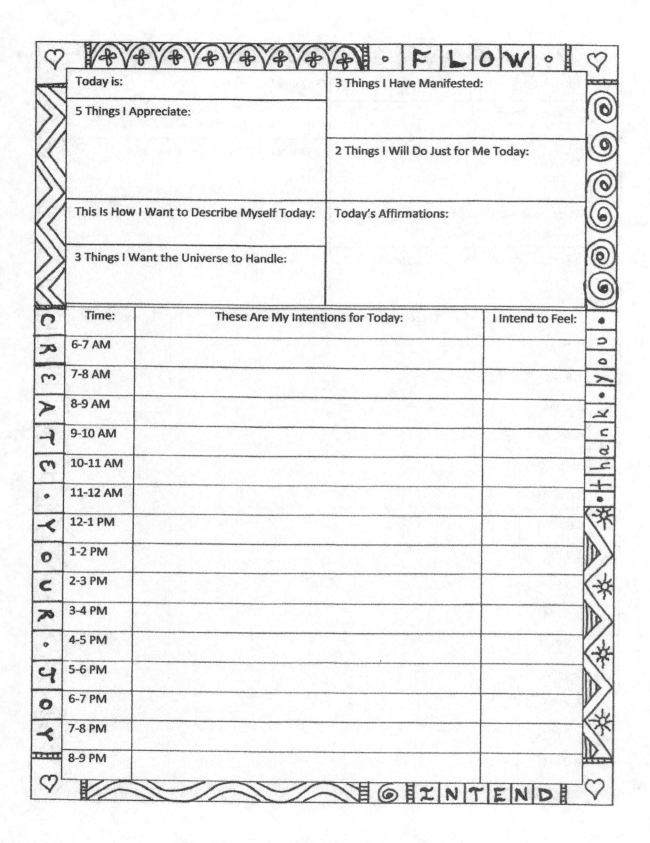

FLOW

| Today is: | 3 Things I Have Manifested: |

5 Things I Appreciate:

2 Things I Will Do Just for Me Today:

This Is How I Want to Describe Myself Today:

Today's Affirmations:

3 Things I Want the Universe to Handle:

CREATE • YOUR • JOY

thank you

INTEND

Time:	These Are My Intentions for Today:	I Intend to Feel:
6-7 AM		
7-8 AM		
8-9 AM		
9-10 AM		
10-11 AM		
11-12 AM		
12-1 PM		
1-2 PM		
2-3 PM		
3-4 PM		
4-5 PM		
5-6 PM		
6-7 PM		
7-8 PM		
8-9 PM		

176

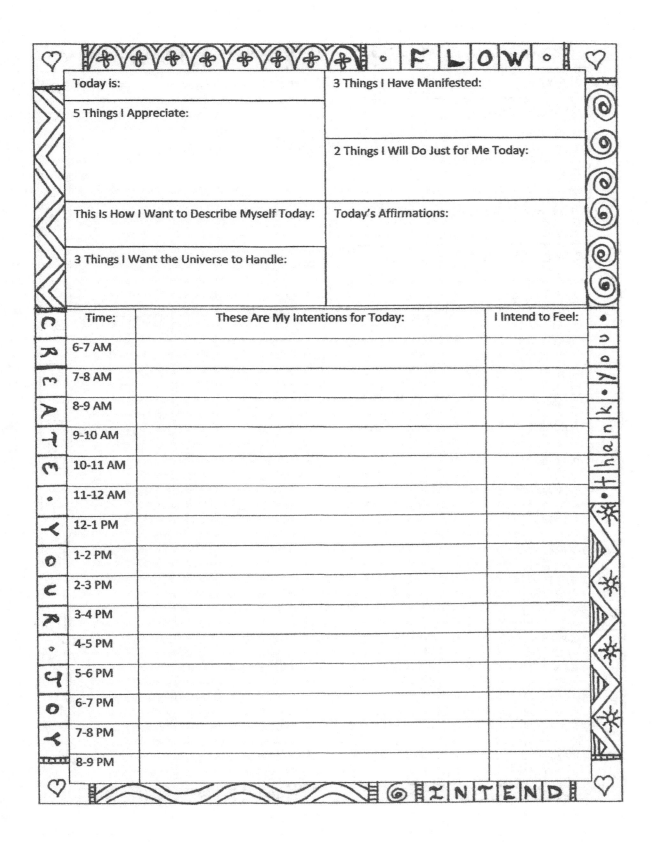

FLOW

Today is:	3 Things I Have Manifested:
5 Things I Appreciate:	
	2 Things I Will Do Just for Me Today:
This Is How I Want to Describe Myself Today:	**Today's Affirmations:**
3 Things I Want the Universe to Handle:	

	Time:	These Are My Intentions for Today:	I Intend to Feel:
C	6-7 AM		
R	7-8 AM		
E	8-9 AM		
A	9-10 AM		
T	10-11 AM		
E	11-12 AM		
	12-1 PM		
Y	1-2 PM		
O	2-3 PM		
U	3-4 PM		
R	4-5 PM		
	5-6 PM		
J	6-7 PM		
O	7-8 PM		
Y	8-9 PM		

CREATE YOUR JOY · *thank you* · **INTEND**

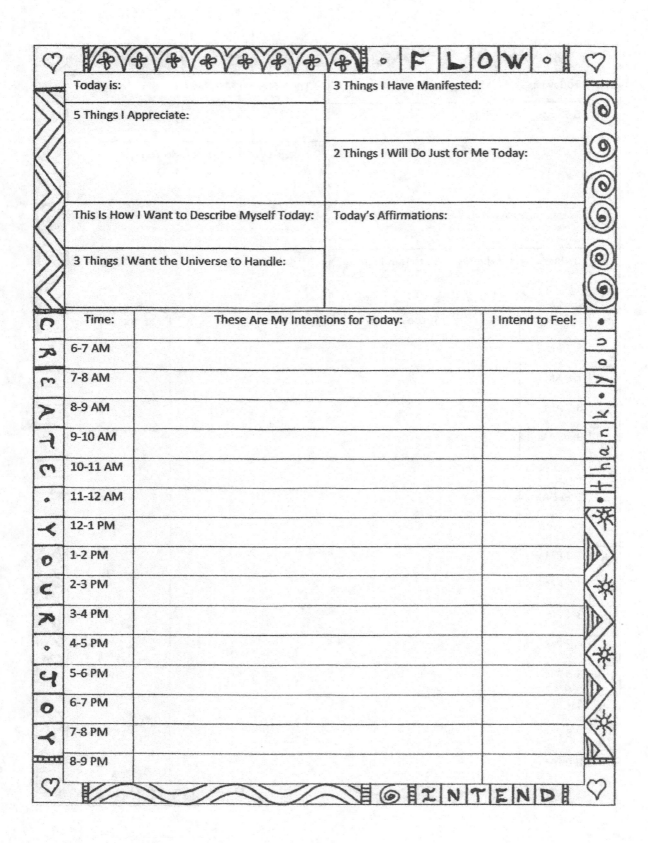

FLOW

Today is:	3 Things I Have Manifested:
5 Things I Appreciate:	
	2 Things I Will Do Just for Me Today:
This Is How I Want to Describe Myself Today:	Today's Affirmations:
3 Things I Want the Universe to Handle:	

Time:	These Are My Intentions for Today:	I Intend to Feel:
6-7 AM		
7-8 AM		
8-9 AM		
9-10 AM		
10-11 AM		
11-12 AM		
12-1 PM		
1-2 PM		
2-3 PM		
3-4 PM		
4-5 PM		
5-6 PM		
6-7 PM		
7-8 PM		
8-9 PM		

CREATE . YOUR . JOY

thank . you

INTEND

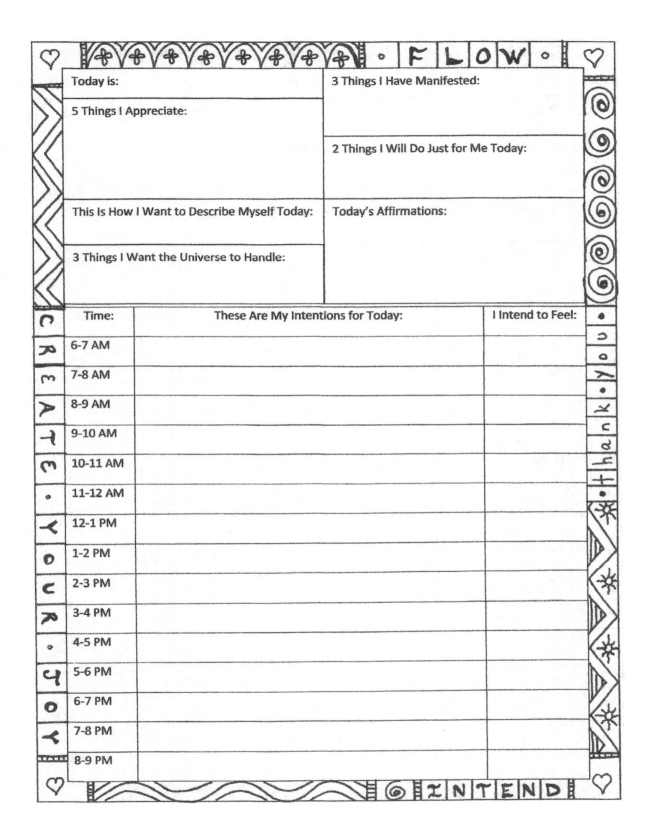

FLOW

Today is:	3 Things I Have Manifested:
5 Things I Appreciate:	
	2 Things I Will Do Just for Me Today:
This Is How I Want to Describe Myself Today:	Today's Affirmations:
3 Things I Want the Universe to Handle:	

Time:	These Are My Intentions for Today:	I Intend to Feel:
6-7 AM		
7-8 AM		
8-9 AM		
9-10 AM		
10-11 AM		
11-12 AM		
12-1 PM		
1-2 PM		
2-3 PM		
3-4 PM		
4-5 PM		
5-6 PM		
6-7 PM		
7-8 PM		
8-9 PM		

INTEND

179

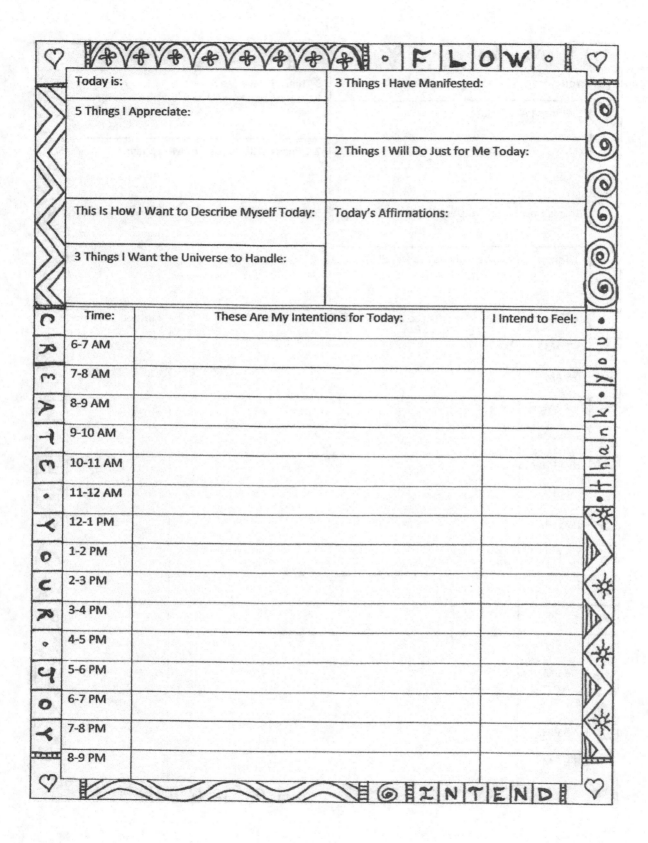

FLOW

Today is:	3 Things I Have Manifested:
5 Things I Appreciate:	
	2 Things I Will Do Just for Me Today:
This Is How I Want to Describe Myself Today:	Today's Affirmations:
3 Things I Want the Universe to Handle:	

Time:	These Are My Intentions for Today:	I Intend to Feel:
6-7 AM		
7-8 AM		
8-9 AM		
9-10 AM		
10-11 AM		
11-12 AM		
12-1 PM		
1-2 PM		
2-3 PM		
3-4 PM		
4-5 PM		
5-6 PM		
6-7 PM		
7-8 PM		
8-9 PM		

CREATE · YOUR · JOY

thank · you

INTEND

FLOW

Today is:	**3 Things I Have Manifested:**
5 Things I Appreciate:	
	2 Things I Will Do Just for Me Today:
This Is How I Want to Describe Myself Today:	**Today's Affirmations:**
3 Things I Want the Universe to Handle:	

Time:	These Are My Intentions for Today:	I Intend to Feel:
6-7 AM		
7-8 AM		
8-9 AM		
9-10 AM		
10-11 AM		
11-12 AM		
12-1 PM		
1-2 PM		
2-3 PM		
3-4 PM		
4-5 PM		
5-6 PM		
6-7 PM		
7-8 PM		
8-9 PM		

CREATE • YOUR • JOY

thank you

INTEND

181

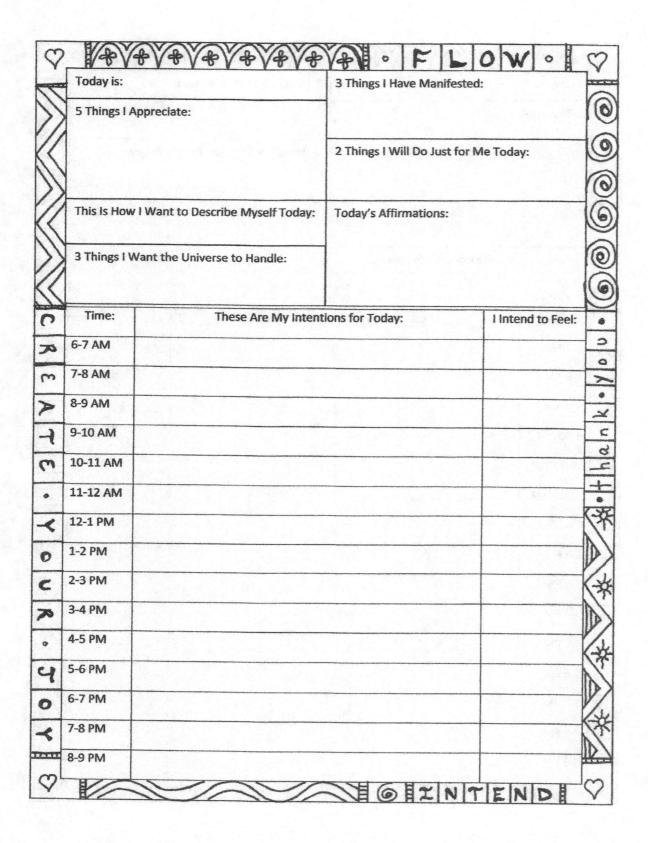

FLOW

| Today is: | 3 Things I Have Manifested: |

5 Things I Appreciate:

2 Things I Will Do Just for Me Today:

This Is How I Want to Describe Myself Today:

Today's Affirmations:

3 Things I Want the Universe to Handle:

CREATE . YOUR . JOY

thank you

INTEND

Time:	These Are My Intentions for Today:	I Intend to Feel:
6-7 AM		
7-8 AM		
8-9 AM		
9-10 AM		
10-11 AM		
11-12 AM		
12-1 PM		
1-2 PM		
2-3 PM		
3-4 PM		
4-5 PM		
5-6 PM		
6-7 PM		
7-8 PM		
8-9 PM		

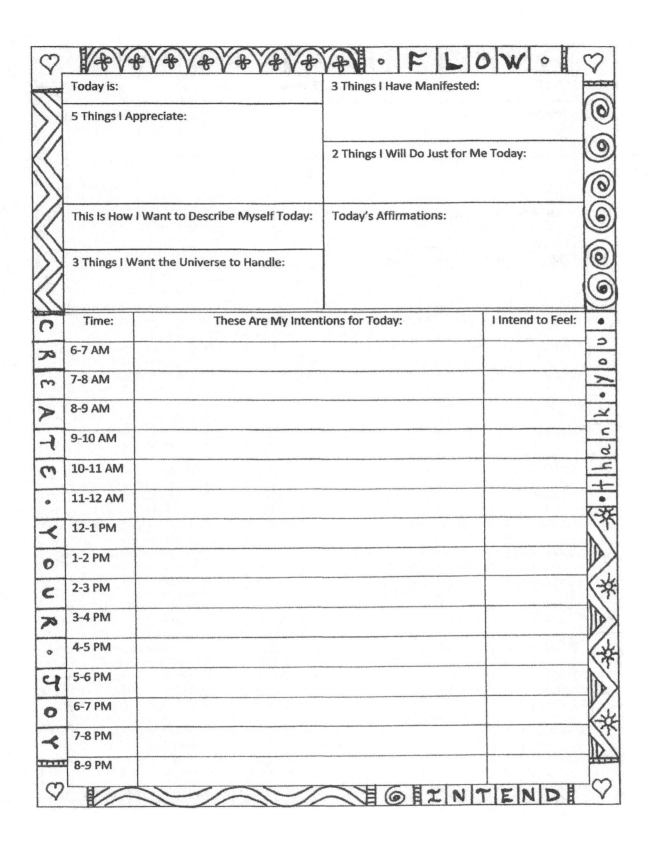

FLOW

Today is:	3 Things I Have Manifested:
5 Things I Appreciate:	
	2 Things I Will Do Just for Me Today:
This Is How I Want to Describe Myself Today:	**Today's Affirmations:**
3 Things I Want the Universe to Handle:	

CREATE · YOUR · JOY

thank you · co

Time:	These Are My Intentions for Today:	I Intend to Feel:
6-7 AM		
7-8 AM		
8-9 AM		
9-10 AM		
10-11 AM		
11-12 AM		
12-1 PM		
1-2 PM		
2-3 PM		
3-4 PM		
4-5 PM		
5-6 PM		
6-7 PM		
7-8 PM		
8-9 PM		

INTEND

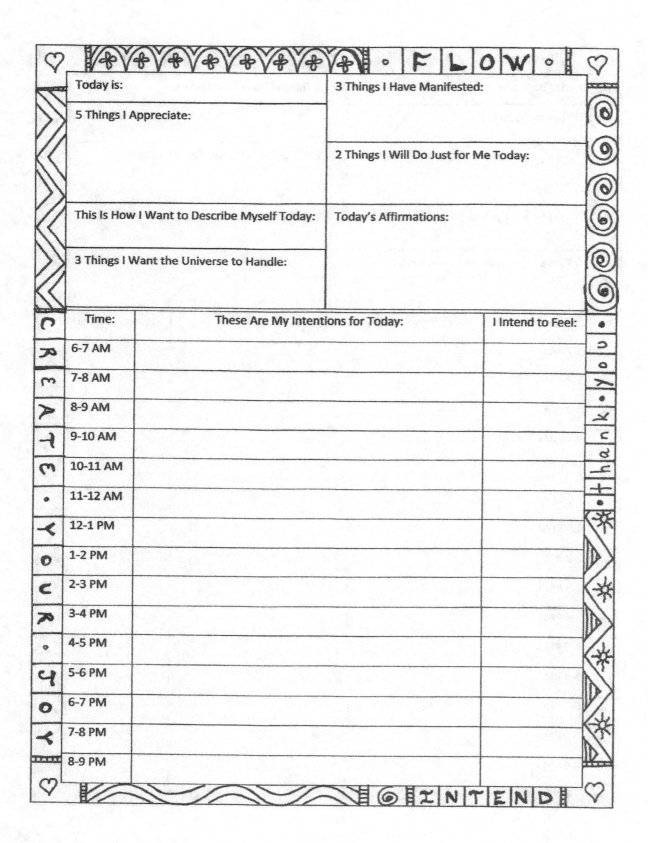

FLOW

| Today is: | 3 Things I Have Manifested: |

5 Things I Appreciate:

2 Things I Will Do Just for Me Today:

| This Is How I Want to Describe Myself Today: | Today's Affirmations: |

3 Things I Want the Universe to Handle:

CREATE · YOUR · JOY

thank you ·

Time:	These Are My Intentions for Today:	I Intend to Feel:
6-7 AM		
7-8 AM		
8-9 AM		
9-10 AM		
10-11 AM		
11-12 AM		
12-1 PM		
1-2 PM		
2-3 PM		
3-4 PM		
4-5 PM		
5-6 PM		
6-7 PM		
7-8 PM		
8-9 PM		

INTEND

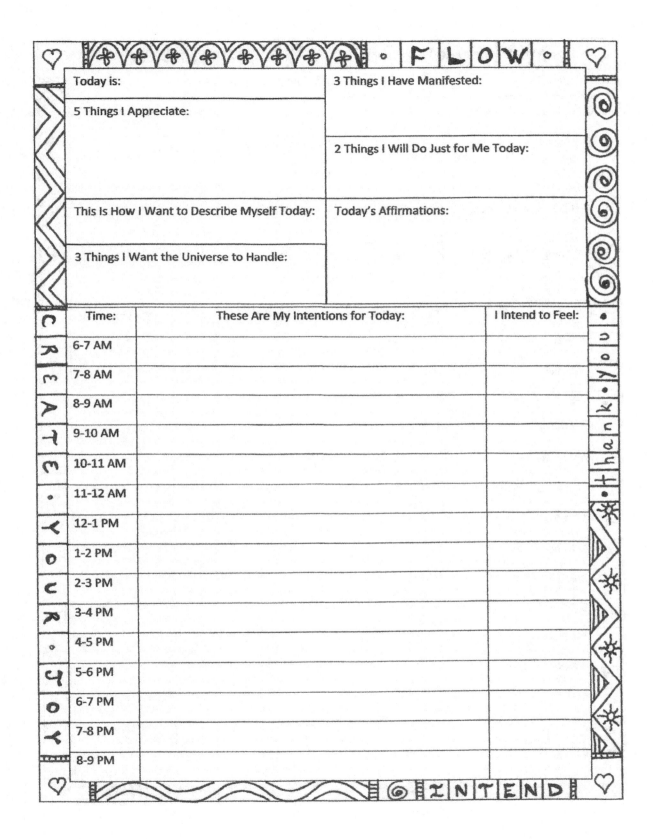

FLOW

Today is:	3 Things I Have Manifested:

5 Things I Appreciate:

2 Things I Will Do Just for Me Today:

This Is How I Want to Describe Myself Today:

Today's Affirmations:

3 Things I Want the Universe to Handle:

Time:	These Are My Intentions for Today:	I Intend to Feel:
6-7 AM		
7-8 AM		
8-9 AM		
9-10 AM		
10-11 AM		
11-12 AM		
12-1 PM		
1-2 PM		
2-3 PM		
3-4 PM		
4-5 PM		
5-6 PM		
6-7 PM		
7-8 PM		
8-9 PM		

CREATE. YOUR. JOY

thank you

INTEND

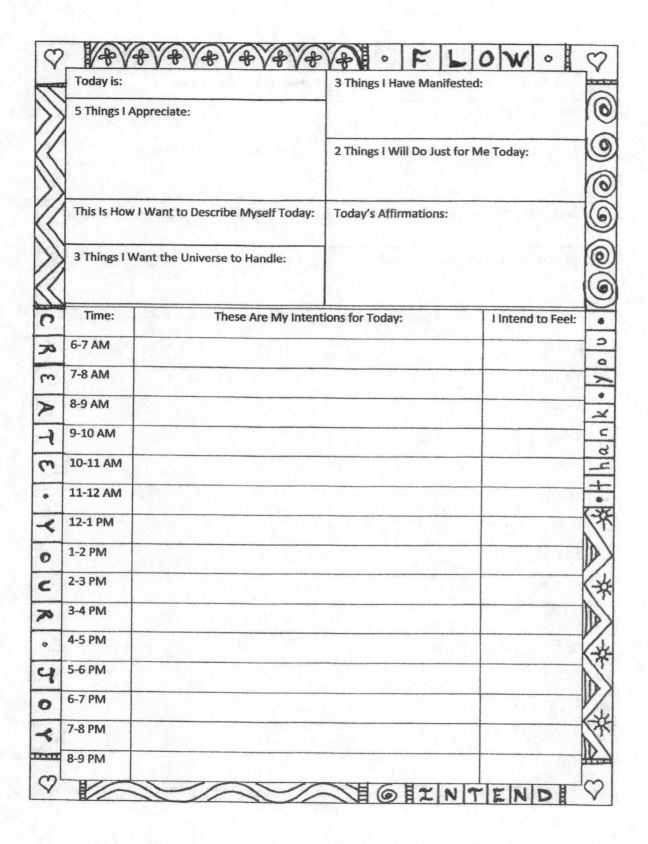

FLOW

Today is:

5 Things I Appreciate:

This Is How I Want to Describe Myself Today:

3 Things I Want the Universe to Handle:

3 Things I Have Manifested:

2 Things I Will Do Just for Me Today:

Today's Affirmations:

Time:	These Are My Intentions for Today:	I Intend to Feel:
6-7 AM		
7-8 AM		
8-9 AM		
9-10 AM		
10-11 AM		
11-12 AM		
12-1 PM		
1-2 PM		
2-3 PM		
3-4 PM		
4-5 PM		
5-6 PM		
6-7 PM		
7-8 PM		
8-9 PM		

CREATE • YOUR • JOY

thank you

INTEND

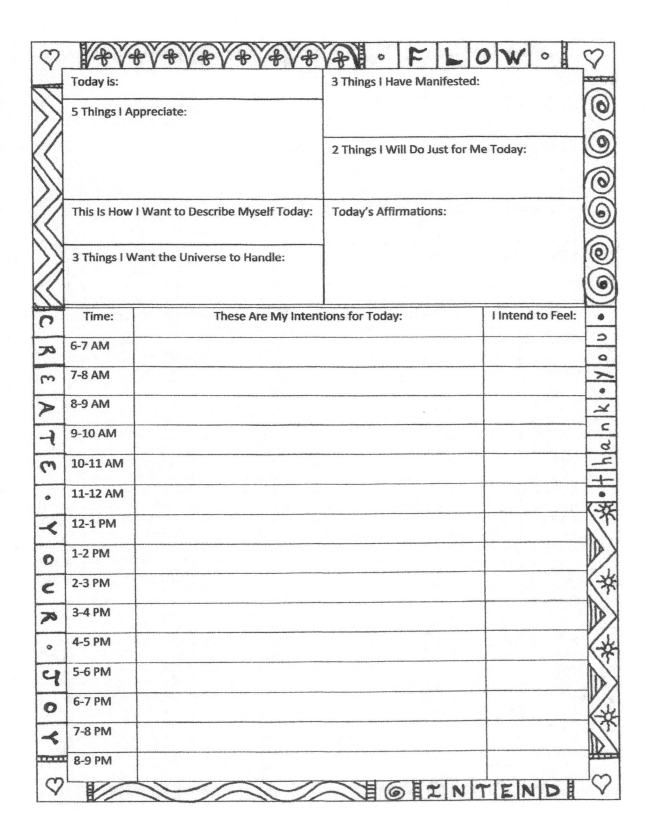

FLOW

Today is:	3 Things I Have Manifested:
5 Things I Appreciate:	
	2 Things I Will Do Just for Me Today:
This Is How I Want to Describe Myself Today:	Today's Affirmations:
3 Things I Want the Universe to Handle:	

CREATE . YOUR . JOY

Time:	These Are My Intentions for Today:	I Intend to Feel:
6-7 AM		
7-8 AM		
8-9 AM		
9-10 AM		
10-11 AM		
11-12 AM		
12-1 PM		
1-2 PM		
2-3 PM		
3-4 PM		
4-5 PM		
5-6 PM		
6-7 PM		
7-8 PM		
8-9 PM		

thank . you

INTEND

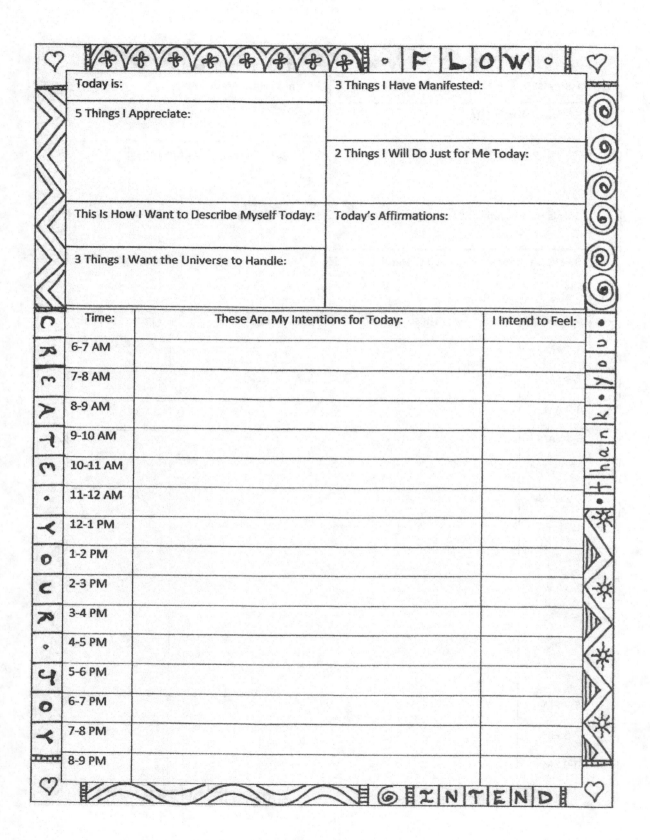

FLOW

Today is:

5 Things I Appreciate:

This Is How I Want to Describe Myself Today:

3 Things I Want the Universe to Handle:

3 Things I Have Manifested:

2 Things I Will Do Just for Me Today:

Today's Affirmations:

Time:	These Are My Intentions for Today:	I Intend to Feel:
6-7 AM		
7-8 AM		
8-9 AM		
9-10 AM		
10-11 AM		
11-12 AM		
12-1 PM		
1-2 PM		
2-3 PM		
3-4 PM		
4-5 PM		
5-6 PM		
6-7 PM		
7-8 PM		
8-9 PM		

CREATE • YOUR • JOY

thank you

INTEND

Month: July

Sunday	Monday	Tuesday	Wednesday	Thursday	Friday	Saturday

Do at least one thing every day that brings you joy and record it on this page.

Affirmations:

" Talk about your joys. "

--Rita Schiano

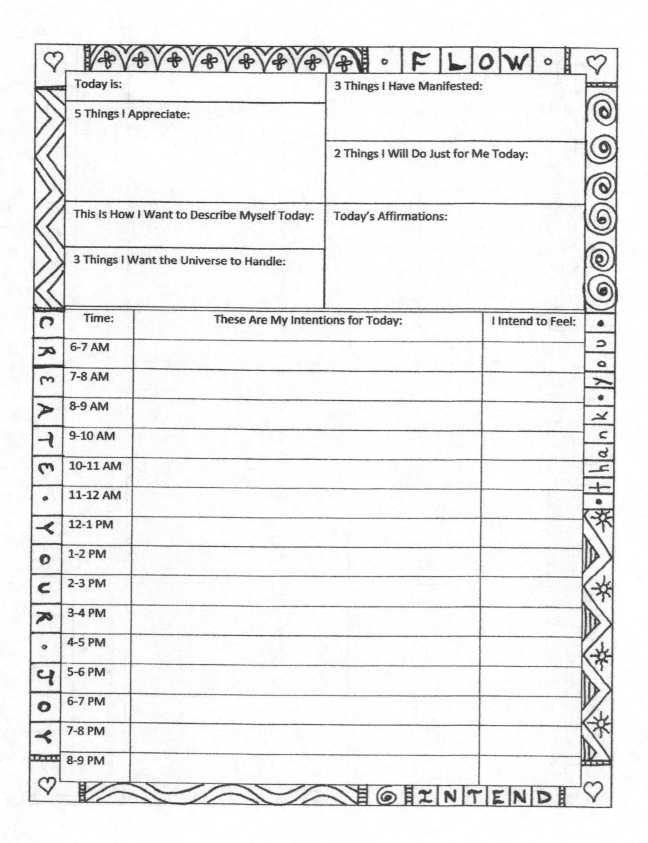

FLOW

Today is:

5 Things I Appreciate:

3 Things I Have Manifested:

2 Things I Will Do Just for Me Today:

This Is How I Want to Describe Myself Today:

Today's Affirmations:

3 Things I Want the Universe to Handle:

CREATE • YOUR • JOY	Time:	These Are My Intentions for Today:	I Intend to Feel:	thank you
	6-7 AM			
	7-8 AM			
	8-9 AM			
	9-10 AM			
	10-11 AM			
	11-12 AM			
	12-1 PM			
	1-2 PM			
	2-3 PM			
	3-4 PM			
	4-5 PM			
	5-6 PM			
	6-7 PM			
	7-8 PM			
	8-9 PM			

INTEND

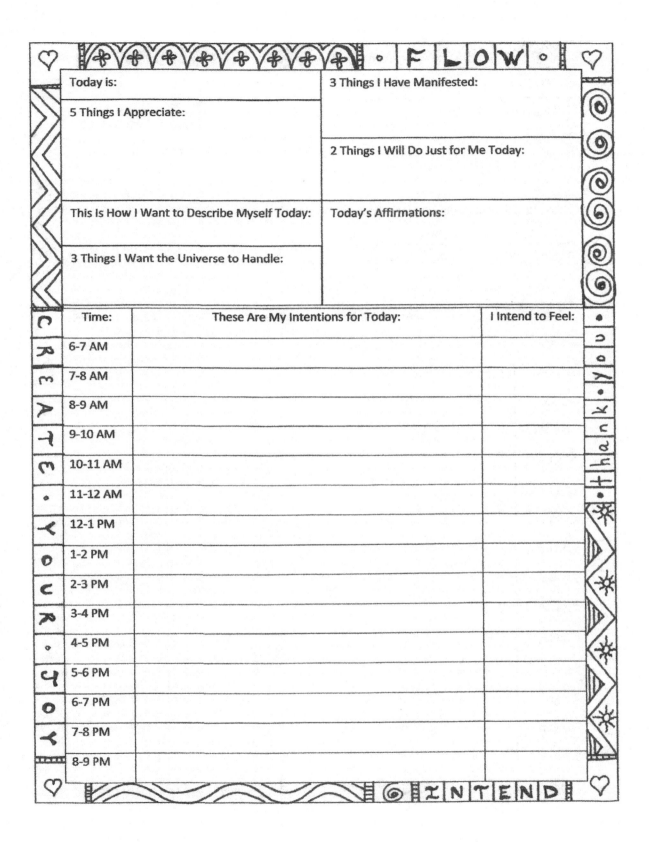

FLOW

Today is:	3 Things I Have Manifested:
5 Things I Appreciate:	
	2 Things I Will Do Just for Me Today:
This Is How I Want to Describe Myself Today:	Today's Affirmations:
3 Things I Want the Universe to Handle:	

Time:	These Are My Intentions for Today:	I Intend to Feel:
6-7 AM		
7-8 AM		
8-9 AM		
9-10 AM		
10-11 AM		
11-12 AM		
12-1 PM		
1-2 PM		
2-3 PM		
3-4 PM		
4-5 PM		
5-6 PM		
6-7 PM		
7-8 PM		
8-9 PM		

CREATE • YOUR • JOY

thank you • thank you

I INTEND

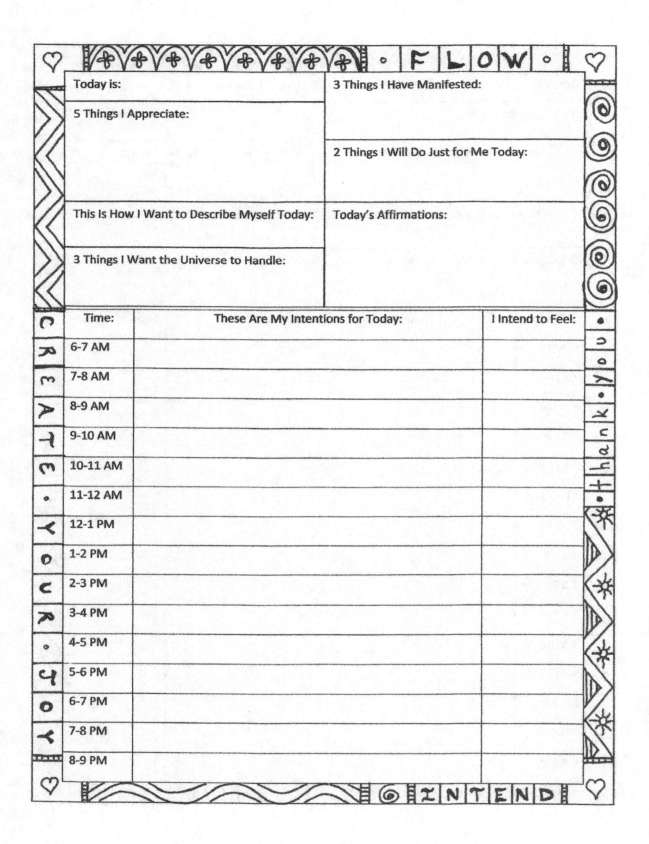

F L O W

| Today is: |
| 5 Things I Appreciate: |

| 3 Things I Have Manifested: |

| 2 Things I Will Do Just for Me Today: |

| This Is How I Want to Describe Myself Today: |

| Today's Affirmations: |

| 3 Things I Want the Universe to Handle: |

Time:	These Are My Intentions for Today:	I Intend to Feel:
6-7 AM		
7-8 AM		
8-9 AM		
9-10 AM		
10-11 AM		
11-12 AM		
12-1 PM		
1-2 PM		
2-3 PM		
3-4 PM		
4-5 PM		
5-6 PM		
6-7 PM		
7-8 PM		
8-9 PM		

CREATE . YOUR . JOY

thank you .

INTEND

FLOW

Today is:	3 Things I Have Manifested:
5 Things I Appreciate:	
	2 Things I Will Do Just for Me Today:
This Is How I Want to Describe Myself Today:	**Today's Affirmations:**
3 Things I Want the Universe to Handle:	

	Time:	These Are My Intentions for Today:	I Intend to Feel:
C	6-7 AM		
R	7-8 AM		
E	8-9 AM		
A	9-10 AM		
T	10-11 AM		
E	11-12 AM		
•	12-1 PM		
Y	1-2 PM		
O	2-3 PM		
U	3-4 PM		
R	4-5 PM		
•	5-6 PM		
J	6-7 PM		
O	7-8 PM		
Y	8-9 PM		

INTEND

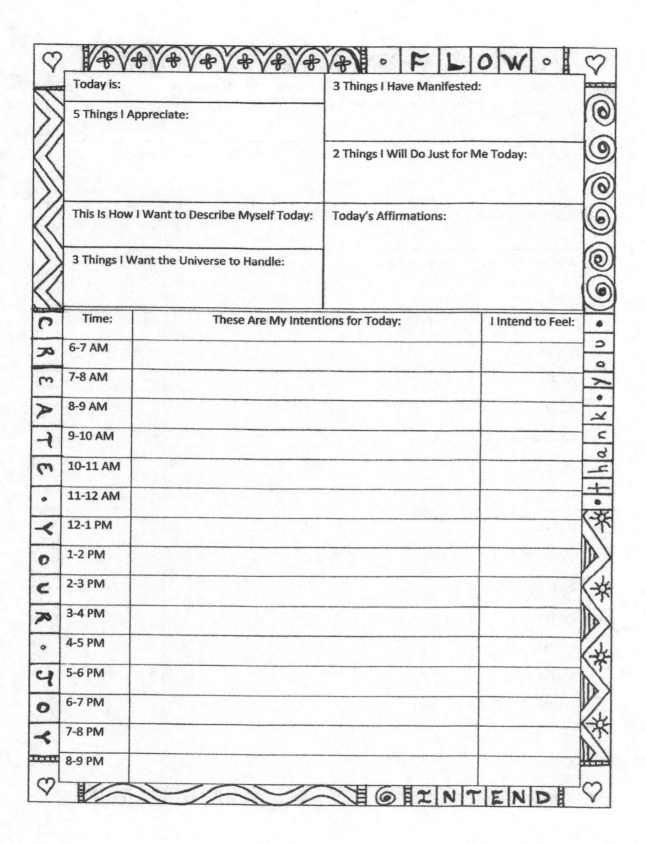

FLOW

Today is:	3 Things I Have Manifested:
5 Things I Appreciate:	
	2 Things I Will Do Just for Me Today:
This Is How I Want to Describe Myself Today:	Today's Affirmations:
3 Things I Want the Universe to Handle:	

CREATE • YOUR • JOY

thank you •

Time:	These Are My Intentions for Today:	I Intend to Feel:
6-7 AM		
7-8 AM		
8-9 AM		
9-10 AM		
10-11 AM		
11-12 AM		
12-1 PM		
1-2 PM		
2-3 PM		
3-4 PM		
4-5 PM		
5-6 PM		
6-7 PM		
7-8 PM		
8-9 PM		

INTEND

194

FLOW

Today is:	3 Things I Have Manifested:
5 Things I Appreciate:	
	2 Things I Will Do Just for Me Today:
This Is How I Want to Describe Myself Today:	Today's Affirmations:
3 Things I Want the Universe to Handle:	

Time:	These Are My Intentions for Today:	I Intend to Feel:
6-7 AM		
7-8 AM		
8-9 AM		
9-10 AM		
10-11 AM		
11-12 AM		
12-1 PM		
1-2 PM		
2-3 PM		
3-4 PM		
4-5 PM		
5-6 PM		
6-7 PM		
7-8 PM		
8-9 PM		

CREATE YOUR JOY

INTEND

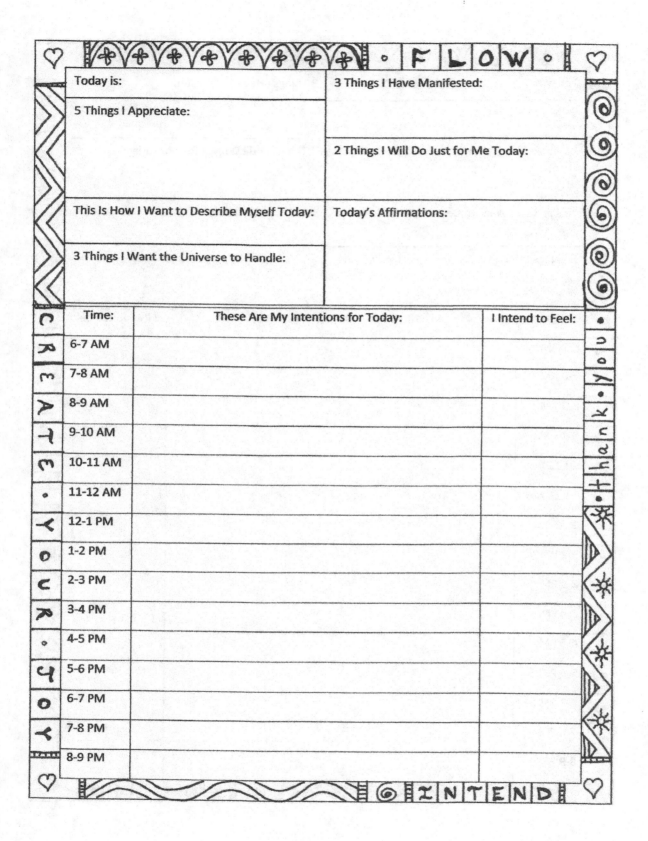

FLOW

Today is:	3 Things I Have Manifested:
5 Things I Appreciate:	
	2 Things I Will Do Just for Me Today:
This Is How I Want to Describe Myself Today:	**Today's Affirmations:**
3 Things I Want the Universe to Handle:	

CREATE • YOUR • JOY

Time:	These Are My Intentions for Today:	I Intend to Feel:
6-7 AM		
7-8 AM		
8-9 AM		
9-10 AM		
10-11 AM		
11-12 AM		
12-1 PM		
1-2 PM		
2-3 PM		
3-4 PM		
4-5 PM		
5-6 PM		
6-7 PM		
7-8 PM		
8-9 PM		

thank you • INTEND

196

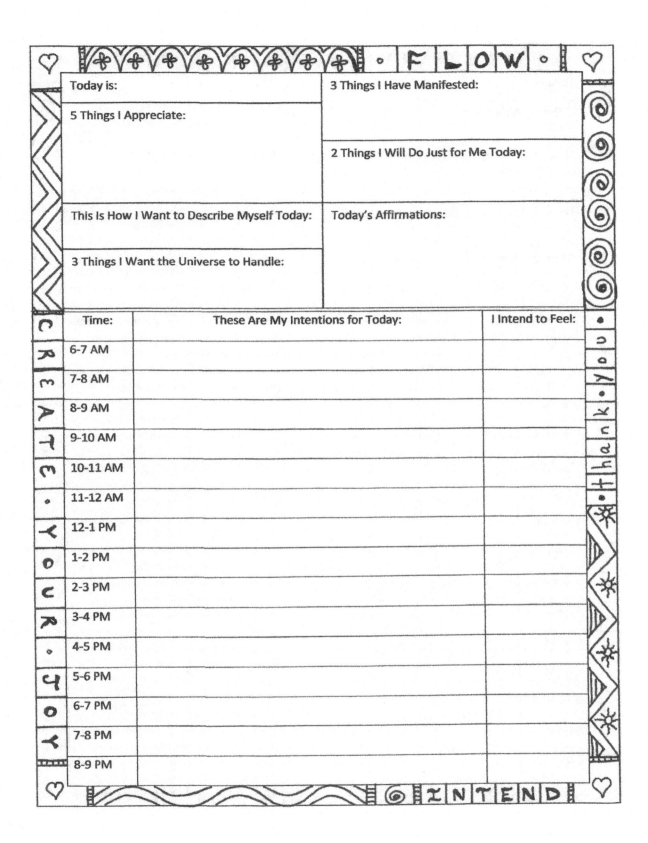

FLOW

Today is:	3 Things I Have Manifested:
5 Things I Appreciate:	
	2 Things I Will Do Just for Me Today:
This Is How I Want to Describe Myself Today:	Today's Affirmations:
3 Things I Want the Universe to Handle:	

CREATE · YOUR · JOY

Time:	These Are My Intentions for Today:	I Intend to Feel:
6-7 AM		
7-8 AM		
8-9 AM		
9-10 AM		
10-11 AM		
11-12 AM		
12-1 PM		
1-2 PM		
2-3 PM		
3-4 PM		
4-5 PM		
5-6 PM		
6-7 PM		
7-8 PM		
8-9 PM		

INTEND

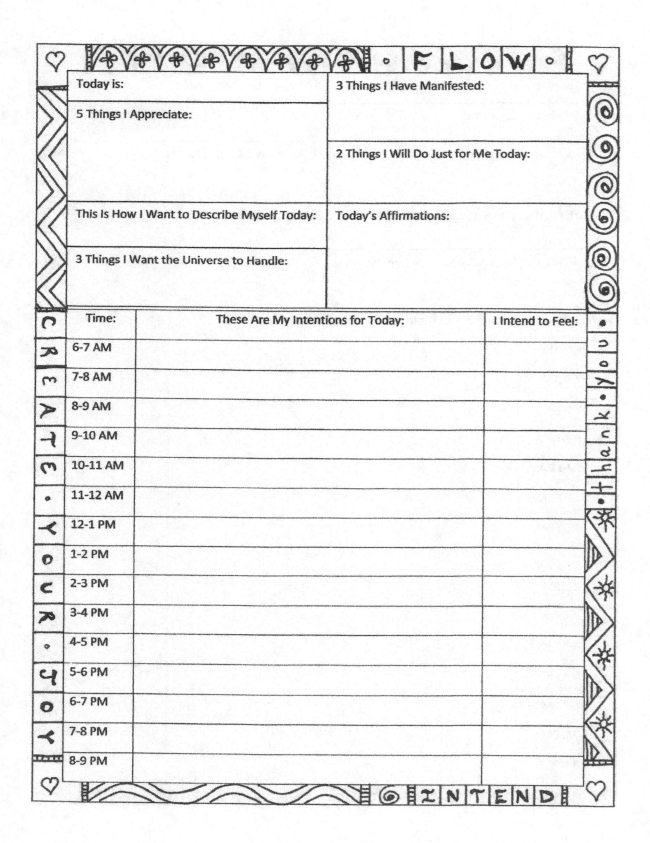

FLOW

Today is:	3 Things I Have Manifested:
5 Things I Appreciate:	
	2 Things I Will Do Just for Me Today:
This Is How I Want to Describe Myself Today:	Today's Affirmations:
3 Things I Want the Universe to Handle:	

CREATE · YOUR · JOY

thank you

Time:	These Are My Intentions for Today:	I Intend to Feel:
6-7 AM		
7-8 AM		
8-9 AM		
9-10 AM		
10-11 AM		
11-12 AM		
12-1 PM		
1-2 PM		
2-3 PM		
3-4 PM		
4-5 PM		
5-6 PM		
6-7 PM		
7-8 PM		
8-9 PM		

INTEND

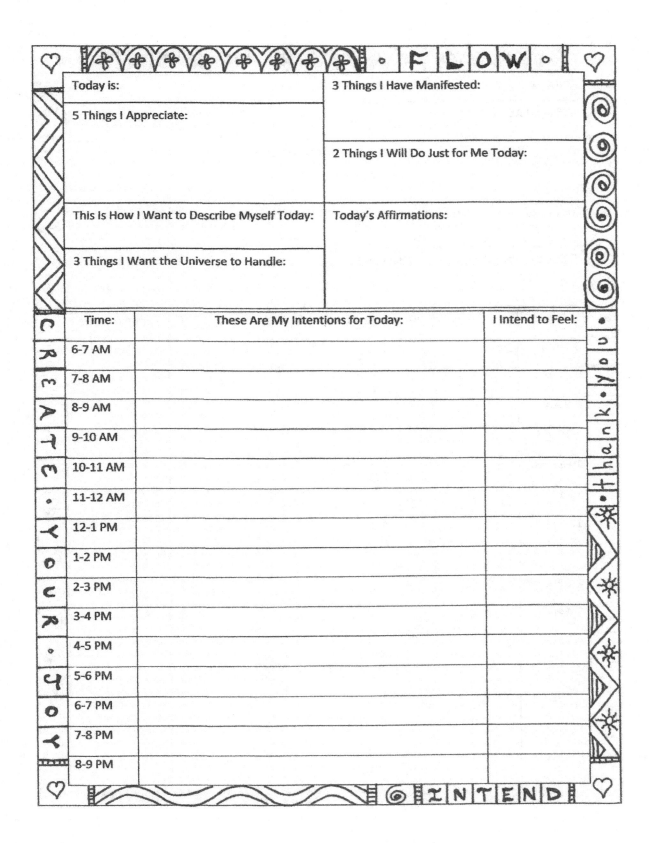

FLOW

Today is:	3 Things I Have Manifested:
5 Things I Appreciate:	
	2 Things I Will Do Just for Me Today:
This Is How I Want to Describe Myself Today:	**Today's Affirmations:**
3 Things I Want the Universe to Handle:	

CREATE • YOUR • JOY

thank you

Time:	These Are My Intentions for Today:	I Intend to Feel:
6-7 AM		
7-8 AM		
8-9 AM		
9-10 AM		
10-11 AM		
11-12 AM		
12-1 PM		
1-2 PM		
2-3 PM		
3-4 PM		
4-5 PM		
5-6 PM		
6-7 PM		
7-8 PM		
8-9 PM		

INTEND

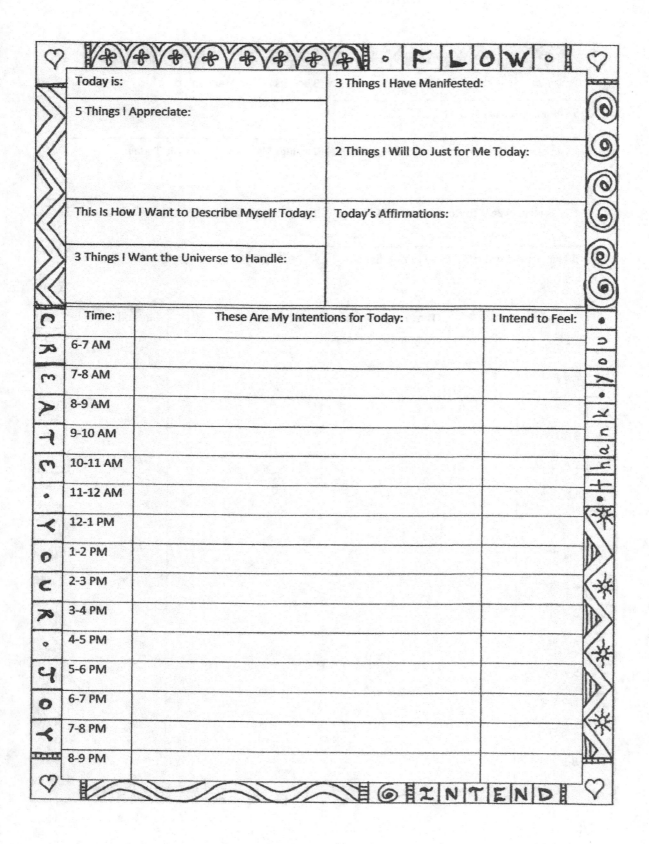

FLOW

Today is:	3 Things I Have Manifested:
5 Things I Appreciate:	
	2 Things I Will Do Just for Me Today:
This Is How I Want to Describe Myself Today:	**Today's Affirmations:**
3 Things I Want the Universe to Handle:	

Time:	These Are My Intentions for Today:	I Intend to Feel:
6-7 AM		
7-8 AM		
8-9 AM		
9-10 AM		
10-11 AM		
11-12 AM		
12-1 PM		
1-2 PM		
2-3 PM		
3-4 PM		
4-5 PM		
5-6 PM		
6-7 PM		
7-8 PM		
8-9 PM		

CREATE . YOUR . JOY

thank you

INTEND

FLOW

Today is:	3 Things I Have Manifested:
5 Things I Appreciate:	
	2 Things I Will Do Just for Me Today:
This Is How I Want to Describe Myself Today:	Today's Affirmations:
3 Things I Want the Universe to Handle:	

CREATE · YOUR · JOY

Time:	These Are My Intentions for Today:	I Intend to Feel:
6-7 AM		
7-8 AM		
8-9 AM		
9-10 AM		
10-11 AM		
11-12 AM		
12-1 PM		
1-2 PM		
2-3 PM		
3-4 PM		
4-5 PM		
5-6 PM		
6-7 PM		
7-8 PM		
8-9 PM		

thank you · INTEND

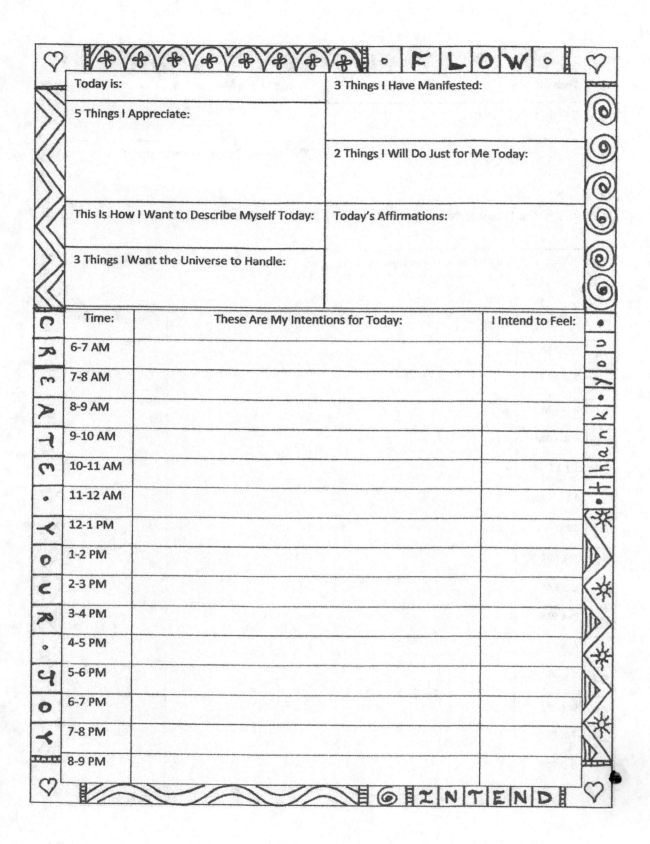

FLOW

Today is:

5 Things I Appreciate:

This Is How I Want to Describe Myself Today:

3 Things I Want the Universe to Handle:

3 Things I Have Manifested:

2 Things I Will Do Just for Me Today:

Today's Affirmations:

CREATE . YOUR . JOY

Time:	These Are My Intentions for Today:	I Intend to Feel:
6-7 AM		
7-8 AM		
8-9 AM		
9-10 AM		
10-11 AM		
11-12 AM		
12-1 PM		
1-2 PM		
2-3 PM		
3-4 PM		
4-5 PM		
5-6 PM		
6-7 PM		
7-8 PM		
8-9 PM		

thank . you

INTEND

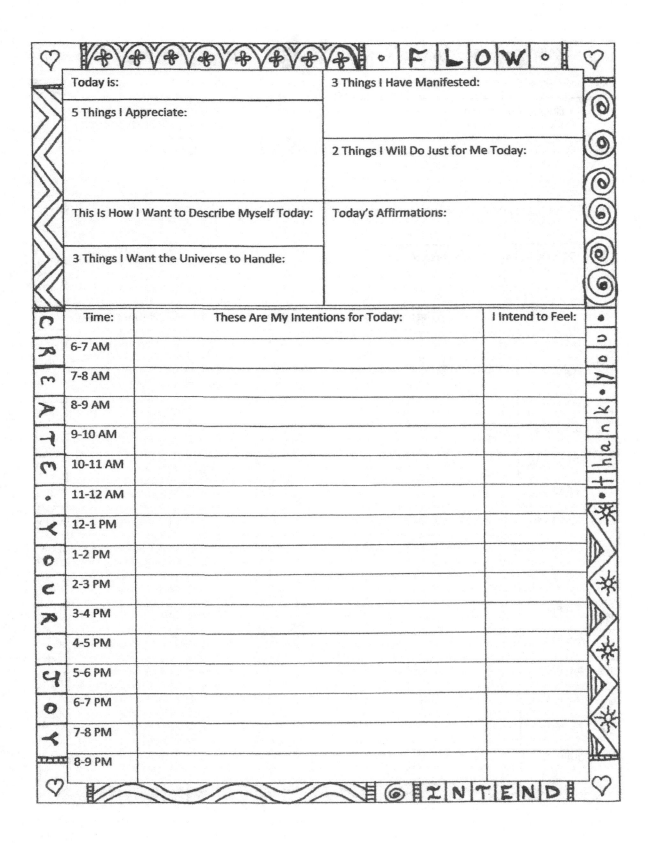

FLOW

Today is:		3 Things I Have Manifested:
5 Things I Appreciate:		
		2 Things I Will Do Just for Me Today:
This Is How I Want to Describe Myself Today:		**Today's Affirmations:**
3 Things I Want the Universe to Handle:		

	Time:	These Are My Intentions for Today:	I Intend to Feel:
C	6-7 AM		
R	7-8 AM		
E	8-9 AM		
A	9-10 AM		
T	10-11 AM		
E	11-12 AM		
•	12-1 PM		
Y	1-2 PM		
O	2-3 PM		
U	3-4 PM		
R	4-5 PM		
•	5-6 PM		
J	6-7 PM		
O	7-8 PM		
Y	8-9 PM		

INTEND

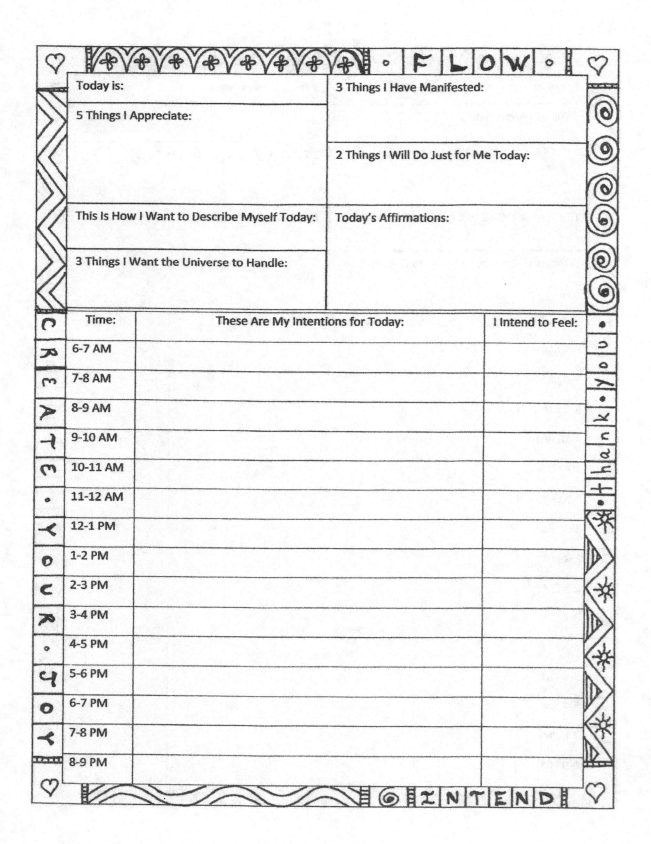

FLOW

Today is:	3 Things I Have Manifested:
5 Things I Appreciate:	
	2 Things I Will Do Just for Me Today:
This Is How I Want to Describe Myself Today:	Today's Affirmations:
3 Things I Want the Universe to Handle:	

Time:	These Are My Intentions for Today:	I Intend to Feel:
6-7 AM		
7-8 AM		
8-9 AM		
9-10 AM		
10-11 AM		
11-12 AM		
12-1 PM		
1-2 PM		
2-3 PM		
3-4 PM		
4-5 PM		
5-6 PM		
6-7 PM		
7-8 PM		
8-9 PM		

CREATE · YOUR · JOY

thank · you

INTEND

• F L O W •

Today is:	3 Things I Have Manifested:
5 Things I Appreciate:	
	2 Things I Will Do Just for Me Today:
This Is How I Want to Describe Myself Today:	**Today's Affirmations:**
3 Things I Want the Universe to Handle:	

Time:	These Are My Intentions for Today:	I Intend to Feel:
6-7 AM		
7-8 AM		
8-9 AM		
9-10 AM		
10-11 AM		
11-12 AM		
12-1 PM		
1-2 PM		
2-3 PM		
3-4 PM		
4-5 PM		
5-6 PM		
6-7 PM		
7-8 PM		
8-9 PM		

CREATE • YOUR • CROY

thank you

INTEND

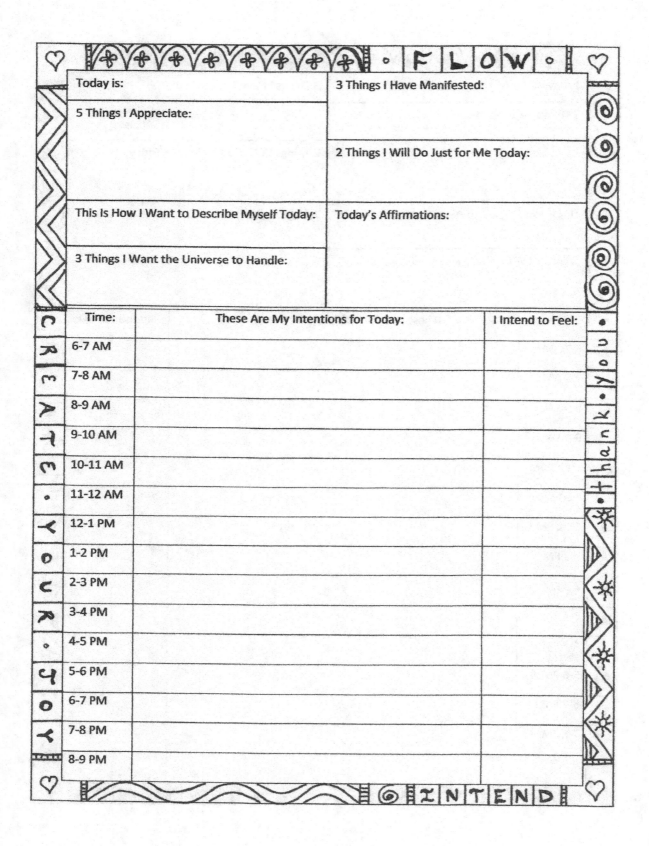

FLOW

Today is:

5 Things I Appreciate:

This Is How I Want to Describe Myself Today:

3 Things I Want the Universe to Handle:

3 Things I Have Manifested:

2 Things I Will Do Just for Me Today:

Today's Affirmations:

Time:	These Are My Intentions for Today:	I Intend to Feel:
6-7 AM		
7-8 AM		
8-9 AM		
9-10 AM		
10-11 AM		
11-12 AM		
12-1 PM		
1-2 PM		
2-3 PM		
3-4 PM		
4-5 PM		
5-6 PM		
6-7 PM		
7-8 PM		
8-9 PM		

CREATE • YOUR • JOY

thank you

INTEND

FLOW

Today is:	3 Things I Have Manifested:
5 Things I Appreciate:	
	2 Things I Will Do Just for Me Today:
This Is How I Want to Describe Myself Today:	Today's Affirmations:
3 Things I Want the Universe to Handle:	

Time:	These Are My Intentions for Today:	I Intend to Feel:
6-7 AM		
7-8 AM		
8-9 AM		
9-10 AM		
10-11 AM		
11-12 AM		
12-1 PM		
1-2 PM		
2-3 PM		
3-4 PM		
4-5 PM		
5-6 PM		
6-7 PM		
7-8 PM		
8-9 PM		

CREATE . YOUR . CR . JOY

Thank you

INTEND

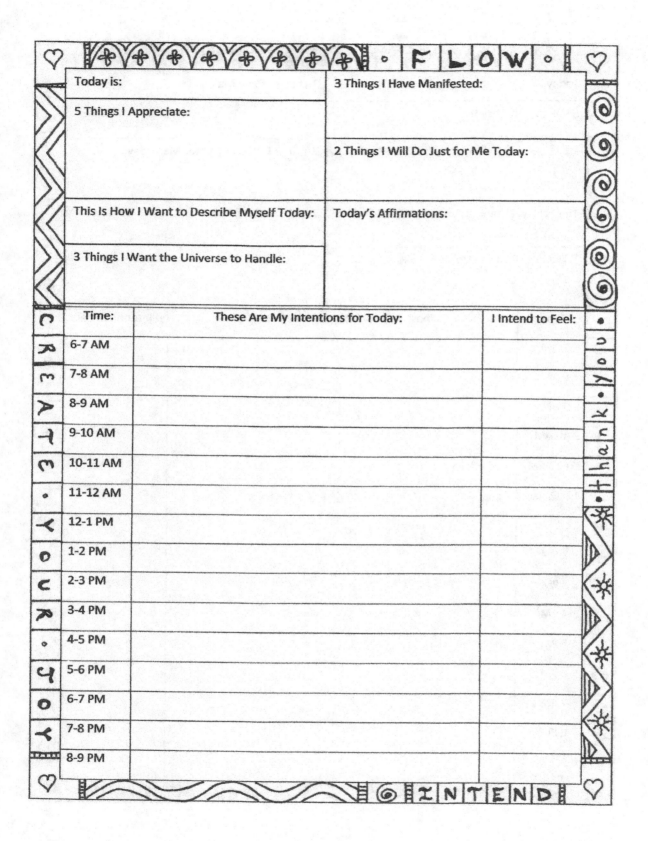

FLOW

Today is:

5 Things I Appreciate:

This Is How I Want to Describe Myself Today:

3 Things I Want the Universe to Handle:

3 Things I Have Manifested:

2 Things I Will Do Just for Me Today:

Today's Affirmations:

Time:	These Are My Intentions for Today:	I Intend to Feel:
6-7 AM		
7-8 AM		
8-9 AM		
9-10 AM		
10-11 AM		
11-12 AM		
12-1 PM		
1-2 PM		
2-3 PM		
3-4 PM		
4-5 PM		
5-6 PM		
6-7 PM		
7-8 PM		
8-9 PM		

CREATE . YOUR . JOY

thank you

INTEND

FLOW

Today is:

5 Things I Appreciate:

This Is How I Want to Describe Myself Today:

3 Things I Want the Universe to Handle:

3 Things I Have Manifested:

2 Things I Will Do Just for Me Today:

Today's Affirmations:

Time:	These Are My Intentions for Today:	I Intend to Feel:
6-7 AM		
7-8 AM		
8-9 AM		
9-10 AM		
10-11 AM		
11-12 AM		
12-1 PM		
1-2 PM		
2-3 PM		
3-4 PM		
4-5 PM		
5-6 PM		
6-7 PM		
7-8 PM		
8-9 PM		

CREATE . YOUR . JOY

thank you

INTEND

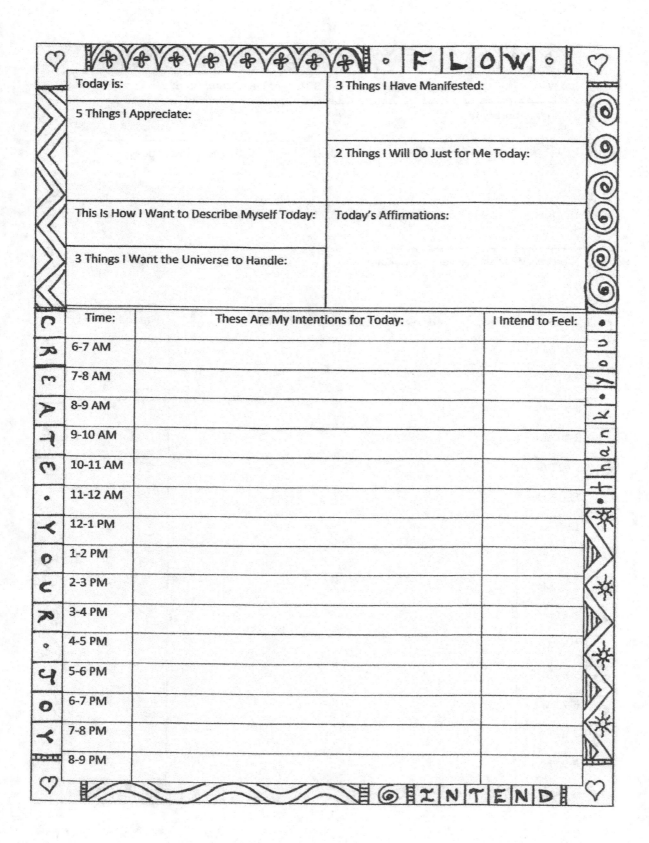

FLOW

Today is:		3 Things I Have Manifested:
5 Things I Appreciate:		
		2 Things I Will Do Just for Me Today:
This Is How I Want to Describe Myself Today:		Today's Affirmations:
3 Things I Want the Universe to Handle:		

CREATE • YOUR • JOY

Time:	These Are My Intentions for Today:	I Intend to Feel:
6-7 AM		
7-8 AM		
8-9 AM		
9-10 AM		
10-11 AM		
11-12 AM		
12-1 PM		
1-2 PM		
2-3 PM		
3-4 PM		
4-5 PM		
5-6 PM		
6-7 PM		
7-8 PM		
8-9 PM		

thank you

INTEND

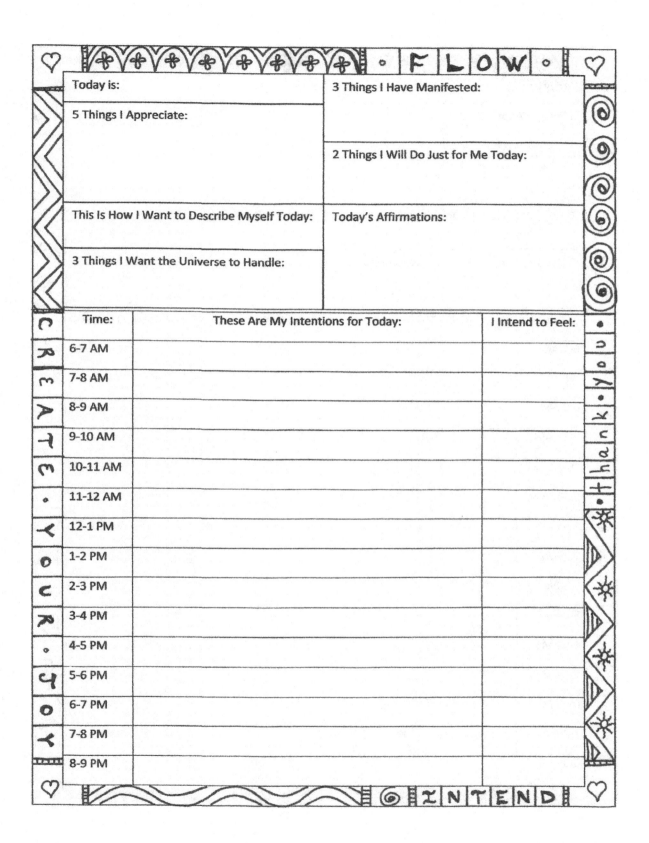

FLOW

Today is:	3 Things I Have Manifested:
5 Things I Appreciate:	
	2 Things I Will Do Just for Me Today:
This Is How I Want to Describe Myself Today:	**Today's Affirmations:**
3 Things I Want the Universe to Handle:	

Time:	These Are My Intentions for Today:	I Intend to Feel:
6-7 AM		
7-8 AM		
8-9 AM		
9-10 AM		
10-11 AM		
11-12 AM		
12-1 PM		
1-2 PM		
2-3 PM		
3-4 PM		
4-5 PM		
5-6 PM		
6-7 PM		
7-8 PM		
8-9 PM		

CREATE . YOUR . JOY

thank you . ×

INTEND

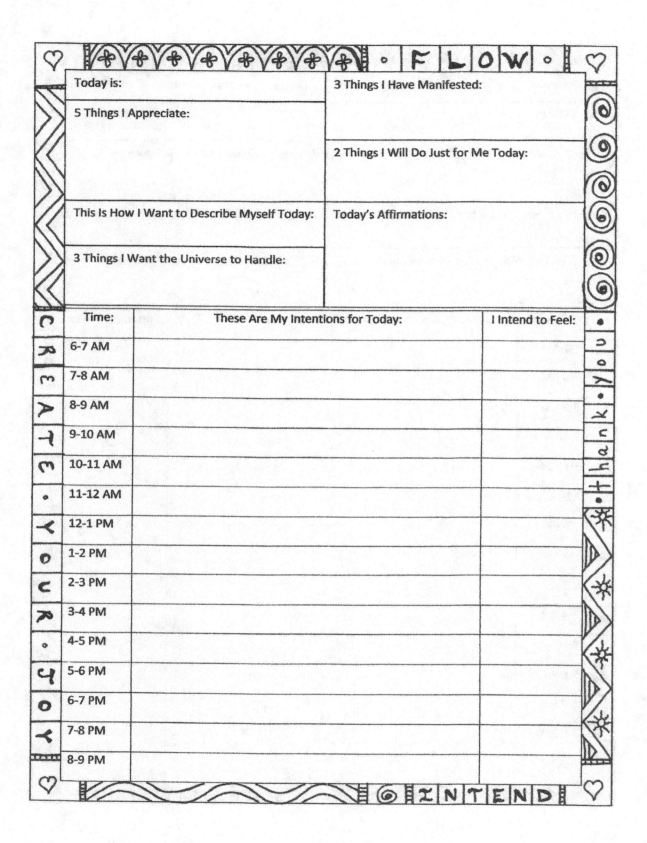

FLOW

Today is:	3 Things I Have Manifested:
5 Things I Appreciate:	
	2 Things I Will Do Just for Me Today:
This Is How I Want to Describe Myself Today:	Today's Affirmations:
3 Things I Want the Universe to Handle:	

Time:	These Are My Intentions for Today:	I Intend to Feel:
6-7 AM		
7-8 AM		
8-9 AM		
9-10 AM		
10-11 AM		
11-12 AM		
12-1 PM		
1-2 PM		
2-3 PM		
3-4 PM		
4-5 PM		
5-6 PM		
6-7 PM		
7-8 PM		
8-9 PM		

CREATE . YOUR . JOY

thank you

INTEND

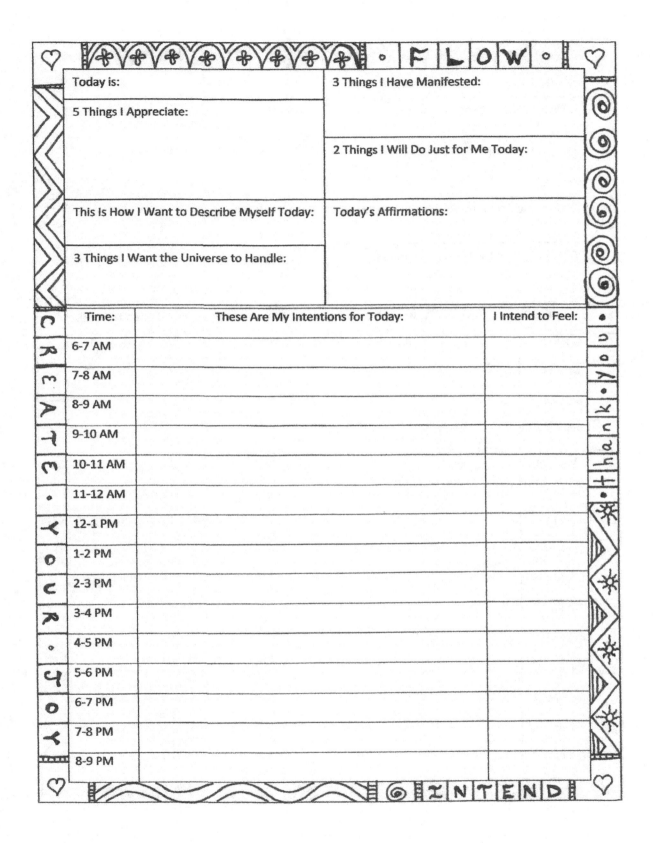

FLOW

Today is:	3 Things I Have Manifested:
5 Things I Appreciate:	
	2 Things I Will Do Just for Me Today:
This Is How I Want to Describe Myself Today:	Today's Affirmations:
3 Things I Want the Universe to Handle:	

Time:	These Are My Intentions for Today:	I Intend to Feel:
6-7 AM		
7-8 AM		
8-9 AM		
9-10 AM		
10-11 AM		
11-12 AM		
12-1 PM		
1-2 PM		
2-3 PM		
3-4 PM		
4-5 PM		
5-6 PM		
6-7 PM		
7-8 PM		
8-9 PM		

CREATE · YOUR · JOY

thank you

INTEND

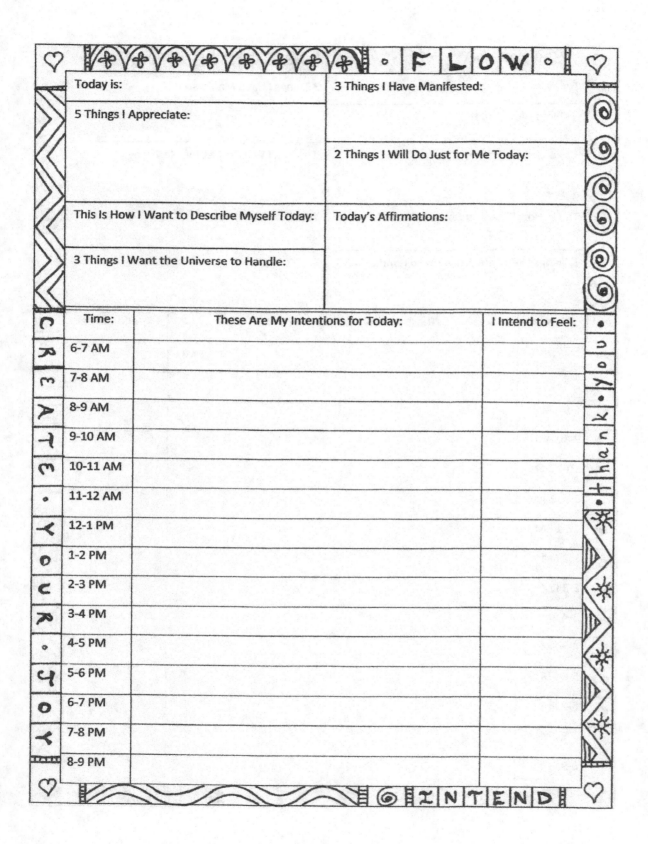

FLOW

Today is:	3 Things I Have Manifested:
5 Things I Appreciate:	
	2 Things I Will Do Just for Me Today:
This Is How I Want to Describe Myself Today:	Today's Affirmations:
3 Things I Want the Universe to Handle:	

Time:	These Are My Intentions for Today:	I Intend to Feel:
6-7 AM		
7-8 AM		
8-9 AM		
9-10 AM		
10-11 AM		
11-12 AM		
12-1 PM		
1-2 PM		
2-3 PM		
3-4 PM		
4-5 PM		
5-6 PM		
6-7 PM		
7-8 PM		
8-9 PM		

CREATE . YOUR . JOY

thank you

INTEND

214

FLOW

Today is:	**3 Things I Have Manifested:**
5 Things I Appreciate:	
	2 Things I Will Do Just for Me Today:
This Is How I Want to Describe Myself Today:	**Today's Affirmations:**
3 Things I Want the Universe to Handle:	

CREATE · YOUR · JOY

Time:	These Are My Intentions for Today:	I Intend to Feel:
6-7 AM		
7-8 AM		
8-9 AM		
9-10 AM		
10-11 AM		
11-12 AM		
12-1 PM		
1-2 PM		
2-3 PM		
3-4 PM		
4-5 PM		
5-6 PM		
6-7 PM		
7-8 PM		
8-9 PM		

thank · you ·

INTEND

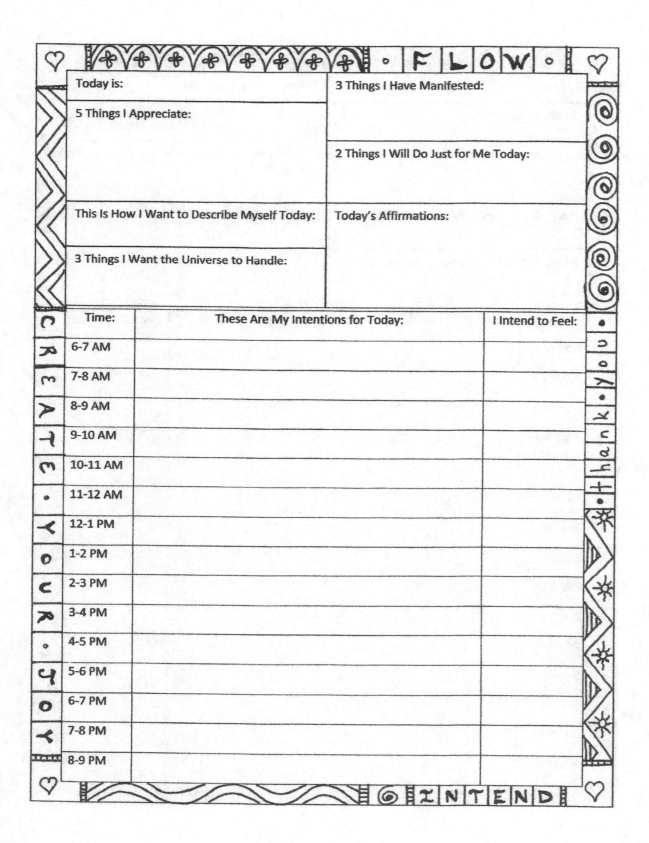

FLOW

Today is:

3 Things I Have Manifested:

5 Things I Appreciate:

2 Things I Will Do Just for Me Today:

This Is How I Want to Describe Myself Today:

Today's Affirmations:

3 Things I Want the Universe to Handle:

CREATE · YOUR · JOY

Time:	These Are My Intentions for Today:	I Intend to Feel:
6-7 AM		
7-8 AM		
8-9 AM		
9-10 AM		
10-11 AM		
11-12 AM		
12-1 PM		
1-2 PM		
2-3 PM		
3-4 PM		
4-5 PM		
5-6 PM		
6-7 PM		
7-8 PM		
8-9 PM		

thank you

INTEND

FLOW

Today is:

5 Things I Appreciate:

3 Things I Have Manifested:

2 Things I Will Do Just for Me Today:

This Is How I Want to Describe Myself Today:

Today's Affirmations:

3 Things I Want the Universe to Handle:

	Time:	These Are My Intentions for Today:	I Intend to Feel:
C	6-7 AM		
R	7-8 AM		
E	8-9 AM		
A	9-10 AM		
T	10-11 AM		
E	11-12 AM		
	12-1 PM		
Y	1-2 PM		
O	2-3 PM		
U	3-4 PM		
R	4-5 PM		
	5-6 PM		
J	6-7 PM		
O	7-8 PM		
Y	8-9 PM		

INTEND

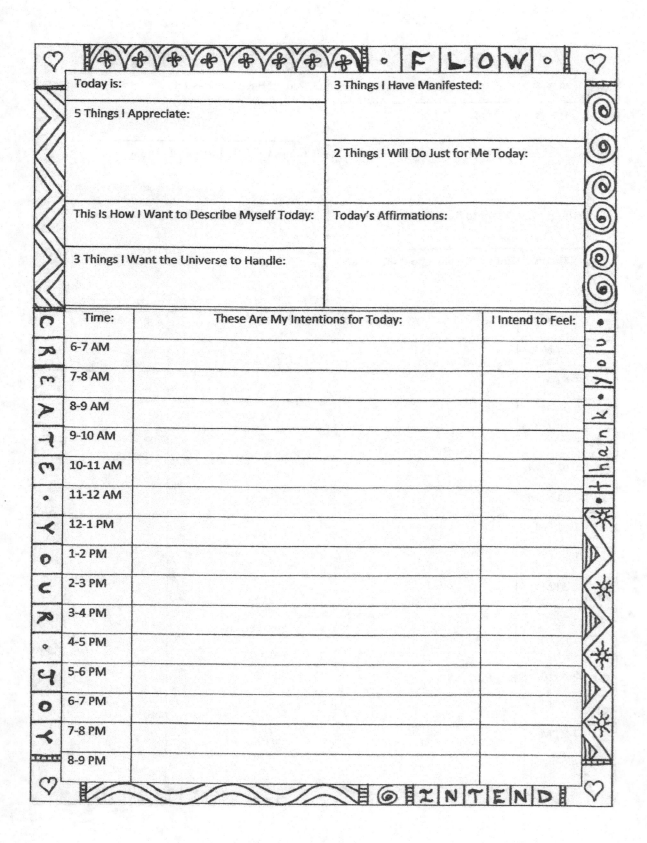

FLOW

Today is:

5 Things I Appreciate:

3 Things I Have Manifested:

2 Things I Will Do Just for Me Today:

This Is How I Want to Describe Myself Today:

Today's Affirmations:

3 Things I Want the Universe to Handle:

CREATE · YOUR · JOY

Time:	These Are My Intentions for Today:	I Intend to Feel:
6-7 AM		
7-8 AM		
8-9 AM		
9-10 AM		
10-11 AM		
11-12 AM		
12-1 PM		
1-2 PM		
2-3 PM		
3-4 PM		
4-5 PM		
5-6 PM		
6-7 PM		
7-8 PM		
8-9 PM		

thank you

INTEND

FLOW

Today is:		3 Things I Have Manifested:
5 Things I Appreciate:		
		2 Things I Will Do Just for Me Today:
This Is How I Want to Describe Myself Today:		**Today's Affirmations:**
3 Things I Want the Universe to Handle:		

Time:	These Are My Intentions for Today:	I Intend to Feel:
6-7 AM		
7-8 AM		
8-9 AM		
9-10 AM		
10-11 AM		
11-12 AM		
12-1 PM		
1-2 PM		
2-3 PM		
3-4 PM		
4-5 PM		
5-6 PM		
6-7 PM		
7-8 PM		
8-9 PM		

CREATE • YOUR • JOY

thank you

INTEND

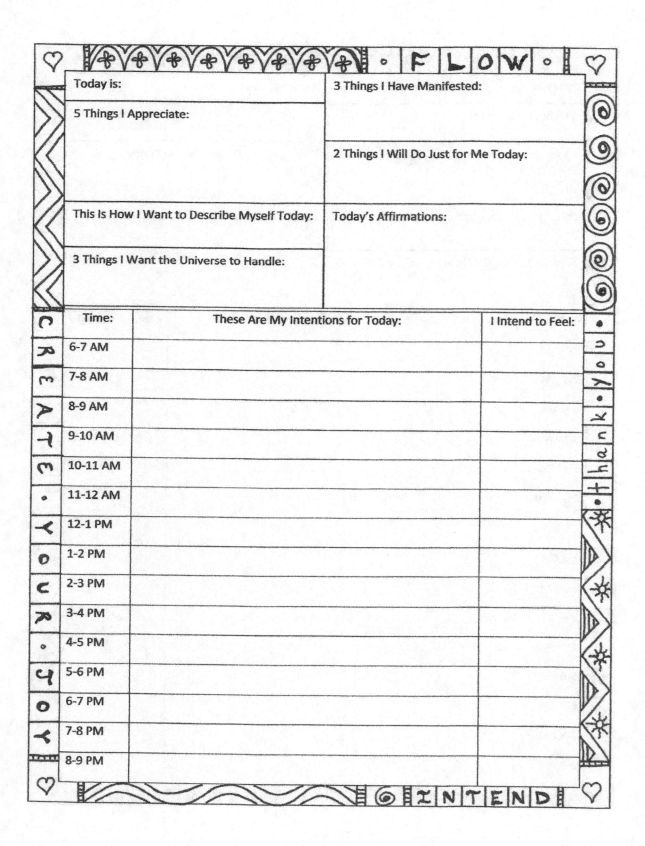

FLOW

Today is:	3 Things I Have Manifested:
5 Things I Appreciate:	
	2 Things I Will Do Just for Me Today:
This Is How I Want to Describe Myself Today:	Today's Affirmations:
3 Things I Want the Universe to Handle:	

	Time:	These Are My Intentions for Today:	I Intend to Feel:
C	6-7 AM		
R	7-8 AM		
E	8-9 AM		
A	9-10 AM		
T	10-11 AM		
E	11-12 AM		
.	12-1 PM		
Y	1-2 PM		
O	2-3 PM		
U	3-4 PM		
R	4-5 PM		
.	5-6 PM		
J	6-7 PM		
O	7-8 PM		
Y	8-9 PM		

INTEND

Month: August

Sunday	Monday	Tuesday	Wednesday	Thursday	Friday	Saturday

Do at least one thing every day that brings you joy and record it on this page.

Affirmations:

" To bring anything into your life, imagine that it's already there. --Richard Back

221

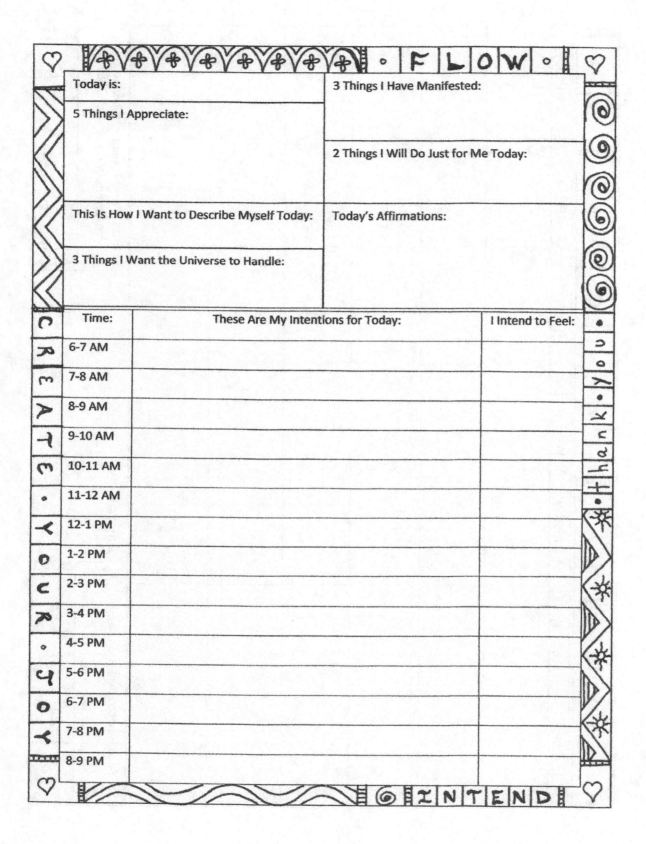

FLOW

Today is:		3 Things I Have Manifested:
5 Things I Appreciate:		
		2 Things I Will Do Just for Me Today:
This Is How I Want to Describe Myself Today:		**Today's Affirmations:**
3 Things I Want the Universe to Handle:		

	Time:	These Are My Intentions for Today:	I Intend to Feel:
C	6-7 AM		
R	7-8 AM		
E	8-9 AM		
A	9-10 AM		
T	10-11 AM		
E	11-12 AM		
Y	12-1 PM		
O	1-2 PM		
U	2-3 PM		
R	3-4 PM		
	4-5 PM		
J	5-6 PM		
O	6-7 PM		
Y	7-8 PM		
	8-9 PM		

INTEND

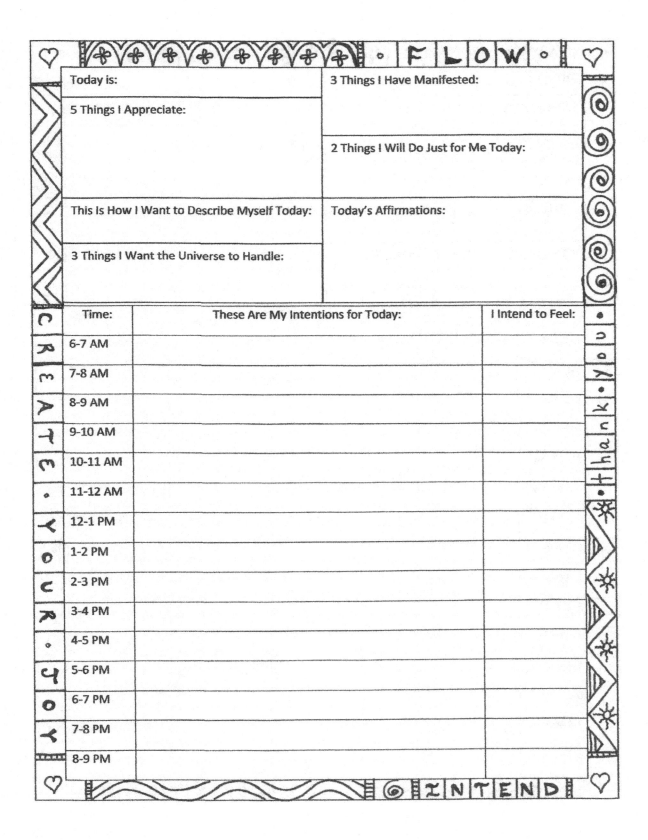

FLOW

Today is:	3 Things I Have Manifested:
5 Things I Appreciate:	
	2 Things I Will Do Just for Me Today:
This Is How I Want to Describe Myself Today:	**Today's Affirmations:**
3 Things I Want the Universe to Handle:	

	Time:	These Are My Intentions for Today:	I Intend to Feel:
C	6-7 AM		
R	7-8 AM		
E	8-9 AM		
A	9-10 AM		
T	10-11 AM		
E	11-12 AM		
Y	12-1 PM		
O	1-2 PM		
U	2-3 PM		
R	3-4 PM		
J	4-5 PM		
O	5-6 PM		
Y	6-7 PM		
	7-8 PM		
	8-9 PM		

INTEND

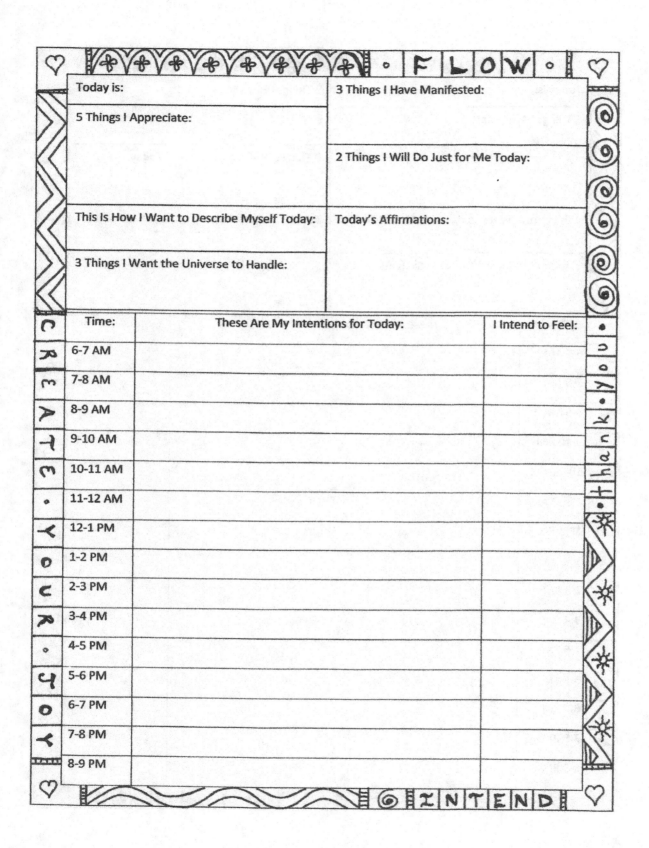

FLOW

Today is:

5 Things I Appreciate:

This Is How I Want to Describe Myself Today:

3 Things I Want the Universe to Handle:

3 Things I Have Manifested:

2 Things I Will Do Just for Me Today:

Today's Affirmations:

Time:	These Are My Intentions for Today:	I Intend to Feel:
6-7 AM		
7-8 AM		
8-9 AM		
9-10 AM		
10-11 AM		
11-12 AM		
12-1 PM		
1-2 PM		
2-3 PM		
3-4 PM		
4-5 PM		
5-6 PM		
6-7 PM		
7-8 PM		
8-9 PM		

CREATE . YOUR . JOY

thank you

INTEND

FLOW

Today is:

5 Things I Appreciate:

This Is How I Want to Describe Myself Today:

3 Things I Want the Universe to Handle:

3 Things I Have Manifested:

2 Things I Will Do Just for Me Today:

Today's Affirmations:

Time:	These Are My Intentions for Today:	I Intend to Feel:
6-7 AM		
7-8 AM		
8-9 AM		
9-10 AM		
10-11 AM		
11-12 AM		
12-1 PM		
1-2 PM		
2-3 PM		
3-4 PM		
4-5 PM		
5-6 PM		
6-7 PM		
7-8 PM		
8-9 PM		

CREATE . YOUR . JOY

thank you

INTEND

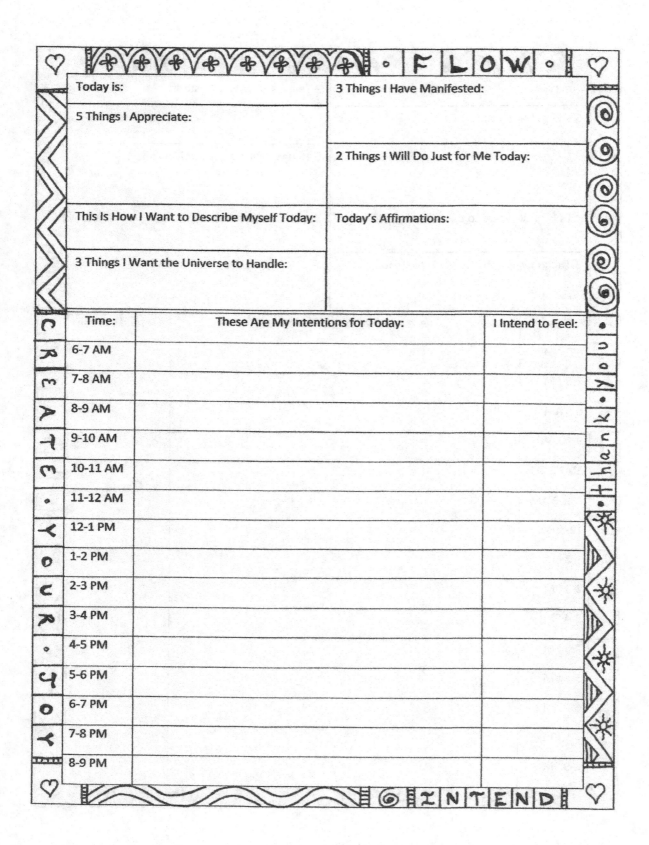

FLOW

Today is:	3 Things I Have Manifested:
5 Things I Appreciate:	
	2 Things I Will Do Just for Me Today:
This Is How I Want to Describe Myself Today:	**Today's Affirmations:**
3 Things I Want the Universe to Handle:	

CREATE · YOUR · JOY

thank you ·

Time:	These Are My Intentions for Today:	I Intend to Feel:
6-7 AM		
7-8 AM		
8-9 AM		
9-10 AM		
10-11 AM		
11-12 AM		
12-1 PM		
1-2 PM		
2-3 PM		
3-4 PM		
4-5 PM		
5-6 PM		
6-7 PM		
7-8 PM		
8-9 PM		

INTEND

· F L O W ·

Today is:		3 Things I Have Manifested:
5 Things I Appreciate:		
		2 Things I Will Do Just for Me Today:
This Is How I Want to Describe Myself Today:		**Today's Affirmations:**
3 Things I Want the Universe to Handle:		

	Time:	These Are My Intentions for Today:	I Intend to Feel:
C	6-7 AM		
R	7-8 AM		
E	8-9 AM		
A	9-10 AM		
T	10-11 AM		
E	11-12 AM		
·	12-1 PM		
Y	1-2 PM		
O	2-3 PM		
U	3-4 PM		
R	4-5 PM		
·	5-6 PM		
J	6-7 PM		
O	7-8 PM		
Y	8-9 PM		

INTEND

227

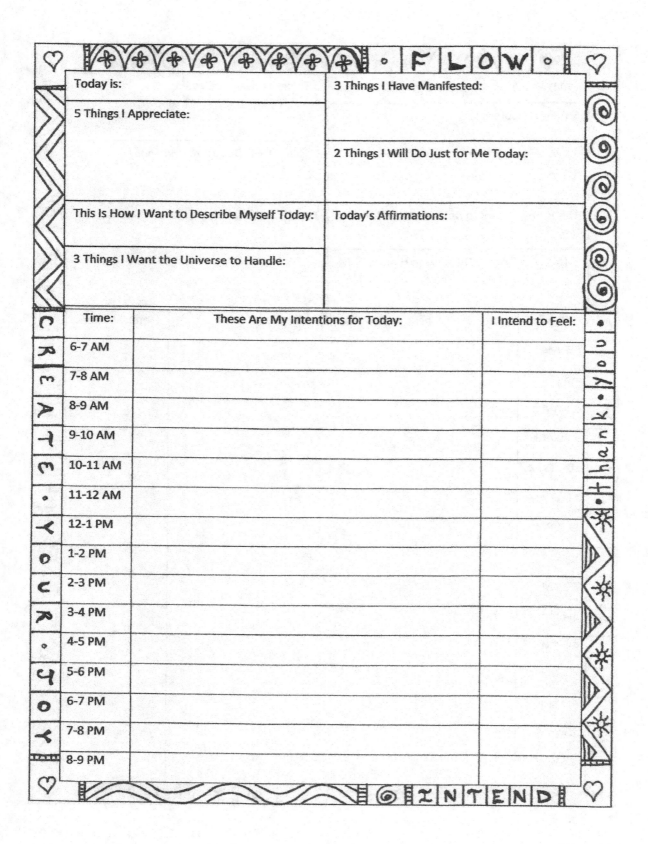

FLOW

Today is:	3 Things I Have Manifested:
5 Things I Appreciate:	
	2 Things I Will Do Just for Me Today:
This Is How I Want to Describe Myself Today:	Today's Affirmations:
3 Things I Want the Universe to Handle:	

Time:	These Are My Intentions for Today:	I Intend to Feel:
6-7 AM		
7-8 AM		
8-9 AM		
9-10 AM		
10-11 AM		
11-12 AM		
12-1 PM		
1-2 PM		
2-3 PM		
3-4 PM		
4-5 PM		
5-6 PM		
6-7 PM		
7-8 PM		
8-9 PM		

CREATE . YOUR . JOY

thank you

INTEND

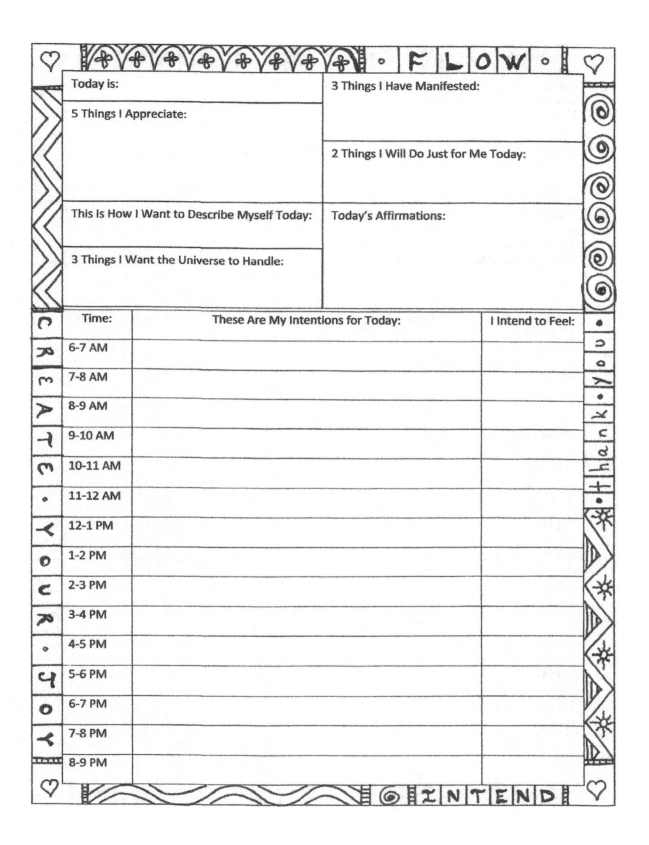

FLOW

Today is:	3 Things I Have Manifested:
5 Things I Appreciate:	
	2 Things I Will Do Just for Me Today:
This Is How I Want to Describe Myself Today:	Today's Affirmations:
3 Things I Want the Universe to Handle:	

Time:	These Are My Intentions for Today:	I Intend to Feel:
6-7 AM		
7-8 AM		
8-9 AM		
9-10 AM		
10-11 AM		
11-12 AM		
12-1 PM		
1-2 PM		
2-3 PM		
3-4 PM		
4-5 PM		
5-6 PM		
6-7 PM		
7-8 PM		
8-9 PM		

CREATE . YOUR . JOY

Thank you.

INTEND

229

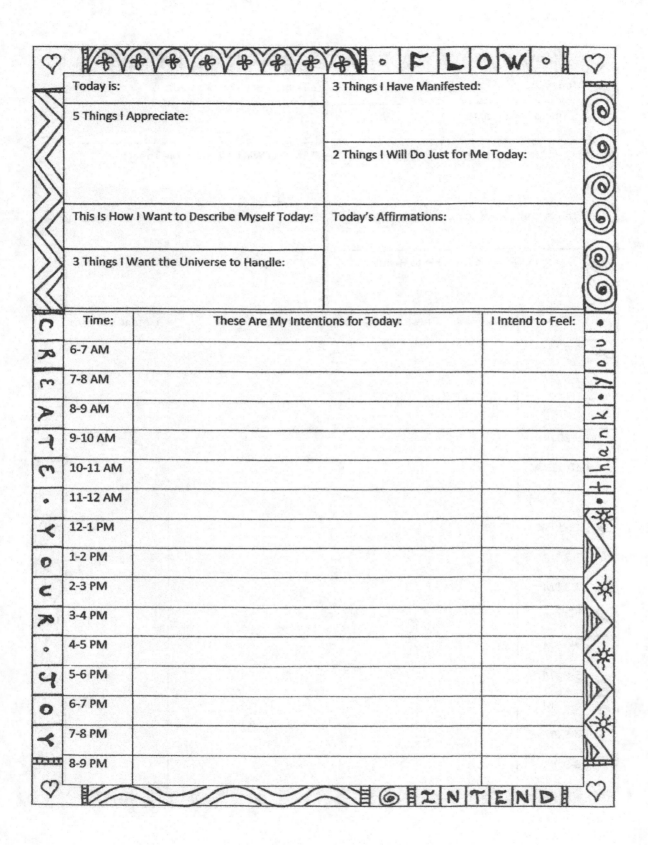

FLOW

Today is:

5 Things I Appreciate:

This Is How I Want to Describe Myself Today:

3 Things I Want the Universe to Handle:

3 Things I Have Manifested:

2 Things I Will Do Just for Me Today:

Today's Affirmations:

Time:	These Are My Intentions for Today:	I Intend to Feel:
6-7 AM		
7-8 AM		
8-9 AM		
9-10 AM		
10-11 AM		
11-12 AM		
12-1 PM		
1-2 PM		
2-3 PM		
3-4 PM		
4-5 PM		
5-6 PM		
6-7 PM		
7-8 PM		
8-9 PM		

CREATE • YOUR • JOY

INTEND

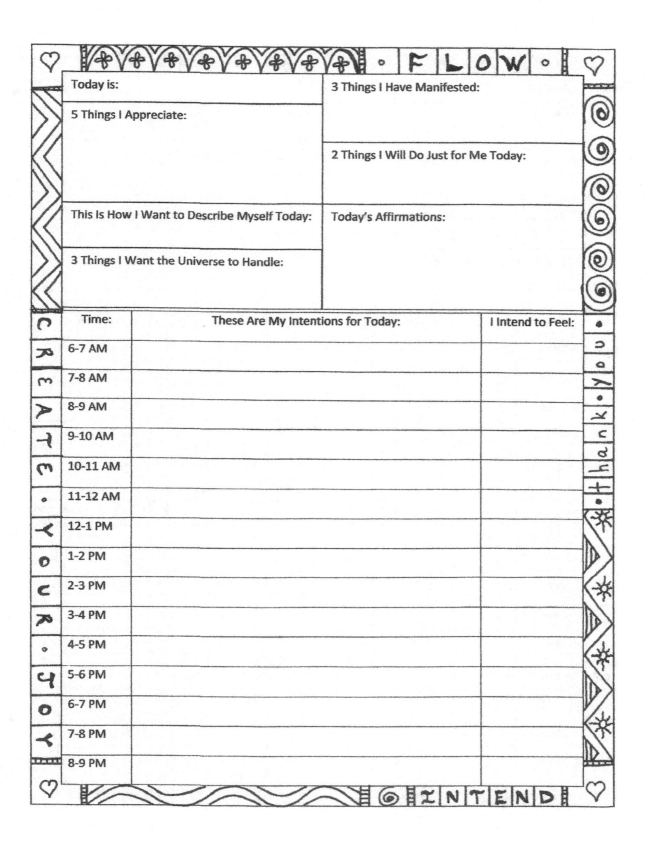

FLOW

Today is:	3 Things I Have Manifested:
5 Things I Appreciate:	
	2 Things I Will Do Just for Me Today:
This Is How I Want to Describe Myself Today:	**Today's Affirmations:**
3 Things I Want the Universe to Handle:	

Time:	These Are My Intentions for Today:	I Intend to Feel:
6-7 AM		
7-8 AM		
8-9 AM		
9-10 AM		
10-11 AM		
11-12 AM		
12-1 PM		
1-2 PM		
2-3 PM		
3-4 PM		
4-5 PM		
5-6 PM		
6-7 PM		
7-8 PM		
8-9 PM		

CREATE . YOUR . JOY

thank you .

INTEND

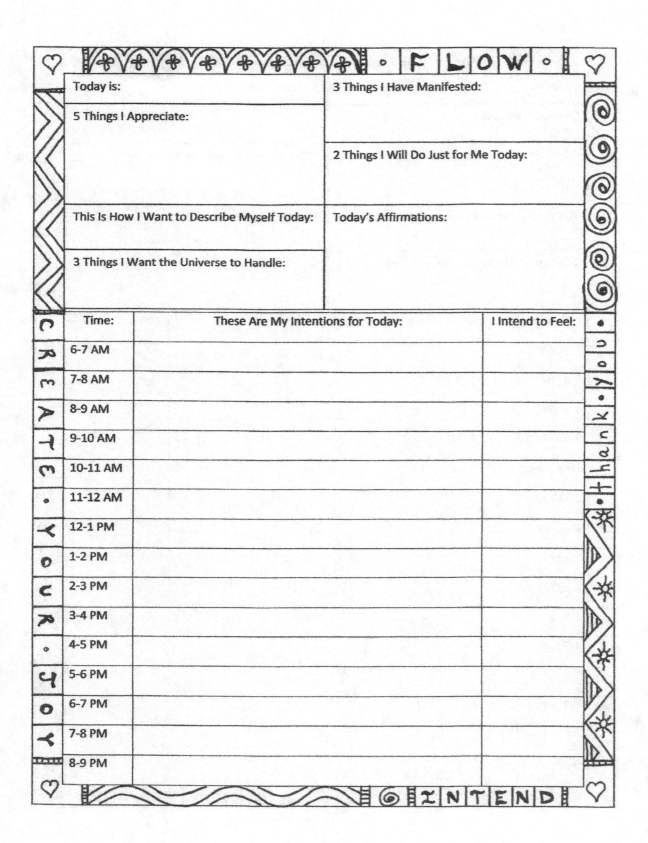

FLOW

Today is:	3 Things I Have Manifested:
5 Things I Appreciate:	
	2 Things I Will Do Just for Me Today:
This Is How I Want to Describe Myself Today:	**Today's Affirmations:**
3 Things I Want the Universe to Handle:	

Time:	These Are My Intentions for Today:	I Intend to Feel:
6-7 AM		
7-8 AM		
8-9 AM		
9-10 AM		
10-11 AM		
11-12 AM		
12-1 PM		
1-2 PM		
2-3 PM		
3-4 PM		
4-5 PM		
5-6 PM		
6-7 PM		
7-8 PM		
8-9 PM		

CREATE . YOUR . JOY

thank you

INTEND

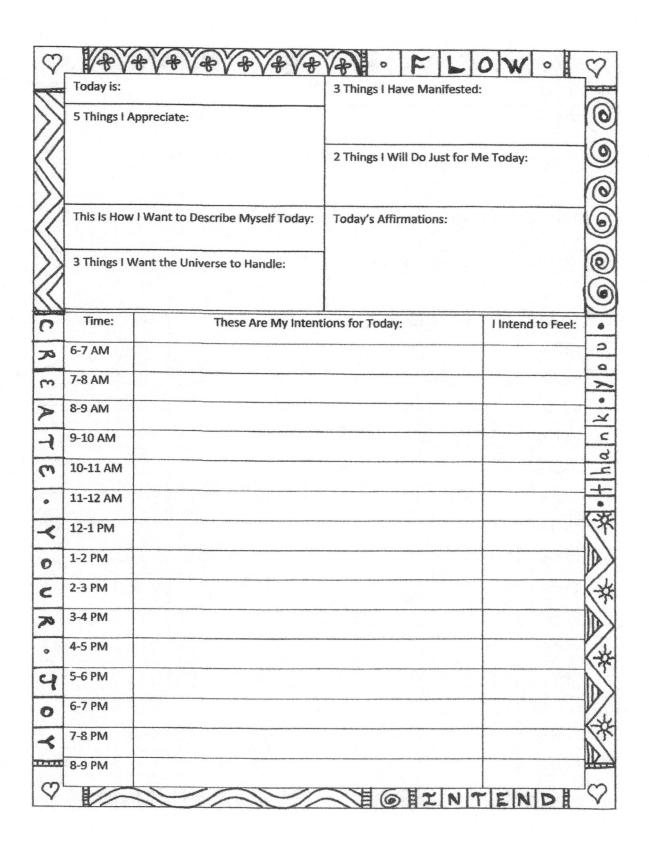

FLOW

Today is:		3 Things I Have Manifested:
5 Things I Appreciate:		
		2 Things I Will Do Just for Me Today:
This Is How I Want to Describe Myself Today:		Today's Affirmations:
3 Things I Want the Universe to Handle:		

Time:	These Are My Intentions for Today:	I Intend to Feel:
6-7 AM		
7-8 AM		
8-9 AM		
9-10 AM		
10-11 AM		
11-12 AM		
12-1 PM		
1-2 PM		
2-3 PM		
3-4 PM		
4-5 PM		
5-6 PM		
6-7 PM		
7-8 PM		
8-9 PM		

CREATE . YOUR . JOY

thank you

INTEND

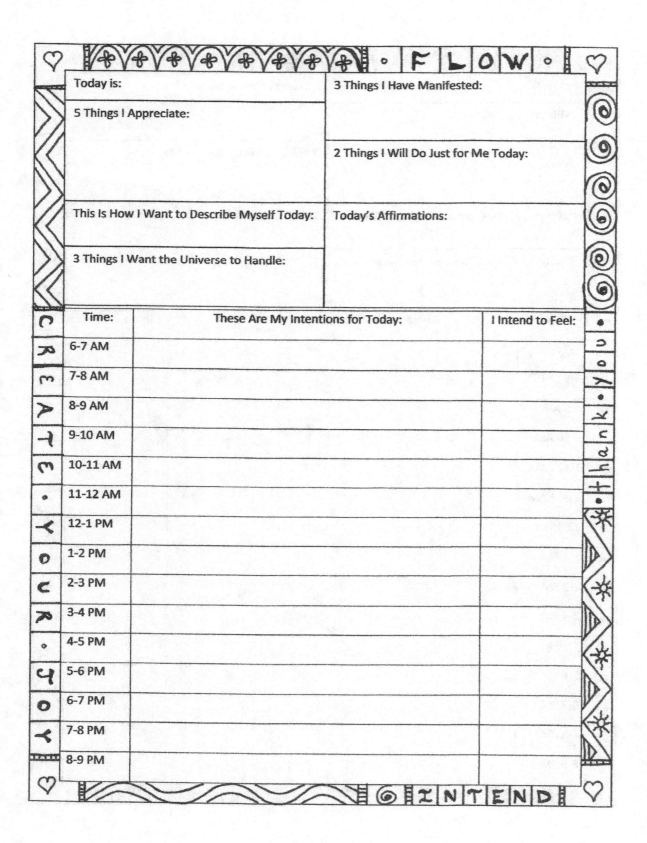

FLOW

Today is:	3 Things I Have Manifested:
5 Things I Appreciate:	
	2 Things I Will Do Just for Me Today:
This Is How I Want to Describe Myself Today:	Today's Affirmations:
3 Things I Want the Universe to Handle:	

CREATE · YOUR · JOY

Thank you · thank you ·

Time:	These Are My Intentions for Today:	I Intend to Feel:
6-7 AM		
7-8 AM		
8-9 AM		
9-10 AM		
10-11 AM		
11-12 AM		
12-1 PM		
1-2 PM		
2-3 PM		
3-4 PM		
4-5 PM		
5-6 PM		
6-7 PM		
7-8 PM		
8-9 PM		

INTEND

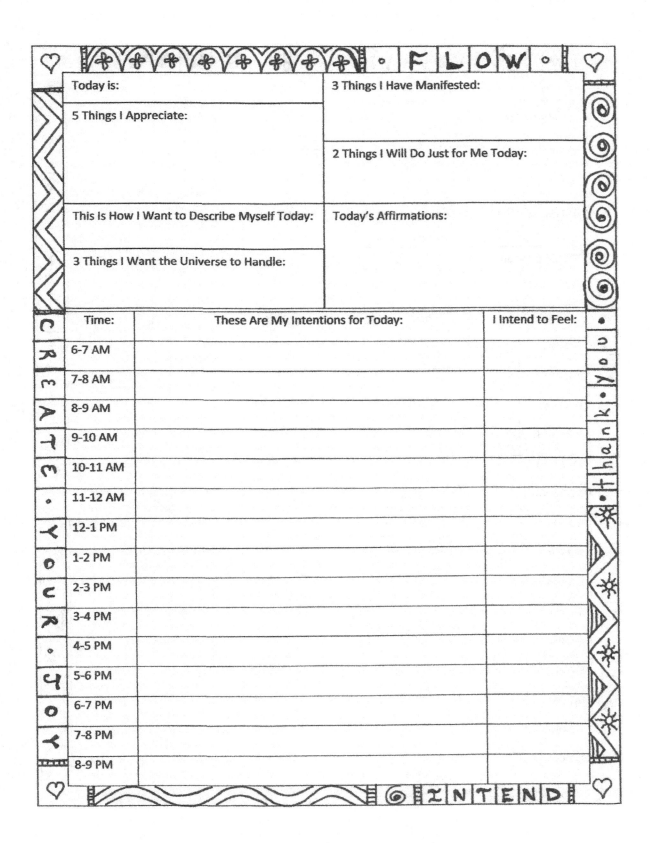

FLOW

Today is:	3 Things I Have Manifested:
5 Things I Appreciate:	
	2 Things I Will Do Just for Me Today:
This Is How I Want to Describe Myself Today:	Today's Affirmations:
3 Things I Want the Universe to Handle:	

Time:	These Are My Intentions for Today:	I Intend to Feel:
6-7 AM		
7-8 AM		
8-9 AM		
9-10 AM		
10-11 AM		
11-12 AM		
12-1 PM		
1-2 PM		
2-3 PM		
3-4 PM		
4-5 PM		
5-6 PM		
6-7 PM		
7-8 PM		
8-9 PM		

INTEND

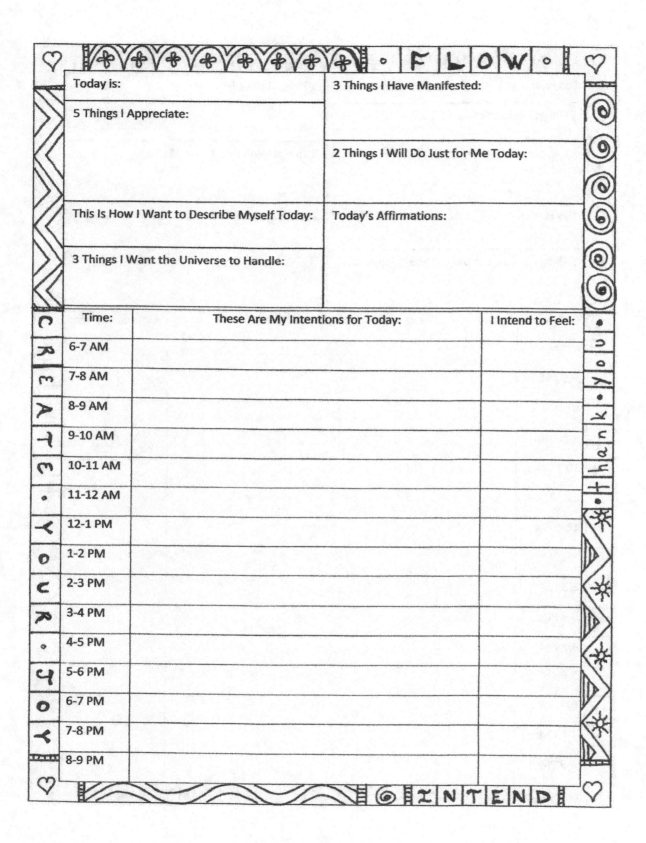

FLOW

| Today is: | 3 Things I Have Manifested: |

5 Things I Appreciate:

| | 2 Things I Will Do Just for Me Today: |

| This Is How I Want to Describe Myself Today: | Today's Affirmations: |

3 Things I Want the Universe to Handle:

	Time:	These Are My Intentions for Today:	I Intend to Feel:
C	6-7 AM		
R	7-8 AM		
E	8-9 AM		
A	9-10 AM		
T	10-11 AM		
E	11-12 AM		
.	12-1 PM		
Y	1-2 PM		
O	2-3 PM		
U	3-4 PM		
R	4-5 PM		
.	5-6 PM		
J	6-7 PM		
O	7-8 PM		
Y	8-9 PM		

thank you

INTEND

FLOW

Today is:	3 Things I Have Manifested:
5 Things I Appreciate:	
	2 Things I Will Do Just for Me Today:
This Is How I Want to Describe Myself Today:	Today's Affirmations:
3 Things I Want the Universe to Handle:	

Time:	These Are My Intentions for Today:	I Intend to Feel:
6-7 AM		
7-8 AM		
8-9 AM		
9-10 AM		
10-11 AM		
11-12 AM		
12-1 PM		
1-2 PM		
2-3 PM		
3-4 PM		
4-5 PM		
5-6 PM		
6-7 PM		
7-8 PM		
8-9 PM		

CREATE . YOUR . JOY

thank you

INTEND

237

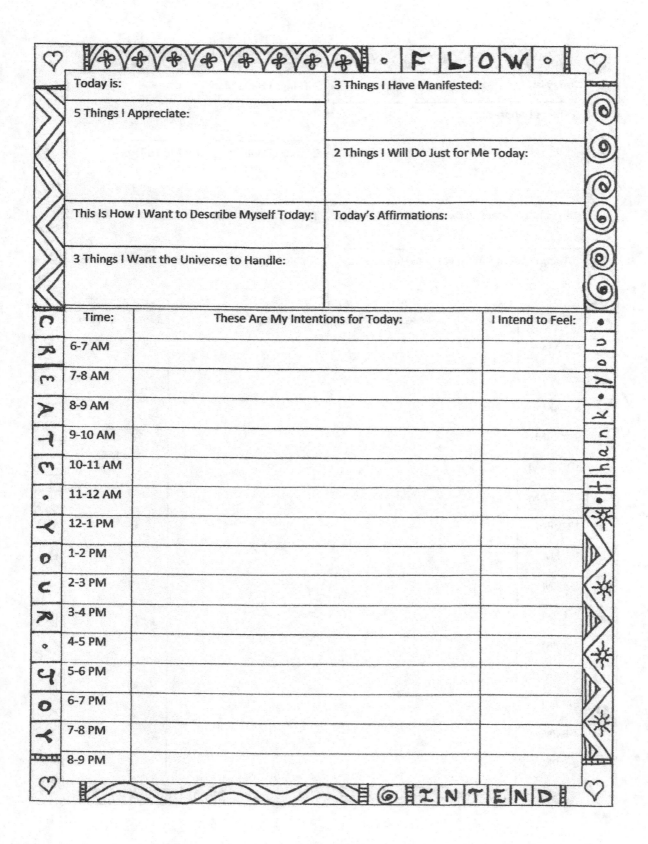

FLOW

Today is:	3 Things I Have Manifested:
5 Things I Appreciate:	
	2 Things I Will Do Just for Me Today:
This Is How I Want to Describe Myself Today:	Today's Affirmations:
3 Things I Want the Universe to Handle:	

Time:	These Are My Intentions for Today:	I Intend to Feel:
6-7 AM		
7-8 AM		
8-9 AM		
9-10 AM		
10-11 AM		
11-12 AM		
12-1 PM		
1-2 PM		
2-3 PM		
3-4 PM		
4-5 PM		
5-6 PM		
6-7 PM		
7-8 PM		
8-9 PM		

CREATE · YOUR · JOY

thank you

INTEND

238

FLOW

Today is:	3 Things I Have Manifested:
5 Things I Appreciate:	
	2 Things I Will Do Just for Me Today:
This Is How I Want to Describe Myself Today:	**Today's Affirmations:**
3 Things I Want the Universe to Handle:	

Time:	These Are My Intentions for Today:	I Intend to Feel:
6-7 AM		
7-8 AM		
8-9 AM		
9-10 AM		
10-11 AM		
11-12 AM		
12-1 PM		
1-2 PM		
2-3 PM		
3-4 PM		
4-5 PM		
5-6 PM		
6-7 PM		
7-8 PM		
8-9 PM		

CREATE • YOUR • JOY

thank you

INTEND

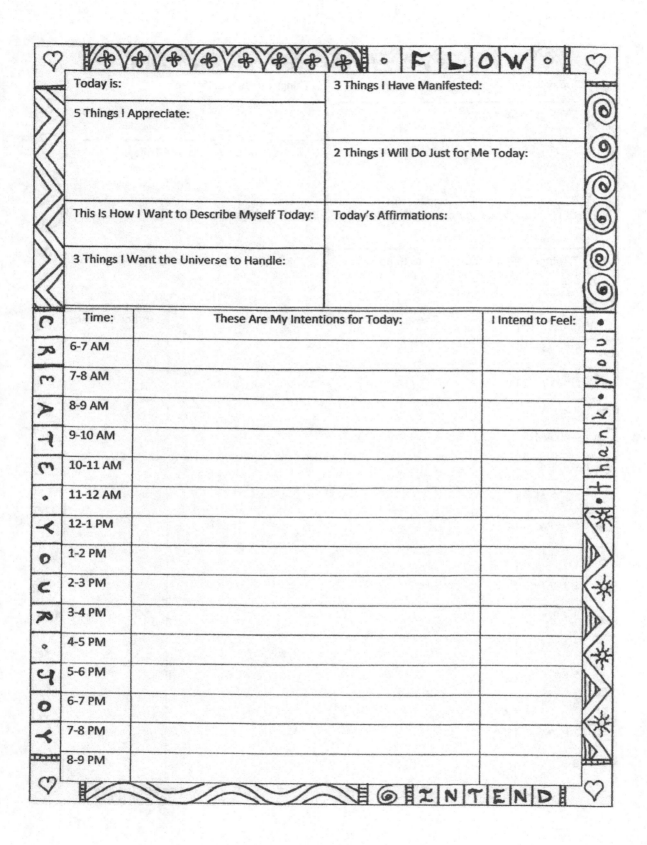

FLOW

Today is:	3 Things I Have Manifested:
5 Things I Appreciate:	
	2 Things I Will Do Just for Me Today:
This Is How I Want to Describe Myself Today:	**Today's Affirmations:**
3 Things I Want the Universe to Handle:	

Time:	These Are My Intentions for Today:	I Intend to Feel:
6-7 AM		
7-8 AM		
8-9 AM		
9-10 AM		
10-11 AM		
11-12 AM		
12-1 PM		
1-2 PM		
2-3 PM		
3-4 PM		
4-5 PM		
5-6 PM		
6-7 PM		
7-8 PM		
8-9 PM		

CREATE . YOUR . JOY

thank you

INTEND

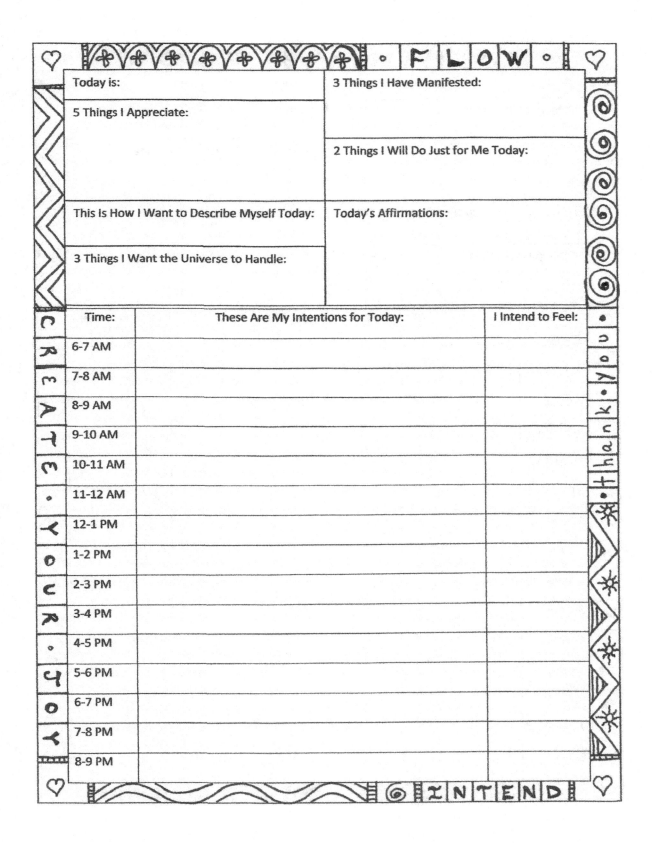

FLOW

	Today is:	3 Things I Have Manifested:
	5 Things I Appreciate:	
		2 Things I Will Do Just for Me Today:
	This Is How I Want to Describe Myself Today:	Today's Affirmations:
	3 Things I Want the Universe to Handle:	

CREATE • YOUR • JOY

Time:	These Are My Intentions for Today:	I Intend to Feel:
6-7 AM		
7-8 AM		
8-9 AM		
9-10 AM		
10-11 AM		
11-12 AM		
12-1 PM		
1-2 PM		
2-3 PM		
3-4 PM		
4-5 PM		
5-6 PM		
6-7 PM		
7-8 PM		
8-9 PM		

thank you

INTEND

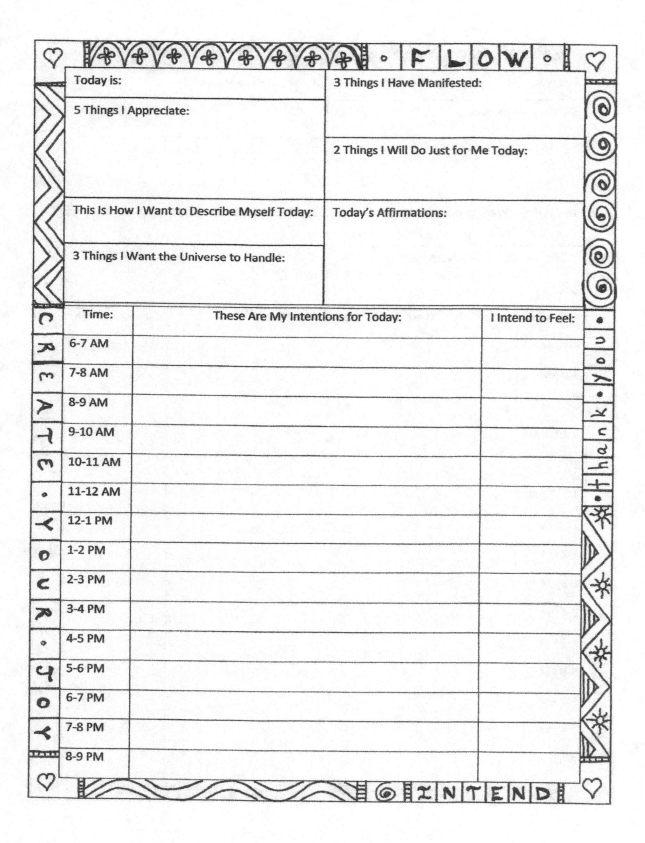

FLOW

Today is:

5 Things I Appreciate:

This Is How I Want to Describe Myself Today:

3 Things I Want the Universe to Handle:

3 Things I Have Manifested:

2 Things I Will Do Just for Me Today:

Today's Affirmations:

	Time:	These Are My Intentions for Today:	I Intend to Feel:
C	6-7 AM		
R	7-8 AM		
E	8-9 AM		
A	9-10 AM		
T	10-11 AM		
E	11-12 AM		
.	12-1 PM		
Y	1-2 PM		
O	2-3 PM		
U	3-4 PM		
R	4-5 PM		
.	5-6 PM		
J	6-7 PM		
O	7-8 PM		
Y	8-9 PM		

CREATE . YOUR . JOY

thank you

INTEND

242

FLOW

Today is:

5 Things I Appreciate:

This Is How I Want to Describe Myself Today:

3 Things I Want the Universe to Handle:

3 Things I Have Manifested:

2 Things I Will Do Just for Me Today:

Today's Affirmations:

Time:	These Are My Intentions for Today:	I Intend to Feel:
6-7 AM		
7-8 AM		
8-9 AM		
9-10 AM		
10-11 AM		
11-12 AM		
12-1 PM		
1-2 PM		
2-3 PM		
3-4 PM		
4-5 PM		
5-6 PM		
6-7 PM		
7-8 PM		
8-9 PM		

CREATE. YOUR. JOY

INTEND

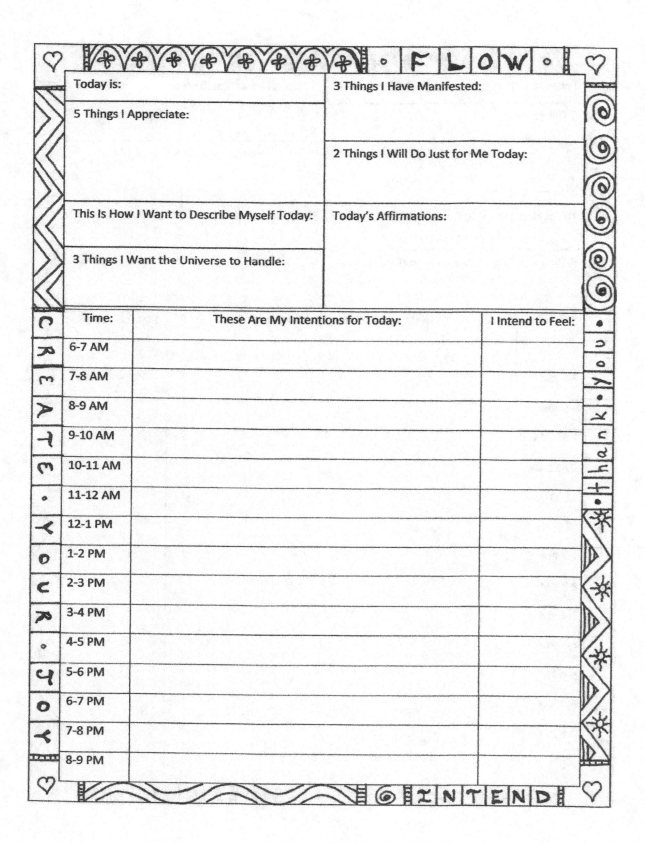

FLOW

Today is:	3 Things I Have Manifested:
5 Things I Appreciate:	
	2 Things I Will Do Just for Me Today:
This Is How I Want to Describe Myself Today:	Today's Affirmations:
3 Things I Want the Universe to Handle:	

Time:	These Are My Intentions for Today:	I Intend to Feel:
6-7 AM		
7-8 AM		
8-9 AM		
9-10 AM		
10-11 AM		
11-12 AM		
12-1 PM		
1-2 PM		
2-3 PM		
3-4 PM		
4-5 PM		
5-6 PM		
6-7 PM		
7-8 PM		
8-9 PM		

INTEND

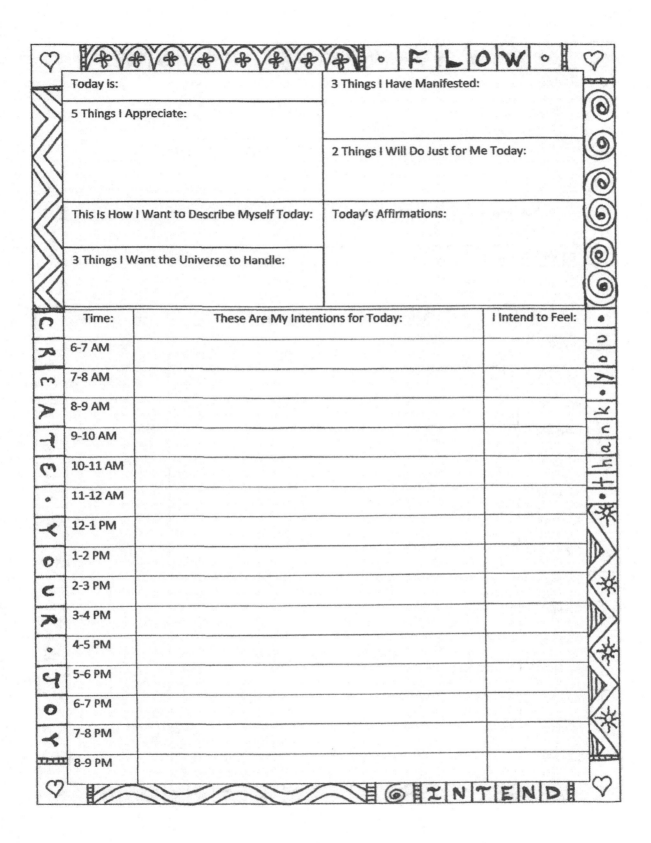

FLOW

Today is:	**3 Things I Have Manifested:**
5 Things I Appreciate:	
	2 Things I Will Do Just for Me Today:
This Is How I Want to Describe Myself Today:	**Today's Affirmations:**
3 Things I Want the Universe to Handle:	

Time:	These Are My Intentions for Today:	I Intend to Feel:
6-7 AM		
7-8 AM		
8-9 AM		
9-10 AM		
10-11 AM		
11-12 AM		
12-1 PM		
1-2 PM		
2-3 PM		
3-4 PM		
4-5 PM		
5-6 PM		
6-7 PM		
7-8 PM		
8-9 PM		

INTEND

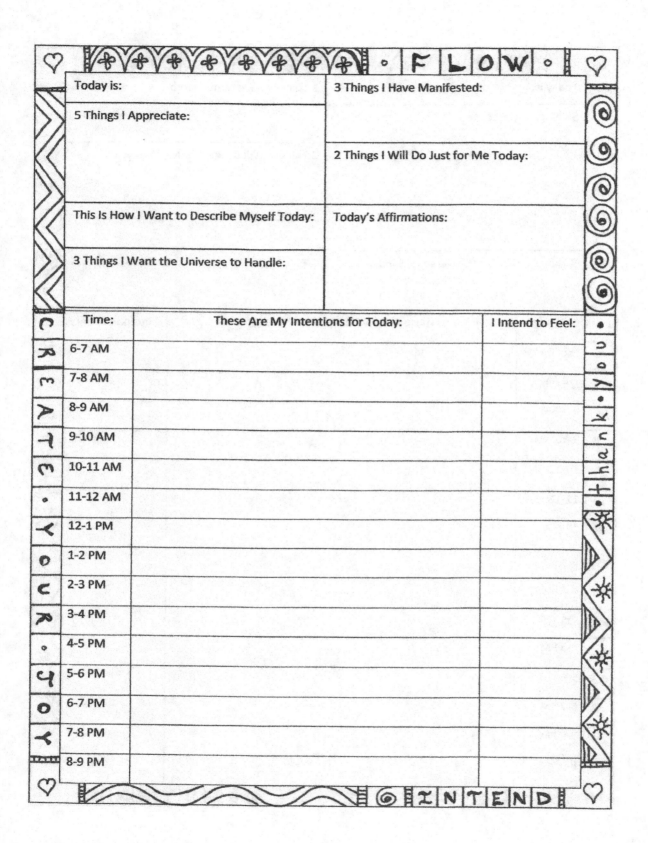

FLOW

Today is:	3 Things I Have Manifested:
5 Things I Appreciate:	
	2 Things I Will Do Just for Me Today:
This Is How I Want to Describe Myself Today:	Today's Affirmations:
3 Things I Want the Universe to Handle:	

	Time:	These Are My Intentions for Today:	I Intend to Feel:
C	6-7 AM		
R	7-8 AM		
E	8-9 AM		
A	9-10 AM		
T	10-11 AM		
E	11-12 AM		
.	12-1 PM		
Y	1-2 PM		
O	2-3 PM		
U	3-4 PM		
R	4-5 PM		
.	5-6 PM		
J	6-7 PM		
O	7-8 PM		
Y	8-9 PM		

INTEND

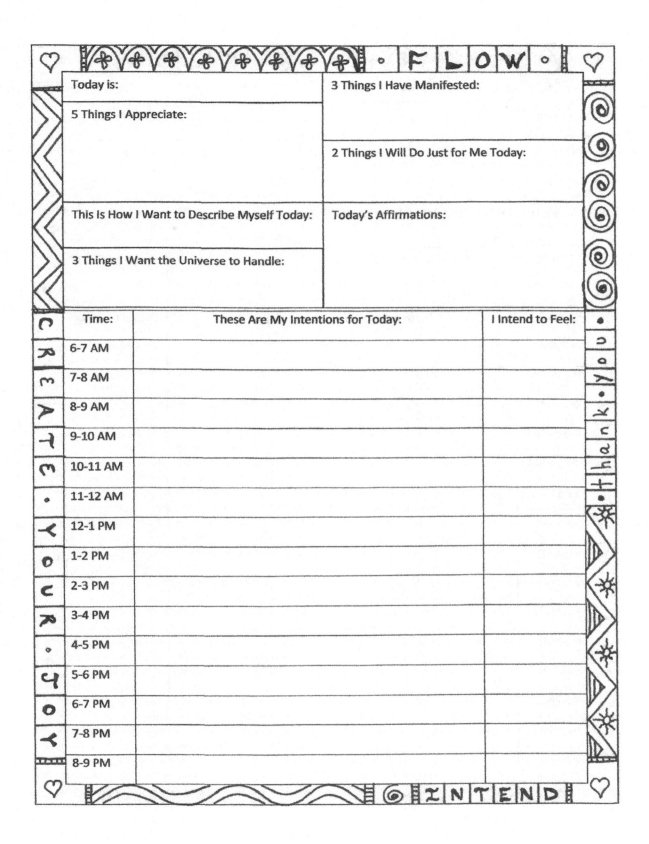

FLOW

Today is:	3 Things I Have Manifested:
5 Things I Appreciate:	
	2 Things I Will Do Just for Me Today:
This Is How I Want to Describe Myself Today:	Today's Affirmations:
3 Things I Want the Universe to Handle:	

Time:	These Are My Intentions for Today:	I Intend to Feel:
6-7 AM		
7-8 AM		
8-9 AM		
9-10 AM		
10-11 AM		
11-12 AM		
12-1 PM		
1-2 PM		
2-3 PM		
3-4 PM		
4-5 PM		
5-6 PM		
6-7 PM		
7-8 PM		
8-9 PM		

CREATE YOUR OWN JOY

thank you

INTEND

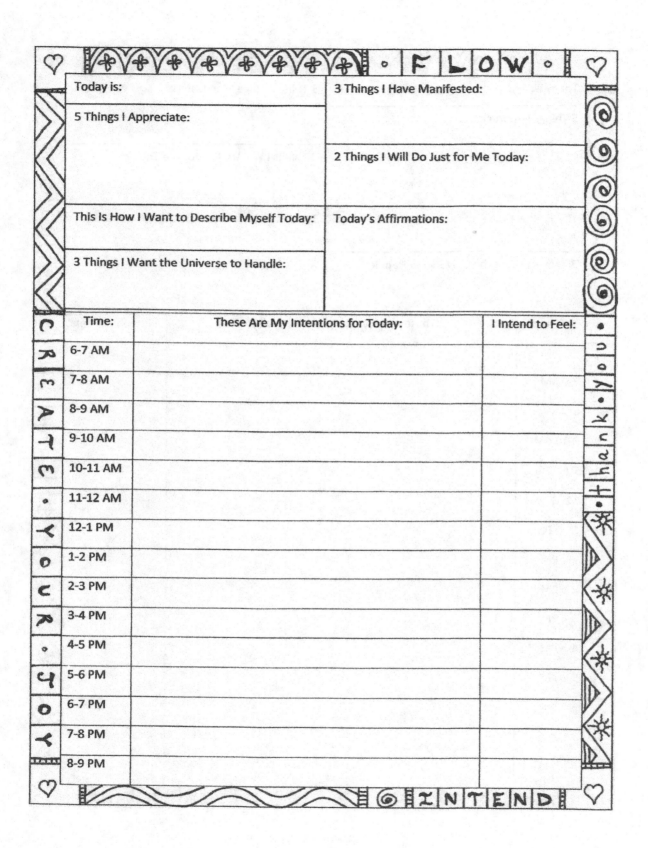

FLOW

Today is:	3 Things I Have Manifested:
5 Things I Appreciate:	
	2 Things I Will Do Just for Me Today:
This Is How I Want to Describe Myself Today:	Today's Affirmations:
3 Things I Want the Universe to Handle:	

CREATE · YOUR · JOY

you · thank

INTEND

Time:	These Are My Intentions for Today:	I Intend to Feel:
6-7 AM		
7-8 AM		
8-9 AM		
9-10 AM		
10-11 AM		
11-12 AM		
12-1 PM		
1-2 PM		
2-3 PM		
3-4 PM		
4-5 PM		
5-6 PM		
6-7 PM		
7-8 PM		
8-9 PM		

FLOW

Today is:	3 Things I Have Manifested:
5 Things I Appreciate:	
	2 Things I Will Do Just for Me Today:
This Is How I Want to Describe Myself Today:	Today's Affirmations:
3 Things I Want the Universe to Handle:	

CREATE · YOUR · JOY

Time:	These Are My Intentions for Today:	I Intend to Feel:
6-7 AM		
7-8 AM		
8-9 AM		
9-10 AM		
10-11 AM		
11-12 AM		
12-1 PM		
1-2 PM		
2-3 PM		
3-4 PM		
4-5 PM		
5-6 PM		
6-7 PM		
7-8 PM		
8-9 PM		

thank you

INTEND

249

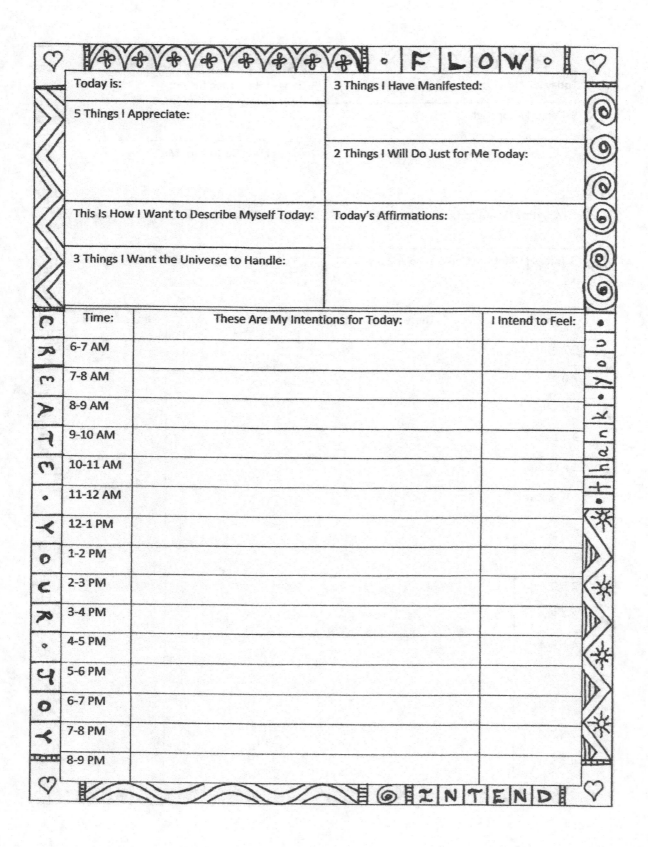

FLOW

Today is:	3 Things I Have Manifested:
5 Things I Appreciate:	
	2 Things I Will Do Just for Me Today:
This Is How I Want to Describe Myself Today:	Today's Affirmations:
3 Things I Want the Universe to Handle:	

Time:	These Are My Intentions for Today:	I Intend to Feel:
6-7 AM		
7-8 AM		
8-9 AM		
9-10 AM		
10-11 AM		
11-12 AM		
12-1 PM		
1-2 PM		
2-3 PM		
3-4 PM		
4-5 PM		
5-6 PM		
6-7 PM		
7-8 PM		
8-9 PM		

CREATE . YOUR . JOY

thank you .

INTEND

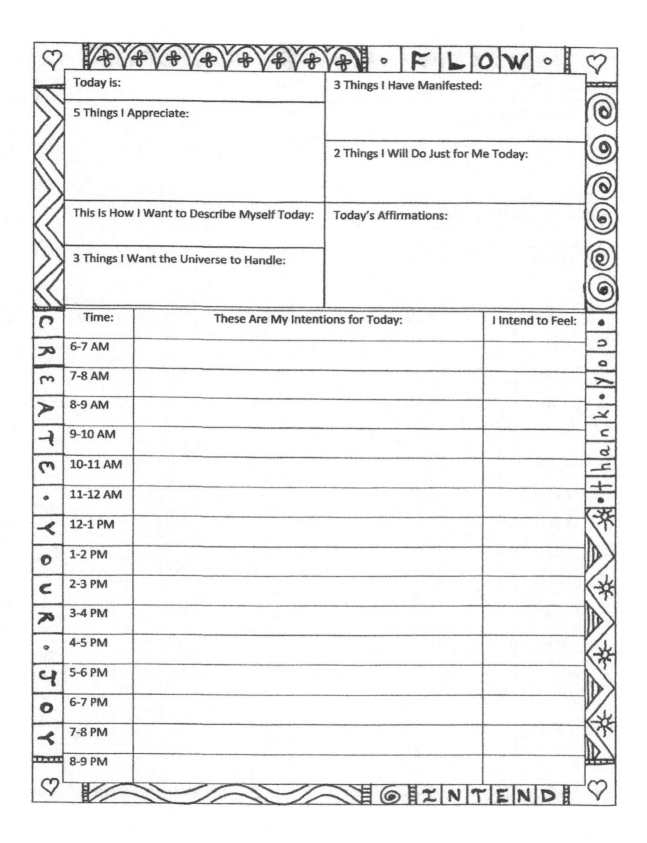

FLOW

Today is:

5 Things I Appreciate:

3 Things I Have Manifested:

2 Things I Will Do Just for Me Today:

This Is How I Want to Describe Myself Today:

Today's Affirmations:

3 Things I Want the Universe to Handle:

Time:	These Are My Intentions for Today:	I Intend to Feel:
6-7 AM		
7-8 AM		
8-9 AM		
9-10 AM		
10-11 AM		
11-12 AM		
12-1 PM		
1-2 PM		
2-3 PM		
3-4 PM		
4-5 PM		
5-6 PM		
6-7 PM		
7-8 PM		
8-9 PM		

CREATE. YOUR. JOY

thank you

INTEND

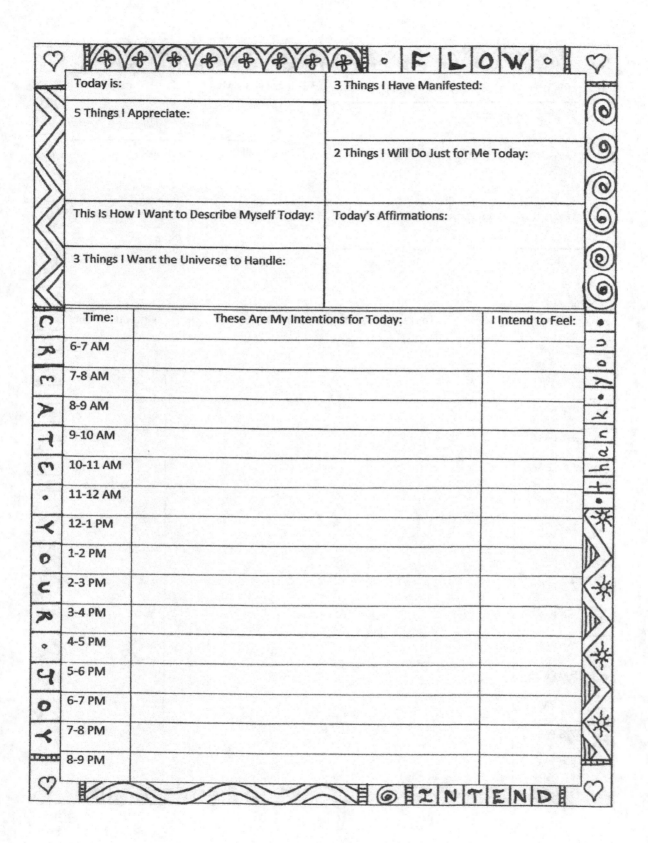

FLOW

Today is:	**3 Things I Have Manifested:**
5 Things I Appreciate:	
	2 Things I Will Do Just for Me Today:
This Is How I Want to Describe Myself Today:	**Today's Affirmations:**
3 Things I Want the Universe to Handle:	

CREATE . YOUR . JOY

thank you

Time:	These Are My Intentions for Today:	I Intend to Feel:
6-7 AM		
7-8 AM		
8-9 AM		
9-10 AM		
10-11 AM		
11-12 AM		
12-1 PM		
1-2 PM		
2-3 PM		
3-4 PM		
4-5 PM		
5-6 PM		
6-7 PM		
7-8 PM		
8-9 PM		

INTEND

Month: September

Sunday	Monday	Tuesday	Wednesday	Thursday	Friday	Saturday

Do at least one thing every day that brings you joy and record it on this page.

Affirmations:

"Doing what you love is the cornerstone of having abundance in your life." –Wayne Dyer

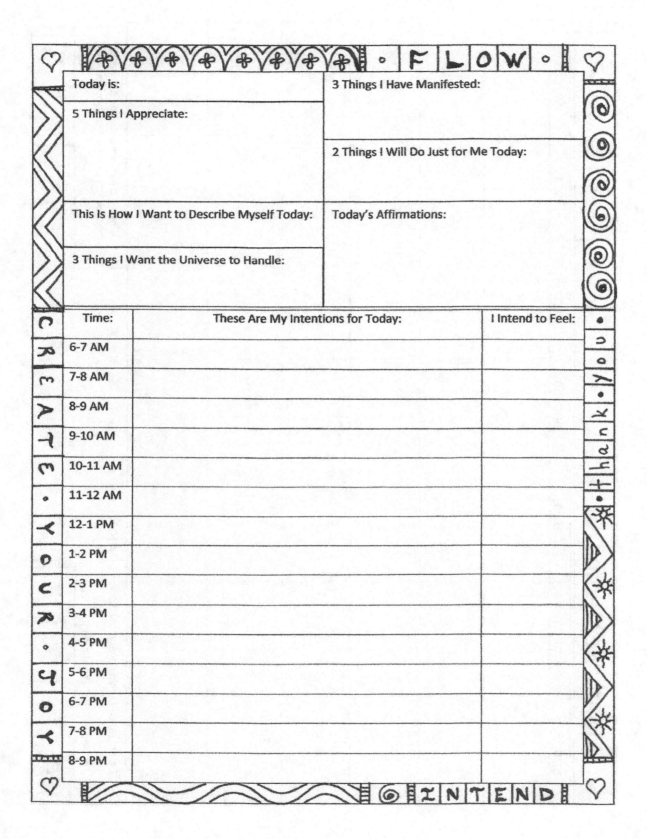

FLOW

Today is:	3 Things I Have Manifested:
5 Things I Appreciate:	
	2 Things I Will Do Just for Me Today:
This Is How I Want to Describe Myself Today:	Today's Affirmations:
3 Things I Want the Universe to Handle:	

Time:	These Are My Intentions for Today:	I Intend to Feel:
6-7 AM		
7-8 AM		
8-9 AM		
9-10 AM		
10-11 AM		
11-12 AM		
12-1 PM		
1-2 PM		
2-3 PM		
3-4 PM		
4-5 PM		
5-6 PM		
6-7 PM		
7-8 PM		
8-9 PM		

INTEND

· F L O W ·

Today is:	3 Things I Have Manifested:
5 Things I Appreciate:	
	2 Things I Will Do Just for Me Today:
This Is How I Want to Describe Myself Today:	Today's Affirmations:
3 Things I Want the Universe to Handle:	

Time:	These Are My Intentions for Today:	I Intend to Feel:
6-7 AM		
7-8 AM		
8-9 AM		
9-10 AM		
10-11 AM		
11-12 AM		
12-1 PM		
1-2 PM		
2-3 PM		
3-4 PM		
4-5 PM		
5-6 PM		
6-7 PM		
7-8 PM		
8-9 PM		

CREATE · YOUR · JOY

thank you

· INTEND ·

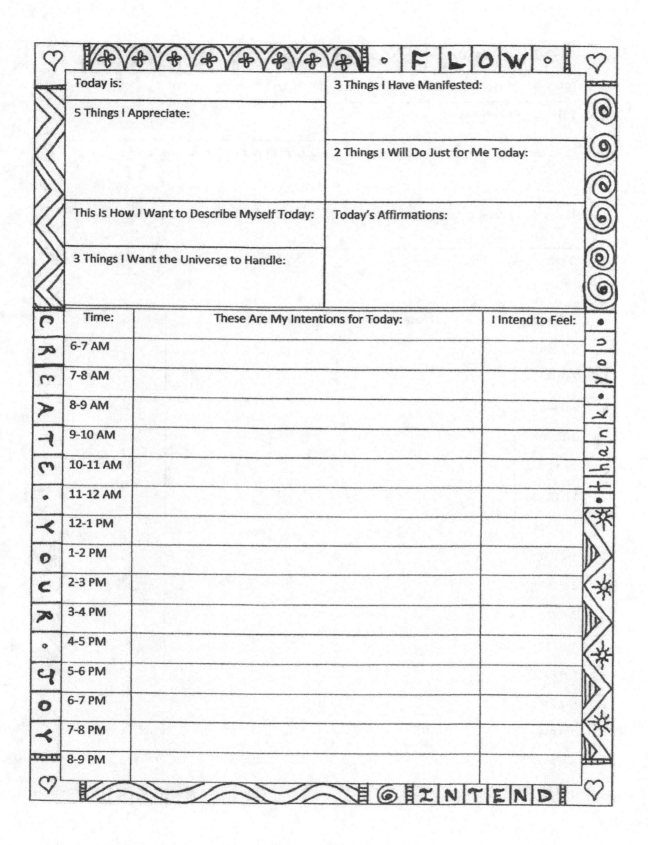

FLOW

Today is:

5 Things I Appreciate:

This Is How I Want to Describe Myself Today:

3 Things I Want the Universe to Handle:

3 Things I Have Manifested:

2 Things I Will Do Just for Me Today:

Today's Affirmations:

Time:	These Are My Intentions for Today:	I Intend to Feel:
6-7 AM		
7-8 AM		
8-9 AM		
9-10 AM		
10-11 AM		
11-12 AM		
12-1 PM		
1-2 PM		
2-3 PM		
3-4 PM		
4-5 PM		
5-6 PM		
6-7 PM		
7-8 PM		
8-9 PM		

CREATE . YOUR . JOY

thank you

INTEND

FLOW

Today is:	3 Things I Have Manifested:
5 Things I Appreciate:	
	2 Things I Will Do Just for Me Today:
This Is How I Want to Describe Myself Today:	Today's Affirmations:
3 Things I Want the Universe to Handle:	

CREATE . YOUR . JOY

Time:	These Are My Intentions for Today:	I Intend to Feel:
6-7 AM		
7-8 AM		
8-9 AM		
9-10 AM		
10-11 AM		
11-12 AM		
12-1 PM		
1-2 PM		
2-3 PM		
3-4 PM		
4-5 PM		
5-6 PM		
6-7 PM		
7-8 PM		
8-9 PM		

thank you

INTEND

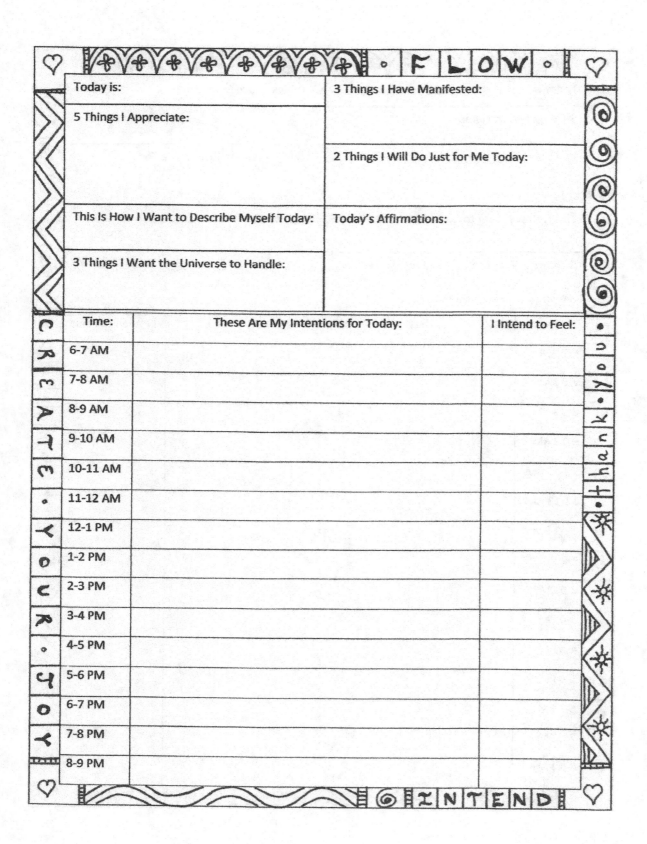

FLOW

Today is:	3 Things I Have Manifested:
5 Things I Appreciate:	
	2 Things I Will Do Just for Me Today:
This Is How I Want to Describe Myself Today:	Today's Affirmations:
3 Things I Want the Universe to Handle:	

CREATE . YOUR . JOY

Time:	These Are My Intentions for Today:	I Intend to Feel:
6-7 AM		
7-8 AM		
8-9 AM		
9-10 AM		
10-11 AM		
11-12 AM		
12-1 PM		
1-2 PM		
2-3 PM		
3-4 PM		
4-5 PM		
5-6 PM		
6-7 PM		
7-8 PM		
8-9 PM		

INTEND

FLOW

Today is:	3 Things I Have Manifested:
5 Things I Appreciate:	
	2 Things I Will Do Just for Me Today:
This Is How I Want to Describe Myself Today:	**Today's Affirmations:**
3 Things I Want the Universe to Handle:	

	Time:	These Are My Intentions for Today:	I Intend to Feel:
C	6-7 AM		
R	7-8 AM		
E	8-9 AM		
A	9-10 AM		
T	10-11 AM		
E	11-12 AM		
	12-1 PM		
Y	1-2 PM		
O	2-3 PM		
U	3-4 PM		
R	4-5 PM		
	5-6 PM		
J	6-7 PM		
O	7-8 PM		
Y	8-9 PM		

CREATE . YOUR . JOY

thank you

INTEND

259

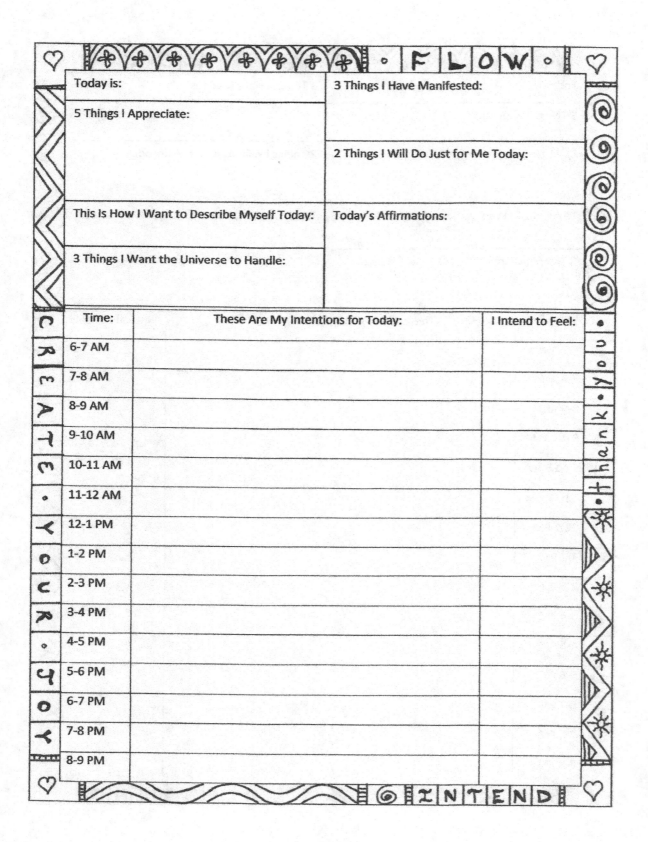

FLOW

Today is:		3 Things I Have Manifested:
5 Things I Appreciate:		
		2 Things I Will Do Just for Me Today:
This Is How I Want to Describe Myself Today:		Today's Affirmations:
3 Things I Want the Universe to Handle:		

CREATE . YOUR . JOY

thank you . thank you

Time:	These Are My Intentions for Today:	I Intend to Feel:
6-7 AM		
7-8 AM		
8-9 AM		
9-10 AM		
10-11 AM		
11-12 AM		
12-1 PM		
1-2 PM		
2-3 PM		
3-4 PM		
4-5 PM		
5-6 PM		
6-7 PM		
7-8 PM		
8-9 PM		

INTEND

FLOW

Today is:

5 Things I Appreciate:

3 Things I Have Manifested:

2 Things I Will Do Just for Me Today:

This Is How I Want to Describe Myself Today:

Today's Affirmations:

3 Things I Want the Universe to Handle:

Time:	These Are My Intentions for Today:	I Intend to Feel:
6-7 AM		
7-8 AM		
8-9 AM		
9-10 AM		
10-11 AM		
11-12 AM		
12-1 PM		
1-2 PM		
2-3 PM		
3-4 PM		
4-5 PM		
5-6 PM		
6-7 PM		
7-8 PM		
8-9 PM		

CREATE • YOUR • JOY

thank you •

INTEND

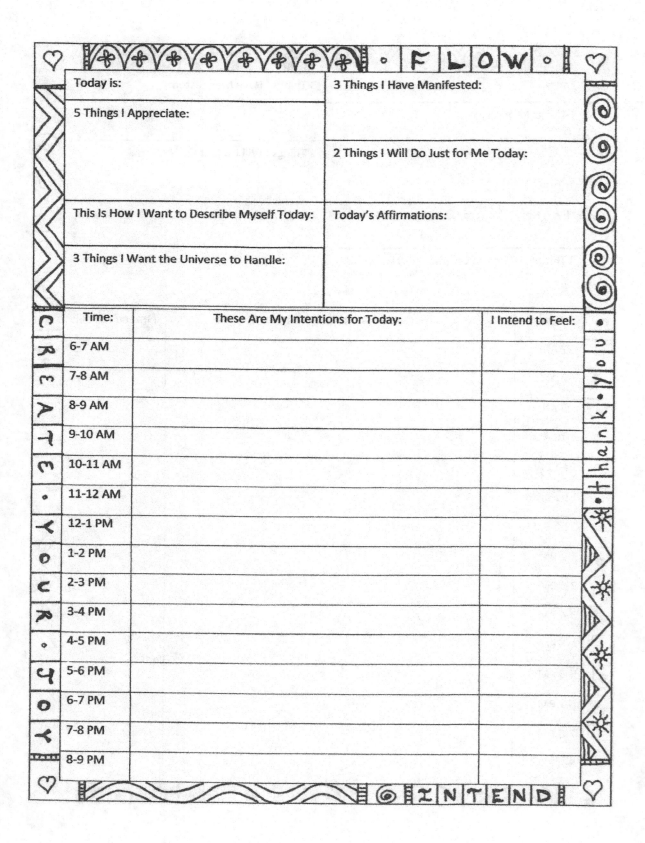

FLOW

Today is:	3 Things I Have Manifested:
5 Things I Appreciate:	
	2 Things I Will Do Just for Me Today:
This Is How I Want to Describe Myself Today:	Today's Affirmations:
3 Things I Want the Universe to Handle:	

	Time:	These Are My Intentions for Today:	I Intend to Feel:
C	6-7 AM		
R	7-8 AM		
E	8-9 AM		
A	9-10 AM		
T	10-11 AM		
E	11-12 AM		
.	12-1 PM		
Y	1-2 PM		
O	2-3 PM		
U	3-4 PM		
R	4-5 PM		
.	5-6 PM		
J	6-7 PM		
O	7-8 PM		
Y	8-9 PM		

INTEND

FLOW

Today is:	3 Things I Have Manifested:
5 Things I Appreciate:	
	2 Things I Will Do Just for Me Today:
This Is How I Want to Describe Myself Today:	Today's Affirmations:
3 Things I Want the Universe to Handle:	

CREATE YOUR OWN JOY

Time:	These Are My Intentions for Today:	I Intend to Feel:
6-7 AM		
7-8 AM		
8-9 AM		
9-10 AM		
10-11 AM		
11-12 AM		
12-1 PM		
1-2 PM		
2-3 PM		
3-4 PM		
4-5 PM		
5-6 PM		
6-7 PM		
7-8 PM		
8-9 PM		

I INTEND

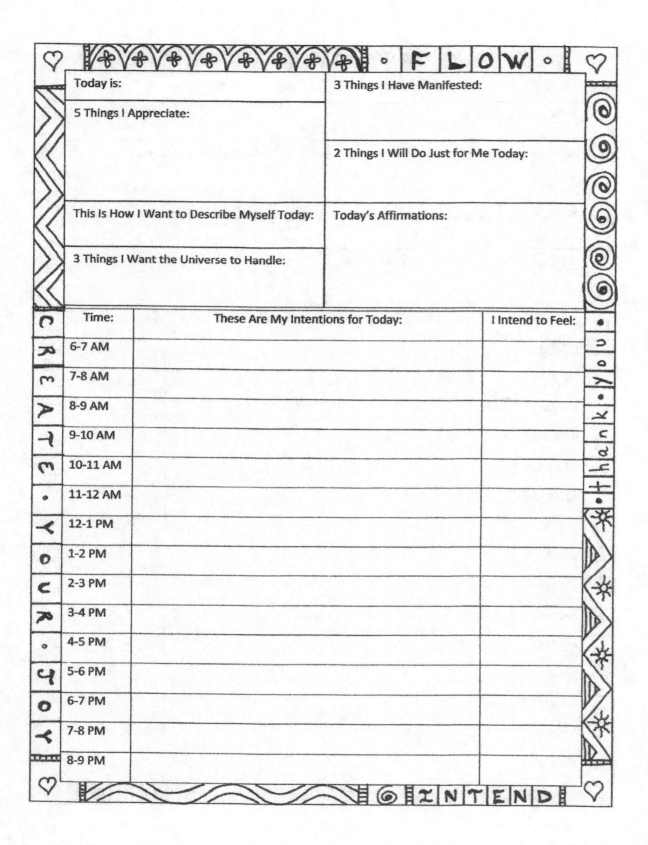

FLOW

Today is:	3 Things I Have Manifested:
5 Things I Appreciate:	
	2 Things I Will Do Just for Me Today:
This Is How I Want to Describe Myself Today:	Today's Affirmations:
3 Things I Want the Universe to Handle:	

CREATE • YOUR • JOY

thank you

Time:	These Are My Intentions for Today:	I Intend to Feel:
6-7 AM		
7-8 AM		
8-9 AM		
9-10 AM		
10-11 AM		
11-12 AM		
12-1 PM		
1-2 PM		
2-3 PM		
3-4 PM		
4-5 PM		
5-6 PM		
6-7 PM		
7-8 PM		
8-9 PM		

INTEND

264

FLOW

Today is:

5 Things I Appreciate:

This Is How I Want to Describe Myself Today:

3 Things I Want the Universe to Handle:

3 Things I Have Manifested:

2 Things I Will Do Just for Me Today:

Today's Affirmations:

Time:	These Are My Intentions for Today:	I Intend to Feel:
6-7 AM		
7-8 AM		
8-9 AM		
9-10 AM		
10-11 AM		
11-12 AM		
12-1 PM		
1-2 PM		
2-3 PM		
3-4 PM		
4-5 PM		
5-6 PM		
6-7 PM		
7-8 PM		
8-9 PM		

CREATE . YOUR . JOY

thank you

INTEND

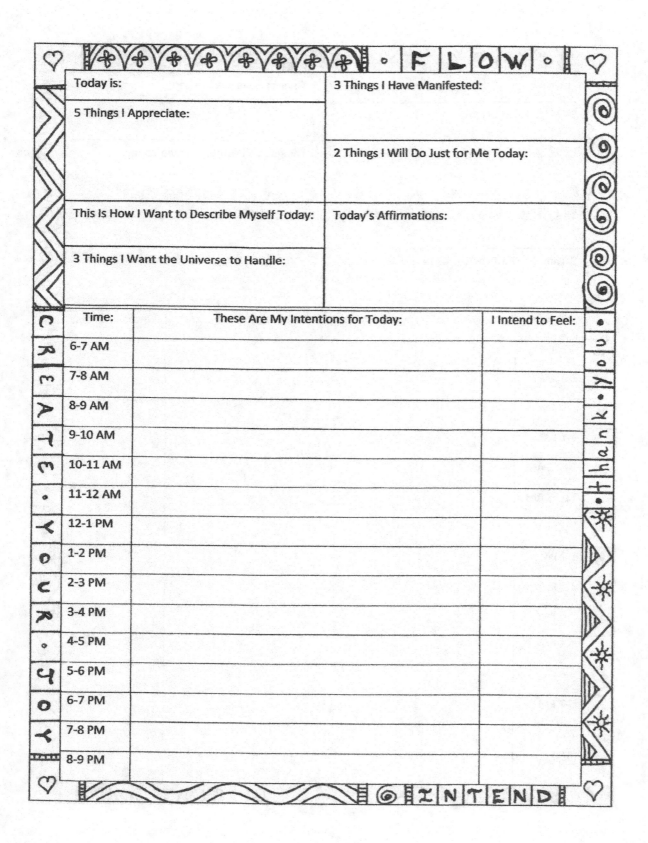

FLOW

Today is:		3 Things I Have Manifested:
5 Things I Appreciate:		
		2 Things I Will Do Just for Me Today:
This Is How I Want to Describe Myself Today:		**Today's Affirmations:**
3 Things I Want the Universe to Handle:		

Time:	These Are My Intentions for Today:	I Intend to Feel:
6-7 AM		
7-8 AM		
8-9 AM		
9-10 AM		
10-11 AM		
11-12 AM		
12-1 PM		
1-2 PM		
2-3 PM		
3-4 PM		
4-5 PM		
5-6 PM		
6-7 PM		
7-8 PM		
8-9 PM		

CREATE · YOUR · JOY

thank you

INTEND

FLOW

Today is:	3 Things I Have Manifested:
5 Things I Appreciate:	
	2 Things I Will Do Just for Me Today:
This Is How I Want to Describe Myself Today:	Today's Affirmations:
3 Things I Want the Universe to Handle:	

CREATE . YOUR . CREATE . JOY

Time:	These Are My Intentions for Today:	I Intend to Feel:
6-7 AM		
7-8 AM		
8-9 AM		
9-10 AM		
10-11 AM		
11-12 AM		
12-1 PM		
1-2 PM		
2-3 PM		
3-4 PM		
4-5 PM		
5-6 PM		
6-7 PM		
7-8 PM		
8-9 PM		

thank you

INTEND

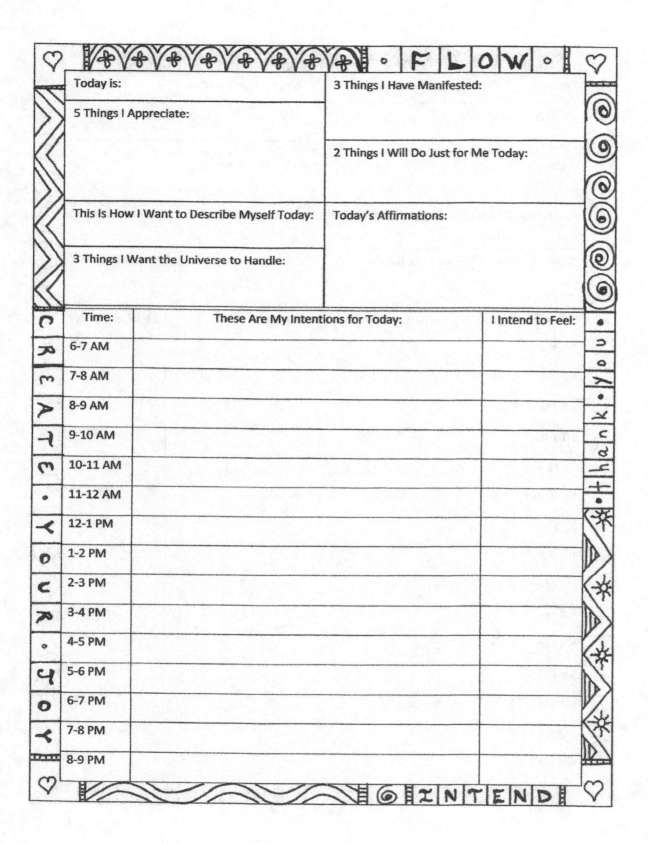

FLOW

Today is:	3 Things I Have Manifested:
5 Things I Appreciate:	
	2 Things I Will Do Just for Me Today:
This Is How I Want to Describe Myself Today:	**Today's Affirmations:**
3 Things I Want the Universe to Handle:	

CREATE · YOUR · JOY

Time:	These Are My Intentions for Today:	I Intend to Feel:
6-7 AM		
7-8 AM		
8-9 AM		
9-10 AM		
10-11 AM		
11-12 AM		
12-1 PM		
1-2 PM		
2-3 PM		
3-4 PM		
4-5 PM		
5-6 PM		
6-7 PM		
7-8 PM		
8-9 PM		

thank you

INTEND

FLOW

Today is:	3 Things I Have Manifested:
5 Things I Appreciate:	
	2 Things I Will Do Just for Me Today:
This Is How I Want to Describe Myself Today:	Today's Affirmations:
3 Things I Want the Universe to Handle:	

Time:	These Are My Intentions for Today:	I Intend to Feel:
6-7 AM		
7-8 AM		
8-9 AM		
9-10 AM		
10-11 AM		
11-12 AM		
12-1 PM		
1-2 PM		
2-3 PM		
3-4 PM		
4-5 PM		
5-6 PM		
6-7 PM		
7-8 PM		
8-9 PM		

CREATE • YOUR • JOY

thank • you

INTEND

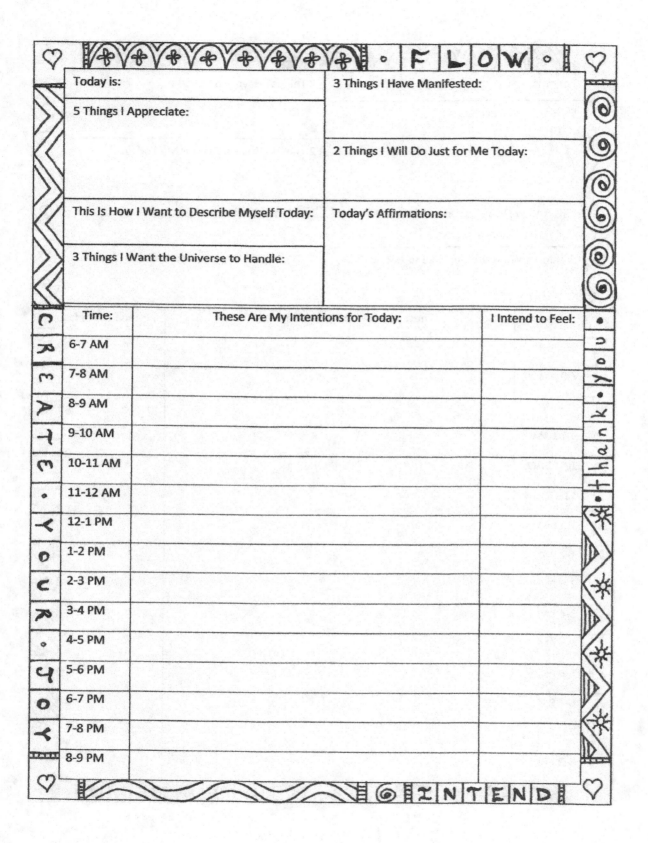

FLOW

Today is:	3 Things I Have Manifested:
5 Things I Appreciate:	
	2 Things I Will Do Just for Me Today:
This Is How I Want to Describe Myself Today:	Today's Affirmations:
3 Things I Want the Universe to Handle:	

Time:	These Are My Intentions for Today:	I Intend to Feel:
6-7 AM		
7-8 AM		
8-9 AM		
9-10 AM		
10-11 AM		
11-12 AM		
12-1 PM		
1-2 PM		
2-3 PM		
3-4 PM		
4-5 PM		
5-6 PM		
6-7 PM		
7-8 PM		
8-9 PM		

CREATE . YOUR . JOY

thank you

INTEND

FLOW

Today is:	3 Things I Have Manifested:
5 Things I Appreciate:	
	2 Things I Will Do Just for Me Today:
This Is How I Want to Describe Myself Today:	**Today's Affirmations:**
3 Things I Want the Universe to Handle:	

Time:	These Are My Intentions for Today:	I Intend to Feel:
6-7 AM		
7-8 AM		
8-9 AM		
9-10 AM		
10-11 AM		
11-12 AM		
12-1 PM		
1-2 PM		
2-3 PM		
3-4 PM		
4-5 PM		
5-6 PM		
6-7 PM		
7-8 PM		
8-9 PM		

CREATE . YOUR . JOY

thank you .

INTEND

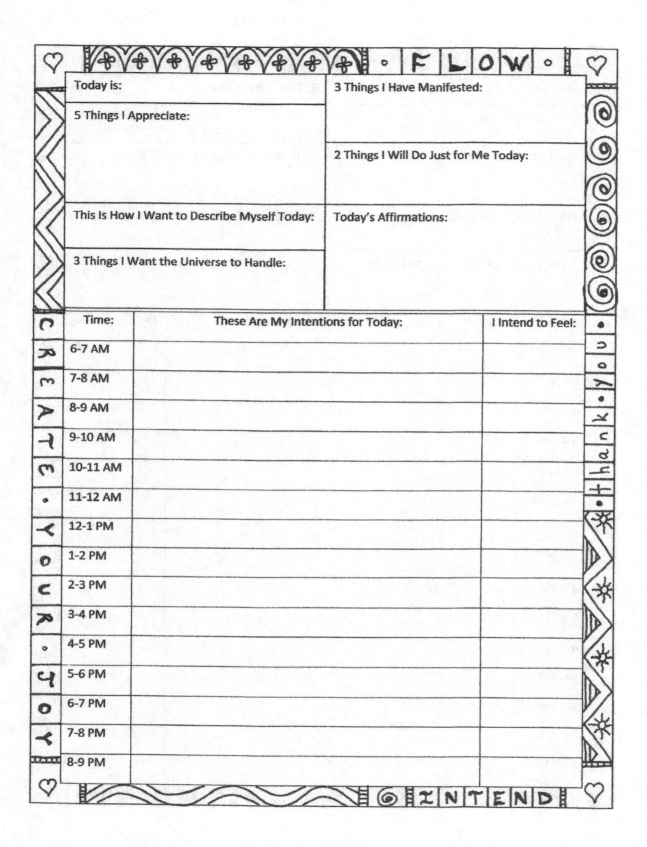

FLOW

Today is:		3 Things I Have Manifested:
5 Things I Appreciate:		
		2 Things I Will Do Just for Me Today:
This Is How I Want to Describe Myself Today:		**Today's Affirmations:**
3 Things I Want the Universe to Handle:		

	Time:	These Are My Intentions for Today:	I Intend to Feel:
C	6-7 AM		
R	7-8 AM		
E	8-9 AM		
A	9-10 AM		
T	10-11 AM		
E	11-12 AM		
.	12-1 PM		
Y	1-2 PM		
O	2-3 PM		
U	3-4 PM		
R	4-5 PM		
.	5-6 PM		
J	6-7 PM		
O	7-8 PM		
Y	8-9 PM		

INTEND

FLOW

Today is:	**3 Things I Have Manifested:**
5 Things I Appreciate:	
	2 Things I Will Do Just for Me Today:
This Is How I Want to Describe Myself Today:	**Today's Affirmations:**
3 Things I Want the Universe to Handle:	

Time:	These Are My Intentions for Today:	I Intend to Feel:
6-7 AM		
7-8 AM		
8-9 AM		
9-10 AM		
10-11 AM		
11-12 AM		
12-1 PM		
1-2 PM		
2-3 PM		
3-4 PM		
4-5 PM		
5-6 PM		
6-7 PM		
7-8 PM		
8-9 PM		

CREATE YOUR JOY

thank you

INTEND

273

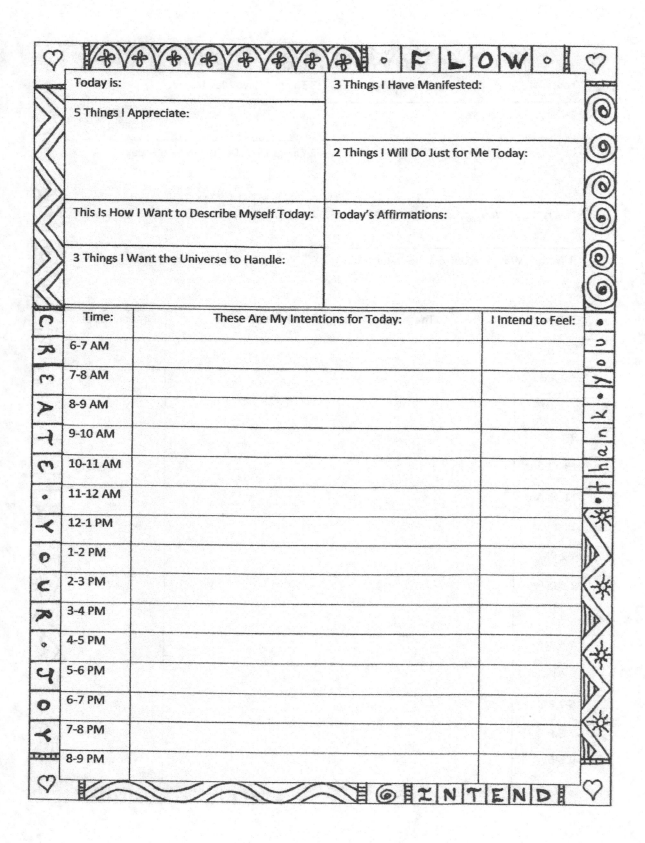

FLOW

Today is:	3 Things I Have Manifested:
5 Things I Appreciate:	
	2 Things I Will Do Just for Me Today:
This Is How I Want to Describe Myself Today:	Today's Affirmations:
3 Things I Want the Universe to Handle:	

Time:	These Are My Intentions for Today:	I Intend to Feel:
6-7 AM		
7-8 AM		
8-9 AM		
9-10 AM		
10-11 AM		
11-12 AM		
12-1 PM		
1-2 PM		
2-3 PM		
3-4 PM		
4-5 PM		
5-6 PM		
6-7 PM		
7-8 PM		
8-9 PM		

CREATE . YOUR . JOY

thank you

INTEND

FLOW

Today is:	3 Things I Have Manifested:
5 Things I Appreciate:	
	2 Things I Will Do Just for Me Today:
This Is How I Want to Describe Myself Today:	Today's Affirmations:
3 Things I Want the Universe to Handle:	

Time:	These Are My Intentions for Today:	I Intend to Feel:
6-7 AM		
7-8 AM		
8-9 AM		
9-10 AM		
10-11 AM		
11-12 AM		
12-1 PM		
1-2 PM		
2-3 PM		
3-4 PM		
4-5 PM		
5-6 PM		
6-7 PM		
7-8 PM		
8-9 PM		

CREATE YOUR JOY

thank you

INTEND

FLOW

Today is:	3 Things I Have Manifested:
5 Things I Appreciate:	
	2 Things I Will Do Just for Me Today:
This Is How I Want to Describe Myself Today:	**Today's Affirmations:**
3 Things I Want the Universe to Handle:	

Time:	These Are My Intentions for Today:	I Intend to Feel:
6-7 AM		
7-8 AM		
8-9 AM		
9-10 AM		
10-11 AM		
11-12 AM		
12-1 PM		
1-2 PM		
2-3 PM		
3-4 PM		
4-5 PM		
5-6 PM		
6-7 PM		
7-8 PM		
8-9 PM		

CREATE . YOUR . JOY

thank you .

INTEND

FLOW

Today is:	3 Things I Have Manifested:
5 Things I Appreciate:	
	2 Things I Will Do Just for Me Today:
This Is How I Want to Describe Myself Today:	Today's Affirmations:
3 Things I Want the Universe to Handle:	

CREATE. YOUR. JOY

Time:	These Are My Intentions for Today:	I Intend to Feel:
6-7 AM		
7-8 AM		
8-9 AM		
9-10 AM		
10-11 AM		
11-12 AM		
12-1 PM		
1-2 PM		
2-3 PM		
3-4 PM		
4-5 PM		
5-6 PM		
6-7 PM		
7-8 PM		
8-9 PM		

thank you

INTEND

277

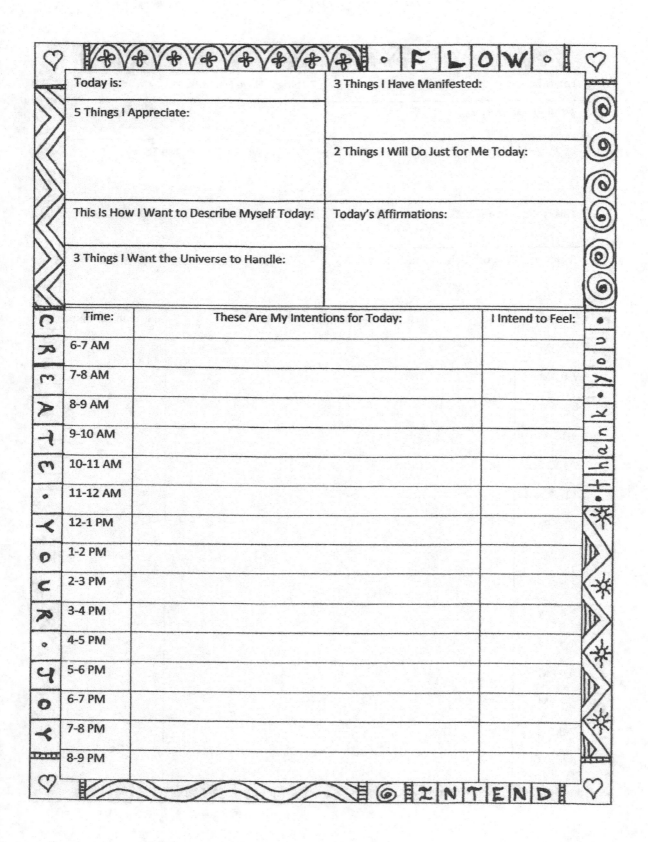

FLOW

Today is:	3 Things I Have Manifested:
5 Things I Appreciate:	
	2 Things I Will Do Just for Me Today:
This Is How I Want to Describe Myself Today:	Today's Affirmations:
3 Things I Want the Universe to Handle:	

CREATE . YOUR . JOY

Time:	These Are My Intentions for Today:	I Intend to Feel:
6-7 AM		
7-8 AM		
8-9 AM		
9-10 AM		
10-11 AM		
11-12 AM		
12-1 PM		
1-2 PM		
2-3 PM		
3-4 PM		
4-5 PM		
5-6 PM		
6-7 PM		
7-8 PM		
8-9 PM		

thank . you

INTEND

• F L O W •

Today is:	3 Things I Have Manifested:
5 Things I Appreciate:	
	2 Things I Will Do Just for Me Today:
This Is How I Want to Describe Myself Today:	**Today's Affirmations:**
3 Things I Want the Universe to Handle:	

Time:	These Are My Intentions for Today:	I Intend to Feel:
6-7 AM		
7-8 AM		
8-9 AM		
9-10 AM		
10-11 AM		
11-12 AM		
12-1 PM		
1-2 PM		
2-3 PM		
3-4 PM		
4-5 PM		
5-6 PM		
6-7 PM		
7-8 PM		
8-9 PM		

CREATE • YOUR • JOY

thank you •

INTEND

279

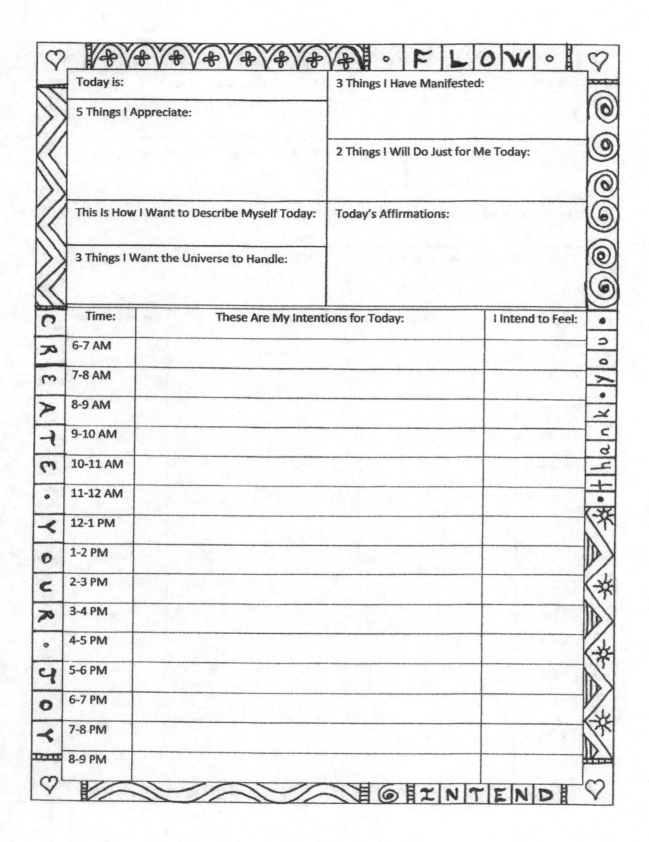

FLOW

Today is:	3 Things I Have Manifested:
5 Things I Appreciate:	
	2 Things I Will Do Just for Me Today:
This Is How I Want to Describe Myself Today:	Today's Affirmations:
3 Things I Want the Universe to Handle:	

Time:	These Are My Intentions for Today:	I Intend to Feel:
6-7 AM		
7-8 AM		
8-9 AM		
9-10 AM		
10-11 AM		
11-12 AM		
12-1 PM		
1-2 PM		
2-3 PM		
3-4 PM		
4-5 PM		
5-6 PM		
6-7 PM		
7-8 PM		
8-9 PM		

CREATE . YOUR . JOY

INTEND

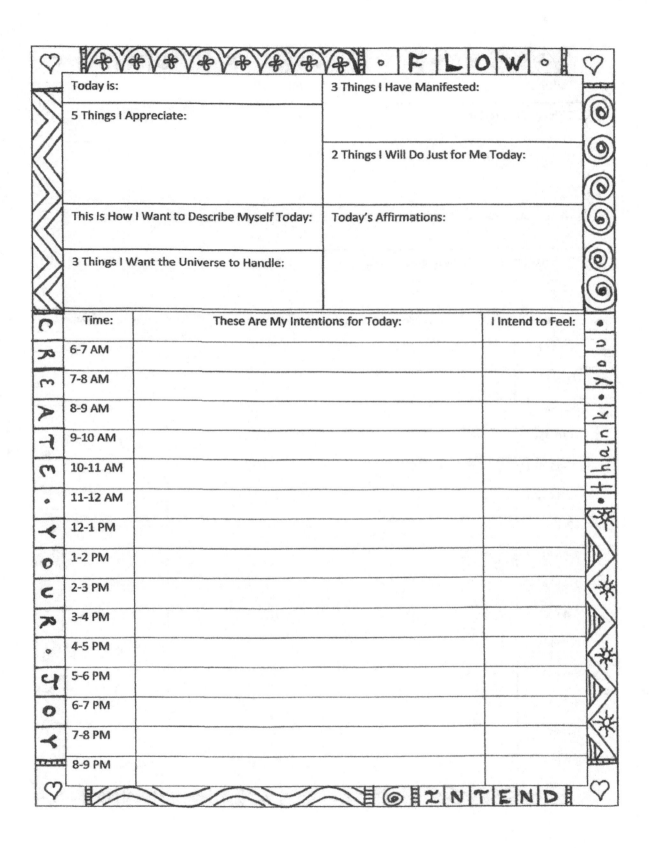

FLOW

Today is:		3 Things I Have Manifested:
5 Things I Appreciate:		
		2 Things I Will Do Just for Me Today:
This Is How I Want to Describe Myself Today:		Today's Affirmations:
3 Things I Want the Universe to Handle:		

	Time:	These Are My Intentions for Today:	I Intend to Feel:
C	6-7 AM		
R	7-8 AM		
E	8-9 AM		
A	9-10 AM		
T	10-11 AM		
E	11-12 AM		
.	12-1 PM		
Y	1-2 PM		
O	2-3 PM		
U	3-4 PM		
R	4-5 PM		
.	5-6 PM		
J	6-7 PM		
O	7-8 PM		
Y	8-9 PM		

INTEND

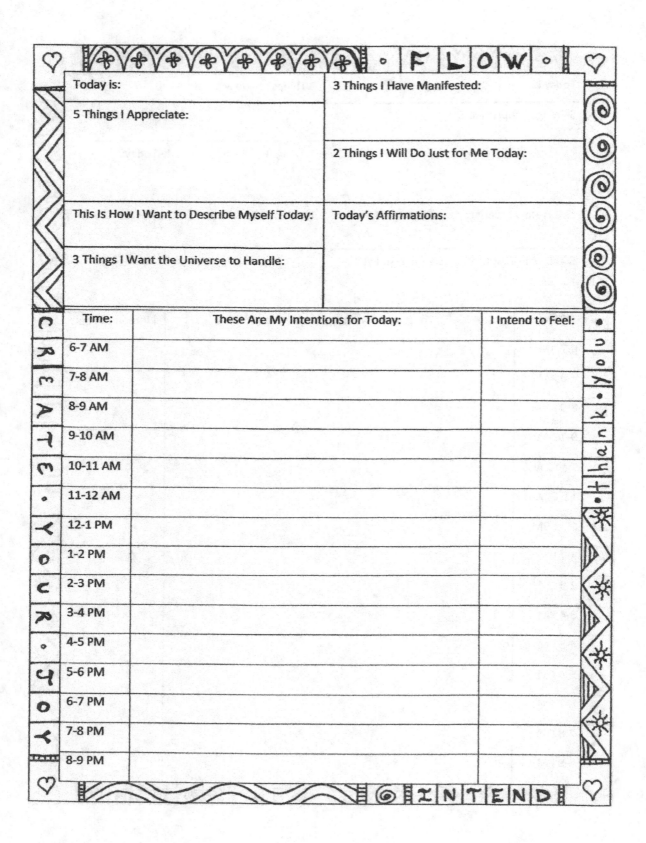

FLOW

Today is:

3 Things I Have Manifested:

5 Things I Appreciate:

2 Things I Will Do Just for Me Today:

This Is How I Want to Describe Myself Today:

Today's Affirmations:

3 Things I Want the Universe to Handle:

CREATE. YOUR. JOY

thank you. u o y

Time:	These Are My Intentions for Today:	I Intend to Feel:
6-7 AM		
7-8 AM		
8-9 AM		
9-10 AM		
10-11 AM		
11-12 AM		
12-1 PM		
1-2 PM		
2-3 PM		
3-4 PM		
4-5 PM		
5-6 PM		
6-7 PM		
7-8 PM		
8-9 PM		

INTEND

· F L O W ·

Today is:

5 Things I Appreciate:

3 Things I Have Manifested:

2 Things I Will Do Just for Me Today:

This Is How I Want to Describe Myself Today:

Today's Affirmations:

3 Things I Want the Universe to Handle:

Time:	These Are My Intentions for Today:	I Intend to Feel:
6-7 AM		
7-8 AM		
8-9 AM		
9-10 AM		
10-11 AM		
11-12 AM		
12-1 PM		
1-2 PM		
2-3 PM		
3-4 PM		
4-5 PM		
5-6 PM		
6-7 PM		
7-8 PM		
8-9 PM		

CREATE · YOUR · JOY

thank you ·

INTEND

Month: October

Sunday	Monday	Tuesday	Wednesday	Thursday	Friday	Saturday

Affirmations:

We live in an unlimited universe!

Do at least one thing every day that brings you joy and record it on this page.

FLOW

Today is:	3 Things I Have Manifested:
5 Things I Appreciate:	
	2 Things I Will Do Just for Me Today:
This Is How I Want to Describe Myself Today:	**Today's Affirmations:**
3 Things I Want the Universe to Handle:	

Time:	These Are My Intentions for Today:	I Intend to Feel:
6-7 AM		
7-8 AM		
8-9 AM		
9-10 AM		
10-11 AM		
11-12 AM		
12-1 PM		
1-2 PM		
2-3 PM		
3-4 PM		
4-5 PM		
5-6 PM		
6-7 PM		
7-8 PM		
8-9 PM		

CREATE . YOUR . JOY

thank you

INTEND

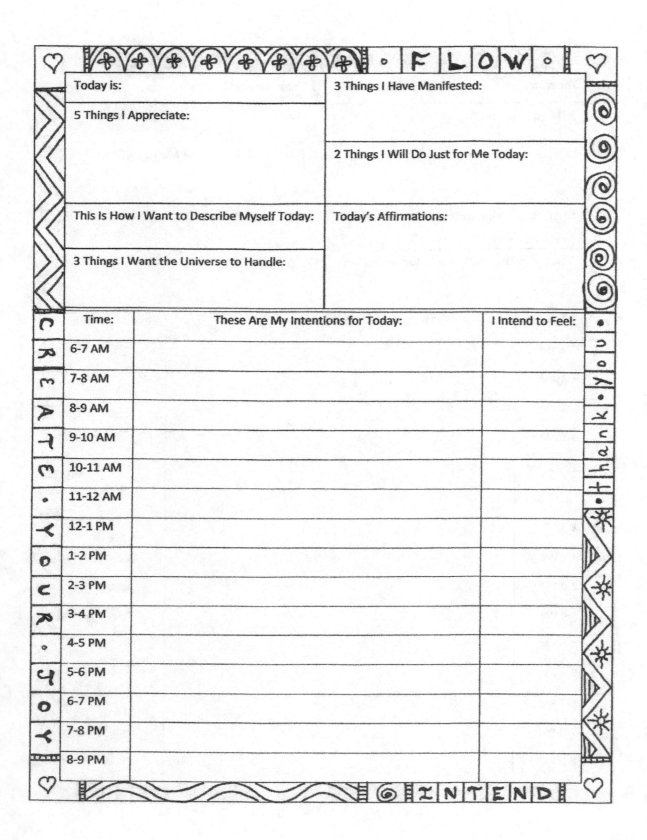

FLOW

Today is:	3 Things I Have Manifested:
5 Things I Appreciate:	
	2 Things I Will Do Just for Me Today:
This Is How I Want to Describe Myself Today:	Today's Affirmations:
3 Things I Want the Universe to Handle:	

	Time:	These Are My Intentions for Today:	I Intend to Feel:	
C	6-7 AM			•
R	7-8 AM			y
E	8-9 AM			o
A	9-10 AM			u
T	10-11 AM			•
E	11-12 AM			k
•	12-1 PM			n
Y	1-2 PM			a
O	2-3 PM			h
U	3-4 PM			t
R	4-5 PM			•
•	5-6 PM			
J	6-7 PM			
O	7-8 PM			
Y	8-9 PM			

INTEND

286

∘ F L O W ∘

Today is:

5 Things I Appreciate:

3 Things I Have Manifested:

2 Things I Will Do Just for Me Today:

This Is How I Want to Describe Myself Today:

Today's Affirmations:

3 Things I Want the Universe to Handle:

Time:	These Are My Intentions for Today:	I Intend to Feel:
6-7 AM		
7-8 AM		
8-9 AM		
9-10 AM		
10-11 AM		
11-12 AM		
12-1 PM		
1-2 PM		
2-3 PM		
3-4 PM		
4-5 PM		
5-6 PM		
6-7 PM		
7-8 PM		
8-9 PM		

CREATE ∘ YOUR ∘ JOY

thank you ∘

∘ INTEND

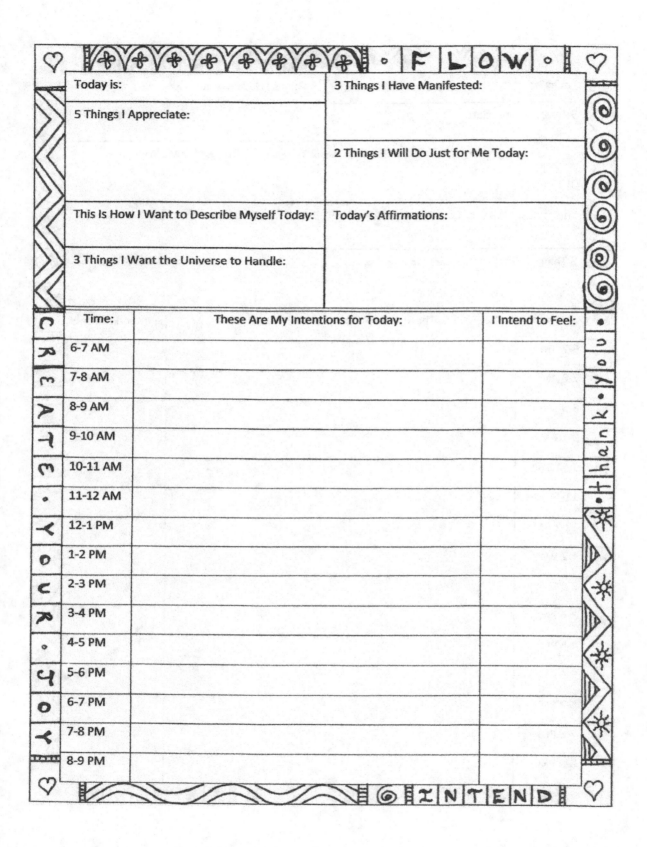

FLOW

Today is:	3 Things I Have Manifested:
5 Things I Appreciate:	
	2 Things I Will Do Just for Me Today:
This Is How I Want to Describe Myself Today:	Today's Affirmations:
3 Things I Want the Universe to Handle:	

CREATE · YOUR · JOY

thank you ·

Time:	These Are My Intentions for Today:	I Intend to Feel:
6-7 AM		
7-8 AM		
8-9 AM		
9-10 AM		
10-11 AM		
11-12 AM		
12-1 PM		
1-2 PM		
2-3 PM		
3-4 PM		
4-5 PM		
5-6 PM		
6-7 PM		
7-8 PM		
8-9 PM		

INTEND

· F L O W ·

Today is:	3 Things I Have Manifested:
5 Things I Appreciate:	
	2 Things I Will Do Just for Me Today:
This Is How I Want to Describe Myself Today:	Today's Affirmations:
3 Things I Want the Universe to Handle:	

Time:	These Are My Intentions for Today:	I Intend to Feel:
6-7 AM		
7-8 AM		
8-9 AM		
9-10 AM		
10-11 AM		
11-12 AM		
12-1 PM		
1-2 PM		
2-3 PM		
3-4 PM		
4-5 PM		
5-6 PM		
6-7 PM		
7-8 PM		
8-9 PM		

CREATE · YOUR · JOY

thank you

I INTEND

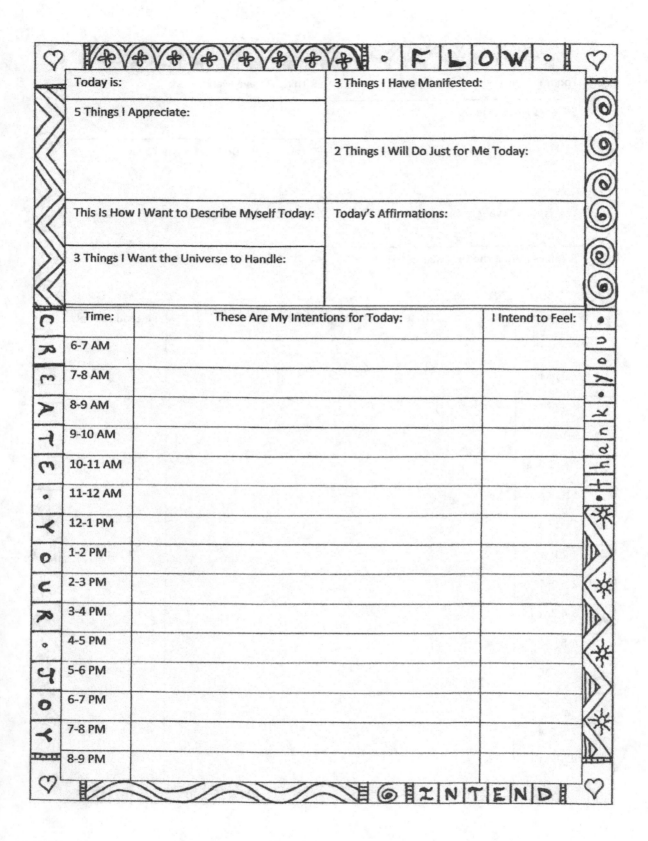

FLOW

Today is:	3 Things I Have Manifested:
5 Things I Appreciate:	
	2 Things I Will Do Just for Me Today:
This Is How I Want to Describe Myself Today:	**Today's Affirmations:**
3 Things I Want the Universe to Handle:	

	Time:	These Are My Intentions for Today:	I Intend to Feel:
C	6-7 AM		
R	7-8 AM		
E	8-9 AM		
A	9-10 AM		
T	10-11 AM		
E	11-12 AM		
Y	12-1 PM		
O	1-2 PM		
U	2-3 PM		
R	3-4 PM		
	4-5 PM		
J	5-6 PM		
O	6-7 PM		
Y	7-8 PM		
	8-9 PM		

CREATE YOUR JOY

thank you

INTEND

FLOW

Today is:	3 Things I Have Manifested:
5 Things I Appreciate:	
	2 Things I Will Do Just for Me Today:
This Is How I Want to Describe Myself Today:	**Today's Affirmations:**
3 Things I Want the Universe to Handle:	

Time:	These Are My Intentions for Today:	I Intend to Feel:
6-7 AM		
7-8 AM		
8-9 AM		
9-10 AM		
10-11 AM		
11-12 AM		
12-1 PM		
1-2 PM		
2-3 PM		
3-4 PM		
4-5 PM		
5-6 PM		
6-7 PM		
7-8 PM		
8-9 PM		

INTEND

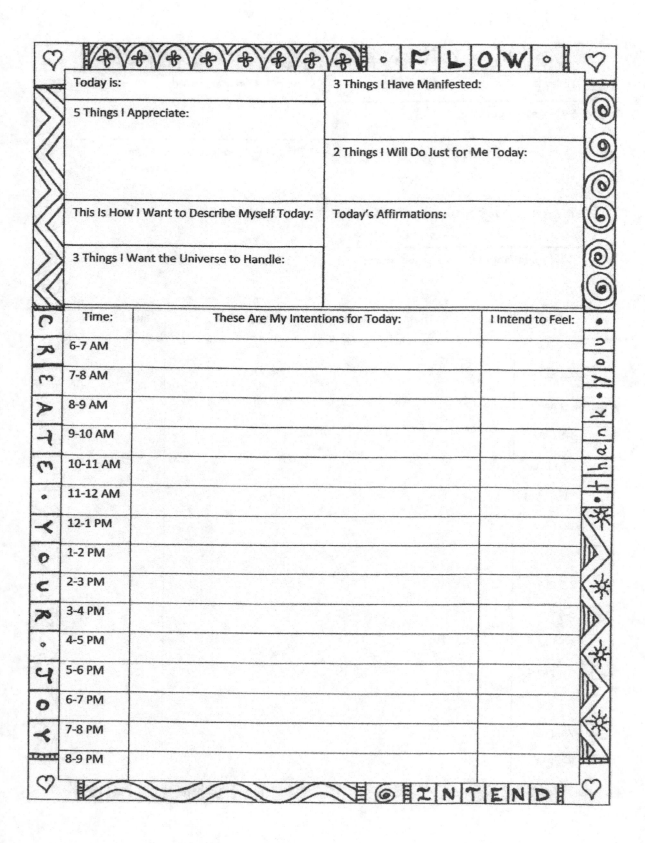

FLOW

Today is:	3 Things I Have Manifested:
5 Things I Appreciate:	
	2 Things I Will Do Just for Me Today:
This Is How I Want to Describe Myself Today:	Today's Affirmations:
3 Things I Want the Universe to Handle:	

Time:	These Are My Intentions for Today:	I Intend to Feel:
6-7 AM		
7-8 AM		
8-9 AM		
9-10 AM		
10-11 AM		
11-12 AM		
12-1 PM		
1-2 PM		
2-3 PM		
3-4 PM		
4-5 PM		
5-6 PM		
6-7 PM		
7-8 PM		
8-9 PM		

CREATE . YOUR . JOY

thank . you

INTEND

• F L O W •

Today is:	3 Things I Have Manifested:
5 Things I Appreciate:	
	2 Things I Will Do Just for Me Today:
This Is How I Want to Describe Myself Today:	Today's Affirmations:
3 Things I Want the Universe to Handle:	

	Time:	These Are My Intentions for Today:	I Intend to Feel:
C	6-7 AM		
R	7-8 AM		
E	8-9 AM		
A	9-10 AM		
T	10-11 AM		
E	11-12 AM		
Y	12-1 PM		
O	1-2 PM		
U	2-3 PM		
R	3-4 PM		
	4-5 PM		
J	5-6 PM		
O	6-7 PM		
Y	7-8 PM		
	8-9 PM		

• INTEND

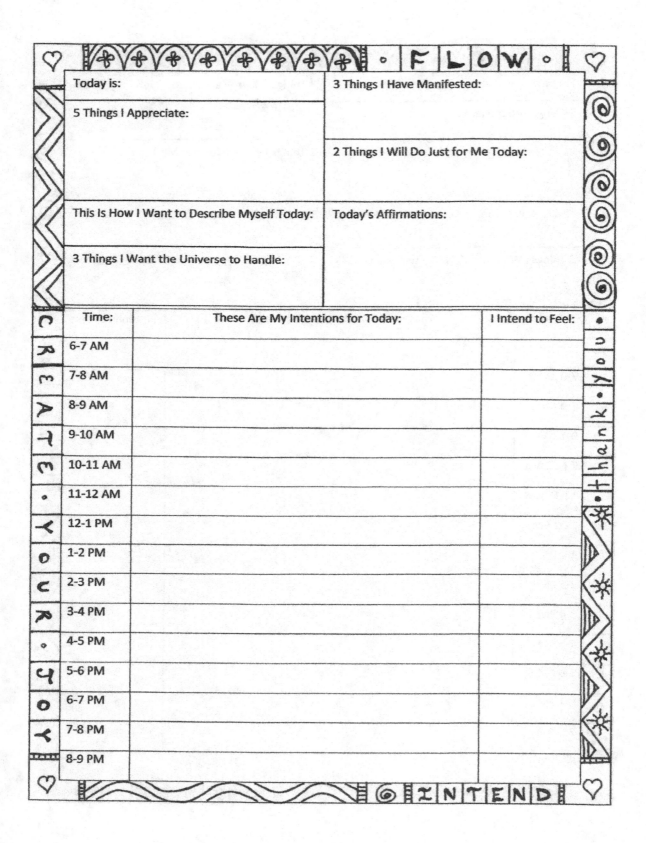

FLOW

Today is:	3 Things I Have Manifested:
5 Things I Appreciate:	
	2 Things I Will Do Just for Me Today:
This Is How I Want to Describe Myself Today:	Today's Affirmations:
3 Things I Want the Universe to Handle:	

CREATE · YOUR · JOY

thank you

Time:	These Are My Intentions for Today:	I Intend to Feel:
6-7 AM		
7-8 AM		
8-9 AM		
9-10 AM		
10-11 AM		
11-12 AM		
12-1 PM		
1-2 PM		
2-3 PM		
3-4 PM		
4-5 PM		
5-6 PM		
6-7 PM		
7-8 PM		
8-9 PM		

INTEND

FLOW

Today is:

5 Things I Appreciate:

This Is How I Want to Describe Myself Today:

3 Things I Want the Universe to Handle:

3 Things I Have Manifested:

2 Things I Will Do Just for Me Today:

Today's Affirmations:

Time:	These Are My Intentions for Today:	I Intend to Feel:
6-7 AM		
7-8 AM		
8-9 AM		
9-10 AM		
10-11 AM		
11-12 AM		
12-1 PM		
1-2 PM		
2-3 PM		
3-4 PM		
4-5 PM		
5-6 PM		
6-7 PM		
7-8 PM		
8-9 PM		

CREATE. YOUR. JOY

Thank you.

INTEND

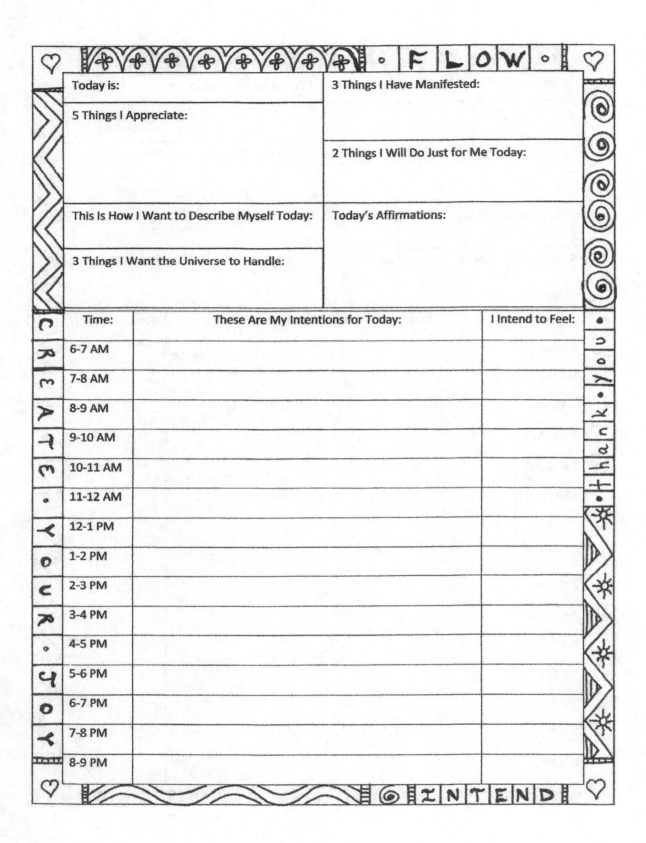

FLOW

Today is:

5 Things I Appreciate:

This Is How I Want to Describe Myself Today:

3 Things I Want the Universe to Handle:

3 Things I Have Manifested:

2 Things I Will Do Just for Me Today:

Today's Affirmations:

Time:	These Are My Intentions for Today:	I Intend to Feel:
6-7 AM		
7-8 AM		
8-9 AM		
9-10 AM		
10-11 AM		
11-12 AM		
12-1 PM		
1-2 PM		
2-3 PM		
3-4 PM		
4-5 PM		
5-6 PM		
6-7 PM		
7-8 PM		
8-9 PM		

CREATE • YOUR • YOU

thank you

INTEND

FLOW

Today is:	3 Things I Have Manifested:
5 Things I Appreciate:	
	2 Things I Will Do Just for Me Today:
This Is How I Want to Describe Myself Today:	**Today's Affirmations:**
3 Things I Want the Universe to Handle:	

Time:	These Are My Intentions for Today:	I Intend to Feel:
6-7 AM		
7-8 AM		
8-9 AM		
9-10 AM		
10-11 AM		
11-12 AM		
12-1 PM		
1-2 PM		
2-3 PM		
3-4 PM		
4-5 PM		
5-6 PM		
6-7 PM		
7-8 PM		
8-9 PM		

CREATE . YOUR . JOY

thank . you

INTEND

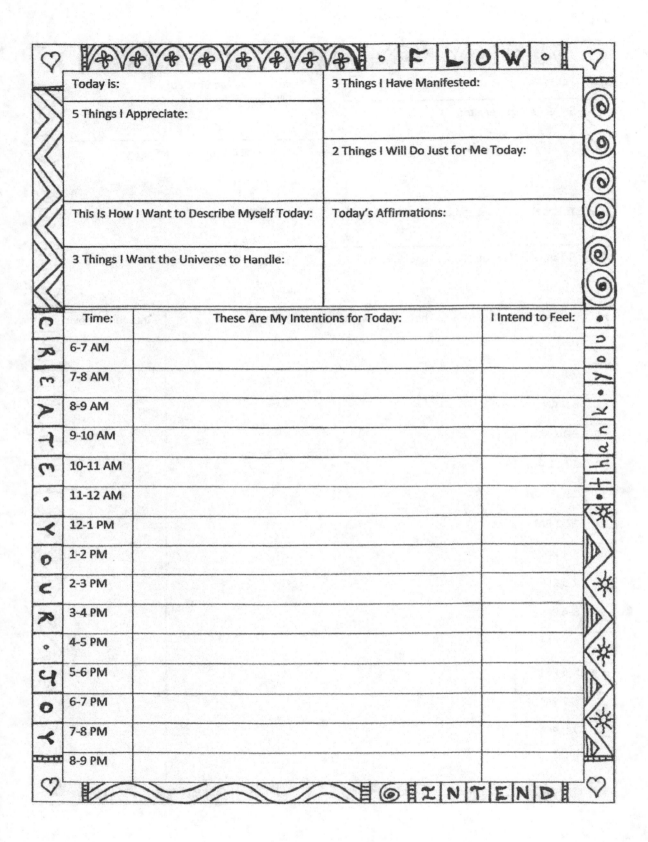

FLOW

Today is:	**3 Things I Have Manifested:**
5 Things I Appreciate:	
	2 Things I Will Do Just for Me Today:
This Is How I Want to Describe Myself Today:	**Today's Affirmations:**
3 Things I Want the Universe to Handle:	

Time:	These Are My Intentions for Today:	I Intend to Feel:
6-7 AM		
7-8 AM		
8-9 AM		
9-10 AM		
10-11 AM		
11-12 AM		
12-1 PM		
1-2 PM		
2-3 PM		
3-4 PM		
4-5 PM		
5-6 PM		
6-7 PM		
7-8 PM		
8-9 PM		

CREATE • YOUR • JOY

thank • you • for

INTEND

FLOW

Today is:	3 Things I Have Manifested:
5 Things I Appreciate:	
	2 Things I Will Do Just for Me Today:
This Is How I Want to Describe Myself Today:	Today's Affirmations:
3 Things I Want the Universe to Handle:	

Time:	These Are My Intentions for Today:	I Intend to Feel:
6-7 AM		
7-8 AM		
8-9 AM		
9-10 AM		
10-11 AM		
11-12 AM		
12-1 PM		
1-2 PM		
2-3 PM		
3-4 PM		
4-5 PM		
5-6 PM		
6-7 PM		
7-8 PM		
8-9 PM		

CREATE • YOUR • JOY

thank you

INTEND

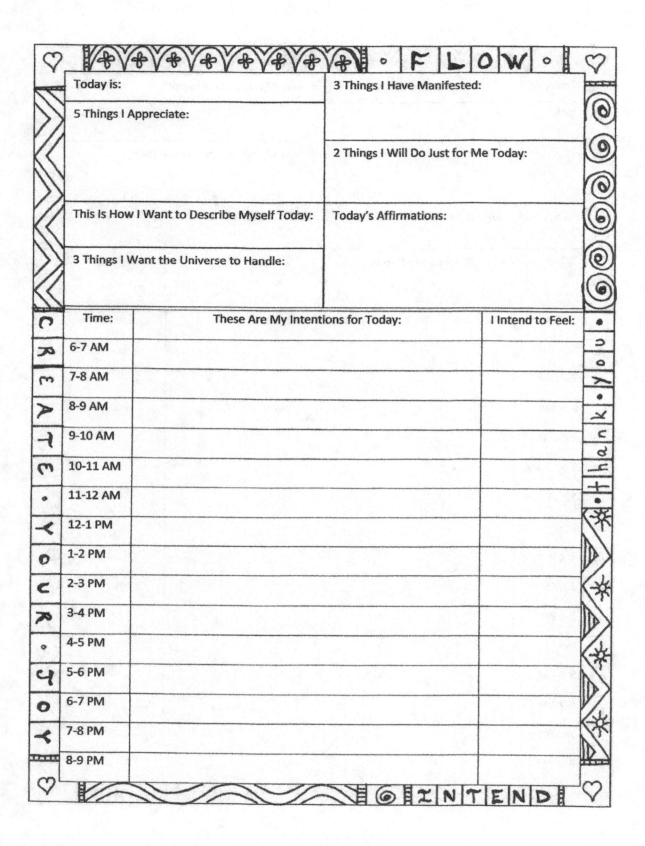

FLOW

Today is:	**3 Things I Have Manifested:**
5 Things I Appreciate:	
	2 Things I Will Do Just for Me Today:
This Is How I Want to Describe Myself Today:	**Today's Affirmations:**
3 Things I Want the Universe to Handle:	

Time:	These Are My Intentions for Today:	I Intend to Feel:
6-7 AM		
7-8 AM		
8-9 AM		
9-10 AM		
10-11 AM		
11-12 AM		
12-1 PM		
1-2 PM		
2-3 PM		
3-4 PM		
4-5 PM		
5-6 PM		
6-7 PM		
7-8 PM		
8-9 PM		

CREATE. YOUR. JOY

thank you

INTEND

FLOW

Today is:	3 Things I Have Manifested:
5 Things I Appreciate:	
	2 Things I Will Do Just for Me Today:
This Is How I Want to Describe Myself Today:	Today's Affirmations:
3 Things I Want the Universe to Handle:	

Time:	These Are My Intentions for Today:	I Intend to Feel:
6-7 AM		
7-8 AM		
8-9 AM		
9-10 AM		
10-11 AM		
11-12 AM		
12-1 PM		
1-2 PM		
2-3 PM		
3-4 PM		
4-5 PM		
5-6 PM		
6-7 PM		
7-8 PM		
8-9 PM		

CREATE . YOUR . JOY

thank you

INTEND

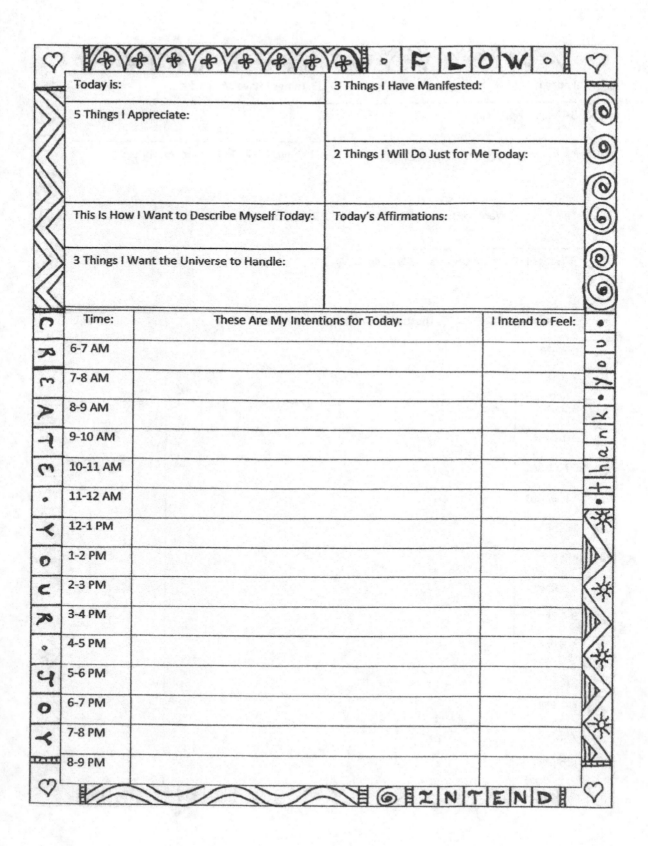

FLOW

Today is:	3 Things I Have Manifested:
5 Things I Appreciate:	
	2 Things I Will Do Just for Me Today:
This Is How I Want to Describe Myself Today:	**Today's Affirmations:**
3 Things I Want the Universe to Handle:	

Time:	These Are My Intentions for Today:	I Intend to Feel:
6-7 AM		
7-8 AM		
8-9 AM		
9-10 AM		
10-11 AM		
11-12 AM		
12-1 PM		
1-2 PM		
2-3 PM		
3-4 PM		
4-5 PM		
5-6 PM		
6-7 PM		
7-8 PM		
8-9 PM		

CREATE • YOUR • JOY

thank you

INTEND

302

FLOW

Today is:	3 Things I Have Manifested:
5 Things I Appreciate:	
	2 Things I Will Do Just for Me Today:
This Is How I Want to Describe Myself Today:	Today's Affirmations:
3 Things I Want the Universe to Handle:	

Time:	These Are My Intentions for Today:	I Intend to Feel:
6-7 AM		
7-8 AM		
8-9 AM		
9-10 AM		
10-11 AM		
11-12 AM		
12-1 PM		
1-2 PM		
2-3 PM		
3-4 PM		
4-5 PM		
5-6 PM		
6-7 PM		
7-8 PM		
8-9 PM		

CREATE. YOUR. JOY

thank you.

INTEND

303

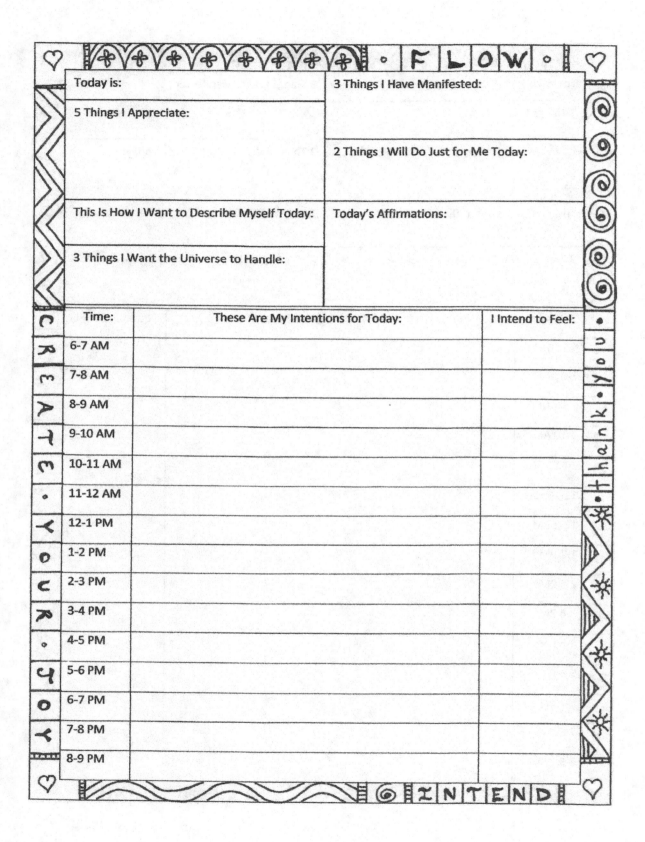

FLOW

Today is:	3 Things I Have Manifested:
5 Things I Appreciate:	
	2 Things I Will Do Just for Me Today:
This Is How I Want to Describe Myself Today:	**Today's Affirmations:**
3 Things I Want the Universe to Handle:	

	Time:	These Are My Intentions for Today:	I Intend to Feel:
C	6-7 AM		
R	7-8 AM		
E	8-9 AM		
A	9-10 AM		
T	10-11 AM		
E	11-12 AM		
.	12-1 PM		
Y	1-2 PM		
O	2-3 PM		
U	3-4 PM		
R	4-5 PM		
.	5-6 PM		
J	6-7 PM		
O	7-8 PM		
Y	8-9 PM		

INTEND

FLOW

Today is:	**3 Things I Have Manifested:**
5 Things I Appreciate:	
	2 Things I Will Do Just for Me Today:
This Is How I Want to Describe Myself Today:	**Today's Affirmations:**
3 Things I Want the Universe to Handle:	

Time:	These Are My Intentions for Today:	I Intend to Feel:
6-7 AM		
7-8 AM		
8-9 AM		
9-10 AM		
10-11 AM		
11-12 AM		
12-1 PM		
1-2 PM		
2-3 PM		
3-4 PM		
4-5 PM		
5-6 PM		
6-7 PM		
7-8 PM		
8-9 PM		

CREATE · YOUR · JOY

thank · you

INTEND

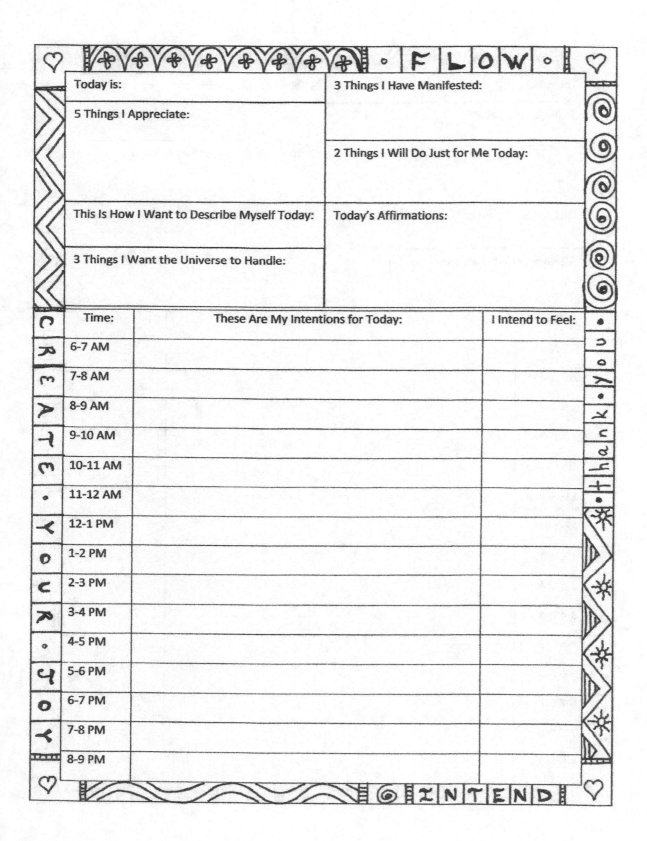

FLOW

Today is:	3 Things I Have Manifested:
5 Things I Appreciate:	
	2 Things I Will Do Just for Me Today:
This Is How I Want to Describe Myself Today:	Today's Affirmations:
3 Things I Want the Universe to Handle:	

Time:	These Are My Intentions for Today:	I Intend to Feel:
6-7 AM		
7-8 AM		
8-9 AM		
9-10 AM		
10-11 AM		
11-12 AM		
12-1 PM		
1-2 PM		
2-3 PM		
3-4 PM		
4-5 PM		
5-6 PM		
6-7 PM		
7-8 PM		
8-9 PM		

CREATE . YOUR . JOY

thank . you

INTEND

· F L O W ·

Today is:

5 Things I Appreciate:

This Is How I Want to Describe Myself Today:

3 Things I Want the Universe to Handle:

3 Things I Have Manifested:

2 Things I Will Do Just for Me Today:

Today's Affirmations:

Time:	These Are My Intentions for Today:	I Intend to Feel:
6-7 AM		
7-8 AM		
8-9 AM		
9-10 AM		
10-11 AM		
11-12 AM		
12-1 PM		
1-2 PM		
2-3 PM		
3-4 PM		
4-5 PM		
5-6 PM		
6-7 PM		
7-8 PM		
8-9 PM		

CREATE · YOUR · JOY

thank · you

· INTEND

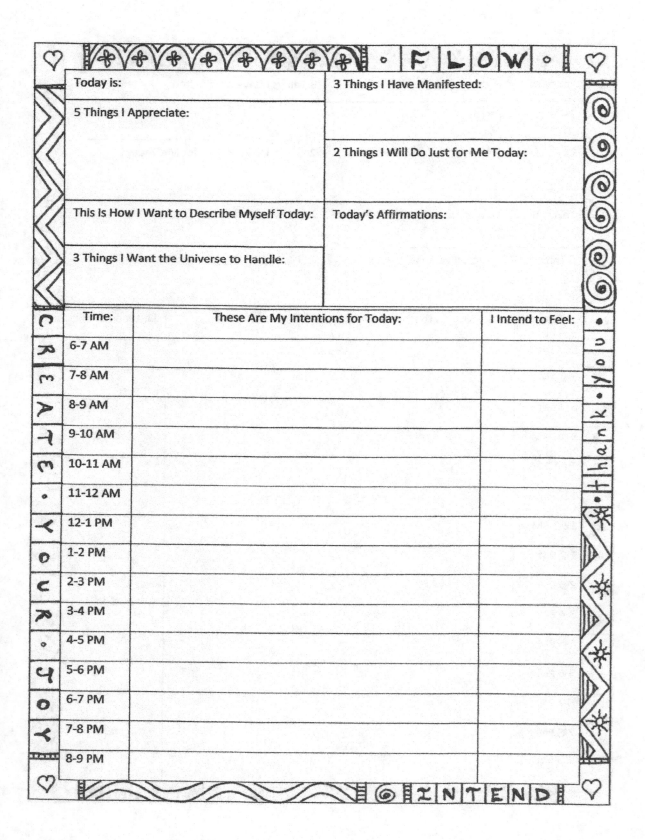

	Time:	These Are My Intentions for Today:	I Intend to Feel:
C	6-7 AM		
R	7-8 AM		
E	8-9 AM		
A	9-10 AM		
T	10-11 AM		
E	11-12 AM		
•	12-1 PM		
Y	1-2 PM		
O	2-3 PM		
U	3-4 PM		
R	4-5 PM		
•	5-6 PM		
J	6-7 PM		
O	7-8 PM		
Y	8-9 PM		

Today is:

5 Things I Appreciate:

This Is How I Want to Describe Myself Today:

3 Things I Want the Universe to Handle:

3 Things I Have Manifested:

2 Things I Will Do Just for Me Today:

Today's Affirmations:

• F L O W •

Today is:	3 Things I Have Manifested:
5 Things I Appreciate:	
	2 Things I Will Do Just for Me Today:
This Is How I Want to Describe Myself Today:	**Today's Affirmations:**
3 Things I Want the Universe to Handle:	

Time:	These Are My Intentions for Today:	I Intend to Feel:
6-7 AM		
7-8 AM		
8-9 AM		
9-10 AM		
10-11 AM		
11-12 AM		
12-1 PM		
1-2 PM		
2-3 PM		
3-4 PM		
4-5 PM		
5-6 PM		
6-7 PM		
7-8 PM		
8-9 PM		

CREATE • YOUR • JOY

thank you

◎ INTEND

309

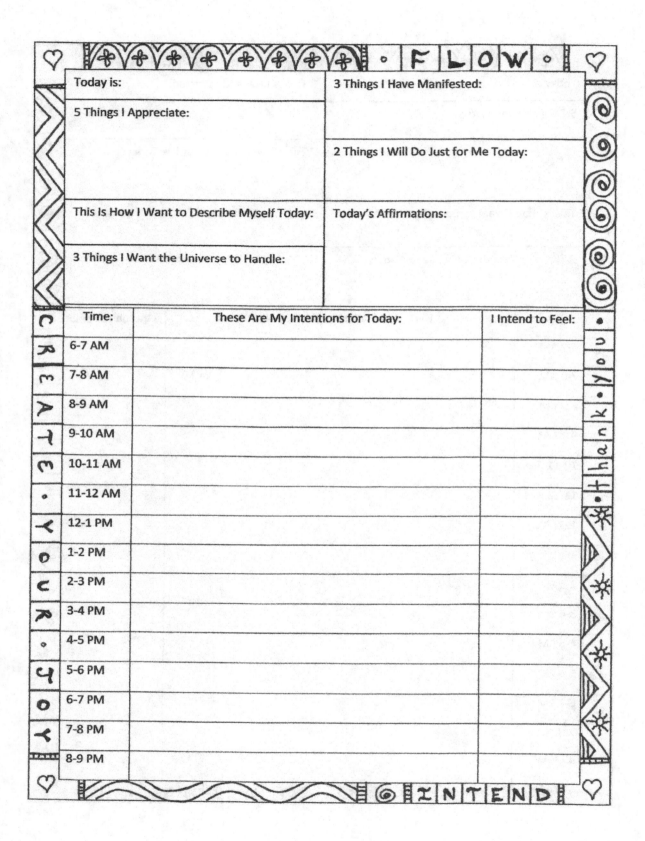

FLOW

Today is:	3 Things I Have Manifested:
5 Things I Appreciate:	
	2 Things I Will Do Just for Me Today:
This Is How I Want to Describe Myself Today:	**Today's Affirmations:**
3 Things I Want the Universe to Handle:	

	Time:	These Are My Intentions for Today:	I Intend to Feel:
C	6-7 AM		
R	7-8 AM		
E	8-9 AM		
A	9-10 AM		
T	10-11 AM		
E	11-12 AM		
·	12-1 PM		
Y	1-2 PM		
O	2-3 PM		
U	3-4 PM		
R	4-5 PM		
·	5-6 PM		
J	6-7 PM		
O	7-8 PM		
Y	8-9 PM		

INTEND

310

FLOW

Today is:	3 Things I Have Manifested:
5 Things I Appreciate:	
	2 Things I Will Do Just for Me Today:
This Is How I Want to Describe Myself Today:	Today's Affirmations:
3 Things I Want the Universe to Handle:	

Time:	These Are My Intentions for Today:	I Intend to Feel:
6-7 AM		
7-8 AM		
8-9 AM		
9-10 AM		
10-11 AM		
11-12 AM		
12-1 PM		
1-2 PM		
2-3 PM		
3-4 PM		
4-5 PM		
5-6 PM		
6-7 PM		
7-8 PM		
8-9 PM		

CREATE. YOUR. JOY

thank you. today

INTEND

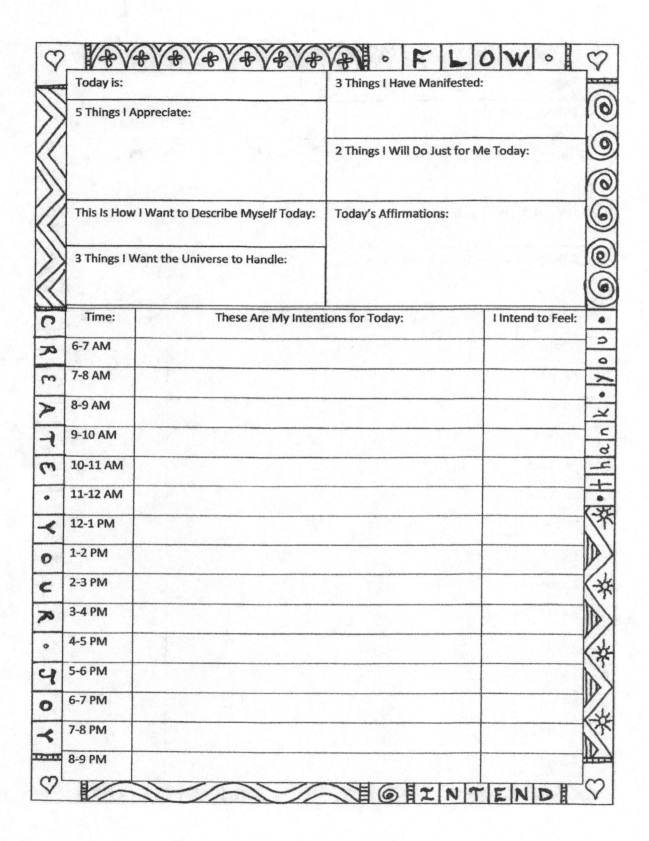

FLOW

| Today is: |
| 5 Things I Appreciate: |
| This Is How I Want to Describe Myself Today: |
| 3 Things I Want the Universe to Handle: |

3 Things I Have Manifested:

2 Things I Will Do Just for Me Today:

Today's Affirmations:

CREATE · YOUR · JOY

THANK YOU ·

Time:	These Are My Intentions for Today:	I Intend to Feel:
6-7 AM		
7-8 AM		
8-9 AM		
9-10 AM		
10-11 AM		
11-12 AM		
12-1 PM		
1-2 PM		
2-3 PM		
3-4 PM		
4-5 PM		
5-6 PM		
6-7 PM		
7-8 PM		
8-9 PM		

INTEND

FLOW

Today is:	3 Things I Have Manifested:
5 Things I Appreciate:	
	2 Things I Will Do Just for Me Today:
This Is How I Want to Describe Myself Today:	Today's Affirmations:
3 Things I Want the Universe to Handle:	

Time:	These Are My Intentions for Today:	I Intend to Feel:
6-7 AM		
7-8 AM		
8-9 AM		
9-10 AM		
10-11 AM		
11-12 AM		
12-1 PM		
1-2 PM		
2-3 PM		
3-4 PM		
4-5 PM		
5-6 PM		
6-7 PM		
7-8 PM		
8-9 PM		

CREATE . YOUR . JOY

thank you

INTEND

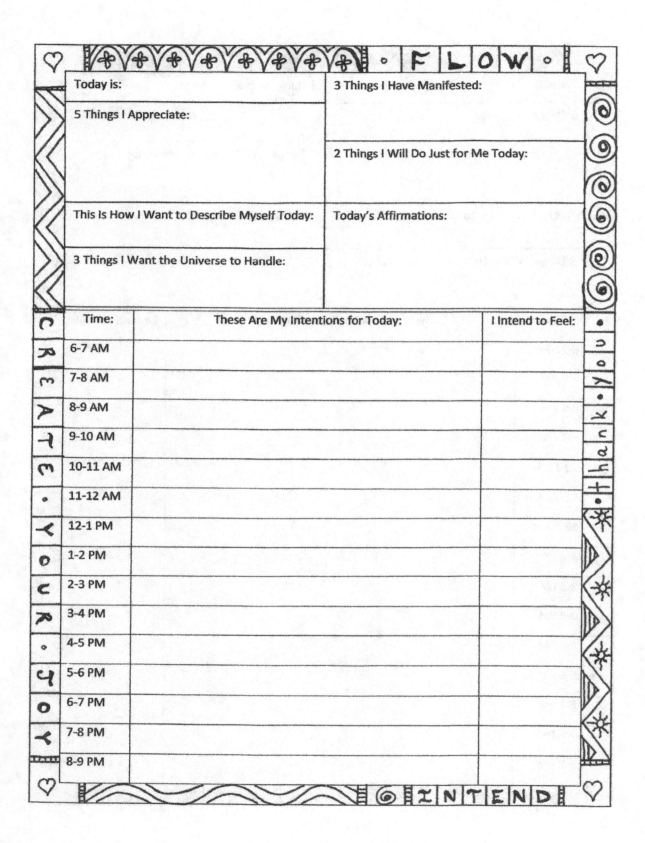

FLOW

Today is:

5 Things I Appreciate:

This Is How I Want to Describe Myself Today:

3 Things I Want the Universe to Handle:

3 Things I Have Manifested:

2 Things I Will Do Just for Me Today:

Today's Affirmations:

CREATE • YOUR • JOY

thank you •

Time:	These Are My Intentions for Today:	I Intend to Feel:
6-7 AM		
7-8 AM		
8-9 AM		
9-10 AM		
10-11 AM		
11-12 AM		
12-1 PM		
1-2 PM		
2-3 PM		
3-4 PM		
4-5 PM		
5-6 PM		
6-7 PM		
7-8 PM		
8-9 PM		

INTEND

FLOW

Today is:	3 Things I Have Manifested:
5 Things I Appreciate:	
	2 Things I Will Do Just for Me Today:
This Is How I Want to Describe Myself Today:	Today's Affirmations:
3 Things I Want the Universe to Handle:	

CREATE . YOUR . JOY

thank you .

Time:	These Are My Intentions for Today:	I Intend to Feel:
6-7 AM		
7-8 AM		
8-9 AM		
9-10 AM		
10-11 AM		
11-12 AM		
12-1 PM		
1-2 PM		
2-3 PM		
3-4 PM		
4-5 PM		
5-6 PM		
6-7 PM		
7-8 PM		
8-9 PM		

INTEND

Month: November

Sunday	Monday	Tuesday	Wednesday	Thursday	Friday	Saturday

Do at least one thing every day that brings you joy and record it on this page.

Affirmations:

"Whatever you pay attention to is what you create." –S. Roman

FLOW

Today is:	3 Things I Have Manifested:
5 Things I Appreciate:	
	2 Things I Will Do Just for Me Today:
This Is How I Want to Describe Myself Today:	Today's Affirmations:
3 Things I Want the Universe to Handle:	

CREATE. YOUR. CROP. JOY

Time:	These Are My Intentions for Today:	I Intend to Feel:
6-7 AM		
7-8 AM		
8-9 AM		
9-10 AM		
10-11 AM		
11-12 AM		
12-1 PM		
1-2 PM		
2-3 PM		
3-4 PM		
4-5 PM		
5-6 PM		
6-7 PM		
7-8 PM		
8-9 PM		

thank you.

INTEND

317

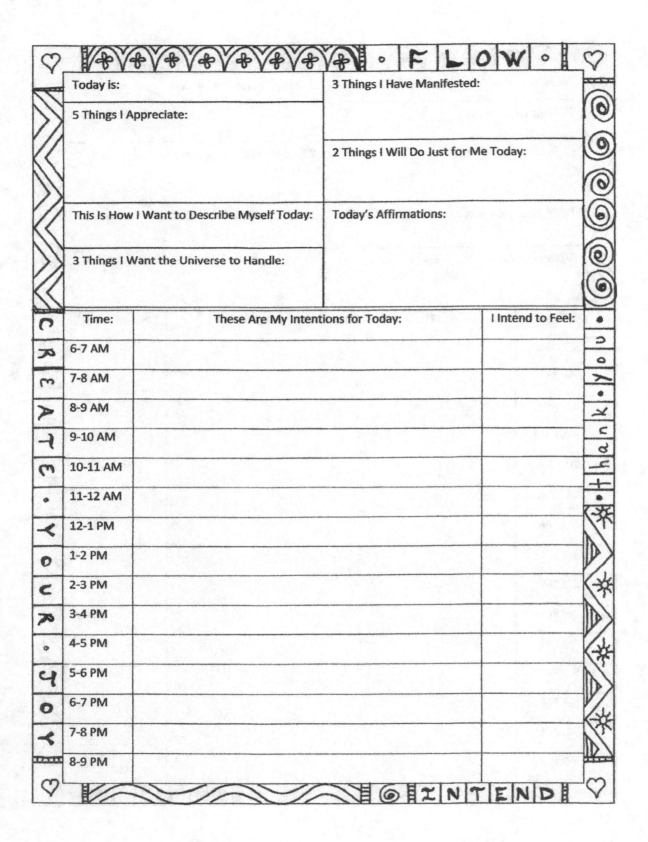

FLOW

Today is:	3 Things I Have Manifested:
5 Things I Appreciate:	
	2 Things I Will Do Just for Me Today:
This Is How I Want to Describe Myself Today:	Today's Affirmations:
3 Things I Want the Universe to Handle:	

CREATE • YOUR • JOY

Time:	These Are My Intentions for Today:	I Intend to Feel:
6-7 AM		
7-8 AM		
8-9 AM		
9-10 AM		
10-11 AM		
11-12 AM		
12-1 PM		
1-2 PM		
2-3 PM		
3-4 PM		
4-5 PM		
5-6 PM		
6-7 PM		
7-8 PM		
8-9 PM		

thank you • INTEND

318

FLOW

Today is:	3 Things I Have Manifested:
5 Things I Appreciate:	
	2 Things I Will Do Just for Me Today:
This Is How I Want to Describe Myself Today:	Today's Affirmations:
3 Things I Want the Universe to Handle:	

Time:	These Are My Intentions for Today:	I Intend to Feel:
6-7 AM		
7-8 AM		
8-9 AM		
9-10 AM		
10-11 AM		
11-12 AM		
12-1 PM		
1-2 PM		
2-3 PM		
3-4 PM		
4-5 PM		
5-6 PM		
6-7 PM		
7-8 PM		
8-9 PM		

CREATE . YOUR . JOY

INTEND

thank you

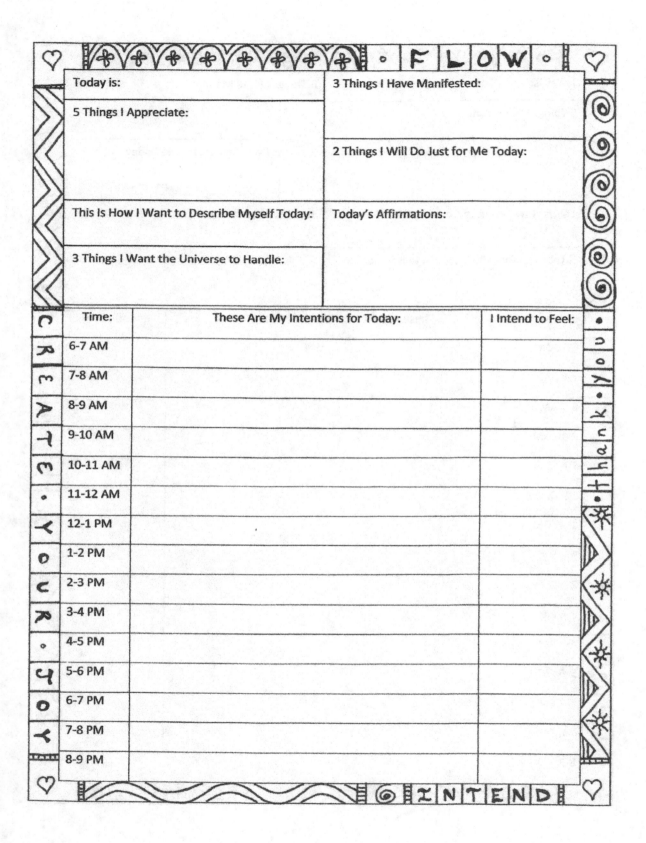

FLOW

Today is:	3 Things I Have Manifested:
5 Things I Appreciate:	
	2 Things I Will Do Just for Me Today:
This Is How I Want to Describe Myself Today:	**Today's Affirmations:**
3 Things I Want the Universe to Handle:	

CREATE YOUR JOY

Time:	These Are My Intentions for Today:	I Intend to Feel:
6-7 AM		
7-8 AM		
8-9 AM		
9-10 AM		
10-11 AM		
11-12 AM		
12-1 PM		
1-2 PM		
2-3 PM		
3-4 PM		
4-5 PM		
5-6 PM		
6-7 PM		
7-8 PM		
8-9 PM		

INTEND

thank you

FLOW

Today is:	3 Things I Have Manifested:
5 Things I Appreciate:	
	2 Things I Will Do Just for Me Today:
This Is How I Want to Describe Myself Today:	Today's Affirmations:
3 Things I Want the Universe to Handle:	

CREATE . YOUR . JOY

Time:	These Are My Intentions for Today:	I Intend to Feel:
6-7 AM		
7-8 AM		
8-9 AM		
9-10 AM		
10-11 AM		
11-12 AM		
12-1 PM		
1-2 PM		
2-3 PM		
3-4 PM		
4-5 PM		
5-6 PM		
6-7 PM		
7-8 PM		
8-9 PM		

thank you

INTEND

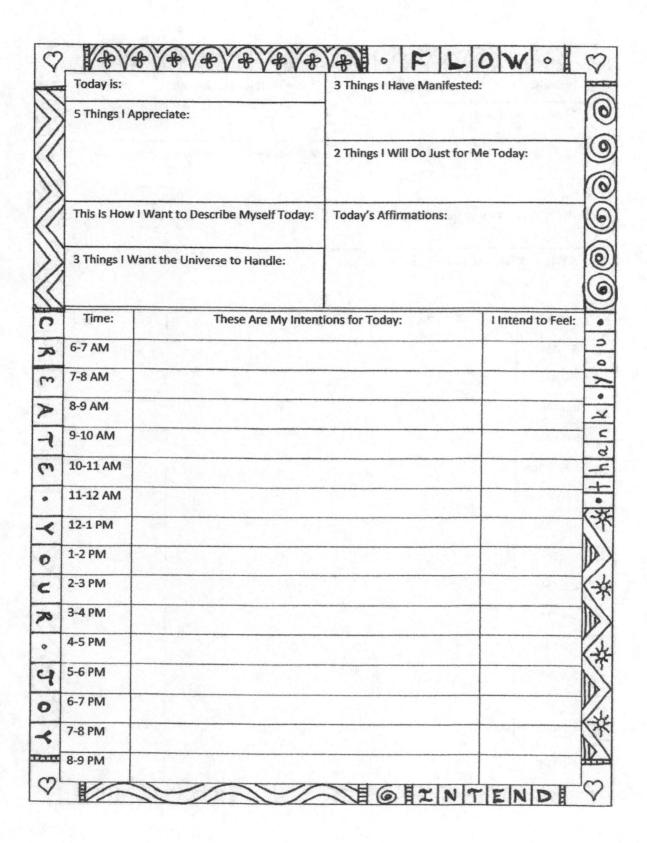

FLOW

Today is:

5 Things I Appreciate:

This Is How I Want to Describe Myself Today:

3 Things I Want the Universe to Handle:

3 Things I Have Manifested:

2 Things I Will Do Just for Me Today:

Today's Affirmations:

Time:	These Are My Intentions for Today:	I Intend to Feel:
6-7 AM		
7-8 AM		
8-9 AM		
9-10 AM		
10-11 AM		
11-12 AM		
12-1 PM		
1-2 PM		
2-3 PM		
3-4 PM		
4-5 PM		
5-6 PM		
6-7 PM		
7-8 PM		
8-9 PM		

CREATE . YOUR . JOY

thank you

INTEND

FLOW

Today is:	**3 Things I Have Manifested:**
5 Things I Appreciate:	
	2 Things I Will Do Just for Me Today:
This Is How I Want to Describe Myself Today:	**Today's Affirmations:**
3 Things I Want the Universe to Handle:	

Time:	These Are My Intentions for Today:	I Intend to Feel:
6-7 AM		
7-8 AM		
8-9 AM		
9-10 AM		
10-11 AM		
11-12 AM		
12-1 PM		
1-2 PM		
2-3 PM		
3-4 PM		
4-5 PM		
5-6 PM		
6-7 PM		
7-8 PM		
8-9 PM		

CREATE . YOUR . JOY

thank . you

INTEND

FLOW

Today is:	**3 Things I Have Manifested:**
5 Things I Appreciate:	
	2 Things I Will Do Just for Me Today:
This Is How I Want to Describe Myself Today:	**Today's Affirmations:**
3 Things I Want the Universe to Handle:	

Time:	These Are My Intentions for Today:	I Intend to Feel:
6-7 AM		
7-8 AM		
8-9 AM		
9-10 AM		
10-11 AM		
11-12 AM		
12-1 PM		
1-2 PM		
2-3 PM		
3-4 PM		
4-5 PM		
5-6 PM		
6-7 PM		
7-8 PM		
8-9 PM		

CREATE · YOUR · CRO · JOY

thank you

INTEND

FLOW

Today is:	3 Things I Have Manifested:
5 Things I Appreciate:	
	2 Things I Will Do Just for Me Today:
This Is How I Want to Describe Myself Today:	Today's Affirmations:
3 Things I Want the Universe to Handle:	

Time:	These Are My Intentions for Today:	I Intend to Feel:
6-7 AM		
7-8 AM		
8-9 AM		
9-10 AM		
10-11 AM		
11-12 AM		
12-1 PM		
1-2 PM		
2-3 PM		
3-4 PM		
4-5 PM		
5-6 PM		
6-7 PM		
7-8 PM		
8-9 PM		

CREATE YOUR JOY

thank you

INTEND

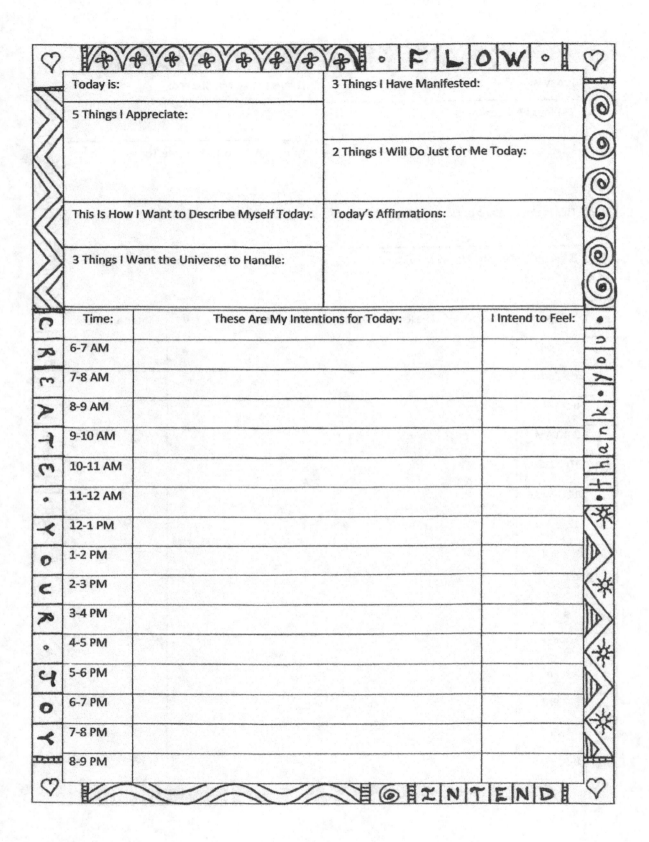

FLOW

Today is:

5 Things I Appreciate:

3 Things I Have Manifested:

2 Things I Will Do Just for Me Today:

This Is How I Want to Describe Myself Today:

Today's Affirmations:

3 Things I Want the Universe to Handle:

Time:	These Are My Intentions for Today:	I Intend to Feel:
6-7 AM		
7-8 AM		
8-9 AM		
9-10 AM		
10-11 AM		
11-12 AM		
12-1 PM		
1-2 PM		
2-3 PM		
3-4 PM		
4-5 PM		
5-6 PM		
6-7 PM		
7-8 PM		
8-9 PM		

CREATE • YOUR • JOY

thank • you

INTEND

· F L O W ·

Today is:	3 Things I Have Manifested:
5 Things I Appreciate:	
	2 Things I Will Do Just for Me Today:
This Is How I Want to Describe Myself Today:	Today's Affirmations:
3 Things I Want the Universe to Handle:	

Time:	These Are My Intentions for Today:	I Intend to Feel:
6-7 AM		
7-8 AM		
8-9 AM		
9-10 AM		
10-11 AM		
11-12 AM		
12-1 PM		
1-2 PM		
2-3 PM		
3-4 PM		
4-5 PM		
5-6 PM		
6-7 PM		
7-8 PM		
8-9 PM		

CREATE • YOUR • JOY

· thank you ·

◎ INTEND

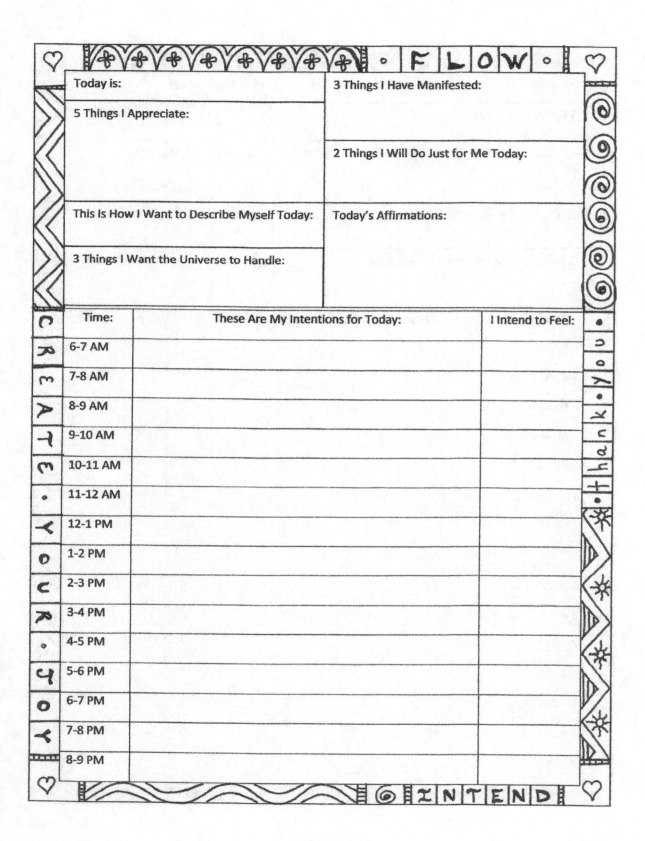

FLOW

Today is:	3 Things I Have Manifested:
5 Things I Appreciate:	
	2 Things I Will Do Just for Me Today:
This Is How I Want to Describe Myself Today:	Today's Affirmations:
3 Things I Want the Universe to Handle:	

	Time:	These Are My Intentions for Today:	I Intend to Feel:
C	6-7 AM		
R	7-8 AM		
E	8-9 AM		
A	9-10 AM		
T	10-11 AM		
E	11-12 AM		
Y	12-1 PM		
O	1-2 PM		
U	2-3 PM		
R	3-4 PM		
J	4-5 PM		
O	5-6 PM		
Y	6-7 PM		
	7-8 PM		
	8-9 PM		

INTEND

328

FLOW

Today is:	3 Things I Have Manifested:
5 Things I Appreciate:	
	2 Things I Will Do Just for Me Today:
This Is How I Want to Describe Myself Today:	Today's Affirmations:
3 Things I Want the Universe to Handle:	

CREATE • YOUR • JOY

Time:	These Are My Intentions for Today:	I Intend to Feel:
6-7 AM		
7-8 AM		
8-9 AM		
9-10 AM		
10-11 AM		
11-12 AM		
12-1 PM		
1-2 PM		
2-3 PM		
3-4 PM		
4-5 PM		
5-6 PM		
6-7 PM		
7-8 PM		
8-9 PM		

INTEND

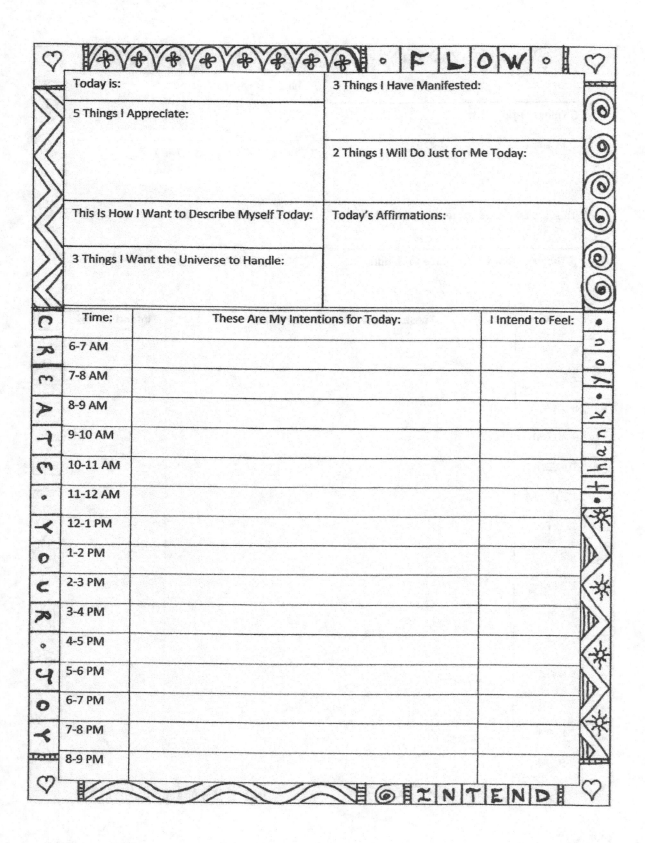

FLOW

Today is:	3 Things I Have Manifested:
5 Things I Appreciate:	
	2 Things I Will Do Just for Me Today:
This Is How I Want to Describe Myself Today:	**Today's Affirmations:**
3 Things I Want the Universe to Handle:	

Time:	These Are My Intentions for Today:	I Intend to Feel:
6-7 AM		
7-8 AM		
8-9 AM		
9-10 AM		
10-11 AM		
11-12 AM		
12-1 PM		
1-2 PM		
2-3 PM		
3-4 PM		
4-5 PM		
5-6 PM		
6-7 PM		
7-8 PM		
8-9 PM		

CREATE • YOUR • JOY

thank you

INTEND

⚬ F L O W ⚬

Today is:	**3 Things I Have Manifested:**
5 Things I Appreciate:	
	2 Things I Will Do Just for Me Today:
This Is How I Want to Describe Myself Today:	**Today's Affirmations:**
3 Things I Want the Universe to Handle:	

Time:	These Are My Intentions for Today:	I Intend to Feel:
6-7 AM		
7-8 AM		
8-9 AM		
9-10 AM		
10-11 AM		
11-12 AM		
12-1 PM		
1-2 PM		
2-3 PM		
3-4 PM		
4-5 PM		
5-6 PM		
6-7 PM		
7-8 PM		
8-9 PM		

CREATE ⚬ YOUR ⚬ JOY

thank you ⚬

⊚ INTEND

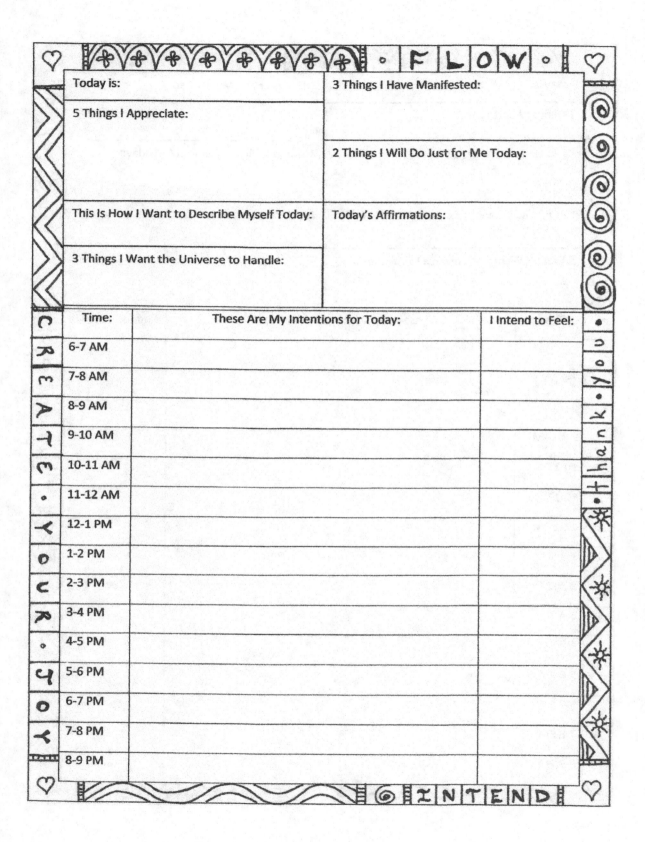

FLOW

Today is:	3 Things I Have Manifested:
5 Things I Appreciate:	
	2 Things I Will Do Just for Me Today:
This Is How I Want to Describe Myself Today:	Today's Affirmations:
3 Things I Want the Universe to Handle:	

Time:	These Are My Intentions for Today:	I Intend to Feel:
6-7 AM		
7-8 AM		
8-9 AM		
9-10 AM		
10-11 AM		
11-12 AM		
12-1 PM		
1-2 PM		
2-3 PM		
3-4 PM		
4-5 PM		
5-6 PM		
6-7 PM		
7-8 PM		
8-9 PM		

CREATE YOUR JOY

thank you

INTEND

FLOW

Today is:	3 Things I Have Manifested:
5 Things I Appreciate:	
	2 Things I Will Do Just for Me Today:
This Is How I Want to Describe Myself Today:	Today's Affirmations:
3 Things I Want the Universe to Handle:	

Time:	These Are My Intentions for Today:	I Intend to Feel:
6-7 AM		
7-8 AM		
8-9 AM		
9-10 AM		
10-11 AM		
11-12 AM		
12-1 PM		
1-2 PM		
2-3 PM		
3-4 PM		
4-5 PM		
5-6 PM		
6-7 PM		
7-8 PM		
8-9 PM		

CREATE · YOUR · JOY

thank you

INTEND

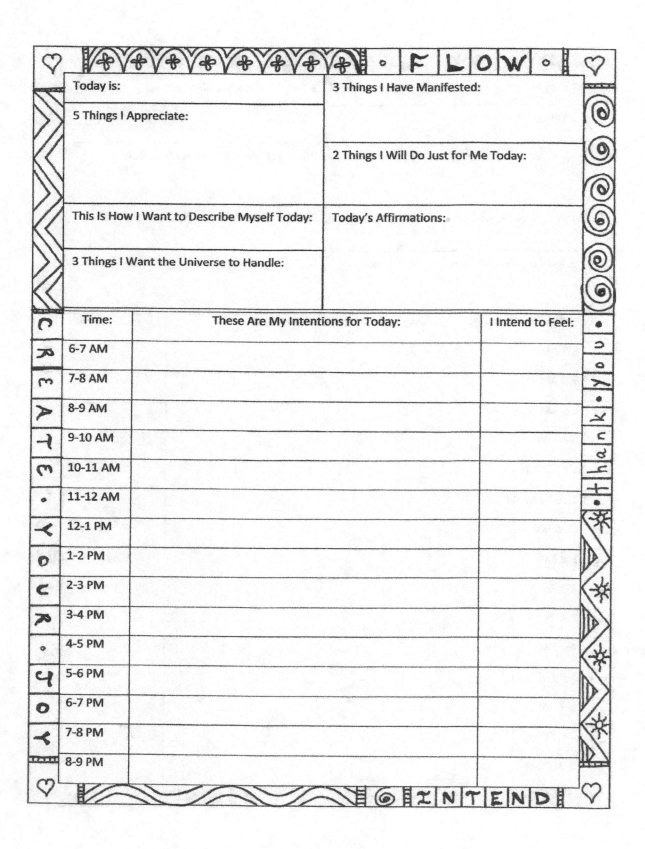

FLOW

Today is:	3 Things I Have Manifested:
5 Things I Appreciate:	
	2 Things I Will Do Just for Me Today:
This Is How I Want to Describe Myself Today:	Today's Affirmations:
3 Things I Want the Universe to Handle:	

	Time:	These Are My Intentions for Today:	I Intend to Feel:
C	6-7 AM		
R	7-8 AM		
E	8-9 AM		
A	9-10 AM		
T	10-11 AM		
E	11-12 AM		
.	12-1 PM		
Y	1-2 PM		
O	2-3 PM		
U	3-4 PM		
R	4-5 PM		
.	5-6 PM		
J	6-7 PM		
O	7-8 PM		
Y	8-9 PM		

INTEND

334

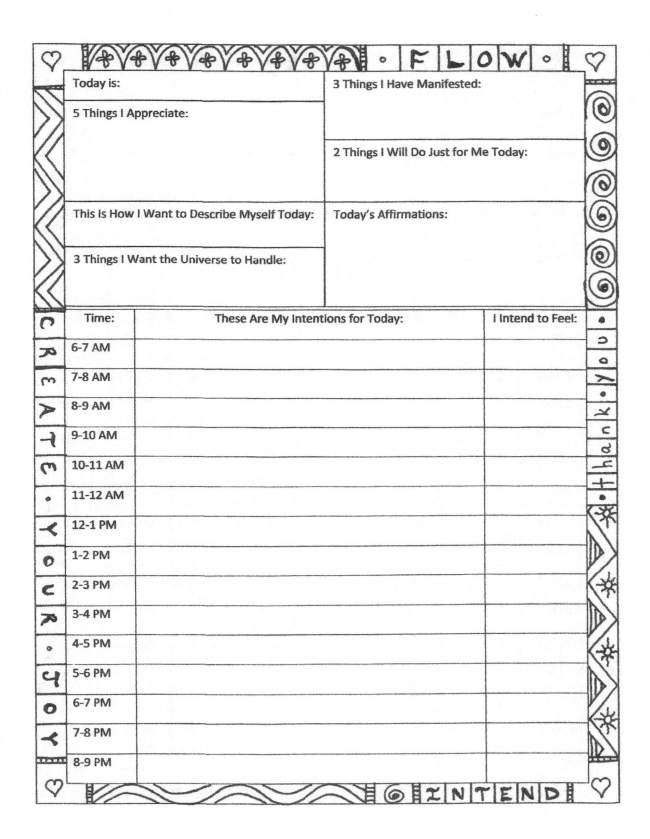

FLOW

Today is:	3 Things I Have Manifested:
5 Things I Appreciate:	
	2 Things I Will Do Just for Me Today:
This Is How I Want to Describe Myself Today:	Today's Affirmations:
3 Things I Want the Universe to Handle:	

Time:	These Are My Intentions for Today:	I Intend to Feel:
6-7 AM		
7-8 AM		
8-9 AM		
9-10 AM		
10-11 AM		
11-12 AM		
12-1 PM		
1-2 PM		
2-3 PM		
3-4 PM		
4-5 PM		
5-6 PM		
6-7 PM		
7-8 PM		
8-9 PM		

CREATE YOUR JOY

thank you

INTEND

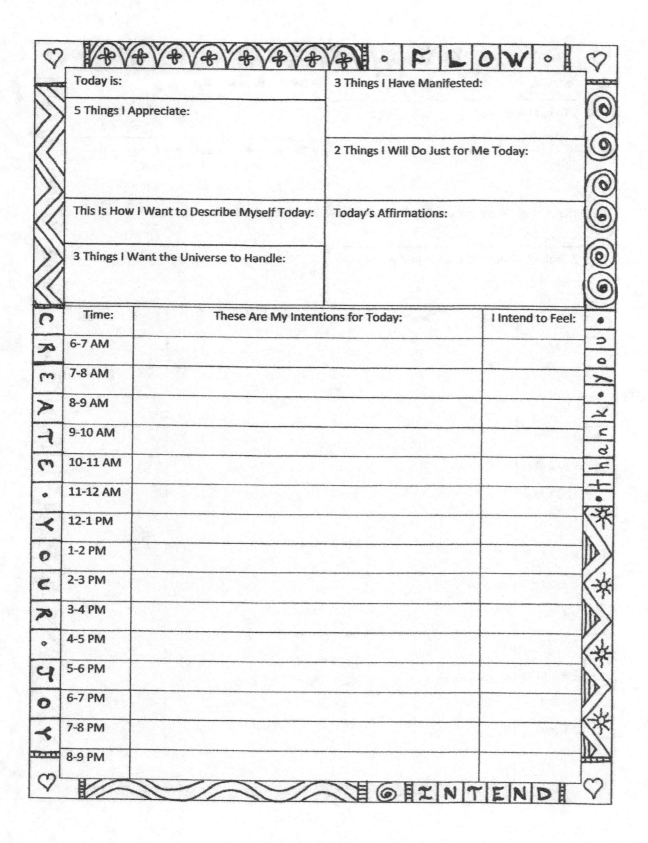

FLOW

| Today is: | 3 Things I Have Manifested: |

5 Things I Appreciate:

2 Things I Will Do Just for Me Today:

This Is How I Want to Describe Myself Today:

Today's Affirmations:

3 Things I Want the Universe to Handle:

CREATE . YOUR . JOY

Time:	These Are My Intentions for Today:	I Intend to Feel:
6-7 AM		
7-8 AM		
8-9 AM		
9-10 AM		
10-11 AM		
11-12 AM		
12-1 PM		
1-2 PM		
2-3 PM		
3-4 PM		
4-5 PM		
5-6 PM		
6-7 PM		
7-8 PM		
8-9 PM		

thank you

INTEND

∘ F L O W ∘

Today is:	**3 Things I Have Manifested:**
5 Things I Appreciate:	
	2 Things I Will Do Just for Me Today:
This Is How I Want to Describe Myself Today:	**Today's Affirmations:**
3 Things I Want the Universe to Handle:	

Time:	These Are My Intentions for Today:	I Intend to Feel:
6-7 AM		
7-8 AM		
8-9 AM		
9-10 AM		
10-11 AM		
11-12 AM		
12-1 PM		
1-2 PM		
2-3 PM		
3-4 PM		
4-5 PM		
5-6 PM		
6-7 PM		
7-8 PM		
8-9 PM		

CREATE ∘ YOUR ∘ JOY

do you ∘ thank ∘

∘ INTEND

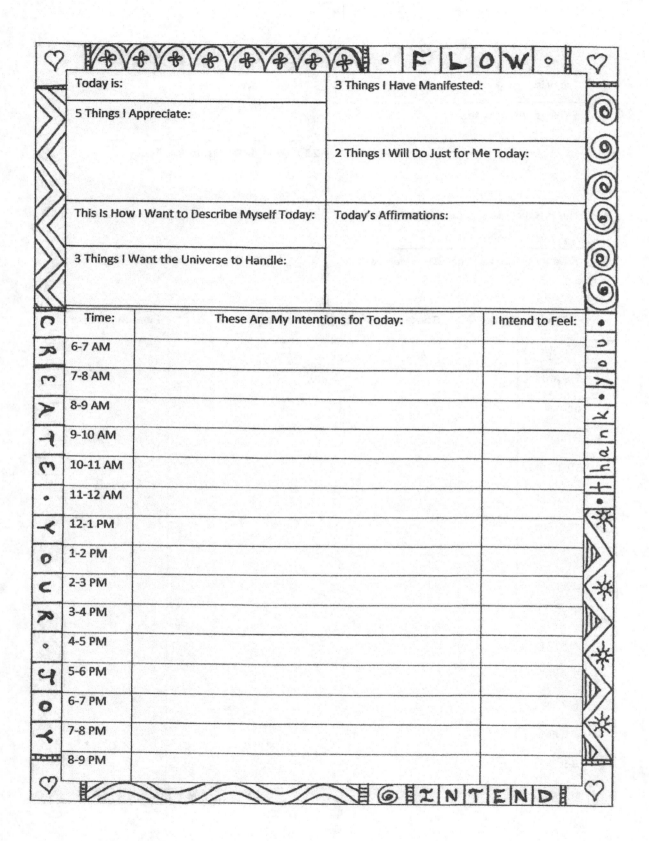

FLOW

| Today is: |
| 5 Things I Appreciate: |

| 3 Things I Have Manifested: |

| 2 Things I Will Do Just for Me Today: |

| This Is How I Want to Describe Myself Today: |
| Today's Affirmations: |

| 3 Things I Want the Universe to Handle: |

CREATE · YOUR · JOY

Time:	These Are My Intentions for Today:	I Intend to Feel:
6-7 AM		
7-8 AM		
8-9 AM		
9-10 AM		
10-11 AM		
11-12 AM		
12-1 PM		
1-2 PM		
2-3 PM		
3-4 PM		
4-5 PM		
5-6 PM		
6-7 PM		
7-8 PM		
8-9 PM		

INTEND

FLOW

Today is:	3 Things I Have Manifested:
5 Things I Appreciate:	
	2 Things I Will Do Just for Me Today:
This Is How I Want to Describe Myself Today:	Today's Affirmations:
3 Things I Want the Universe to Handle:	

Time:	These Are My Intentions for Today:	I Intend to Feel:
6-7 AM		
7-8 AM		
8-9 AM		
9-10 AM		
10-11 AM		
11-12 AM		
12-1 PM		
1-2 PM		
2-3 PM		
3-4 PM		
4-5 PM		
5-6 PM		
6-7 PM		
7-8 PM		
8-9 PM		

CREATE YOUR JOY

INTEND

339

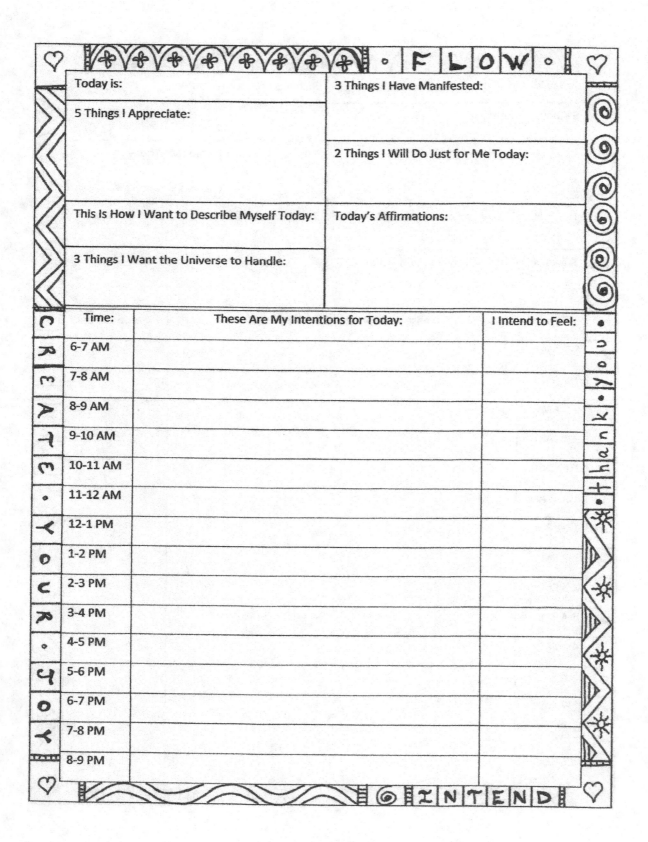

FLOW

Today is:

5 Things I Appreciate:

3 Things I Have Manifested:

2 Things I Will Do Just for Me Today:

This Is How I Want to Describe Myself Today:

Today's Affirmations:

3 Things I Want the Universe to Handle:

Time:	These Are My Intentions for Today:	I Intend to Feel:
6-7 AM		
7-8 AM		
8-9 AM		
9-10 AM		
10-11 AM		
11-12 AM		
12-1 PM		
1-2 PM		
2-3 PM		
3-4 PM		
4-5 PM		
5-6 PM		
6-7 PM		
7-8 PM		
8-9 PM		

CREATE . YOUR . JOY

thank you

INTEND

· F L O W ·

Today is:	3 Things I Have Manifested:
5 Things I Appreciate:	
	2 Things I Will Do Just for Me Today:
This Is How I Want to Describe Myself Today:	Today's Affirmations:
3 Things I Want the Universe to Handle:	

Time:	These Are My Intentions for Today:	I Intend to Feel:
6-7 AM		
7-8 AM		
8-9 AM		
9-10 AM		
10-11 AM		
11-12 AM		
12-1 PM		
1-2 PM		
2-3 PM		
3-4 PM		
4-5 PM		
5-6 PM		
6-7 PM		
7-8 PM		
8-9 PM		

CREATE · YOUR · JOY

thank · you

⊙ INTEND

341

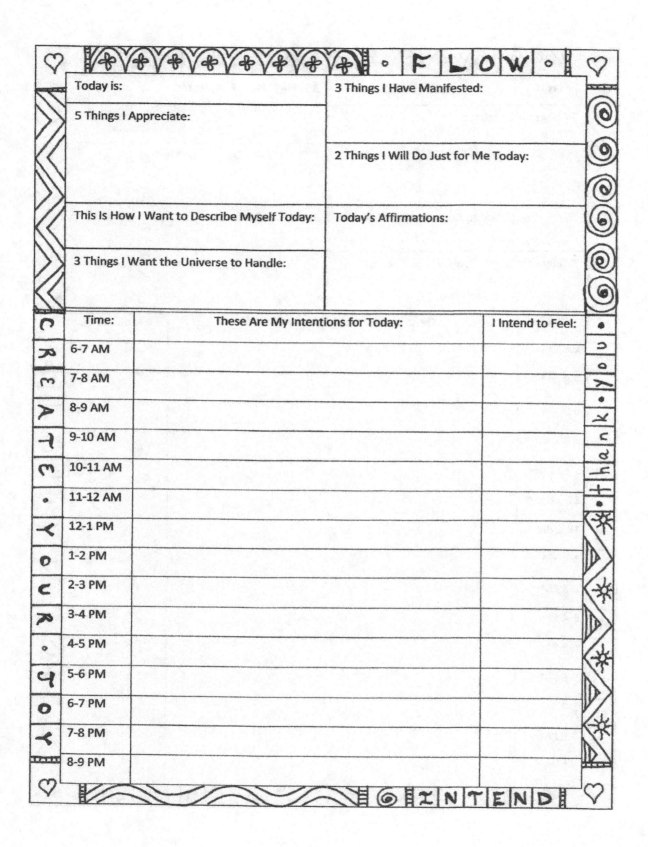

FLOW

Today is:	3 Things I Have Manifested:
5 Things I Appreciate:	
	2 Things I Will Do Just for Me Today:
This Is How I Want to Describe Myself Today:	Today's Affirmations:
3 Things I Want the Universe to Handle:	

Time:	These Are My Intentions for Today:	I Intend to Feel:
6-7 AM		
7-8 AM		
8-9 AM		
9-10 AM		
10-11 AM		
11-12 AM		
12-1 PM		
1-2 PM		
2-3 PM		
3-4 PM		
4-5 PM		
5-6 PM		
6-7 PM		
7-8 PM		
8-9 PM		

CREATE . YOUR . JOY

thank you .

INTEND

FLOW

Today is:	3 Things I Have Manifested:
5 Things I Appreciate:	
	2 Things I Will Do Just for Me Today:
This Is How I Want to Describe Myself Today:	Today's Affirmations:
3 Things I Want the Universe to Handle:	

CREATE • YOUR • JOY

Time:	These Are My Intentions for Today:	I Intend to Feel:
6-7 AM		
7-8 AM		
8-9 AM		
9-10 AM		
10-11 AM		
11-12 AM		
12-1 PM		
1-2 PM		
2-3 PM		
3-4 PM		
4-5 PM		
5-6 PM		
6-7 PM		
7-8 PM		
8-9 PM		

thank • you

INTEND

343

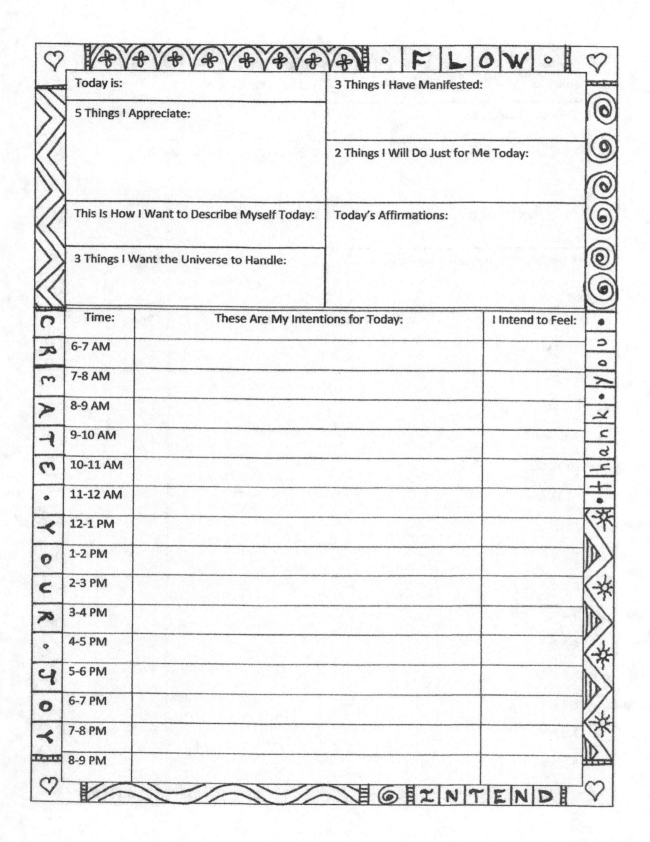

FLOW

Today is:	3 Things I Have Manifested:
5 Things I Appreciate:	
	2 Things I Will Do Just for Me Today:
This Is How I Want to Describe Myself Today:	Today's Affirmations:
3 Things I Want the Universe to Handle:	

Time:	These Are My Intentions for Today:	I Intend to Feel:
6-7 AM		
7-8 AM		
8-9 AM		
9-10 AM		
10-11 AM		
11-12 AM		
12-1 PM		
1-2 PM		
2-3 PM		
3-4 PM		
4-5 PM		
5-6 PM		
6-7 PM		
7-8 PM		
8-9 PM		

CREATE · YOUR · JOY

thank you

INTEND

FLOW

Today is:	**3 Things I Have Manifested:**
5 Things I Appreciate:	
	2 Things I Will Do Just for Me Today:
This Is How I Want to Describe Myself Today:	**Today's Affirmations:**
3 Things I Want the Universe to Handle:	

Time:	These Are My Intentions for Today:	I Intend to Feel:
6-7 AM		
7-8 AM		
8-9 AM		
9-10 AM		
10-11 AM		
11-12 AM		
12-1 PM		
1-2 PM		
2-3 PM		
3-4 PM		
4-5 PM		
5-6 PM		
6-7 PM		
7-8 PM		
8-9 PM		

CREATE · YOUR · JOY

· do you · thank · INTEND

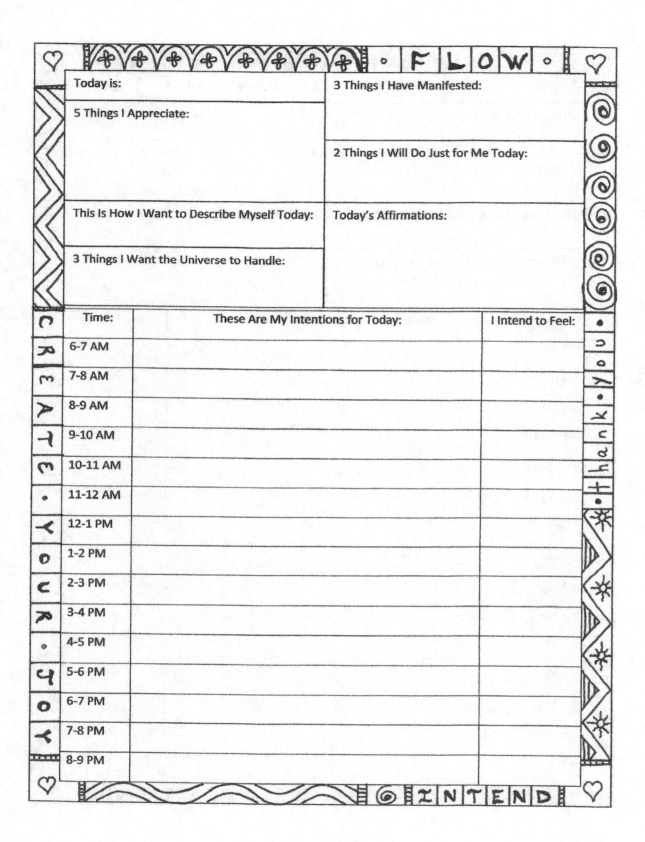

FLOW

Today is:

5 Things I Appreciate:

This Is How I Want to Describe Myself Today:

3 Things I Want the Universe to Handle:

3 Things I Have Manifested:

2 Things I Will Do Just for Me Today:

Today's Affirmations:

Time:	These Are My Intentions for Today:	I Intend to Feel:
6-7 AM		
7-8 AM		
8-9 AM		
9-10 AM		
10-11 AM		
11-12 AM		
12-1 PM		
1-2 PM		
2-3 PM		
3-4 PM		
4-5 PM		
5-6 PM		
6-7 PM		
7-8 PM		
8-9 PM		

CREATE YOUR JOY

thank you

INTEND

Month: **December**

Sunday	Monday	Tuesday	Wednesday	Thursday	Friday	Saturday

Do at least one thing every day that brings you joy and record it on this page.

Affirmations:

"Your attitude determines how you experience the world." -S. Roman

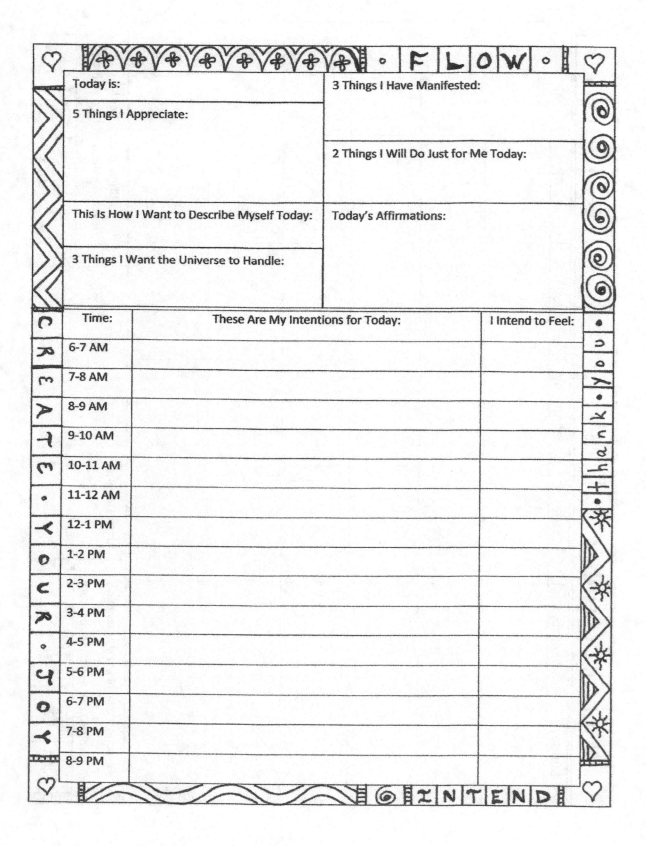

FLOW

Today is:	3 Things I Have Manifested:
5 Things I Appreciate:	
	2 Things I Will Do Just for Me Today:
This Is How I Want to Describe Myself Today:	Today's Affirmations:
3 Things I Want the Universe to Handle:	

Time:	These Are My Intentions for Today:	I Intend to Feel:
6-7 AM		
7-8 AM		
8-9 AM		
9-10 AM		
10-11 AM		
11-12 AM		
12-1 PM		
1-2 PM		
2-3 PM		
3-4 PM		
4-5 PM		
5-6 PM		
6-7 PM		
7-8 PM		
8-9 PM		

CREATE · YOUR · JOY

thank you

INTEND

348

• F L O W •

Today is:	3 Things I Have Manifested:
5 Things I Appreciate:	
	2 Things I Will Do Just for Me Today:
This Is How I Want to Describe Myself Today:	Today's Affirmations:
3 Things I Want the Universe to Handle:	

	Time:	These Are My Intentions for Today:	I Intend to Feel:
C	6-7 AM		
R	7-8 AM		
E	8-9 AM		
A	9-10 AM		
T	10-11 AM		
E	11-12 AM		
·	12-1 PM		
Y	1-2 PM		
O	2-3 PM		
U	3-4 PM		
R	4-5 PM		
·	5-6 PM		
J	6-7 PM		
O	7-8 PM		
Y	8-9 PM		

◎ INTEND

349

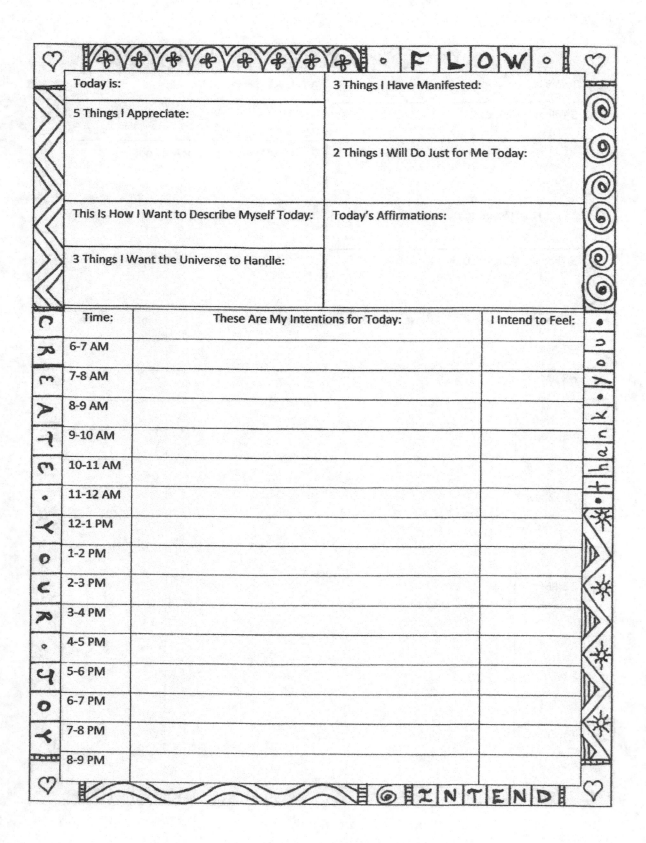

FLOW

Today is:	3 Things I Have Manifested:
5 Things I Appreciate:	
	2 Things I Will Do Just for Me Today:
This Is How I Want to Describe Myself Today:	**Today's Affirmations:**
3 Things I Want the Universe to Handle:	

CREATE • YOUR • JOY

thank you • INTEND

Time:	These Are My Intentions for Today:	I Intend to Feel:
6-7 AM		
7-8 AM		
8-9 AM		
9-10 AM		
10-11 AM		
11-12 AM		
12-1 PM		
1-2 PM		
2-3 PM		
3-4 PM		
4-5 PM		
5-6 PM		
6-7 PM		
7-8 PM		
8-9 PM		

FLOW

Today is:	3 Things I Have Manifested:
5 Things I Appreciate:	
	2 Things I Will Do Just for Me Today:
This Is How I Want to Describe Myself Today:	Today's Affirmations:
3 Things I Want the Universe to Handle:	

CREATE . YOUR . JOY

CULTIVATE . YOUR . thankful . INTEND

Time:	These Are My Intentions for Today:	I Intend to Feel:
6-7 AM		
7-8 AM		
8-9 AM		
9-10 AM		
10-11 AM		
11-12 AM		
12-1 PM		
1-2 PM		
2-3 PM		
3-4 PM		
4-5 PM		
5-6 PM		
6-7 PM		
7-8 PM		
8-9 PM		

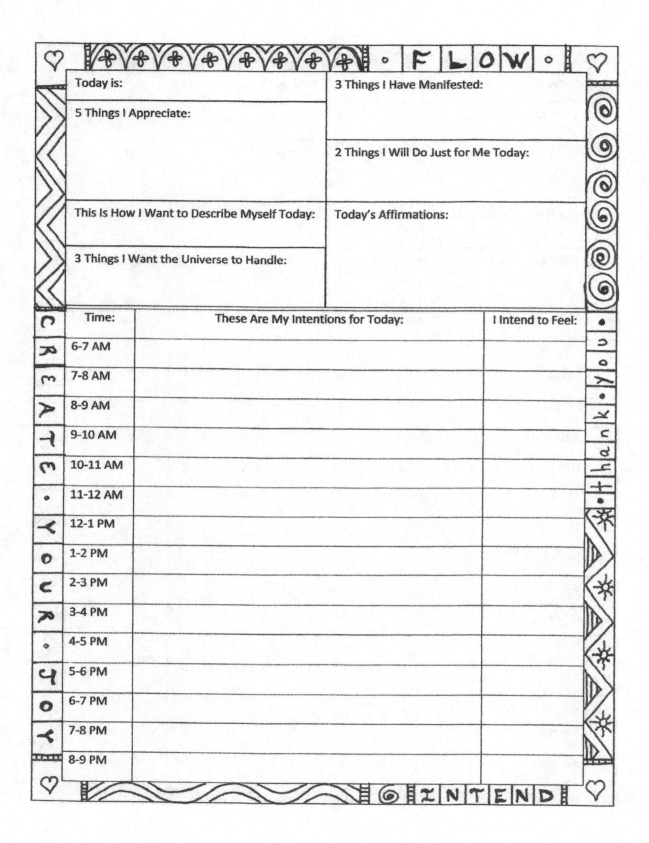

FLOW

Today is:	3 Things I Have Manifested:
5 Things I Appreciate:	
	2 Things I Will Do Just for Me Today:
This Is How I Want to Describe Myself Today:	Today's Affirmations:
3 Things I Want the Universe to Handle:	

CREATE • YOUR • JOY

thank • you •

Time:	These Are My Intentions for Today:	I Intend to Feel:
6-7 AM		
7-8 AM		
8-9 AM		
9-10 AM		
10-11 AM		
11-12 AM		
12-1 PM		
1-2 PM		
2-3 PM		
3-4 PM		
4-5 PM		
5-6 PM		
6-7 PM		
7-8 PM		
8-9 PM		

INTEND

FLOW

Today is:	3 Things I Have Manifested:
5 Things I Appreciate:	
	2 Things I Will Do Just for Me Today:
This Is How I Want to Describe Myself Today:	Today's Affirmations:
3 Things I Want the Universe to Handle:	

Time:	These Are My Intentions for Today:	I Intend to Feel:
6-7 AM		
7-8 AM		
8-9 AM		
9-10 AM		
10-11 AM		
11-12 AM		
12-1 PM		
1-2 PM		
2-3 PM		
3-4 PM		
4-5 PM		
5-6 PM		
6-7 PM		
7-8 PM		
8-9 PM		

CREATE · YOUR · JOY

thank you

INTEND

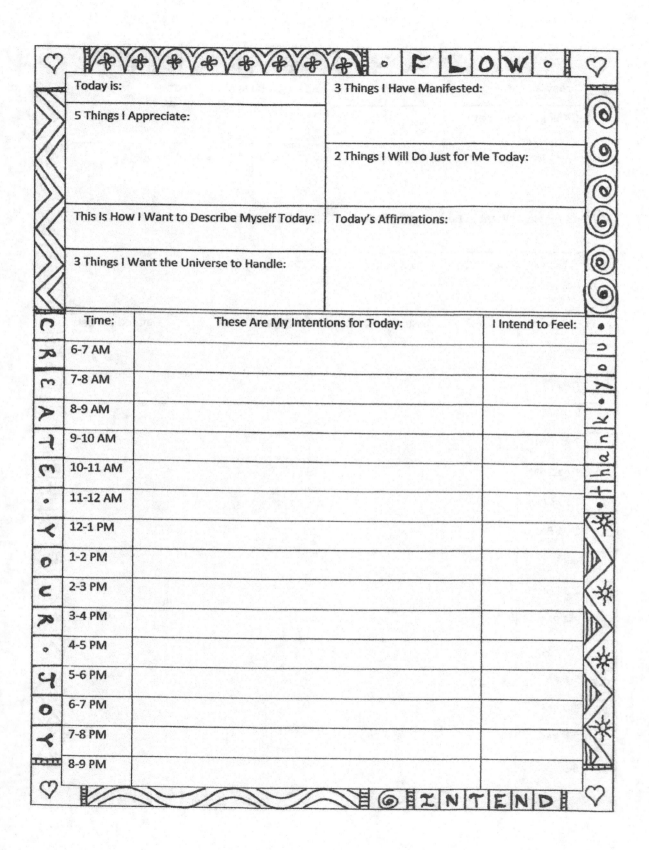

FLOW

Today is:

5 Things I Appreciate:

3 Things I Have Manifested:

2 Things I Will Do Just for Me Today:

This Is How I Want to Describe Myself Today:

Today's Affirmations:

3 Things I Want the Universe to Handle:

Time:	These Are My Intentions for Today:	I Intend to Feel:
6-7 AM		
7-8 AM		
8-9 AM		
9-10 AM		
10-11 AM		
11-12 AM		
12-1 PM		
1-2 PM		
2-3 PM		
3-4 PM		
4-5 PM		
5-6 PM		
6-7 PM		
7-8 PM		
8-9 PM		

CREATE • YOUR • JOY

thank • you

INTEND

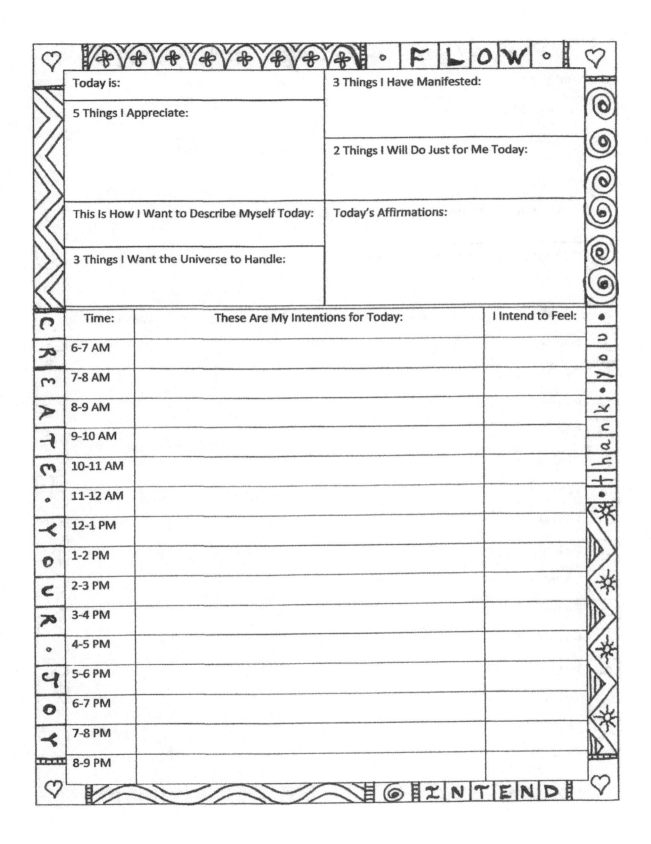

FLOW

Today is:	**3 Things I Have Manifested:**
5 Things I Appreciate:	
	2 Things I Will Do Just for Me Today:
This Is How I Want to Describe Myself Today:	**Today's Affirmations:**
3 Things I Want the Universe to Handle:	

Time:	These Are My Intentions for Today:	I Intend to Feel:
6-7 AM		
7-8 AM		
8-9 AM		
9-10 AM		
10-11 AM		
11-12 AM		
12-1 PM		
1-2 PM		
2-3 PM		
3-4 PM		
4-5 PM		
5-6 PM		
6-7 PM		
7-8 PM		
8-9 PM		

CREATE . YOUR . JOY

INTEND

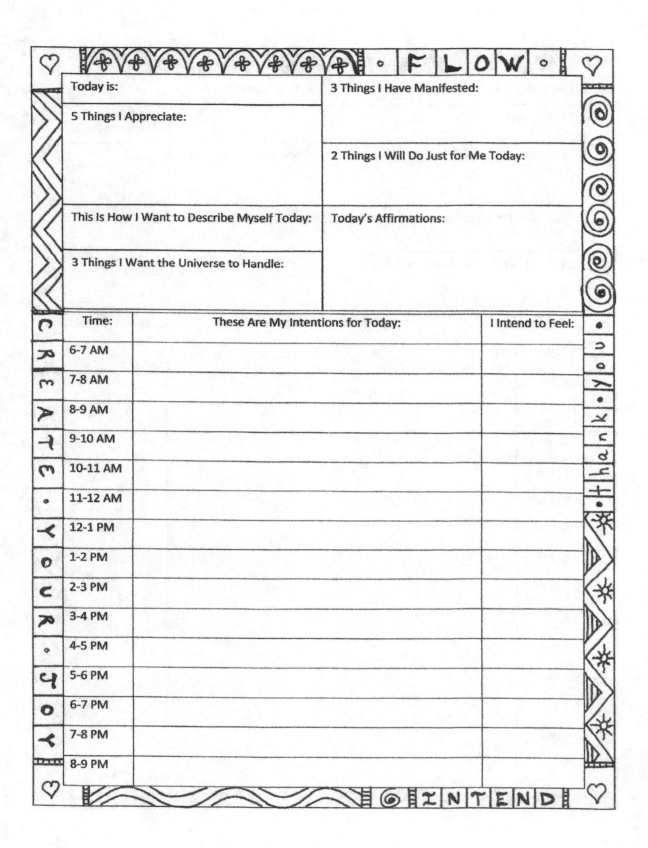

FLOW

Today is:

5 Things I Appreciate:

This Is How I Want to Describe Myself Today:

3 Things I Want the Universe to Handle:

3 Things I Have Manifested:

2 Things I Will Do Just for Me Today:

Today's Affirmations:

Time:	These Are My Intentions for Today:	I Intend to Feel:
6-7 AM		
7-8 AM		
8-9 AM		
9-10 AM		
10-11 AM		
11-12 AM		
12-1 PM		
1-2 PM		
2-3 PM		
3-4 PM		
4-5 PM		
5-6 PM		
6-7 PM		
7-8 PM		
8-9 PM		

CREATE YOUR JOY

thank you

INTEND

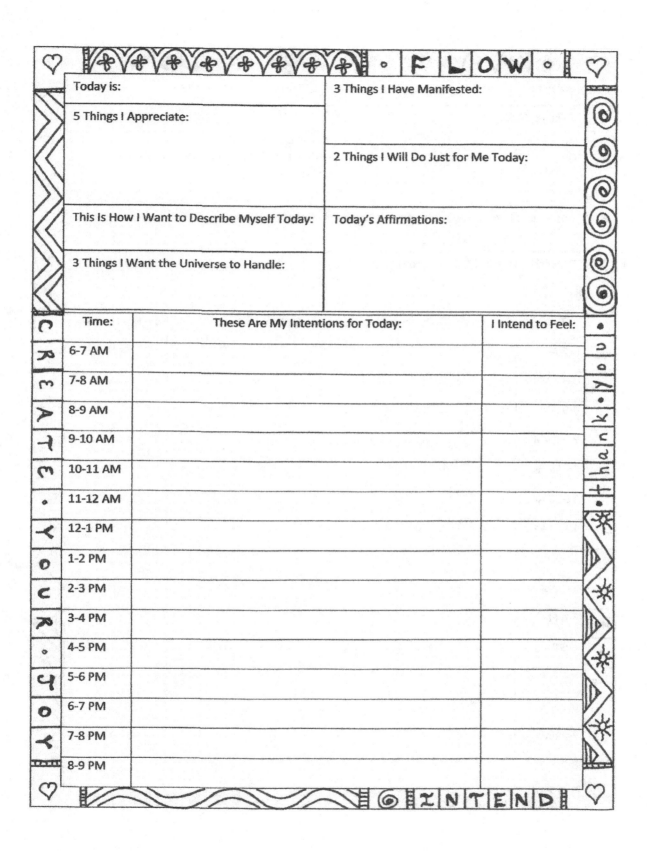

FLOW

Today is:

5 Things I Appreciate:

This Is How I Want to Describe Myself Today:

3 Things I Want the Universe to Handle:

3 Things I Have Manifested:

2 Things I Will Do Just for Me Today:

Today's Affirmations:

Time:	These Are My Intentions for Today:	I Intend to Feel:
6-7 AM		
7-8 AM		
8-9 AM		
9-10 AM		
10-11 AM		
11-12 AM		
12-1 PM		
1-2 PM		
2-3 PM		
3-4 PM		
4-5 PM		
5-6 PM		
6-7 PM		
7-8 PM		
8-9 PM		

CREATE. YOUR. JOY

thank you.

INTEND

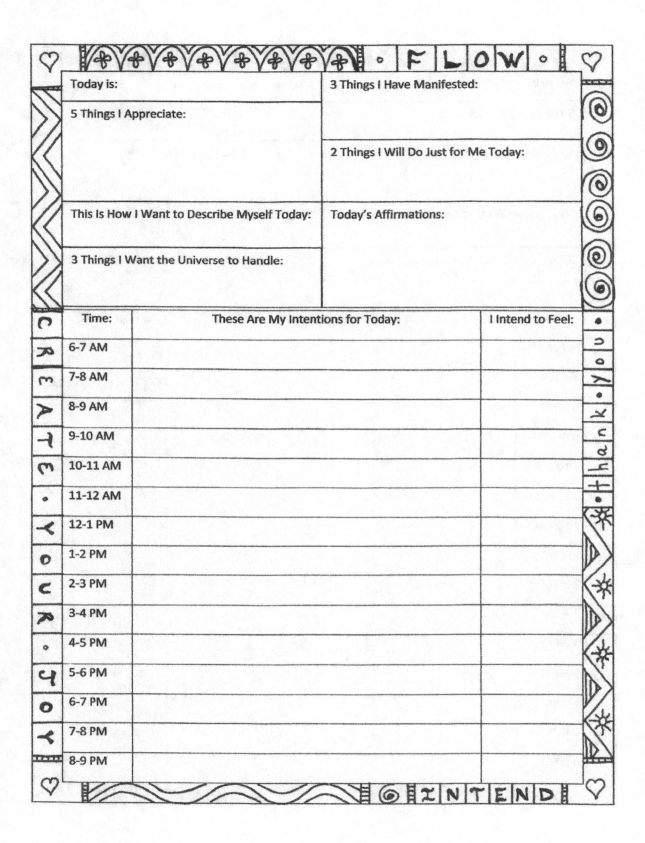

FLOW

Today is:

5 Things I Appreciate:

3 Things I Have Manifested:

2 Things I Will Do Just for Me Today:

This Is How I Want to Describe Myself Today:

Today's Affirmations:

3 Things I Want the Universe to Handle:

Time:	These Are My Intentions for Today:	I Intend to Feel:
6-7 AM		
7-8 AM		
8-9 AM		
9-10 AM		
10-11 AM		
11-12 AM		
12-1 PM		
1-2 PM		
2-3 PM		
3-4 PM		
4-5 PM		
5-6 PM		
6-7 PM		
7-8 PM		
8-9 PM		

CREATE . YOUR . JOY

thank . you

INTEND

FLOW

Today is:	3 Things I Have Manifested:
5 Things I Appreciate:	
	2 Things I Will Do Just for Me Today:
This Is How I Want to Describe Myself Today:	**Today's Affirmations:**
3 Things I Want the Universe to Handle:	

Time:	These Are My Intentions for Today:	I Intend to Feel:
6-7 AM		
7-8 AM		
8-9 AM		
9-10 AM		
10-11 AM		
11-12 AM		
12-1 PM		
1-2 PM		
2-3 PM		
3-4 PM		
4-5 PM		
5-6 PM		
6-7 PM		
7-8 PM		
8-9 PM		

CREATE . YOUR . JOY

thank you .

INTEND

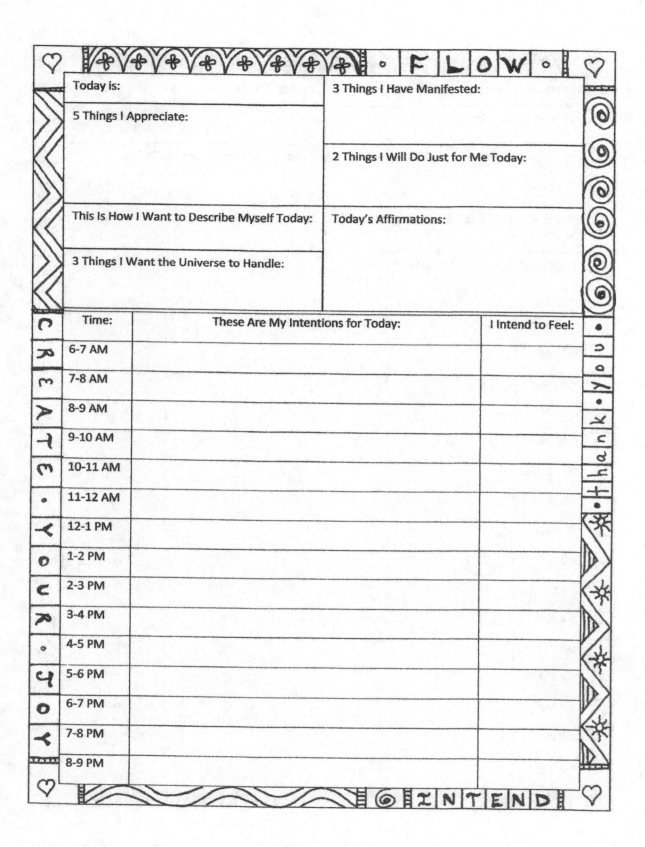

FLOW

Today is:	3 Things I Have Manifested:
5 Things I Appreciate:	
	2 Things I Will Do Just for Me Today:
This Is How I Want to Describe Myself Today:	Today's Affirmations:
3 Things I Want the Universe to Handle:	

Time:	These Are My Intentions for Today:	I Intend to Feel:
6-7 AM		
7-8 AM		
8-9 AM		
9-10 AM		
10-11 AM		
11-12 AM		
12-1 PM		
1-2 PM		
2-3 PM		
3-4 PM		
4-5 PM		
5-6 PM		
6-7 PM		
7-8 PM		
8-9 PM		

CREATE • YOUR • JOY

thank you

INTEND

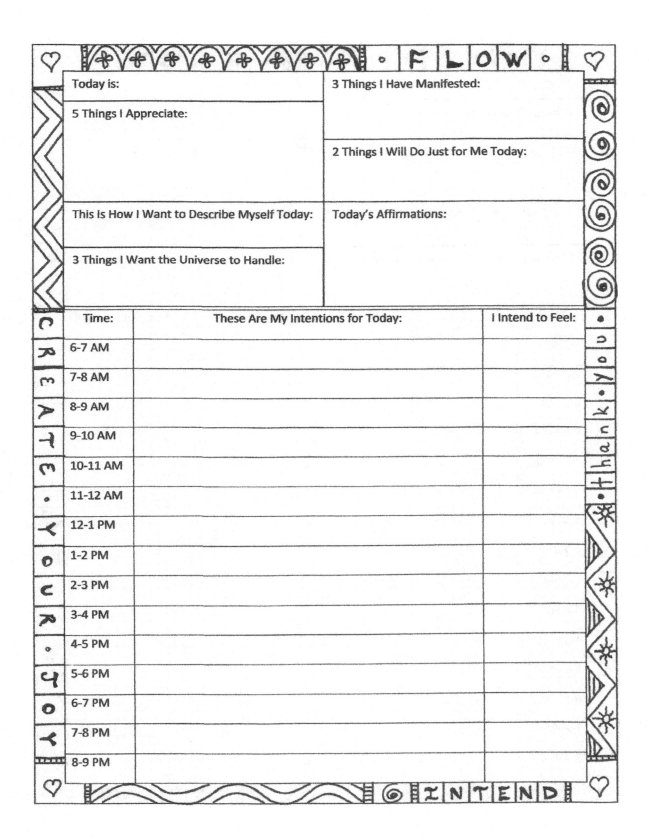

FLOW

Today is:	3 Things I Have Manifested:
5 Things I Appreciate:	
	2 Things I Will Do Just for Me Today:
This Is How I Want to Describe Myself Today:	**Today's Affirmations:**
3 Things I Want the Universe to Handle:	

Time:	These Are My Intentions for Today:	I Intend to Feel:
6-7 AM		
7-8 AM		
8-9 AM		
9-10 AM		
10-11 AM		
11-12 AM		
12-1 PM		
1-2 PM		
2-3 PM		
3-4 PM		
4-5 PM		
5-6 PM		
6-7 PM		
7-8 PM		
8-9 PM		

CREATE • YOUR • JOY

thank you

INTEND

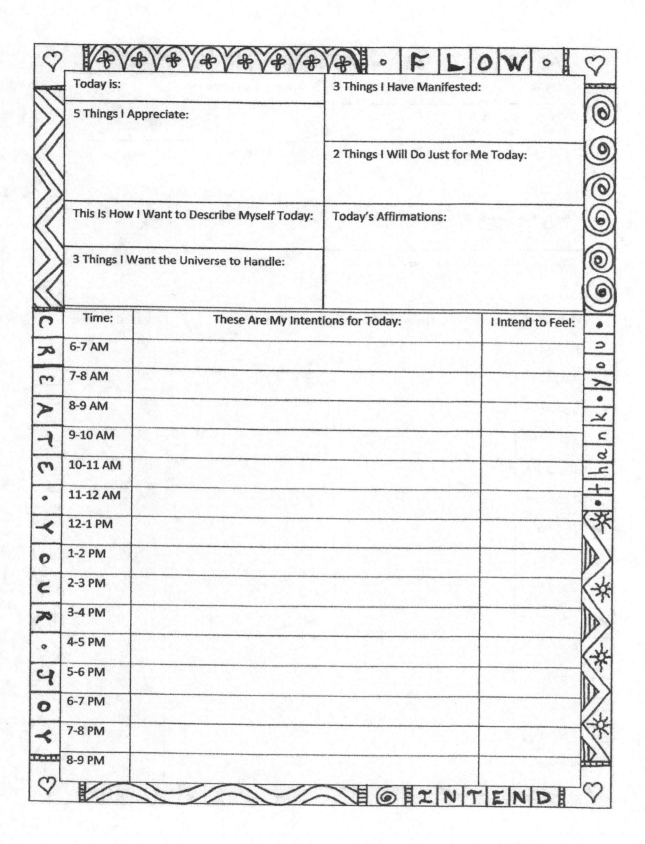

FLOW

Today is:

5 Things I Appreciate:

This Is How I Want to Describe Myself Today:

3 Things I Want the Universe to Handle:

3 Things I Have Manifested:

2 Things I Will Do Just for Me Today:

Today's Affirmations:

Time:	These Are My Intentions for Today:	I Intend to Feel:
6-7 AM		
7-8 AM		
8-9 AM		
9-10 AM		
10-11 AM		
11-12 AM		
12-1 PM		
1-2 PM		
2-3 PM		
3-4 PM		
4-5 PM		
5-6 PM		
6-7 PM		
7-8 PM		
8-9 PM		

CREATE . YOUR . JOY

thank you

INTEND

FLOW

Today is:	3 Things I Have Manifested:
5 Things I Appreciate:	
	2 Things I Will Do Just for Me Today:
This Is How I Want to Describe Myself Today:	Today's Affirmations:
3 Things I Want the Universe to Handle:	

Time:	These Are My Intentions for Today:	I Intend to Feel:
6-7 AM		
7-8 AM		
8-9 AM		
9-10 AM		
10-11 AM		
11-12 AM		
12-1 PM		
1-2 PM		
2-3 PM		
3-4 PM		
4-5 PM		
5-6 PM		
6-7 PM		
7-8 PM		
8-9 PM		

CREATE . YOUR . JOY

THANK YOU

INTEND

363

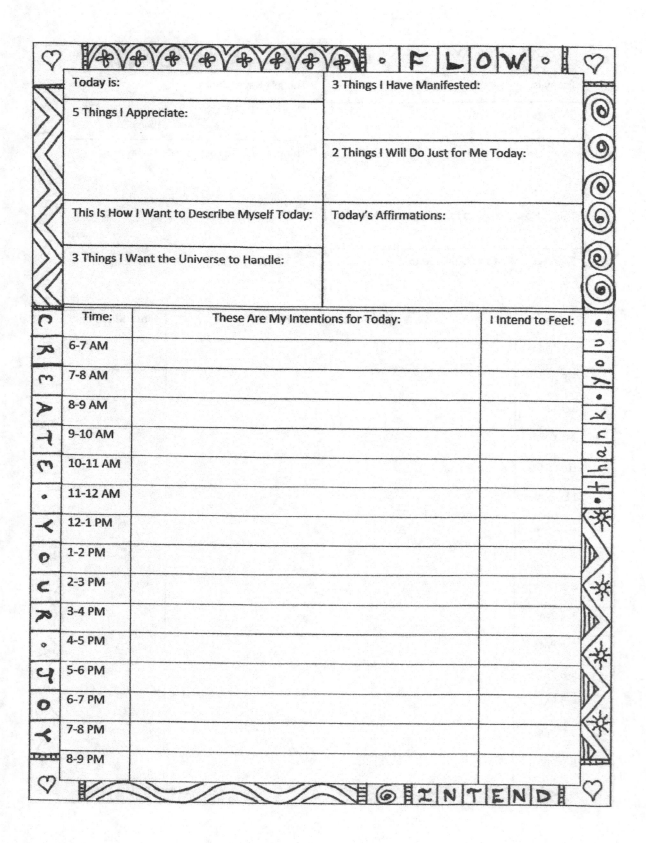

FLOW

Today is:

5 Things I Appreciate:

This Is How I Want to Describe Myself Today:

3 Things I Want the Universe to Handle:

3 Things I Have Manifested:

2 Things I Will Do Just for Me Today:

Today's Affirmations:

	Time:	These Are My Intentions for Today:	I Intend to Feel:
C	6-7 AM		
R	7-8 AM		
E	8-9 AM		
A	9-10 AM		
T	10-11 AM		
E	11-12 AM		
•	12-1 PM		
Y	1-2 PM		
O	2-3 PM		
U	3-4 PM		
R	4-5 PM		
•	5-6 PM		
J	6-7 PM		
O	7-8 PM		
Y	8-9 PM		

INTEND

364

• F L O W •

Today is:	3 Things I Have Manifested:
5 Things I Appreciate:	
	2 Things I Will Do Just for Me Today:
This Is How I Want to Describe Myself Today:	**Today's Affirmations:**
3 Things I Want the Universe to Handle:	

Time:	These Are My Intentions for Today:	I Intend to Feel:
6-7 AM		
7-8 AM		
8-9 AM		
9-10 AM		
10-11 AM		
11-12 AM		
12-1 PM		
1-2 PM		
2-3 PM		
3-4 PM		
4-5 PM		
5-6 PM		
6-7 PM		
7-8 PM		
8-9 PM		

CREATE • YOUR • JOY

thank you

INTEND

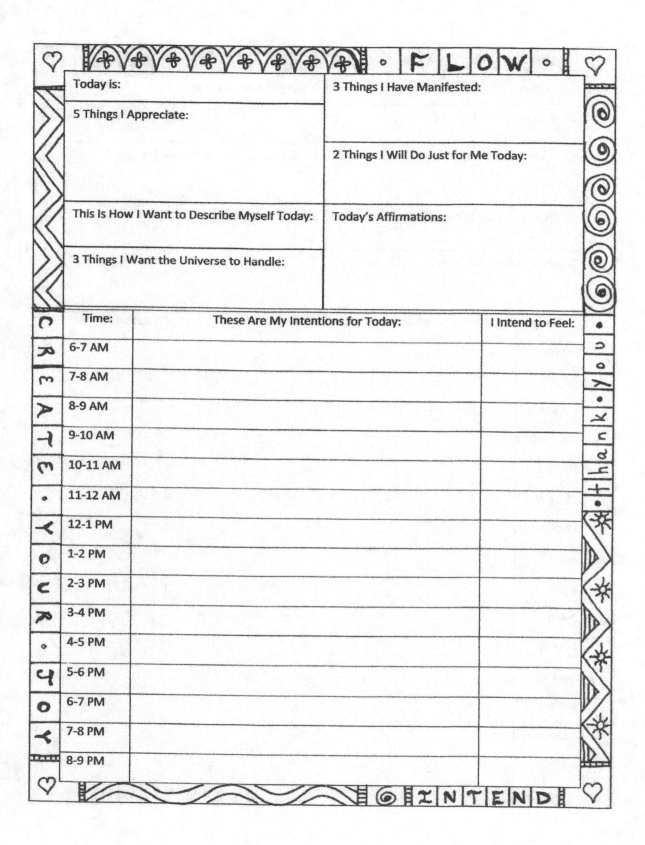

FLOW

Today is:	3 Things I Have Manifested:
5 Things I Appreciate:	
	2 Things I Will Do Just for Me Today:
This Is How I Want to Describe Myself Today:	Today's Affirmations:
3 Things I Want the Universe to Handle:	

	Time:	These Are My Intentions for Today:	I Intend to Feel:
C	6-7 AM		
R	7-8 AM		
E	8-9 AM		
A	9-10 AM		
T	10-11 AM		
E	11-12 AM		
•	12-1 PM		
Y	1-2 PM		
O	2-3 PM		
U	3-4 PM		
R	4-5 PM		
•	5-6 PM		
J	6-7 PM		
O	7-8 PM		
Y	8-9 PM		

INTEND

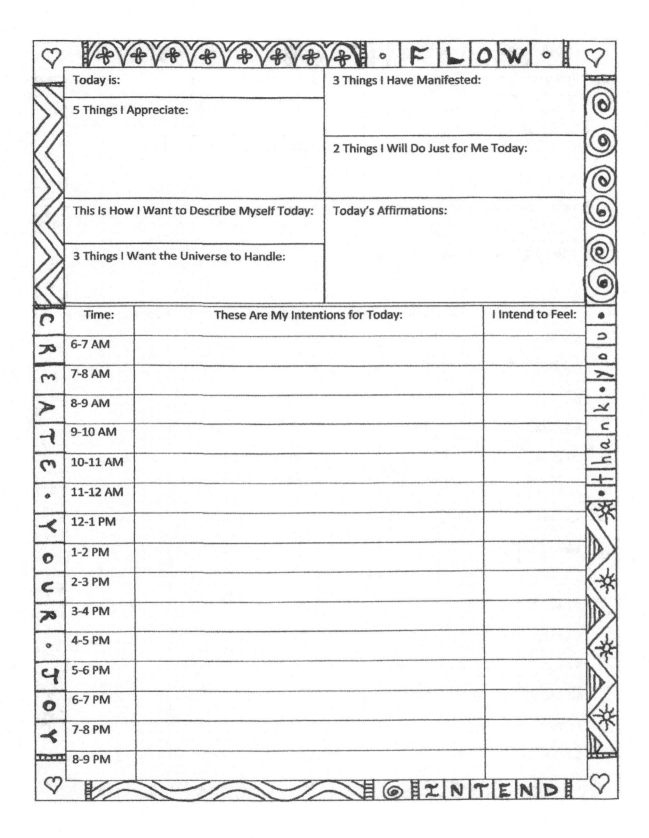

FLOW

Today is:	3 Things I Have Manifested:
5 Things I Appreciate:	
	2 Things I Will Do Just for Me Today:
This Is How I Want to Describe Myself Today:	Today's Affirmations:
3 Things I Want the Universe to Handle:	

Time:	These Are My Intentions for Today:	I Intend to Feel:
6-7 AM		
7-8 AM		
8-9 AM		
9-10 AM		
10-11 AM		
11-12 AM		
12-1 PM		
1-2 PM		
2-3 PM		
3-4 PM		
4-5 PM		
5-6 PM		
6-7 PM		
7-8 PM		
8-9 PM		

CREATE • YOUR • JOY

thank you

INTEND

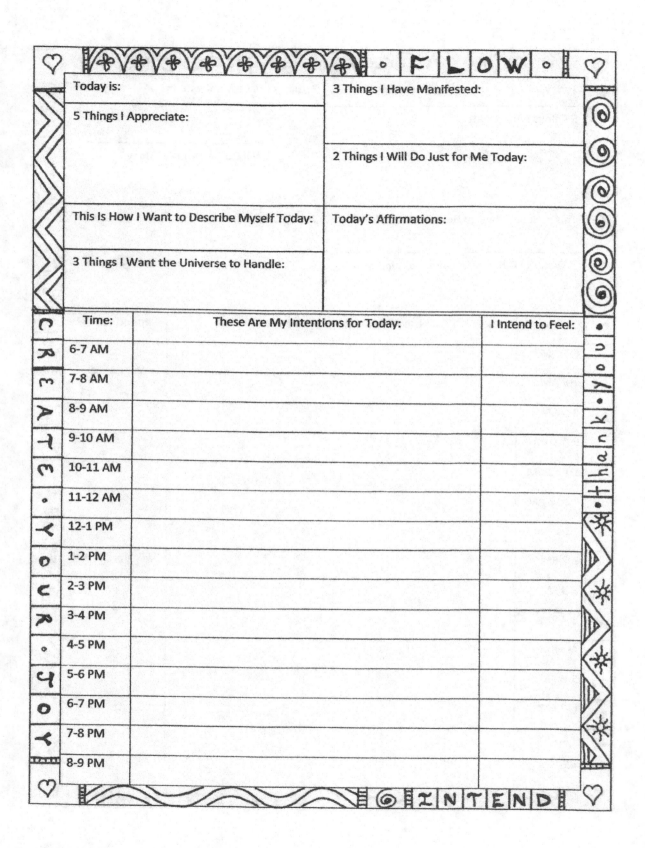

FLOW

Today is:	3 Things I Have Manifested:
5 Things I Appreciate:	
	2 Things I Will Do Just for Me Today:
This Is How I Want to Describe Myself Today:	**Today's Affirmations:**
3 Things I Want the Universe to Handle:	

CREATE . YOUR . JOY

thank you . you

Time:	These Are My Intentions for Today:	I Intend to Feel:
6-7 AM		
7-8 AM		
8-9 AM		
9-10 AM		
10-11 AM		
11-12 AM		
12-1 PM		
1-2 PM		
2-3 PM		
3-4 PM		
4-5 PM		
5-6 PM		
6-7 PM		
7-8 PM		
8-9 PM		

INTEND

· F L O W ·

Today is:	3 Things I Have Manifested:
5 Things I Appreciate:	
	2 Things I Will Do Just for Me Today:
This Is How I Want to Describe Myself Today:	**Today's Affirmations:**
3 Things I Want the Universe to Handle:	

	Time:	These Are My Intentions for Today:	I Intend to Feel:
C	6-7 AM		
R	7-8 AM		
E	8-9 AM		
A	9-10 AM		
T	10-11 AM		
E	11-12 AM		
Y	12-1 PM		
O	1-2 PM		
U	2-3 PM		
R	3-4 PM		
	4-5 PM		
J	5-6 PM		
O	6-7 PM		
Y	7-8 PM		
	8-9 PM		

INTEND

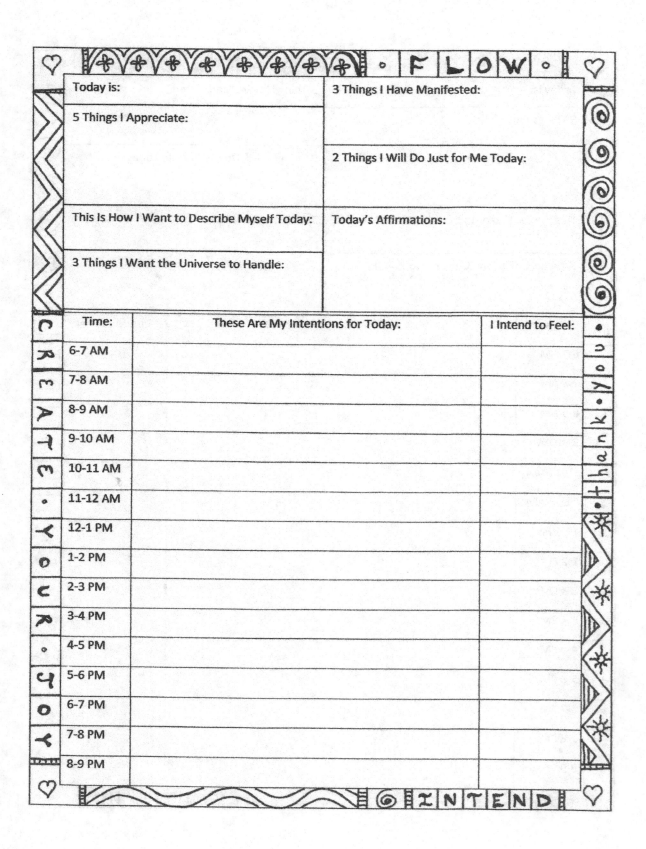

FLOW

Today is:	3 Things I Have Manifested:
5 Things I Appreciate:	
	2 Things I Will Do Just for Me Today:
This Is How I Want to Describe Myself Today:	Today's Affirmations:
3 Things I Want the Universe to Handle:	

CREATE · YOUR · JOY

thank you

Time:	These Are My Intentions for Today:	I Intend to Feel:
6-7 AM		
7-8 AM		
8-9 AM		
9-10 AM		
10-11 AM		
11-12 AM		
12-1 PM		
1-2 PM		
2-3 PM		
3-4 PM		
4-5 PM		
5-6 PM		
6-7 PM		
7-8 PM		
8-9 PM		

INTEND

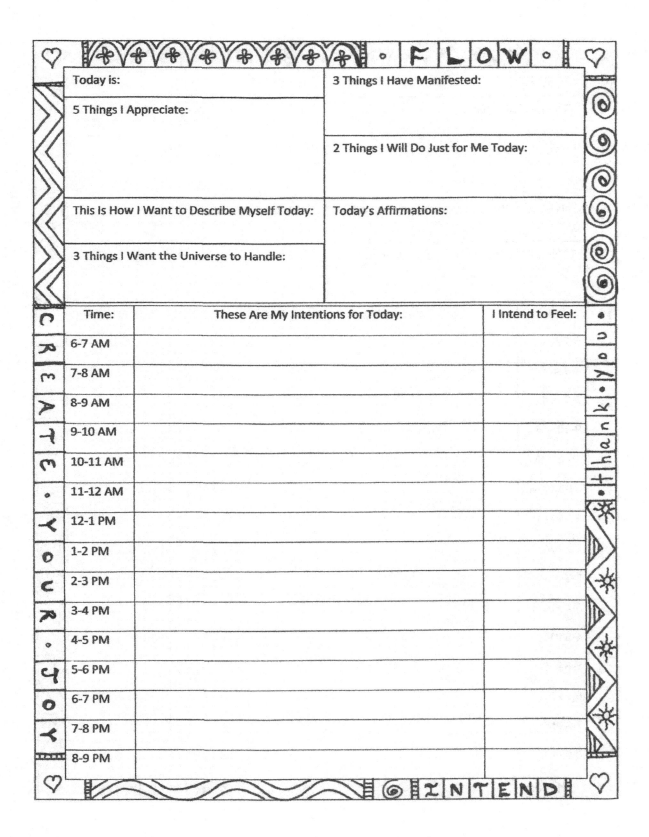

FLOW

Today is:	3 Things I Have Manifested:
5 Things I Appreciate:	
	2 Things I Will Do Just for Me Today:
This Is How I Want to Describe Myself Today:	Today's Affirmations:
3 Things I Want the Universe to Handle:	

Time:	These Are My Intentions for Today:	I Intend to Feel:
6-7 AM		
7-8 AM		
8-9 AM		
9-10 AM		
10-11 AM		
11-12 AM		
12-1 PM		
1-2 PM		
2-3 PM		
3-4 PM		
4-5 PM		
5-6 PM		
6-7 PM		
7-8 PM		
8-9 PM		

CREATE . YOUR . JOY

thank you

INTEND

371

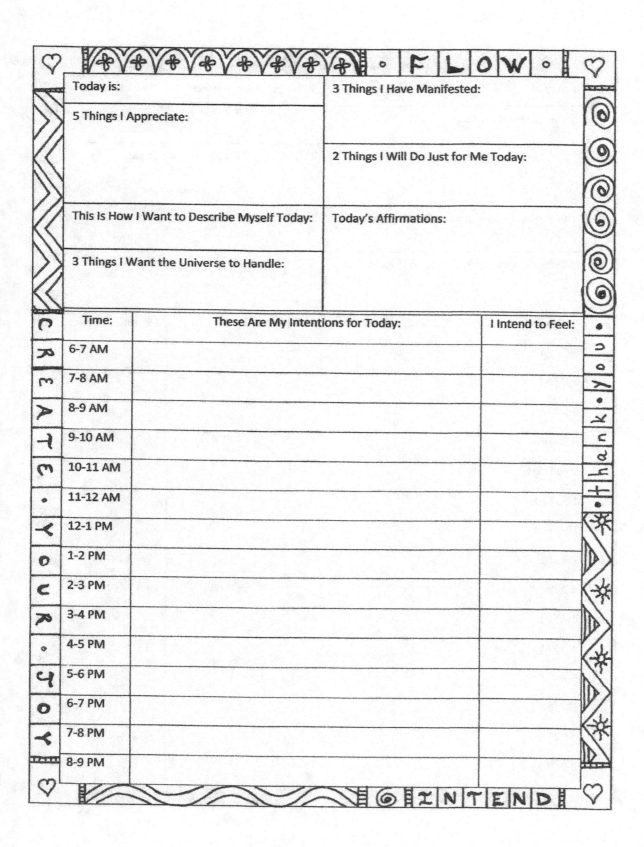

F L O W

Today is:	3 Things I Have Manifested:
5 Things I Appreciate:	
	2 Things I Will Do Just for Me Today:
This Is How I Want to Describe Myself Today:	**Today's Affirmations:**
3 Things I Want the Universe to Handle:	

CREATE • YOUR • JOY

thank you • 404

Time:	These Are My Intentions for Today:	I Intend to Feel:
6-7 AM		
7-8 AM		
8-9 AM		
9-10 AM		
10-11 AM		
11-12 AM		
12-1 PM		
1-2 PM		
2-3 PM		
3-4 PM		
4-5 PM		
5-6 PM		
6-7 PM		
7-8 PM		
8-9 PM		

INTEND

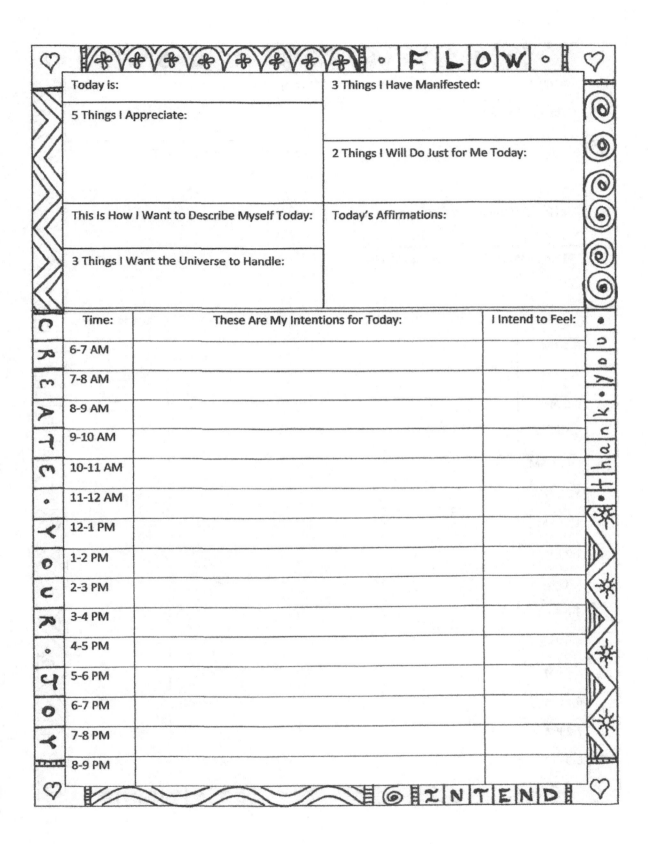

FLOW

Today is:	3 Things I Have Manifested:
5 Things I Appreciate:	
	2 Things I Will Do Just for Me Today:
This Is How I Want to Describe Myself Today:	Today's Affirmations:
3 Things I Want the Universe to Handle:	

Time:	These Are My Intentions for Today:	I Intend to Feel:
6-7 AM		
7-8 AM		
8-9 AM		
9-10 AM		
10-11 AM		
11-12 AM		
12-1 PM		
1-2 PM		
2-3 PM		
3-4 PM		
4-5 PM		
5-6 PM		
6-7 PM		
7-8 PM		
8-9 PM		

CREATE . YOUR . JOY

thank you

INTEND

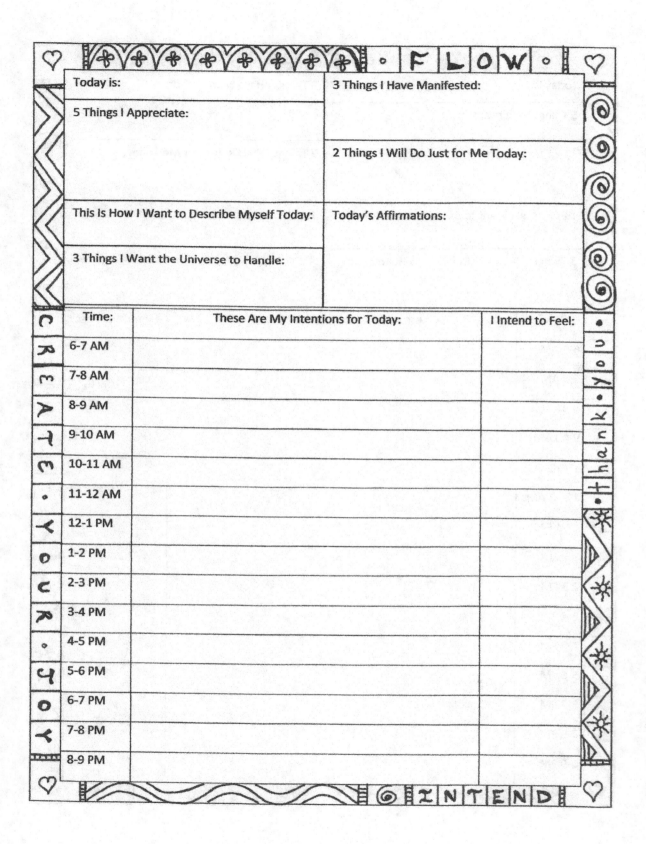

FLOW

Today is:	3 Things I Have Manifested:
5 Things I Appreciate:	
	2 Things I Will Do Just for Me Today:
This Is How I Want to Describe Myself Today:	Today's Affirmations:
3 Things I Want the Universe to Handle:	

Time:	These Are My Intentions for Today:	I Intend to Feel:
6-7 AM		
7-8 AM		
8-9 AM		
9-10 AM		
10-11 AM		
11-12 AM		
12-1 PM		
1-2 PM		
2-3 PM		
3-4 PM		
4-5 PM		
5-6 PM		
6-7 PM		
7-8 PM		
8-9 PM		

CREATE . YOUR . JOY

thank you

INTEND

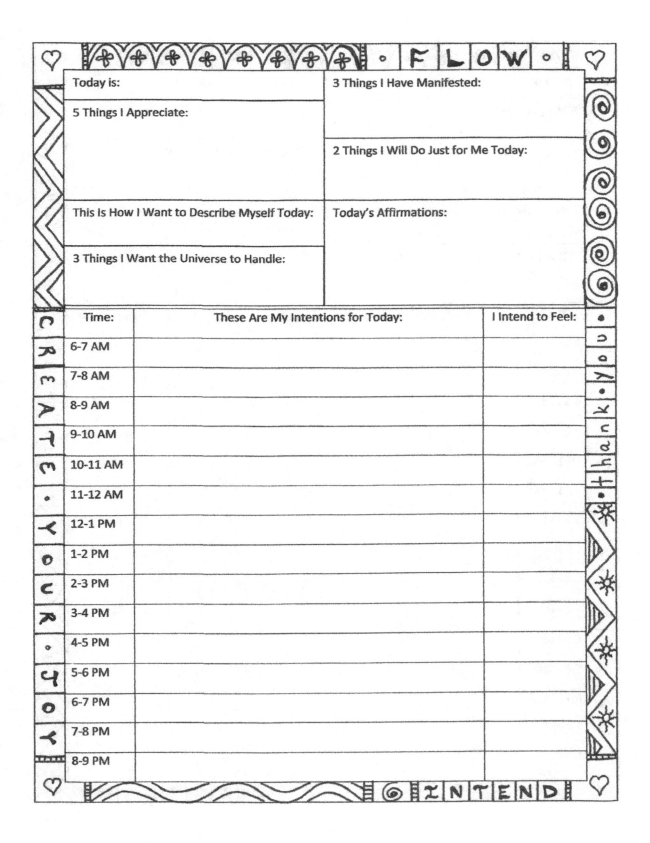

FLOW

Today is:	3 Things I Have Manifested:
5 Things I Appreciate:	
	2 Things I Will Do Just for Me Today:
This Is How I Want to Describe Myself Today:	Today's Affirmations:
3 Things I Want the Universe to Handle:	

CREATE · YOUR · JOY

Time:	These Are My Intentions for Today:	I Intend to Feel:
6-7 AM		
7-8 AM		
8-9 AM		
9-10 AM		
10-11 AM		
11-12 AM		
12-1 PM		
1-2 PM		
2-3 PM		
3-4 PM		
4-5 PM		
5-6 PM		
6-7 PM		
7-8 PM		
8-9 PM		

thank you · INTEND

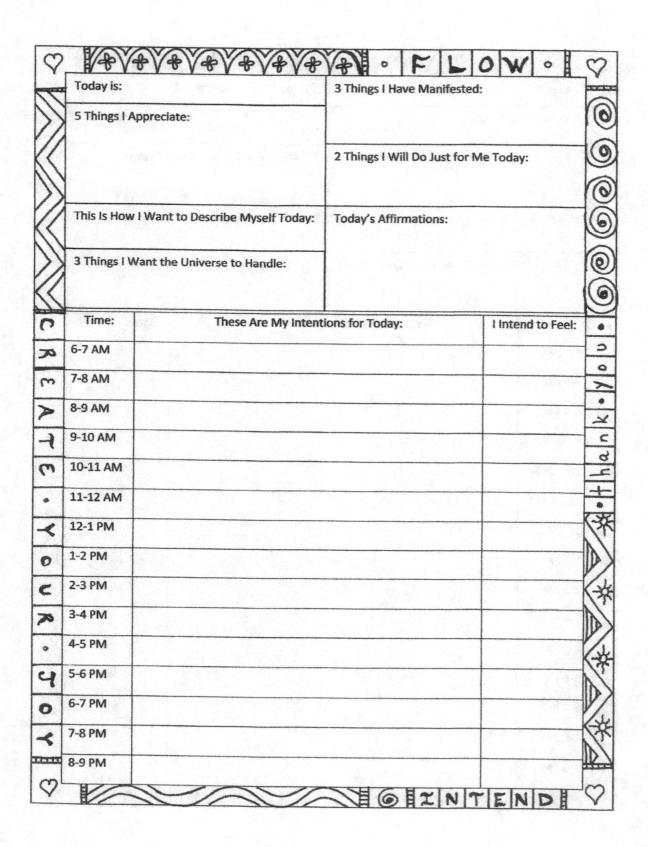

FLOW

Today is:	3 Things I Have Manifested:
5 Things I Appreciate:	
	2 Things I Will Do Just for Me Today:
This Is How I Want to Describe Myself Today:	Today's Affirmations:
3 Things I Want the Universe to Handle:	

CREATE • YOUR • JOY

• thank you •

Time:	These Are My Intentions for Today:	I Intend to Feel:
6-7 AM		
7-8 AM		
8-9 AM		
9-10 AM		
10-11 AM		
11-12 AM		
12-1 PM		
1-2 PM		
2-3 PM		
3-4 PM		
4-5 PM		
5-6 PM		
6-7 PM		
7-8 PM		
8-9 PM		

INTEND

Today is:	3 Things I Have Manifested:
5 Things I Appreciate:	
	2 Things I Will Do Just for Me Today:
This Is How I Want to Describe Myself Today:	Today's Affirmations:
3 Things I Want the Universe to Handle:	

Time:	These Are My Intentions for Today:	I Intend to Feel:
6-7 AM		
7-8 AM		
8-9 AM		
9-10 AM		
10-11 AM		
11-12 AM		
12-1 PM		
1-2 PM		
2-3 PM		
3-4 PM		
4-5 PM		
5-6 PM		
6-7 PM		
7-8 PM		
8-9 PM		

CREATE • YOUR • JOY

thank you

° INTEND

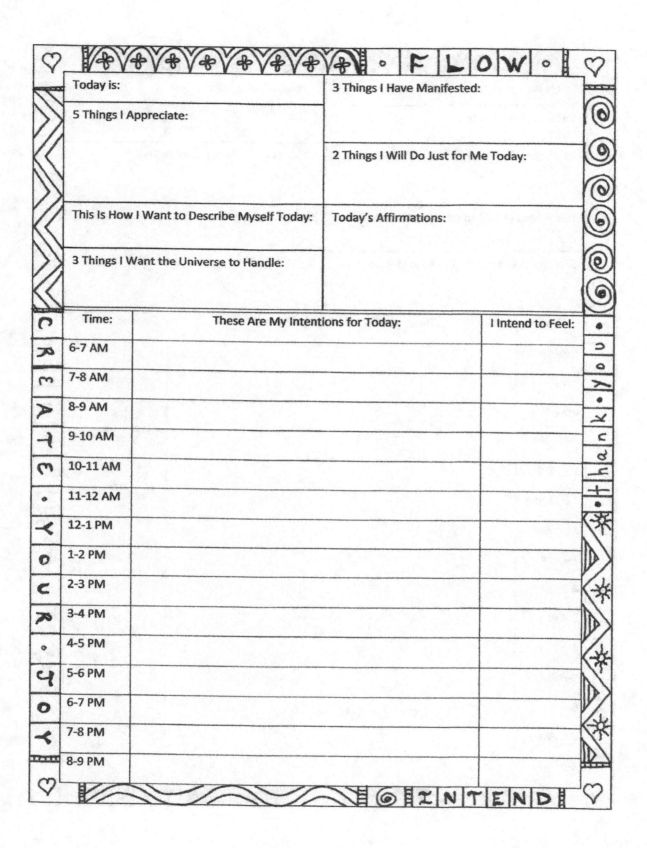

FLOW

Today is:	3 Things I Have Manifested:
5 Things I Appreciate:	
	2 Things I Will Do Just for Me Today:
This Is How I Want to Describe Myself Today:	**Today's Affirmations:**
3 Things I Want the Universe to Handle:	

CREATE • YOUR • JOY

thank you •

Time:	These Are My Intentions for Today:	I Intend to Feel:
6-7 AM		
7-8 AM		
8-9 AM		
9-10 AM		
10-11 AM		
11-12 AM		
12-1 PM		
1-2 PM		
2-3 PM		
3-4 PM		
4-5 PM		
5-6 PM		
6-7 PM		
7-8 PM		
8-9 PM		

INTEND

Contacts

Name	Phone #s	Addresses

Contacts

Name	Phone #s	Addresses

Contacts

Name	Phone #s	Addresses

Contacts

Name	Phone #s	Addresses

Contacts

Name	Phone #s	Addresses

About Tess

    Tess is a passionate life coach, educator, author of *What the Restorative Approach Looks Like in My Classroom*, documentary filmmaker (*Celebrating our Circles*), speaker, EFT practitioner, artist and musician.

    Tess lives in Nova Scotia, Canada with her husband, two stepdaughters and three fur babies.